Victorian Comedy and Laughter

Louise Lee
Editor

Victorian Comedy and Laughter

Conviviality, Jokes and Dissent

Editor
Louise Lee
Department of English
and Creative Writing
University of Roehampton
London, UK

ISBN 978-1-137-57881-5   ISBN 978-1-137-57882-2   (eBook)
https://doi.org/10.1057/978-1-137-57882-2

This Palgrave Macmillan imprint is published by the registered company Springer Nature Limited
The registered company address is: The Campus, 4 Crinan Street, London, N1 9XW, United Kingdom

ACKNOWLEDGEMENTS

Many thanks to Jane Darcy, who organised the 'Victorian Comedy' Conference at University College London, from which many of these articles are drawn, and to the contributors for their enthusiasm, patience and good humour. I am greatly indebted, too, to Milena Kozic, friend and former Ph.D. student at King's College London, who has acted as an invaluable consultant and assistant on this book, and to Alastair Sherwood, without whose help it might never have been finished. Thanks, also, to Camille Davies, Shaun Vigil and Rebecca Hinsley at Palgrave for steering it wisely and kindly to completion. The students of the third-year undergraduate course Laughing Victorians at Roehampton University, London, deserve a special mention for their many excellent ideas and insights. Much gratitude, too, to my husband Johnny Lee and daughter Georgina for their wisecracking fun and encouragement. This book is dedicated to my parents Carole and Charles Walker—both consummately good gigglers—and to the memory of my brother, Sam Walker (1966–2015), whose awesome puns are missed every day.

CONTENTS

NOTES ON CONTRIBUTORS

Malcolm Y. Andrews is an Emeritus Professor of Victorian and Visual Arts at the University of Kent. He is currently Editor of *The Dickensian*, the journal of the Dickens Fellowship, and has published on Dickens and on landscape art.

Jonathan Buckmaster is an Honorary Research Fellow at the University of Buckingham and Associate Editor of *Dickens Journals Online*. He was awarded his doctorate for his thesis on Charles Dickens and the pantomime clown in February 2013. This work reinterprets Dickens's *Memoirs of Joseph Grimaldi* (1838) and examines a number of Dickens's comic figures in relation to the tropes of pantomime. His monograph, *Dickens's Clowns: Charles Dickens, Joseph Grimaldi and the Pantomime of Life*, has recently been published by Edinburgh University Press (2019).

Oliver Double is a Reader in Drama at the University of Kent. He is the author of *Stand-Up! On Being a Comedian* (1997), *Britain had Talent: A History of Variety Theatre* (2012) and *Getting the Joke: The Inner Workings of Stand-Up Comedy* (2nd edition, 2014), and he is the co-editor of *Popular Performance* (2017). In 2013, he established the British Stand-Up Comedy Archive, and is the creator and co-presenter of a podcast based on the items it contains, *A History of Comedy in Several Objects*.

Ann Featherstone is an Honorary Research Fellow in Theatre History in the Department of Drama at the University of Manchester. Her research interests have always been located in nineteenth-century popular entertainment. She has contributed chapters and articles on the Victorian portable theatre, pantomime, theatrical advertising and circus. With Professor Jacky Bratton, she co-wrote *The Victorian Clown* (CUP, 2006) and edited *The Journals of Sydney Race 1892–1900: A Provincial View of Popular Entertainment* (2007) for the Society for Theatre Research, where she is a member of the Publications Committee. She has written two novels, published by John Murray, set in the world of Victorian circus and music hall. She has contributed to BBC television programmes on music hall and circus and has recently appeared on *Who Do You Think You Are?*

Peter T. A. Jones teaches at the New College of the Humanities at Northeastern and Queen Mary. His work examines the discursive intersection between literary culture, popular entertainment and urban locality during the nineteenth century. Peter has published on the history of street markets and is working on two books examining the rise of cockney popular culture and the creative history of railway arches. Peter is an Editorial Fellow at History Workshop Online and Vice-President of the Literary London Society. He co-ordinated 'Stray Voices', a research network which explored the unsettled history of homelessness.

Matthew Kaiser is Associate Professor and Chair of English at University of California, Merced. He is the author of *The World in Play: Portraits of a Victorian Concept* (Stanford UP, 2012), the translator of Leopold von Sacher-Masoch's *Venus in Furs* (Cognella, 2017), and the editor of seven books, including the forthcoming *A Cultural History of Comedy in the Age of Empire* (Bloomsbury, 2020).

Louise Lee is a Senior Lecturer in Victorian Literature at the University of Roehampton, London. She is completing a monograph, *The Call to Levity: Laughter, Evolution & the Victorian Literary Imagination 1830–1910* (forthcoming Oxford University Press and the British Academy, 2021), and with Martin Priestman, co-edited a special edition of *Romanticism on the Net*, 'Evolution and Literature: The Two Darwins' (2016). She has published essays on Emily Brontë, Charles Kingsley and Mary Elizabeth Braddon, and with Mark Knight co-edited *Religion, Literature and the Imagination: Sacred Worlds* (Bloomsbury, 2010).

Bob Nicholson is a Reader in History and the Digital Humanities at Edge Hill University in the UK. He works on the history of nineteenth-century popular culture, with a particular focus on jokes, journalism, popular entertainment and transatlantic relations. His research appears in publications such as the *Journal of Victorian Culture*, *Media History*, the *Victorian Periodicals Review* and across a range of edited collections. He is currently working with the British Library on a project that aims to create a digital archive of one million historical jokes, starting with material from the Victorian era. He tweets @DigiVictorian.

Peter Swaab is a Professor of English Literature at University College London. He is the editor of *'Over the Land and Over the Sea': Selected Nonsense and Travel Writings of Edward Lear* (Carcanet, 2005), and further essays on Lear. With Philip Horne, he edited *Thorold Dickinson: A World of Film* (Manchester University Press, 2008) while his other publications include a BFI Film Classics book, *Bringing Up Baby* (2010), and *The Regions of Sara Coleridge's Thought* (Palgrave, 2012). He is currently writing a book on Sylvia Townsend Warner.

Jonathan Wild is a Senior Lecturer in English Literature at the University of Edinburgh. He has published widely on late Victorian and Edwardian topics and is author of *The Rise of the Office Clerk in Literary Culture, 1880–1939* (Palgrave, 2006), and *Literature of the 1900s: The Great Edwardian Emporium* (Edinburgh University Press, 2017).

Louise Wingrove is an independent Researcher who received her Ph.D. in Performance History from the University of Bristol. Her research focuses on re-imagining and reclaiming the repertoires, careers and image cultivation of music hall and vaudeville serio-comediennes on British and Australian stages.

LIST OF FIGURES

Edward Lear's Travels in Nonsense and Europe

'Capital Company': Writing and Telling Jokes in Victorian
Britain

Introduction: Victorian Comedy and Laughter—Conviviality, Jokes and Dissent

Louise Lee

'Fagin, do look at him! I can't bear it; it is such a jolly game, I can't bear it. Hold me, somebody, while I laugh it out.' With this irrepressible ebullition of mirth, Master Bates laid himself flat on the floor: and kicked convulsively for five minutes, in an ecstasy of facetious joy. (Charles Dickens, *Oliver Twist*, 1837–9)

Why does Charley Bates laugh? The answer seems straightforward enough: the newly genteel attire of Oliver Twist, a recent guest of the Brownlows, now back in Fagin's den, causes a surge of 'facetious joy'. And yet, this appears to be only a partial answer. For Charley is helplessly, haplessly, hopelessly, laid to waste by laughter in a way that is not quite fully accounted for by the circumstances. 'Hold me, somebody, while I laugh it out', he pleads. And, if we take Dickens at his word, Charley spends a full *five* minutes, lying on the floor, kicking his legs in the air, in a kind of joyfully fetal re-imagining of Oliver's far more ghastly entrance into the world. 'It is such a jolly game', Charley cries breathlessly between convulsions, 'I can't bear it'.[1]

L. Lee (✉)
Department of English and Creative Writing,
University of Roehampton, London, UK

© The Author(s) 2020
L. Lee (ed.), *Victorian Comedy and Laughter*,
https://doi.org/10.1057/978-1-137-57882-2_1

1

Bearing it. The Victorian novel, and indeed Victorian culture more generally, is interested in such unbearable moments, but cannot quite contain them, nor indeed depict them. For it is a contradictory aspect of laughter that despite an undeniable corporeal reality that qualifies it to be considered, in the words of one critic, as an 'event' in its own right (rather than merely a response to something), it is too quickly over, too summarily haunted by its own pastness, even before the last sigh and whimper of amusement fades away and equanimity is restored.[2] This fragility of representation, caught between what Anca Parvulescu calls the robust and affirmative 'now' of laughter, but also its amnesiac and passifying propensities, is *one* reason (among many) why it is both under-determined and over-determined in the Victorian novel, and indeed, in Victorian studies more generally.[3] It is also perhaps, why, as James Kincaid suggests, modern critics read a novel like *Oliver Twist* and laugh along to its scabrously funny scenes, yet end up writing essays on its 'bleak effects'.[4]

A similar ellipsis between the experience of laughter, and its textual remediation, occurs at the end of the Victorian period in Bram Stoker's *Dracula* (1897), where 'King Laugh' is enigmatically transformed into a force described by vampire-hunter Professor Abraham Van Helsing, as, like death, both unconquerable, but also quixotic: 'When King Laugh come he make them all dance to the tune he plays'. Laughter is depicted here as a sovereign force *visiting* the body, rather than coming from within it, while Van Helsing's quasi-prophetic and quasi-Biblical language ('come') renders it as determinedly unknowable, even ineffable: a laughing sublime that resists interpretation.[5] The nineteenth-century thinker who most closely captured this fugitive sense of laughter's infinite and endlessly replicating multiplicities, but also its strange immutability, was Friedrich Nietzsche, who, in the work that proclaimed the death of Judeo-Christianity's God, *The Gay Science* (1882), also pursued laughter, or what Sara Crangle has termed 'risibility', as a tool of self-knowledge:

At times we need to have a rest from ourselves by looking at and down at ourselves and, from an artistic distance, laughing *at* ourselves or crying *at* ourselves; we have to discuss the *hero* no less than the *fool* in our passion for knowledge; we must now and then be pleased about our folly in order [...] to stay pleased about our wisdom [...] nothing does us as much good as the fool's cap: we need it against ourselves[...].[6]

The glorious understatement of 'need[ing] to have a rest from ourselves'—with all the inanition and weariness of consciousness it implies—is certainly one of the meanings that can be applied to Van Helsing, who often appears unconscionably strung out in the novel. Yet it seems insufficient to fully do justice to the boyish vitality of Charley Bates, depicted three generations earlier, whose 'ecstasy' is not quite the Nietzschean 'self-tickling' limned by Crangle; the autonomous and subjective laughter that is 'associated with divinity' and a desire for 'the infinite' that 'transcend[s] our brief existences'.[7]

But, then, in the sixty years that elapsed between Charley's giddy 'ebullition of mirth' in the 1830s, and Van Helsing's far more compromised iteration of it in the 1890s, laughter grew up or grew down. It became more eerily freighted with dreams of the social, but also with the private and personal, and bearing witness to these shifts in tone, value and feeling, is a commitment shown by all the contributors of *Victorian Comedy and Laughter: Conviviality, Jokes and Dissent*. The essays presented here embrace many disciplines from literature, science, aesthetics, performance studies, philosophy, cultural studies and materialist cultures of the body. They underscore the profound interest Victorians had in laughter as a force of social cohesion, but also as a marker of charged subjectivity, and also replicate the experience of writing about laughter that the Victorians themselves encountered: that in an age of emergent professional methodologies, it is often necessary to trespass on other disciplines to talk about it. Yet laughter is good to think with, as the many disciplinary co-trespassers of this collection show, and, as the many eminent Victorians who wrote on the subject acknowledged, from Dickens himself to Thomas Carlyle, Alexander Bain, Leslie Stephen, George Eliot, George Meredith, Charles Darwin, G. H. Lewes and James Sully (to name but a few).

None of the contributors to this volume would subscribe to what might be termed, borrowing from Michel Foucault, the 'repressive hypothesis' of Victorian laughter perpetuated in Western culture during the first half of the twentieth century: that is, the widespread belief that Victorians were either too glum or uptight to laugh.[8] The 'turn to affect' and the rise in performance studies in the past thirty years has put a final stake in the heart of that particular critical revenant. And indeed, we might go even further in reversing this paradigm and say that, reading from the breadth of essays presented here, the Victorians were the first age to experience the kind of modernity which is close to our own today, punctuated by laugh-out-loud moments produced in response to an exponentially expanding mass culture. By the 1860s and 1870s, laughter was part of everyday Victorian life through myriad platforms: from periodicals such as *Punch*, *Fun* and *Judy*, to late-century magazines like *Pick-Me-Up* and *Ally Sloper's Half Holiday*, to comic novels, songs and poetry, nonsense fiction and burlesques, to endless squibs, spoofs and parodies, and to the gags, ditties and 'patter' of fin de siècle music-hall comedians and comediennes, circus clowns and the proponents of 'New Humour'.

But not only did the Victorians conspicuously enjoy laughter, they also, to re-deploy further Foucauldian vernacular, transformed it into discourse. By the 1870s, a national debate was being staged across provincial and metropolitan periodicals and journals about the nature of laughter, its causes, targets and effects. Today, though, we might miss some of the heterogeneity of this dialogue because a large portion of it, excluding the notable contributions by those mentioned above, was distinguished by its commonplace un-distinguishability. As R. B. Martin observed, in still one of the best books to be written on the subject, *The Triumph of Wit* (1974), the 'large group of writings' on nineteenth-century laughter and comedy was conducted in an echo chamber of 'tediously familiar' material, often plagiarised and re-heated, without any accompanying analysis. As Martin observes, 'the vague tickle of a phrase may drive one to locate the source from which the echo emanates, only to find that phrases, sentences, paragraphs have been shamelessly lifted'.[9]

This critical or rather *un*-critical state of affairs in Victorian middlebrow writing about laughter was further compounded by a literary 'protocol' that Nicholas Dames has recently discussed: the use of the prolonged textual excerpt in reviews. As Dames argues, the concept of the twenty-first-century 'close reading' has been enshrined from the mid-twentieth century onwards in a privileged position in the academy, and requires the critic to engage with the 'higher literacy that scholars are enjoined to teach' in universities. But the pervasive Victorian habit, on the other hand, of deploying 'lengthy inset quotations' with little accompanying critical commentary results in a form of appreciation that, by Dames's account, is also 'utterly innocuous'. 'Innocuous', as Dames says, because, as a 'protocol', it is 'neither innovative' nor 'scandalous' and entails little professional risk. But the risky aspect of writing about laughter and comedy is that it requires creativity, and often a world view, and rendering the experience only implicitly (rather than explicitly) by merely quoting a text's 'amusing' parts under-explains, even effaces, its complications.[10] As Rachel Ablow comments on this kind of critical excerpt, it proffers an illustrative '"see, it *feels* [italics added] this way"' interpretation rather than a more analytic '"see, it works this way" epistemology of close reading [...]'. This 'feelings' approach, while valuable of itself, renders often unsaid and tantalisingly beyond reach, any sustained collective discussion regarding laughter's ontological, aesthetic or ethical implications.[11]

This does take us back to the perennial problem about laughter, though, both in the case of the Victorians, specifically, but also, historically: how to adduce meaning, through language, to a phenomenon that is fundamentally a-textual, even *anti*-textual. And writings on the subject have often been characterised by evasion and velleity: from famously, Aristotle's lost second book on laughter and comedy from *The Poetics*—which forms the basis of the plot of Umberto Eco's *The Name of the Rose*—to, for example, Charles Darwin's grandfather, Erasmus's, planned but not undertaken *An Examination of Wit*, to a number of other works and treatises, half-finished or un-written.[12] For one of the trickier aspects of laughter, as with Charley Bates's 'mirthful' outburst above, is its unfailing tendency to start as one thing and to become another. To compare, one need only look at the complex responses provoked by the enormously successful cross-class phenomenon, Douglas Jerrold's *Mrs Caudle's Curtain Lectures* (1845), little read or studied today, but which sustained *Punch*'s financial fortunes in the 1840s, in which a hen-pecked husband is haunted by the ghost of his dead wife's tongue.[13] The trials and tribulations of Job Caudle, with all its hilarities, but also, importantly, its labile sympathies between husband and wife, render an uncanny sense that what seemed like moments of knowledge or certainty, are not; and what's more, the perception of this arises, not in any earth-shaking revelation, but through an aggregate of minor, comic, but also increasingly painful glimpses at other truths, in which laughter appears to fall back on, and into, itself. But then, as Parvulescu observes:

> To read in laughter's archive is to decipher nuances. It is a voyage into the microscopic, into the difference of the bit of nuance. It is also an exercise in closeness, in intimacy. Close reading or close listening is intimate reading. An infinite spectrum of nuances—tones, timbres, accents, resonances—unfold in laughter. And yet we do not quite have a vocabulary to talk about laughter.[14]

The 'vocabulary' that evades laughter then refers to language but also to the possession of a resilient-enough affective and critical repertoire to talk about laughter when faced with the inordinate amount of questions it generates: for it requires the theorist of laughter (and that may mean everyone, for after Freud, we *all* theorise our own laughter in the way we do our own dreams) to invite a state of negative capability, and of intellectual uncertainty. In a bid to vitiate this state of unknowingness, or not-fully-knowingness, Erasmus Darwin even proposed a grammatical mark—an inverted question mark—to connote irony.[15] Yet, as with irony, to engage with the experience of laughter itself, it is also necessary to invert questions, and send any answers right back, with even more questions. For laughter is not 'innocuous', even if some of the appreciative, though muted, responses to it in the Victorian period, were.

But then there must be a caveat in modern scholarship, too, about any treatment of Victorian laughter which falsely renders aspects of the discussion 'innocuous' or amorphous when it is not. For, in the absence of a commonality of language on the subject, and indeed, when referring to a critical world before such useful aids to modern thinking about laughter as the vernacular of psychology, and even modern literary criticism itself, Victorian usages of cognate terms that surround laughter like 'wit', 'humour', 'comedy', the 'incongruous', and 'fancy' provide a much-needed control mechanism to track laughter's changing relation to subjectivity. If these cultural templates appear to some extent pre-formed, and even recondite, or outmoded, they are certainly never static, for it is at such acute marginals of difference that culture is made and re-made. It is not pettifogging, therefore, to linger on the contrast, say, between William Hazlitt, writing in 1819, about wit as 'the salt of conversation, not the food',[16] and Walter Pater's surprisingly religious and dissonantal echoing of *Ecclesiastes*, proposing in 1878, that wit is 'that unreal and transitory mirth, which is as the crackling of thorns under the pot'.[17] Whether Victorians aphorise or flatten out the experience of laughter, or else, endow it with agelastic (or laughter-fearing) Biblical connotations, tells much in miniature about its pressure points in relation to autonomy, individualism and the social.

Yet listening, or close-listening, to Victorian debates about laughter from the vantage point of the twenty-first century often obliges us to fall back on what Parvulescu terms 'description', which, as she observes, gets a bad press for ornateness and 'detail', and also, after André Breton, for 'naïvité' because of its implicit claims about an 'unmediated relation to the real'.[18] Swap the word 'real' for 'vitality', however, and the stakes are changed, for in those 'descriptive' moments, a world that might seem irrecoverably lost to the past's vortices, is suddenly, and briefly, revivified, not through access to the material realm though, but rather to the fleeting one: to reverse Karl Marx's famous reflection from *The Communist Manifesto* (1848), all that is melted into air becomes momentarily solid. Ralph Waldo Emerson caught both this sense of laughter's 'meltingness' and also its materiality when he visited London in 1847, and observed: 'It is a new trait of the nineteenth century that the wit and humor of England,—as in *Punch*, so in the humorists, Jerrold, Dickens, Thackeray, Hood,—have taken the direction of humanity and freedom'.[19] To laugh in the world is to imagine new 'directions', new ontologies, into which that laughter might belong. And whether this impulse is radical or conservative—or both—to see life through comedy is to resist what Robert Pfaller has called Western culture's 'subtle hegemony of the tragic'.[20]

This collection is thus organised around new 'directions' for comedy and laughter staged across the three generations of the Victorian period: the first concerns 'Conviviality' (1837–1870), the utopian dream of laughing togetherness that emerges from within a system of literary production but also reaches beyond it; the second, 'Jokes' (1850–1890), concerns the rise-on-rise of a textual (and age-old oral) form to rival even the pre-eminence of the Victorian three-decker novel, and traces the joke's hyper-transmissibility and multiple formulations in Victorian print culture, and also on the nineteenth-century stage; and the final section, 'Dissent' (1870–1900), traces how in the latter part of the nineteenth-century 'joke culture', now embedded in Victorian life, reaches towards new punchlines and new voices.

1   CONVIVIALITY

The volume begins with Malcolm Andrews's argument for the redemptive power of laughter in Dickens's early novels as a force that brings 'together ideas and people that cultural habit and social conformity have separated'. If, as Marx argued, under conditions of capitalism 'all that is holy is profaned',[21] the logic of Andrews's argument in 'Laughter and Conviviality', suggests a new locale for the sacred: the laughing interpersonal. But there is a caveat, as Andrews observes, for it must be the '*right* [italics added] sort of merriment'. This phrase is Dickens's own, and comes from a representative scene, in Chapter Six of *Pickwick Papers* (1836–1837), during the playing of the card game Pope Joan at Dingley Dell, where, as Andrews observes, 'the euphoria' and 'community laughter [...] run[s] on a loop'.[22]

What Andrews pursues specifically in regard to this animated tableau is a distinctive form of phenomenological fun, which Dickens states, comes from 'the heart and not the lips'. This may not necessarily include (although it doesn't actually *pre*clude) the verbal contrivances of the scene—the 'jokes' being rehearsed by Mr. Winkle to the assembled throng—which, we are told, are 'very well known in town, but [...] not at all known in the country'.[23] But it *does* most decidedly embrace what Andrews calls the 'heady conviviality', the feeling of all-inclusive interstitial connectedness—the 'social glue'—which lies within the scene's, and indeed, conviviality's, 'core meaning [of] living together'. Conviviality has two main impetuses, as Andrews argues: the first is a theoretical one, and owes much to that highly influential and also improbable (considering his later reputation as a jeremiad) theorist of early Victorian humour, Thomas Carlyle. Re-scripting the Romantic writer Jean Paul Richter's theory of the 'inverse sublime', Carlyle praised the welcoming spirit of humour which eschews the artifice and cleverness of wit in favour of a humane and even lachrymose fondness: for him, 'true humour' exalts 'into our affections what is below us, while sublimity draws down into our affections what is above us', and it manifests itself in 'warm, tender fellow-feeling with all forms of existence'.[24]

The extent of this democratic togetherness, as Andrews suggests, is realised in *Pickwick Papers*, in many 'manic' scenes of laughter, and also, even, from a ground-up textual level by grammatical devices such as polysyndeton, in which multiple clauses are conjoined, and through breathless repetitive refrains, which underwrite the 'emphatic bind[ing] together' of the novel's 'disparate' energies. As Andrews asserts '[polysyndeton] is the appropriate rhetorical instrument for generating community and conviviality—which are themselves forms of social conjunction'. But this takes Andrews towards a new consideration of how conviviality might operate in terms of Dickens's authorial self-fashioning, orchestrating the responses of his new and heterogeneous readership in the 1830s: ideas which have particular resonance with regards to *Pickwick Papers* and the bold new experiment of serial publication. A number of critics have addressed this issue, particularly in regard to Benedict Anderson's paradigmatic concept of the simultaneity or the 'meanwhile' of print periodical time, and its creation of imagined communities, with Dickens writing as if inhabiting one intimate and congenial domestic space—the hearth—addressing his readers in another.[25] Andrews builds on these palliative thematics but also conjures a far more frenetic hearth, and a far more frenetic Dickens. As he suggests:

> I think of such techniques [as those displayed in *Pickwick Papers*] as the literary equivalent of Dickens's behaviour at family dancing parties. According to his daughter Mamie's account, even when Dickens was not dancing, 'he would insist upon the sides keeping up a kind of jig step, and clapping his hands to add to the fun, and dancing at the backs of those whose enthusiasm he thought needed rousing, and was himself never still for a moment.'[26] [...]So Dickens dances at our backs rhetorically to rouse us into joining the festive community of his characters. He is then not only the author of the novel we are reading: he is also our insistently genial party host. Dickensian conviviality is not just what happens in the pages of his novels; it is a community event, bringing author, characters and readers into one big festivity.

The dancing author, the genial host, both mirroring and exhorting his readers to take part in the festive fun, not only through the kinetic revivals to readerly energy produced by multiple jokes, quips, comic asides, misdirects and funny anecdotes, but also through what Andrews observes is a kind of suggestive textual determinism, particularly evident in the Pope Joan scene, where 'the repetition of the words "laughter" or "merriment," supply[...] the keynote and the refrain', acting as an exuberant recitative, a physiological call to linking arms of the perpetual renewal of laughing togetherness. Andrews's conception of Dickens's party poetics comes close to the form of authorship that Roland Barthes describes in *The Pleasure of the Text* (1973), as 'writing aloud'; one that produces 'pulsional incidents, the language lined with flesh, a text where we can hear the grain of the throat, the patina of consonants, the voluptuousness of vowels, a whole carnal stereophony: the articulation of the body, of the tongue, not that of meaning, of language.'[27]

There are implications, here, for *Pickwick Papers*, a novel which is characterised by its sprawling, messy, indeterminacy, and where, as John Bowen has observed, the written world of 'papers', notes, letters, and apparently illegible inscriptions, is subject to misreading, *over*-reading and editorialising; and where voices, too, with their multifarious humbugs, intrigues and stratagems, are just as unreliable.[28] In this world, to laugh along with Dickens—to be, as Andrews puts it, 'roused' to his 'jig-step'—represents a value of itself: it is to be aware of one's own heaving body, but also to forget oneself temporarily. Through conviviality, Dickens 'writing aloud' as the somaticised author, emerging from within the disparate papers of his first novel, inaugurates the 'reading aloud' of his somaticised readers.

But while it might be tempting to consider that laughter here represents a vestigial trace of the 'natural', there is an extent to which, as Andrews suggests, it requires 'coaxing'. Such benign coercions means that small resistances are spotted, but then overcome, and that readers, like the characters in the Pope Joan scene, are 'laughed out' of their private tensions and worries, or led to laughter through, what Andrews calls a series of 'calculated shocks,' which 'break down [the reader's] sober detachment.'[29] The limits of this detachment are what Jonathan Buckmaster explores in 'Brutal Buffoonery and Clown Atrocity: Dickens's Pantomime Violence'. As he details, Dickens was once asked, in a purifying corrective spirit that is still recognisable today, to pen a new and morally improving version of *Punch and Judy*, but declined, characterising both the puppet show (and also the pantomimes that he had grown up with) as 'extravagant reliefs from the realities of life which would lose [their] hold upon people if [they] were made moral and instructive'.[30] Such entertainments were 'quite harmless' in their influence, he said, consisting of 'outrageous joke[s] which no-one [...] would think of regarding as an incentive to any course of action, or a model of any kind of conduct'.[31]

The lack of piety is refreshing, but as Buckmaster notes, this relation changed throughout Dickens's career, as audiences progressively became more squeamish about such stock feats of Georgian pantomime as mock-babies squashed flat to look like pancakes, or Pantaloon the clown being chased by red-hot pokers. By the 1860s, as Buckmaster notes, slapstick moments like these became 'something [both] to relish and to repudiate'. This is a negotiation that also plays out in the clown's onstage and on-page antics in Dickens's works, which produces what Buckmaster calls a 'double palliative', combining 'the communal laughter of a shared humanity' with 'the retributive laughter of an oppressor brought low'.

Yet while the cultural work of slapstick in the polyphonic space of the Victorian novel (and in Victorian culture more broadly), still remains a relatively under-developed field, Buckmaster is highly attentive to the ways in which specific techniques such as pantomime 'slosh' scenes are textualised, and re-interpreted, in Dickens's novels.[32] What such tableaux demonstrate, as he asserts, is the clown, not as a peripheral, but as a *central*, figure in the Dickensian imagination; and, also, as is limned in tales of suffering clowns in *Pickwick Papers*, as a *worker*, who like other workers in Victorian modernity, endures bodily hardships—and slapstick is a sign of this. The clown in Dickens's work can be read as a comic hierophant of an aesthetic that heralds new relations between self and community, positing a parallel world, that Dickens calls 'pantomime time',[33] which, like the elastic body of the clown, demonstrates its own extendable logic, while inflecting and changing the everyday.

Buckmaster's interests in discrete comic worlds—but ones that also re-direct animus towards new ways of thinking about the quotidian—talks to conviviality of a specifically *generic* kind in Peter Swaab's 'Edward Lear's Travels in Nonsense and Europe'. As Swaab suggests, Lear's works start by 'exploit[ing] the relation between sense and nonsense', and end by 'calling a new realm into being'. Lear's topographic imaginary is built on tensions, as Swaab details, both fugitive and home-loving, pivoting between 'questing' and 'nesting'. And, as with Dickens, the textual dream of a utopian community is powered by a perennial and incurable sense of 'outsiderliness'. But while Victorian nonsense writing has often been read as an analogue of the imperial project, Lear's terms of engagement are naturally more horizontal and resistant to such 'hermetic positions', and, from within this maelstrom of messy hybridities and cluttered everythings, rich possibilities arise for new relations and affiliations, crossing boundaries between human and animal; between animate and inanimate. As Swaab suggests about Lear's works: 'Bringing creatures unprecedentedly together is something nonsense writing can do'.

As with other writing in this edition, the comic never quite deserts seriousness, but finds new ways to interrogate and express it, playfully deploying multiple perspectives and literary forms—often short ones. Taking up Lear's limericks written across thirty years, from *A Book of Nonsense* in 1846, and *More Nonsense* in 1872, Swaab argues: 'Though brief they are not trifling'. The resonance of the limerick triumphs even when it is formally, as Adam Mars-Jones notes, 'oddly unsatisfying' like 'a bicycle with stabilisers'—ending, as it often does, with a repeated rhyme.[34] But this perennial state of a purposively self-thwarting *un*-development in the rhythm of Lear's work may be one of his wisdoms, as it relocates agonistic emphasis elsewhere: for, in not being fully grown-up, there are different potentials for adulthood. As Swaab suggests, 'nonsenses are dreams of metamorphosis. In them [Lear] imagines ways of not being human, but being still a happy creature'.

But it is as a traveller, as Swaab notes, that Lear's nonsense characters, and indeed perhaps Lear himself, makes *most* sense, particularly in his journals across the Abruzzi, Calabria and Albania—which still remain under-studied—but which feature a number of Lear episodes (in what Swaab calls comic 'Pickwickian' mode) in which traveller and indigenous inhabitant are mutually and reciprocally involved in exploring language, food and customs, and finding 'each is an object of energetic wonderment to the other'. This is no cool-headed anthropological exercise or experiment, however: in one scene at Episkopì, described in his Albanian journal, Lear finds a river full of watercresses, and immediately starts to eat them (accompanied by hunks of bread and cheese), much to the convulsed amusement of the local population, who waggishly supply a selection of equally strange accompaniments for the 'oddball' Englishman's dining experience—including handfuls of grass and a grasshopper. As Swaab comments:

> They become friends not in a conventional traveller's way by learning to understand each other's ways—and not via the explorations of history and archaeology and textiles which the journals also include —but from shouts of laughter, from exulting in their differences. The world of difference is the condition of friendship.

2   Jokes

The joke, too, can be seen as a form of traveller in the Victorian period, albeit a hyperactive and unruly one. For, in the age of the voluminous three-decker novel, or what Henry James famously called 'large, loose, baggy monsters', there is the pithy and piercing effect of a joke, which, given its formal qualities of condensation and contraction, threatens, as an impudent arriviste, Victorian culture's most pre-eminent literary construct—with an after-shock increasingly felt as part of a wider pan-European and transatlantic phenomenon.[35] As Freud remarks, at the beginning of the twentieth century, in *The Joke and Its Relation to the Unconscious* (1905):

A new joke has almost the same effect as an event of the widest interest; it is passed on from one to another like the news of the latest victory. Even great men who think it worth their while to tell us of their education, what cities and lands they have seen, and what outstanding people they have met, do not scorn to include in their memoirs the fact that they have heard this or that excellent joke.[36]

Although, as Daniel Wickberg has shown, the joke is, of itself, nothing new to Britain, having been a feature of national life since the 'classical *ana* and collections of *facetiae*' and 'jestbooks of the early modern' era, what *does* provide the distinct difference in the Victorian age is its excessive mercantile transmissibility: the new and myriad pathways for dissemination through exponentially expanding local, national and international print cultures, theatrical performances, circuses and revues.[37] For what began life as a figure of oral and folk culture, as Wickberg has shown, becomes, like many other commodities in the period, produced on an ever-expanding scale—industrialised even—with the voracious appetite for new material often outstripping supply.

And it is the implications of this new phenomenon, particularly the tensions it produces with regard to the nature of authorship, that Bob Nicholson discusses in his essay, '"Capital Company": Writing and Telling Jokes in Victorian Britain.' For while, as Nicholson argues, from the 1840s onwards, 'columns of jokes, jests, puns, witticisms, and humorous anecdotes [are] a staple feature of the press', an important new cultural figure begins to emerge from the 1850s and 1860s onwards: that of the professional and semi-professional joke-writer. Yet for these 'droll dogs' and 'agreeable rattlers' (just some of the many 'appellations', as Nicholson observes, that are applied to this new, and in some ways, hyper-modern profession) the joke-writer's art, unlike that of the professional novelist or journalist, is often anonymised and effaced, in the process of telling and retelling jests across numerous cultural platforms. As Nicholson notes:

> It is easy to imagine the novelist seated at a desk, quill in hand, engaged in the solitary production of a new manuscript [...] Indeed, representations of this creative 'brain work' circulated very widely in Victorian culture [...] Even [at a lower level of production] the most disreputable kind of reporting was understood to have been *deliberately written by somebody* [...] Professional joke-writers [however] were less fortunate.

For, as Nicholson asserts, the status of joke-work as a form of artistic production was also hampered by two contradictory impulses: the first of these was premised on the historical precariousness of the form itself, that 'jokes were supposed to be *observed*, *recorded*, *revived*, or *caught*; they were not meant to be *written*'. But then, against this, there was the extraordinary valency, even promiscuity, of a joke once committed to the air or to the page:

> [A joke] might be retold around dinner tables in return for a plate of venison, shared with a friend while strolling an art gallery, performed at a family concert, written on a postcard and submitted to a joke competition, or printed in newspapers from London to New York. At various stages of its life, it might be attributed to different wits, but the connection between a joke and its author was easily invented and even more easily severed.

Nonetheless, the comparative invisibility, even the spectral place of the joke-writer as a figure of cultural production in the latter half of the century, should not be mistaken for marginalisation. For while many jokes in the period were customised, as Nicholson explains, from old ones, and others were taken from the sayings of wits or the well-known, increasingly, many *more* were taken from the speech of real life, and this gives Victorian joke-writing and joke-writers, a distinctive character. To demonstrate this, Nicholson charts the origins and trajectory of some notable jokes from the 1880s and 1890s—drawn, as above, from quotidian observation—including one based on the overheard expostulation of a visiting Glaswegian to London, indignantly complaining about extortionate costs in the capital: 'Bang went saxpence!' After its first overhearing in the galleries of the Royal Water Colour Society, this was later reprinted as one of *Punch*'s most successful cartoons, with the phrase entering the language, and, as Nicholson observes, still in use a century later.[38] As he comments:

> Jokes, in this observational model of authorship, were not deliberately *written* or *manufactured*, but accidentally *encountered*, *captured* and *adapted*. There are echoes here of Baudelaire's *flâneur*, of would-be jokers strolling casually through life, subjecting the environment and the unsuspecting people around them to a hidden, humour-seeking gaze.

As Nicholson rightly points out, the *flâneur's* spectacularised position as observer, immersed in bohemian and classed masculine culture, is

implicated in the birth of the 'saxpence' joke, for there is a strong sense
that the Glaswegian, himself, did not *realise* he was being funny—even if
the wits of *Punch* did.

But there is an extent, here, to which the vocabulary of the period
could be broadened to name this new cultural figure, either as a *jokist*
(a term used by contemporary newspapers and journals), or as a *jokeur*,
the latter, drawing on the cultural repertoire of Baudelaire and Walter
Benjamin's entitled boulevardier—but also, departing from it.[39] For, by
dint of the joke-writer's invisibility and ubiquity, entry into this particular Victorian club does not rely on the explicit privileges of class or gender, but merely on an eye—or, as more often is the case, an *ear*—for
the quirky, the amusing, and the overheard incongruous phrase. *Punch's*
ledgers show, as Nicholson notes, that hundreds of *female* contributors submitted jokes to its annals in this mode (belying the prevailing
Victorian notion that women had no sense of humour), while up and
down the country, journals, and magazines, as well as national and local
newspapers, openly invited readers to offer up similar jokes or pithy sayings as part of competitions, or else, public appeals to collate and collect jokes to 'preserve' the culture of a particular newspaper's circulation
area. In the national jokescape of mid-to-late century Victorian Britain,
joke-writing was not only a new profession, but an attitude of mind—
and increasingly, this was a populist, rather than an elitist, pursuit.

It would be difficult, perhaps, to think of an author in the nineteenth
century *less* apparently associated with the joke than George Eliot. As
Dames has shown, if there is a tempo (what he calls 'affective mechanics')[40] connected to her work, it is one of duration and elongation,
suggestive, as he asserts, of her seriousness; and indeed, seriousness,
in its many guises, is the way that the Victorians, and Victorian readers, are characterised by Franco Moretti in his important recent work,
The Bourgeois: Between History and Literature.[41] But, in my own essay,
'George Eliot's Jokes', I take up her forgotten 1856 article on laughter, 'German Wit: Heinrich Heine' to argue that attention paid to Eliot's
undoubted interest in wit and humour (both, changing and dynamic
categories in the period) grants us new ways to think about the terms
of realism and sympathy in her work, and the relation between author,
narrators and readers. As I discuss, the essay on the German Romantic
writer Heine, penned anonymously for the *Westminster Review*, is
one of several that she wrote on this extraordinarily iconoclastic

and controversial figure—a cultural exile admired by among others, Nietzsche—and yet it has received no more than a name-check in two major critical companions to Eliot's work in the past twenty years.[42] This is despite the fact that Heine is the author who *also* provides the literary mainstay of Freud's work on the joke. Attending to Eliot's two-step theory of wit and humour, with humour coming from the *heart* of culture, and wit, or the joke (the German word 'witz' translates both as 'wit' *and* 'joke') striking 'violently' in Eliot's account, like an 'electric shock'—and often, *before* 'moral sympathies' are engaged—proffers new ways of reading her novels.[43]

In a broader sense, though, what is intriguing about Eliot's work is the degree to which even such an apparently 'eminent' Victorian (to borrow Lytton Strachey's satirical term for great nineteenth-century worthies) is immersed in joke culture.[44] One of the earliest recorded memories of her, as Kathryn Hughes has shown, is of Eliot, as a precocious seven-year-old in her childhood home at Nuneaton, reciting verbatim, and to any astonished adult who would listen, jokes from the eighteenth-century familiar, *Joe Miller's Jest book*.[45] A similar activity is also described by the scientific writer Philip Henry Gosse—later a member of the strict Protestant sect, the Plymouth Brethren—who, as a shy office boy in the 1820s, 'toilfully copied' out jokes from *Joe Miller's* to rehearse them in wider company.[46] Such childhood transcriptions and feats of memory provide a tantalising glimpse into subtle, ground-up shifts in the period: suggesting apocryphal but also meaningful ways in which the social capital of jokes rendered an experience that was at once both quasi-literary and quasi-scriptural.

This linkage is also suggested in a heated comparison of a jestbook to the Bible in the opening chapter of Eliot's first published novel, *Adam Bede* (1859). Even *Middlemarch* (1871–2), seen by many as the high point of Eliot's seriousness, and the summative moment of Victorian realism, was criticised by a young Henry James, for a tendency to 'make light of the serious elements of the story and to sacrifice them to the more trivial ones'.[47] 'Sacrifice' again stages a conflict, and a decidedly active one, between religion and comedy in the period. Eliot's knowledge of the circulatory systems of jokes is also demonstrated in *Middlemarch*, when the occasionally feckless, but well-meaning, Fred Vincy—whose horse has gone lame—must suffer the boasts of a horse-trader, not just about his equine charge's breathing problems, but about a joke on a similar subject that went the Victorian equivalent of 'viral':

'If you set him cantering, he goes on like twenty sawyers. I never heard but one worse roarer in my life, and that was a roan: it belonged to Pegwell, the corn-factor; he used to drive him in his gig seven years ago, and he wanted me to take him, but I said, "Thank you, Peg, I don't deal in wind-instruments." That was what I said. It went the round of the country, that joke did.'[48]

The punchline might be as tired out as the horse, but nonetheless, by the 1870s, going 'the round of the country' is, as we have seen, a feasible trajectory for a joke. What is less so, however, is that Eliot, herself, is, at one point, constructed as part of the new and ever-expanding invis-ible army of *jokeurs*. In a review of her historical Italian novel, *Romola* (1862), which contains, incidentally, a chapter entitled 'A Florentine Joke', one critic wrote in *Home and Foreign Review* in 1863:

[Eliot's] wit is not of that refined *malin*, and careless kind which befits the drawing-room. It is more the wit of the wine-party or club, or the professed joker whose facetiousness is manufactured by rule and line. [...] Sometimes she ventures on a pun; she tells us that beans were, in more than one sense, the political pulse of Florence. One who has so deep a fund of humour ought not to need reminding of the laborious ineffective-ness of this kind of wit.[49]

The jibe about the stale or over-worked gag also reveals the self-reflex-ive debates about the national sense of humour, that, as Wickberg sug-gests, were increasingly a part of late-Victorian life.[50] Leslie Stephen, for example, averred in his 1876 essay 'Humour' for the *Cornhill Magazine*:

A fashion has sprung up of late years regarding the sense of humour as one of the cardinal virtues. It naturally follows that everybody supposes that he possesses the quality himself, and that his neighbours do not. It is indeed rarer to meet man, woman, or child who will confess to any deficiency in humour than to a want of logic. Many people will confess that they are indolent, superstitious, unjust, fond of money, of good living, or of flat-tery [...] but nobody ever admits that he or she can't see a joke or take an argument [...] everybody has shrunk like a coward at one time or another from the awful imputation—'You have no sense of humour'.[51]

Surprisingly often, what mobilised an indignant critic or letter-writer in the period was a hackneyed or oft-heard punchline: for the Victorians, as for generations since, jokes required a perpetual sense of topical up-to-dateness. And it is caught on the horns of this temporal dilemma that Ann Featherstone depicts the circus clown in 'The Game of Words: A Victorian Clown's Gag-Book and Circus Performance'. For, as she describes, one of the changing aspects of the clown in the latter half of the century, is that, rather than being centre stage, he was the continuity man—given the job of 'keeping the ball rolling'—when many circus tricks (often involving complex equestrian feats and high-stakes acrobatics) didn't quite go to plan. In these interim moments, clowns fell back on 'wheezes'—prepared routines or asides, 'parodies of melodrama or Shakespeare, stump speeches on topics close to an audience's heart [and …] re-workings of familiar songs, short gags and backchat, all […] delivered within the close confines of the circus ring'.

But, as Featherstone notes, clowns—figures both of nostalgia to Victorian audiences and also more utilitarian comic every men—were expected to, as one disgruntled red-nosed artiste put it, 'vault, ride in saddle, hold balloons and banners, ride comic ponies, act combats and play parts in pieces [and] practise every day[…]'. Yet they were the focus of regular complaints (like the one about Eliot) from critical spectators who tired of the '"stale, flat and unprofitable" quality' of their verbal repertoire. As one letter to *The Era* protested in 1883:

> Why are the same old wearisome jokes and time belaboured jests repeated year after year? […] If [clowns] have not the ability themselves can they not get someone to write them something original? Or, barring this, why don't they read the comic and American papers?[52]

The exigencies of multiple performances meant time spent topping-up scripts was limited, but what Featherstone explores in her essay—as do the final two contributions to this section by Louise Wingrove and Oliver Double—is what Wingrove calls the 'non-verbal and paralinguistic techniques' deployed by performers to mediate jokes, as part of the 'communal circuitry' between audiences and comedians, often involving Deleuzian flights of the self.[53] Drawing on previously un-discussed and unpublished notes from the well-thumbed working (rather than complete) copy of the Victorian clown Thomas Lawrence's joke-book, Featherstone describes how this negotiation often meant rising *above* the material, to, as one wily circus ringmaster put it—'just gag it'—meaning that 'by a little physical exertion an immense deal of fun may be made out of nothing'.[54] *Nothing* is always something in comedy, though, and, as Featherstone explains, 'gagging' is a term which 'often meant ad-libbing' but also more often, an 'energetic performance, verbally and physically, using the circus ring and the clown's proximity to the audience'. Exploring the many ways, as Featherstone does, in which clowns breached, but also creatively utilised, this liminal space explains how they maintained their appeal—despite the sometimes *forced* quality of their wheezes, examples of which are rendered below:

> The height of nonsense is kissing an old Woman when there's a young one close by.
> Don't I look like a descendent of the seasons—my father was a season—he was a bumbailiff, he often used to seize.
> Why are the ladies the biggest thieves in the world—they crib their babies, they bone their stays and they steel their petticoats.[55]

As Featherstone notes, these lines 'sit awkwardly on the page and only really come alive in the delivery', but they nonetheless capture moments where 'verbose conceit and the self-conscious pun, so popular in Victorian print, might be realised with "side"' in the Victorian circus ring. What is inherent in the jests above, of course, is a kind of tamely commodified and family-friendly Victorian misogyny, yet gendered dynamics take a different turn in Louise Wingrove's essay, '"Sassin' Back"': Victorian Serio-Comediennes and Their Audiences'. For, like Featherstone, Wingrove is as interested in the *mode* of jokes' delivery, and their aftershock, as their verbal content—in the complex interplay between audience and performer.

And while Freud depicted wit as an almost exclusively male activity in *The Joke And Its Relation to the Unconscious*, particularly in the retort (as in, for example, the famous 'famillionairely' opening joke quoted from the pages of Heine), Wingrove's essay proffers an alternative account of gendered situational mastery.[56] While, as she notes, few verbatim details exist of the repartee deployed by working-class comediennes like Bessie Bellwood and Jenny Hill to control and manage hecklers in their audiences, there are descriptions of the spectacularised *effects* of these encounters. One of Wingrove's foci is the 'punitive patter' deployed by both women, a weaponised version of the licensed music hall cross-talk that one northern newspaper reviewer (in a description of Bellwood) called 'sassin' back'.[57] To 'sass', as Wingrove observes, has decidedly gendered connotations. It means:

[T]o reply or speak to someone impertinently, to answer back, and derives from the Latin *salsus*, or *salsa*—feminine for *salted*. It connotes vigour and spirit, but also provocation and conceit, all energies that were welcome in the music hall [...]. Here, sass also connotes an indomitable, specifically female spirit, talking back, fighting back, and raising her voice, and in this sense the off-the-cuff, feisty extemporising that is sass is political.

While it is oft-said that female Victorian music hall stars were transgressive, 'sassin' back' reloads the nature of the insult, and the vituperation of the cultural act, dramatising what Wingrove calls the 'demonic apotheosis of the comedienne', utilising the penetrative animus of the joke, to differentiate herself, as Wingrove suggests, from the serious 'Galateas' of the acting world, often portrayed via 'sculptural metaphor[s]' as 'beautiful, composed, and immaculate'.[58] Comic performers like Bellwood gave loud, skilful and intricate expression to verbal excess as a form of both unruly autonomy and appropriation, becoming the fierce metonymic 'tongue' of thoughtless patriarchal discourse, surreally replicated as *many* tongues, in the famous account by Jerome K. Jerome in 1892, where Bellwood—as Wingrove discusses—rebarbatively berates an unsuspecting coal-heaver who had been leading 'booing and hissing' against her. In just under six minutes, and through a virtuoso performance that transformed the audience's hostility into standing ovation, she left the 'forlorn' heckler eerily and spectrally bereft—by Jerome's account, 'surrounded by space, and language'.[59]

One of the English etymologies of 'joke' is from the Old High German word 'gehan'—'to utter'—and such moments reveal the singular logic of the Victorian music hall's dream-space, in which stars like Bellwood, as much *audience*-created as self-created, deploy their own, but also a communal comic utterance, as both insiders and outsiders to the theatres in which they operate.[60] In many ways, the negotiations of a serio-comedienne like Bellwood talks to the 'jubilant alterity' of another performer and household name of the period, Harry Relph, or 'Little Tich'.[61] As Oliver Double demonstrates in his essay, '"Deliberately Shaped for Fun by the High Gods": Little Tich, Size and Respectability in the Music Hall', the verbal gag becomes the 'sight gag' in Tich's works.[62] At four foot six inches high, Little Tich (whose name lives on in the language today) was famed for both his Big Boot Dance and for acting alongside Britain's tallest actor, Picton Roxborough (who was six foot five). The outpourings of popular affection for Little Tich were prodigious, literalising, at one point, the phrase 'hard act to follow', when, as Double discusses, an adoring Manchester audience *refused* to allow him to leave the stage in preparation for the next act. But Relph's success is testament to a kind of comic self-spectacularisation, where he appears to join in—and enjoy the jokes about his size—while also simultaneously and notably distancing himself from them, deploying a gestural and verbal meta-language admired by among others, J. B. Priestley:

> His act, for all its mad energy, kept moving into another and cool dimension, where we observed and estimated it with him. The clever eyes would give us a wink or at least a twinkle, asking us to join him as a sophisticated performer, pretending for our amusement to be an indignant jockey or outraged lady in court dress. He would suddenly take us behind the scenes with him, doing it with a single remark. He would offer us a joke and then confide that it went better the night before.[63]

Such techniques are redolent of fourth wall-breaking twenty-first-century comedians like Stewart Lee but, as Double also discusses, the self-ironising exuberance disguises what, offstage, was a decidedly strained ambivalence about what Lillian Craton has called 'the Victorian fascination with physical difference'.[64] Choosing Paris rather than London as a home, Relph, beyond his stage persona, was a gifted painter, musician and speaker of many languages, who, as Double observes, counted among his friends artists like Paul Nash and Henri de Toulouse-Lautrec. Indeed, as Nash commented, Relph's 'private character [...] was rather grave and inclined to studiousness'.[65] This is borne out in an extant film of Little Tich doing his Big Boot Dance during the Paris Exposition of 1900, viewable on YouTube.[66] For alongside the athletic skill, the creative 'angularity' that would also be a feature of Charlie Chaplin's works, and Priestley's 'wink, or at least a twinkle', there is also an intriguing *sang froid*.[67] One contemporary critic observed, as Double notes, that Tich's performance had 'a spontaneity—or a splendid imitation of it—that is irresistible'.[68] This doubleness is perhaps what made him so beguiling to late nineteenth-century audiences—embodying what Tom Paulus and Rob King call the 'paradoxes of the modern subject'.[69] In this respect, Little Tich's boots are themselves something of a temporal conundrum: for they are neither wellington nor hobnail boots, but long thin shoes—of about two foot—which bear far more resemblance to the old wooden slapstick than boots, making the distinctive slapstick report when they hit the stage floor. It is fitting, perhaps, in the transition between the nineteenth and twentieth centuries, that the phantom 'violence' of Grimaldi's slapstick should be replaced with the phantom 'fun' of Little Tich—imbricated in a joke which he may (or may not) enjoy.

3   DISSENT

If the Victorian age began with laughter as a form of resistance, it ends with a resistance *to* laughter, or particular iterations of it. The final three essays in the collection consider the different ways in which late-Victorian intellectuals, authors and critics dispossess and re-possess comic modes as part of new debates about literary style, aesthetics and subjectivity. Dickens operates here either as a nostalgic totem of a bygone age, or as the prototype for a commodified popular collective whose cultural logic can still be seen in the apparently giddy cohesion of the music halls. And this is the starting point for Peter Jones's essay, 'Laughing Out of Turn: *Fin de Siècle* Literary Realism and the Vernacular Humours of the Music Hall'. As he observes:

> As the geniality and '*charmisma*' associated with the Dickensian or Thackerean corpus faded away, the disenchanted stance of naturalism became entrenched. Laughter gained little purchase with the socially conscious narratives of George Gissing, Emile Zola, Arthur Morrison or Thomas Hardy, which sought to illuminate the enervating effects of modern conditions on the individual and the masses.[70]

But such positions are liable to be self-defeating, as Jones argues, for there is a 'tonal' crisis inherent in the genre: the problem is that a commitment to the faithful mimetic representation of modern life meant also being attentive to 'forms of merriment in pubs, streets or dwellings', which seemed 'glaringly dissonant' within these works. In this respect, Jones's particular focus is the ways in which the 'gestures and routines' of the music hall are subsumed into the 'pessimistic creed' of late nineteenth-century realism. This conflict can be seen in a number of Gissing's works, including a short story, published in the *English Illustrated Magazine* in 1893, 'The Muse of the Halls'. It concerns the ambitions of a 'serious' composer who marries a former music hall star, Lillian Dove. Lillian, whose real name is Hilda, speaks in the patter of the halls, even in private domestic spaces:

'The corruption of the music-hall, already! I can't help it. If I degrade myself, I am only following the general example of our time. Everybody, in every kind of art, is beginning to play to the gallery. We have to be democratic, or starve. And we don't like starving. We've got to *climb down*—there's a phrase for you, Denis! We have to *get a show*—there's another! We must find tunes that'll *knock 'em'*—[71]

Yet while Hilda's husband Denis attempts to retain something like artistic autonomy, this proves a fruitless quest that ends in a form of aesthetic capitulation (or 'playing to the gallery') as he abandons his attempt at writing a 'Cantata' and instead becomes the pseudonymous writer of catchy music hall ditties, famed through the land.[72] John Carey has commented that Gissing was one of the earliest English writers to 'formulate the intellectuals' case against mass culture'—an argument, that he suggests, was done 'so thoroughly that nothing essential has been added […] since'.[73] What is striking about Gissing, though—as for other writers of the 'novel of misery'—is that it is not only laughter's connection with populism that made it a suspicious activity, but laughter *itself*: for it signified a fundamental misreading of life. In this respect, the work of Gissing and others was seen as an aesthetic riposte to the 'humane Idealism of Victor Hugo and […] Dickens', who 'lacked the central conviction that the life of man was a nightmare of sensuality, crime, drunkenness and nervous disorders'.[74] Nonetheless, it is perhaps a capitulation of the kind that Gissing himself fictionalised, that despite his own commitment, as Jones observes, to a 'mordant solemnity', he also, at one point, 'played to the gallery', and enjoyed commercial success by writing a novel that was a 'knowing parody of the Dickensian comic method', *The Town Traveller*. This became an unexpected hit, universally praised.[75]

It is a different sort of protest to laughter—but nonetheless an impassioned one—that is taken up in Jonathan Wild's essay, 'What Was *New* About the "New Humour"?: Barry Pain's "Divine Carelessness".' Faced with reading the work of the 1890s writer Pain, whose humour, as Wild observes, is a surreal forerunner of *Monty Python*, the critic Andrew Lang complained: 'These new jokes vanquish me; they make me feel more than commonly suicidal. Anyone can put together incongruous bosh'. In an essay for *Longman's Magazine*, in 1891, and responding to a favourable *Punch* review of Pain's first book, *In a Canadian Canoe*, Lang commented that, 'it seems pretty certain that the same mind cannot appreciate both the New Humour and the old'.[76] Yet, as Wild notes, it is odd—considering Pain *inspired* the 'pejorative' category of New Humour—that his work is not more representative of other notable and enduring writers of this school like Jerome K. Jerome. Wild's discussion focuses on the aspect of Pain's work that so exasperated Lang, particularly the serio-comic device of the apologue, or moral fable, which rendered what Pain called the 'spirit of divine carelessness' that he argued was essential to all humour:

> If there is one gift more than another which opens to a man the world of the imagination, that gift is humour. Here that divine carelessness which is essential to true humour can move unimpeded: there are no stupid limitations; one needs no paltry research to acquire the local colour; one need not consult the lawyer, the doctor, nor the antiquarian, in order to gain a mean and stupid accuracy. The world of the imagination has no laws and no limitations but those which the instinct of the artist imposes upon him. It is not easy, as it may seem to some, to acquit one's self well in that world; it is not true that anyone can write a story of the imaginary world. There is a distinction between carelessness, the habit of merely making mistakes, and that divine carelessness which belongs to true humour.[77]

Pain's philosophical interests in humour are echoes of the work of earlier Romantic comedic metaphysicians like Jean Paul Richter, but are also inflected with a strong dose of everyday detail and anthropomorphism. Particularly characteristic of the stories from *In a Canadian Canoe* are 'On Art and Sardines' which features a 'doe sardine', swimming beneath a rowing boat moored by the Cambridge Backs, reading a novel by Ouida thrown overboard in disgust by a young man on a steamer.[78] Another apologue, 'The Girl and the Beetle', features a dying beetle called Thomas, who has lived a life of 'immorality' and is encouraged by his beetle wife Mary, and a pious acquaintance, Dear Friend (also a beetle) to repent his life, but, at one point, this process of spiritual purification is interrupted by 'a curious stridulating noise' which Thomas makes, and which he explains thus[79]:

> 'It is caused,' he answered dryly, 'by the friction of a transversely striated elevation on the posterior border of the hinder coxa against the hinder margin of the acctabulum, into which it fits.'
> 'Ah!' gasped the Dear Friend; but he speedily recovered himself. 'That is indeed interesting— really, extremely interesting.' He was trying to think in what way it would be possible to connect this with more

important matters. 'Talking about fits,' he said, 'I have just come away from such a sad case, quite a young-'
'I was not talking about fits, sir,' interrupted Thomas, a little irritably.[80]

As Wild notes, this story becomes a satire of Victorian attitudes to death, but the apologue offered, a 'format capable of providing fresh impetus for literature, being "much less exhausted than the lump of stirring incidents which is welcomed as a novel of adventure"'.[81] A story in similar mode is 'The Celestial Grocery', which focuses on a shop that deals in abstract concepts rather than material goods—for example, 'Requited Love', 'Political Success', and 'Personal Charm'—and culminates, as Wild suggests, with 'a pathetically sombre conclusion'. Despite enthusiastic reviews elsewhere, Lang regarded Pain's humour as, at best, undergraduate tomfoolery ('Cambridge fun'), or, at worst, the result of what Wild calls a 'deeply corrupted sensibility', or an unhealthy 'decadent variety' of humour that Lang distinguished from an earlier 'healthy nonsense' such as that exemplified by the work of Edward Lear.

The discourse of what constituted *healthy* humour—or not—in the 1890s is taken up more explicitly in the final essay of the collection, Matthew Kaiser's 'Just Laughter: Neurodiversity in Oscar Wilde's "Pen, Pencil and Poison".' Here, the focus is on a work which is often regarded as relatively minor in the Wildean canon, but which Kaiser argues is 'theoretically innovative', and deserves reassessment for its anticipation of debates 'for which we only now are developing a vocabulary'. It concerns the life of the Regency dandy, forger, critic and notorious poisoner—Thomas Griffiths Wainewright—who 'murdered two women and two men and attempted to kill two Australians'. Kaiser's interest is in the affective dissonance caused by the undoubtedly grim (and reputedly real-life) subject matter of Wainewright's dastardliness, and its witty and mercurial treatment by Wilde. This includes, at one point, Wainewright's justification for murdering his sister-in-law—'the lovely' Helen Abercrombie—whose 'life he had insured for 18,000*l*. As Wilde notes, 'when a friend reproached [Wainewright] with [her] murder, he shrugged his shoulders and said, "Yes; it was a dreadful thing to do, but she had very thick ankles."'[82] Such moments, as Kaiser observes, unsettle all sense of what a morally or 'mentally fit' reader might be.

Yet repeatedly, as Kaiser argues, twenty-first-century critics and readers of 'Pen, Pencil & Poison' have displaced their focus away from the essay's ethical complexity to more palatable concerns such as forgery, Paterian aesthetics, or rhetoric—*anything*, in other words, to take the sting out of the tale. But to acknowledge, indeed to *reclaim*, these unpleasant aspects, grants new revelations about the nature of laughter, and about reading itself at the end of the century:

> We must be prepared as readers to poison our minds, to read against the grain of our cognitive health. Forget, for a moment, the 'remarkable' Wainewright, or the witty Wilde: the *reader* is the true hero, or anti-hero, in 'Pen, Pencil and Poison'. The subject of Wilde's essay is our laughter: our susceptibility or resistance to his cruel jokes. Wilde prods us into questioning our ideological—our neuronormative—investment in being perceived by our peers as intellectually 'healthy' readers.

These are debates, he asserts, which strike at the very heart of English literary studies, both as an emergent discipline in the Victorian period— which 'justified [its] enterprise ideologically on therapeutic grounds'— and also one that speaks today through a differentiated language of neuroscientific investigation, and 'the nascent neurodiversity movement'. Unexpectedly, as Kaiser argues, it is one of Wilde's most vociferous, and conservative critics, who got closest to understanding, as Wilde did, the 'neural plasticity' inherent in reading. Though Max Nordau—author of *Degeneration* (1892)—was sent into a 'wordless rage' about 'Pen, Pencil and Poison', nonetheless, 'uncanny similarities' exist between Wilde and Nordau in regard to their views on the 'reader as physically susceptible to literary texts'.

The difference, suggests Kaiser, is one of degree rather than kind: while Nordau assumes one 'neurotypical reader'—a divergence from which is bound up with accusations of deviance and deficits—Wilde assumes *many* readers and 'actively encourages his readers to be of two minds, indeed, to be of four minds[...]'. As Kaiser suggests:

> 'Pen, Pencil and Poison' addresses itself simultaneously to at least four implied or mock readers: a socially conscious reader fascinated but troubled by the idea of Wainewright; a dispassionate and clinically detached reader who views Wainewright as a metaphor or conceptual abstraction rather than as an actual person; a sociopathic reader who smiles indulgently

at Wainewright's unconventional and unsentimental attitude; and an aesthetically sensitive reader engrossed in the play of Wilde's language, in the illusion produced. All four of these implied readers think the joke is on the other three readers. All four are correct. In 'Pen, Pencil and Poison', Wilde encourages us to laugh behind our own multiple backs.

Notes

1. Charles Dickens, *Oliver Twist*, ed. Philip Horne (London: Penguin, 2003), 128.
2. Alfie Bown, *In the Event of Laughter: Psychoanalysis, Literature and Comedy* (New York: Bloomsbury, 2018), 2. See also Alain Badiou, *Being and Event* (London: Continuum, 2005).
3. Anca Parvulescu, *Laughter: Notes on a Passion* (Cambridge, MA: MIT Press, 2010), 14.
4. James Kincaid, 'Laughter and "Oliver Twist",' *PMLA* 83, no. 1 (March 1968): 63.
5. Bram Stoker, *Dracula* (London: Penguin Books, 2009), 186–187.
6. Friedrich Nietzsche, *The Gay Science: With a Prelude in German Rhymes and an Appendix of Songs*, trans. Josefine Nauckhoff and Adrian Del Caro (Cambridge: Cambridge University Press, 2001), 104.
7. Sara Crangle, *Prosaic Desires: Modernist Knowledge, Boredom, Laughter, and Anticipation* (Edinburgh: Edinburgh University Press, 2010), 112.
8. Michel Foucault, *The History of Sexuality: An Introduction*, vol. 1, trans. Robert Hurley (New York: Vintage Books, 1990), 15–50.
9. R. B. Martin, *The Triumph of Wit: A Study of Victorian Comic Theory* (Oxford: Clarendon Press, 1974), 82.
10. Nicholas Dames, 'On Not Close Reading: The Prolonged Excerpt as Victorian Critical Protocol,' in *The Feeling of Reading: Affective Experience and Victorian Literature*, ed. Rachel Ablow (Ann Arbor, MI: The University of Michigan Press, 2010), 12–15.
11. Rachel Ablow, 'Introduction: The Feeling of Reading,' in *The Feeling of Reading*, 5.
12. Parvulescu, *Laughter*, 7. Also the subject of a commemorative conference keynote speech given by Sir Kenneth Calman, 'An Examination of Wit: Erasmus Darwin's Unwritten Book', in Lichfield, April 19–22, 2002.
13. See Richard D. Altick, *Punch: The Lively Youth of a British Institution, 1841–1851* (Athens: Ohio State University Press, 1997), 13–15.
14. Ibid., 19.
15. D. M. Hassler, *The Comedian as the Letter D: Erasmus Darwin's Comic Materialism* (New York: Springer, 2012), 22, n. 50.

16. William Hazlitt, 'On Wit and Humour,' in *Lectures on the English Comic Writers* (New York: Russell & Russell, 1969), 29.
17. Walter Pater, 'Charles Lamb,' in *Appreciations: With an Essay on Style* (London: Macmillan & Co., 1889), 107.
18. Parvulescu, *Laughter* 19–20.
19. Ralph Waldo Emerson, *English Traits* (Boston: Houghton, Mifflin, & Co., 1886), 256.
20. Robert Pfaller, ed. *Stop that Comedy! On the Subtle Hegemony of the Tragic in Our Culture* (Vienna: Sonderzahl, 2005).
21. Karl Marx, *The Communist Manifesto* (New York: Simon & Schuster, 2013), 63.
22. Charles Dickens, *The Pickwick Papers* (Hertfordshire: Wordsworth Editions, 1993), 74.
23. Dickens, *Pickwick Papers*, 73–74.
24. Thomas Carlyle, 'John Paul Friedrich Richter,' in *Critical and Miscellaneous Essays Collected and Republished* (New York: Alden, 1885), 19–20.
25. Benedict Anderson, *Imagined Communities: Reflections on the Origin and Spread of Nationalism* (London: Verso, 1991), 25.
26. Mamie Dickens, *My Father As I Recall Him* (Westminster: Roxburghe Press, 1897), 31.
27. Roland Barthes, *The Pleasure of the Text*, trans. Richard Miller (New York: Hill and Wang, 1975), 66.
28. John Bowen, *Other Dickens: Pickwick to Chuzzlewit* (Oxford: Oxford University Press, 1999), 44–82.
29. Malcolm Andrews, *Dickensian Laughter* (Oxford: Oxford University Press, 2013), 43.
30. Charles Dickens, 'Letter to Mary Tayler,' 6 November 1849, in *The Letters of Charles Dickens: 1847–1849*, ed. Graham Storey and K. J. Fielding (Oxford: Clarendon Press, 1980), 640.
31. Ibid., 640.
32. Jeffrey Richards, *The Golden Age of Pantomime: Slapstick, Spectacle and Subversion in Victorian England* (London: I.B. Tauris, 2014) is a magnificent starting point for reading into the cultural significance of Victorian slapstick; as is Maggie Hennefeld's consideration of the post-Victorian moment in *Specters of Slapstick and Silent Film Comediennes* (New York: Columbia University Press, 2018).
33. Charles Dickens, ed. *The Memoirs of Joseph Grimaldi*, 2 vols. (London: Richard Bentley, 1838), xi.
34. Adam Mars-Jones, 'Queerer and Queerer: "Edward Lear: The Complete Verse and Other Nonsense",' *The Guardian*, November 11, 2001, https://www.theguardian.com/books/2001/nov/11/classics.highereducation.

35. Henry James, *The Tragic Muse* (London: Macmillan and Co., 1921), xi.
36. Sigmund Freud, *The Joke and Its Relation to the Unconscious*, trans. Joyce Crick (London: Penguin, 2003), 9.
37. Daniel Wickberg, *The Senses of Humor: Self and Laughter in Modern America* (Ithaca, NY: Cornell University Press, 1998), 122.
38. For the joke as Victorian commodity, see also Wickberg, *The Senses of Humor*, chapter four.
39. Walter Benjamin, *Selected Writings Vol. 4, 1938–40*, ed. Howard Eiland and Michael W. Jennings (Cambridge, MA: Belknap Press of Harvard University Press, 2003), 18–35.
40. Nicholas Dames, *The Physiology of the Novel: Reading, Neural Science, and the Form of Victorian Fiction* (Oxford: Oxford University Press, 2007), 56.
41. Franco Moretti, *The Bourgeois: Between History and Literature* (London: Verso Books, 2013), 74.
42. See chapter six: 175, n.24.
43. George Eliot, 'German Wit: Heinrich Heine,' *Westminster Review* 65 (January 1856): 3.
44. Lytton Strachey, *Cornerstones: Portraits of Four Eminent Victorians* (Tucson, AZ: Fireship Press, 2009). Eliot, however, wasn't included in Strachey's list.
45. Kathryn Hughes, *George Eliot: The Last Victorian* (Lanham, MD: Rowman and Littlefield, 2001), 19.
46. Simon Dickie, *Cruelty and Laughter: Forgotten Comic Literature and the Unsentimental Eighteenth Century* (Chicago: University of Chicago Press, 2011), 36. See also, Ann Thwaite, *Glimpses of the Wonderful: The Life of Philip Henry Gosse* (London: Faber and Faber, 2002), 34–35.
47. Henry James, unsigned review, *Galaxy* 15 (March 1873): 424–428.
48. George Eliot, *Middlemarch* (Hertfordshire: Wordsworth Editions, 1994), 197.
49. Richard Simpson, 'Richard Simpson on George Eliot,' in *George Eliot: The Critical Heritage*, ed. David Carroll (Abingdon-on-Thames: Routledge, 2013), 233.
50. *The Senses of Humor*, 123–134.
51. Leslie Stephen, 'Humour,' *Cornhill Magazine* 33 (March 1876): 318–326.
52. *The Era*, August 4, 1883.
53. Barry J. Faulk, *Music Hall and Modernity: The Late-Victorian Discovery of Popular Culture* (Athens, OH: Ohio University Press, 2004), 30.
54. Peter Paterson, *Glimpses of Real Life, As Seen in the Theatrical World and in Bohemia: Being the Confessions of Peter Paterson* (Edinburgh: William P. Nimmo, 1864), 115.

55. For details about transcribing Lawrence's notes, see Ann Featherstone's essay for this volume: 203, n.8.
56. Freud, *The Joke*, 11.
57. 'Chips,' *The North-Eastern Daily Gazette*, January 22, 1894, 4.
58. Gail Marshall, *Actresses on the Victorian Stage: Feminine Performance and the Galatea Myth* (Cambridge: Cambridge University Press, 1998).
59. Jerome K. Jerome, 'Variety Patter,' *The Idler* 1, no. 2 (March 1892): 123–135. See also Peter Jones's discussion of the scene in his essay for this edition.
60. Donald Phillip Verene, *The Philosophy of Literature: Four Studies* (Eugene, OR: Cascade Books, 2018), 60.
61. Tom Paulus and Rob King, 'Introduction,' in *Slapstick Comedy*, ed. Tom Paulus and Rob King (Abingdon-on-Thames: Routledge, 2010), 5.
62. See Nöel Carroll's discussion of the sight gag in *Comedy/Cinema/Theory* (Berkeley, CA: University of California Press, 1991).
63. J. B. Priestley, *Particular Pleasures* (London: Heinemann, 1975), 189.
64. Lillian Craton, *The Victorian Freak Show: The Significance of Disability and Physical Differences in 19th-Century Fiction* (Amherst, NY: Cambria Press, 2009), 2.
65. Paul Nash, *Outline: An Autobiography* (London: Columbus Books, 1988), 170.
66. See chapter nine: 258, n.63.
67. Alan Burton and Laraine Porter, *Crossing the Pond: Anglo-American Film Relations Before 1930* (Towbridge: Flicks Books, 2002), 98.
68. 'Variety Theatres,' *Manchester Guardian*, December 16, 1908, 14.
69. Paulus and King, 15.
70. William Oddie, 'Mr. Micawber and the Redefinition of Experience,' in *Charles Dickens*, ed. Harold Bloom, rev. edn (New York: Infobase Publishing, 2006), 98.
71. George Gissing, 'The Muse of the Halls,' *The Gissing Journal* 42, no. 3 (2006): 8.
72. Ibid., 10.
73. John Carey, *The Intellectuals and the Masses: Pride and Prejudice Among the Literary Intelligentsia* (London: Faber and Faber, 1992), 93.
74. 'The Novel of Misery,' *Quarterly Review* 196, no. 392 (October 1902): 391–414.
75. Simon J. James, *Unsettled Accounts: Money and Narrative in the Novels of George Gissing* (London: Anthem Press, 2003), 52, 98.
76. Andrew Lang, 'At the Sign of the Ship: The New Humour,' *Longman's Magazine* 18, no. 108 (October 1891): 660–662.
77. Barry Pain, 'The Old Humour and the New,' *The Speaker* 4 (December 19, 1891): 741.

78. Barry Pain, *In a Canadian Canoe* (London: Henry & Co., 1891), 5–6.
79. Ibid., 168.
80. Ibid., 168–169.
81. Pain, 'The Old Humour and the New,' 741.
82. Oscar Wilde, *Intentions*, in *The Artist as Critic: Critical Writings of Oscar Wilde*, ed. Richard Ellmann (Chicago: University of Chicago Press, 1969), 377.

WORKS CITED

Ablow, Rachel. 'Introduction: The Feeling of Reading.' In *The Feeling of Reading: Affective Experience and Victorian Literature*, edited by Rachel Ablow, 1–10. Ann Arbor, MI: The University of Michigan Press, 2010.

Altick, Richard, D. *Punch: The Lively Youth of a British Institution, 1841–1851*. Athens: Ohio State University Press, 1997.

Anderson, Benedict. *Imagined Communities: Reflections on the Origin and Spread of Nationalism*. London: Verso, 1991.

Andrews, Malcolm. *Dickensian Laughter*. Oxford: Oxford University Press, 2013.

Anonymous. 'Chips.' *The North-Eastern Daily Gazette*, January 22, 1894.

Anonymous. 'The Novel of Misery.' *Quarterly Review* 196, no. 392 (October 1902): 391–414.

Anonymous. 'Unsigned Letter.' *The Era*, August 4, 1883.

Anonymous. 'Variety Theatres.' *Manchester Guardian*, December 16, 1908.

Barthes, Roland. *The Pleasure of the Text*. Translated by Richard Miller. New York: Hill and Wang, 1975.

Benjamin, Walter. *Selected Writings. Vol. 4, 1938–1940*, edited by Howard Eiland and Michael W. Jennings. Cambridge, MA: Belknap Press of Harvard University Press, 2003.

Bowen, John. *Other Dickens: Pickwick to Chuzzlewit*. Oxford: Oxford University Press, 1999.

Bown, Alfie. 'Eventual Laughter: Dickens and Comedy.' PhD thesis, University of Manchester, 2014.

Bown, Alfie. *In the Event of Laughter: Psychoanalysis, Literature and Comedy*. New York: Bloomsbury, 2018.

Burton, Alan and Laraine Porter. *Crossing the Pond: Anglo-American Film Relations Before 1930*. Towbridge: Flicks Books, 2002.

Carey, John. *The Intellectuals and the Masses: Pride and Prejudice Among the Literary Intelligentsia*. London: Faber and Faber, 1992.

Carlyle, Thomas. 'John Paul Friedrich Richter.' In *Critical and Miscellaneous Essays Collected and Republished*, 5–27. New York: Alden, 1885.

Carroll, Nöel. *Comedy/Cinema/Theory.* Berkeley, CA: University of California Press, 1991.

Crangle, Sara. *Prosaic Desires: Modernist Knowledge, Boredom, Laughter, and Anticipation.* Edinburgh: Edinburgh University Press, 2010.

Craton, Lillian. *The Victorian Freak Show: The Significance of Disability and Physical Differences in 19th-Century Fiction.* Amherst, NY: Cambria Press, 2009.

Dames, Nicholas. 'On Not Close Reading: The Prolonged Excerpt as Victorian Critical Protocol.' In *The Feeling of Reading: Affective Experience and Victorian Literature,* edited by Rachel Ablow, 11–26. Ann Arbor, MI: The University of Michigan Press, 2010.

Dames, Nicholas. *The Physiology of the Novel: Reading, Neural Science, and the Form of Victorian Fiction.* Oxford: Oxford University Press, 2007.

Dickens, Charles. 'Letter to Mary Tayler,' 6 November 1849. In *The Letters of Charles Dickens: 1847–1849,* edited by Graham Storey and K. J. Fielding, 640. Oxford: Clarendon Press, 1980.

Dickens, Charles. *Oliver Twist,* edited by Philip Horne. London: Penguin Books, 2003.

Dickens, Charles. *The Pickwick Papers.* Hertfordshire: Wordsworth Editions, 1993.

Dickens, Charles, ed. *The Memoirs of Joseph Grimaldi,* 2 vols. London: Richard Bentley, 1838.

Dickie, Simon. *Cruelty and Laughter: Forgotten Comic Literature and the Unsentimental Eighteenth Century.* Chicago, IL: University of Chicago Press, 2011.

Eliot, George. 'German Wit: Heinrich Heine.' *Westminster Review* 65 (January 1856): 1–33.

Eliot, George. *Middlemarch.* Hertfordshire: Wordsworth Editions, 1994.

Emerson, Ralph Waldo. *English Traits.* Boston: Houghton, Mifflin, and Co., 1886.

Faulk, Barry J. *Music Hall and Modernity: The Late-Victorian Discovery of Popular Culture.* Athens, OH: Ohio University Press, 2004.

Foucault, Michel. *The History of Sexuality: An Introduction.* 1st vol. Translated by Robert Hurley. New York: Vintage Books, 1990.

Freud, Sigmund. *The Joke and Its Relation to the Unconscious.* Translated by Joyce Crick. London: Penguin, 2003.

Gissing, George. 'The Muse of the Halls.' *The Gissing Journal* 42, no. 3 (2006): 1–14.

Hazlitt, William. 'On Wit and Humour.' In *Lectures on the English Comic Writers,* 1–31. New York: Russell & Russell, 1969.

Hennefeld, Maggie. *Specters of Slapstick and Silent Film Comediennes.* New York: Columbia University Press, 2018.

Hughes, Kathryn. *George Eliot: The Last Victorian*. Lanham, MD: Rowman and Littlefield, 2001.

James, Henry. *The Tragic Muse*. London: Macmillan and Co., 1921.

James, Henry. Unsigned Review. *Galaxy* 15 (March 1873): 424–428.

James, Simon J. *Unsettled Accounts: Money and Narrative in the Novels of George Gissing*. London: Anthem Press, 2003.

Jerome, Jerome K.. 'Variety Patter.' *The Idler* 1, no. 2 (March 1892): 123–135.

Kincaid, James. 'Laughter and "Oliver Twist".' *PMLA* 83, no. 1 (March 1968): 63–70.

Lang, Andrew. 'At the Sign of the Ship: The New Humour.' *Longman's Magazine* 18, no. 108 (October 1891): 660–666.

Mars-Jones, Adam. 'Queerer and Queerer: "Edward Lear: The Complete Verse and Other Nonsense".' *The Guardian*, November 11, 2001. https://www.theguardian.com/books/2001/nov/11/classics.highereducation.

Marshall, Gail. *Actresses on the Victorian Stage: Feminine Performance and the Galatea Myth*. Cambridge: Cambridge University Press, 1998.

Martin, Robert Bernard. *The Triumph of Wit: A Study of Victorian Comic Theory*. Oxford: Clarendon Press, 1974.

Marx, Karl. *The Communist Manifesto*. New York: Simon and Schuster, 2013.

Moretti, Franco. *The Bourgeois: Between History and Literature*. London: Verso Books, 2013.

Nash, Paul. *Outline: An Autobiography*. London: Columbus Books, 1988.

Nietzsche, Friedrich. *The Gay Science: With a Prelude in German Rhymes and an Appendix of Songs*. Translated by Josefine Nauckhoff and Adrian Del Caro. Cambridge: Cambridge University Press, 2001.

Oddie, William. 'Mr. Micawber and the Redefinition of Experience.' In *Charles Dickens*, edited by Harold Bloom, revised edition, 91–104. New York: Infobase Publishing, 2006.

Pain, Barry. *In a Canadian Canoe*. London: Henry & Co., 1891.

Pain, Barry. 'The Old Humour and the New.' *The Speaker* 4 (December 19, 1891): 740–742.

Parvulescu, Anca. *Laughter: Notes on a Passion*. Cambridge, MA: MIT Press, 2010.

Pater, Walter. 'Charles Lamb.' In *Appreciations: With an Essay on Style*, 107–127. London: Macmillan and Co., 1889.

Paterson, Peter. *Glimpses of Real Life, As Seen in the Theatrical World and in Bohemia: Being the Confessions of Peter Paterson*. Edinburgh: William P. Nimmo, 1864.

Paulus, Tom and Rob King. 'Introduction.' In *Slapstick Comedy*, edited by Tom Paulus and Rob King, 1–18. Abingdon-on-Thames: Routledge, 2010.

Pfaller, Robert. *Stop That Comedy! On the Subtle Hegemony of the Tragic in Our Culture*. Wien: Sonderzahl, 2005.

Priestley, J. B. *Particular Pleasures*. London: Heinemann, 1975.

Richards, Jeffrey. *The Golden Age of Pantomime: Slapstick, Spectacle and Subversion in Victorian England*. London: I.B. Tauris, 2014.

Simpson, Richard. 'Richard Simpson on George Eliot.' In *George Eliot: The Critical Heritage*, edited by David Carroll, 221–250. Abingdon-on-Thames: Routledge, 2013.

Stephen, Leslie. 'Humour.' *Cornhill Magazine* 33 (March 1876): 318–326.

Stoker, Bram. *Dracula*. London: Penguin Books, 2009.

Strachey, Lytton. *Cornerstones: Portraits of Four Eminent Victorians*. Tucson, AZ: Fireship Press, 2009.

Verene, Donald Phillip. *The Philosophy of Literature: Four Studies*. Eugene, OR: Cascade Books, 2018.

Welsh, Alexander. *The City of Dickens*. Cambridge, MA: Harvard University Press, 1986.

Wickberg, Daniel. *The Senses of Humor: Self and Laughter in Modern America*. Ithaca, NY: Cornell University Press, 1998.

Wilde, Oscar. *Intentions*. In *The Artist as Critic: Critical Writings of Oscar Wilde*, edited by Richard Ellmann, 290–432. Chicago: University of Chicago Press, 1969.

Conviviality

Laughter and Conviviality

Malcolm Y. Andrews

In *Pickwick Papers*, chapter 6, the Pickwickians are at Dingley Dell and assemble for a game of cards with their host and his family. Pope Joan is one of the games they play, and it involves various terms such as Intrigue and Matrimony:

> Old Mr. Wardle was in the very height of his jollity; and he was so funny in his management of the board, and the old ladies were so sharp after their winnings, that the whole table was in a perpetual roar of merriment and laughter. There was one old lady who always had about half-a-dozen cards to pay for, at which everybody laughed, regularly every round; and when the old lady looked cross at having to pay, they laughed louder than ever; on which the old lady's face gradually brightened up, till at last she laughed louder than any of them. Then, when the spinster aunt got "matrimony," the young ladies laughed afresh, and the spinster aunt seemed disposed to be pettish; till, feeling Mr. Tupman squeezing her hand under the table, she brightened up too, and looked rather knowing, as if matrimony in reality were not quite so far off as some people thought for; whereupon everybody laughed again, and especially old Mr. Wardle, who enjoyed a joke as much as the youngest. As to Mr. Snodgrass, he did nothing but whisper poetical sentiments into his partner's ear, which made one

M. Y. Andrews (✉)
Canterbury, UK

© The Author(s) 2020 37
L. Lee (ed.), *Victorian Comedy and Laughter*,
https://doi.org/10.1057/978-1-137-57882-2_2

old gentleman facetiously sly, about partnerships at cards and partnerships for life, and caused the aforesaid old gentleman to make some remarks thereupon, accompanied with divers winks and chuckles, which made the company very merry and the old gentleman's wife especially so. And Mr. Winkle came out with jokes which are very well known in town, but are not at all known in the country: and as everybody laughed at them very heartily, and said they were very capital, Mr. Winkle was in a state of great honour and glory. And the benevolent clergyman looked pleasantly on; for the happy faces which surrounded the table made the good old man feel happy too; and though the merriment was rather boisterous, still it came from the heart and not from the lips: and this is the right sort of merriment, after all.[1]

This is heady conviviality. The community laughter seems to be running on a loop. The euphoria at Dingley Dell is sustained at a manic level, and it comes from a good-humoured companionship that crosses all the boundaries of age and sex. This is a good starting point for thinking about the relationship between laughter and conviviality. There are several points to be made about the nature and quality of the convivial laughter here, and I would like to register these before broadening discussion of this theme.

Let us take those last remarks, about the 'right sort of merriment'. This qualification echoes contemporary debates about wit and humour and the distinction between them. Wit was seen as a demonstration of intellectual sophistication, often of a competitive kind, as in who can outdo whom in witty repartee. Wit is 'artificial and a thing of culture; humour lies nearer to nature',[2] wrote one critic in 1860. Wit segregates and marks out a sophisticated élite. Humour, on the other hand, is inclusive and harmonises individuals and groups. Wit springs from the head; humour from the heart. The Dingley Dell merriment is the 'right sort' because 'it came from the heart and not from the lips'.

One of the most eloquent and influential spokesmen for this new understanding of humour was Thomas Carlyle. In his essay on the German Romantic writer Jean Paul Richter in 1827, nine years before this *Pickwick* passage, he declared:

True humour springs not more from the head than from the heart; it is not contempt, its essence is love; it issues not in laughter, but in still smiles, which lie far deeper.[3]

'Not in laughter', says Carlyle. But six years later, in *Sartor Resartus*, he welcomed robust laughter: 'the man who cannot laugh is not only fit for treasons, stratagems, and spoils; but his whole life is already a treason and a stratagem'.[4] The essence of this true humour is love. Carlyle borrows the term 'inverse sublimity' from Richter to gloss this belief in the close relationship between humour and love (in the same 1827 essay):

> True humour exalts into our affections what is below us, while sublimity draws down into our affections what is above us [and it manifests itself in] warm, tender fellow-feeling with all forms of existence.[5]

Humour, laughter, conviviality and 'tender fellow-feeling' form a nexus, and that *Pickwick* paragraph is a celebration of the combination. Indeed, it is at the heart of the novel: the Dingley Dell Christmas is narrated in the chapter called 'A *Good-humoured* Christmas Chapter' (my emphasis). Let us look back on that passage again.

Much of what provokes the community laughter has to do with teasing hints of romance and matrimony (usually ridiculous subjects in *Pickwick*). Thereby, the normal social conviviality of a party is extended and deepened into the promise of more intimate emotional bondings between some of the individuals. Conviviality has as its core meaning 'living together', and that's the sense which I will be emphasising, rather more than its current secondary meaning.

Then we might think about the language and structure of that Dingley Dell passage. Most obvious, perhaps, is the repetition of the words 'laughter' or 'merriment', supplying the keynote and the refrain of the passage. Every interaction seems to lead to laughter and merriment as the description pans across the crowded scene. In terms of the passage's structural organisation, we have a long paragraph of about 330 words, but just six sentences. Heavier and more insistent punctuation would jam the momentum generated as the convivial energy intensifies and spreads epidemically. The prose thus *enacts* the sense of cementing merry community. The conjunctions are frequent and insistent, dragging every single person into the same festive frame, so that it feels like one long breathless sentence, punctuated only by roars of laughter. The last two sentence beginnings are effectively uninterrupted continuations of their predecessors, since they start with 'And...'. In fact, 'and' is as frequent a figure in this paragraph as 'laughter' and 'merriment'.

Polysyndeton is the term for this use of multiple conjunctions. Polysyndeton emphatically binds together disparate components: as such, it is the appropriate rhetorical instrument for generating community and conviviality—which are themselves forms of social conjunction.

Keynote verbal refrains, breathless polysyndeton, these are familiar strategies in Dickens for coaxing his characters into conviviality and at the same time coaxing his reader into their company to share their high spirits. I think of such techniques as the literary equivalent of Dickens's behaviour at family dancing parties. According to his daughter Mamie's account, even when Dickens was not dancing, 'he would insist upon the sides keeping up a kind of jig step, and clapping his hands to add to the fun, and dancing at the backs of those whose enthusiasm he thought needed rousing, was himself never still for a moment'.[6] As their author, of course Dickens could coerce his fictional characters into conviviality at any time. What was more difficult was to ensure that the *reader*—whose party enthusiasm might need rousing a bit more—was joining the narrative dance in the same festive spirit. Dickens exploits all the rhetorical means at his command to cajole his readers into expansive good humour and conviviality, because they *should* belong to the party. When you keep narrative company with Dickens, you can't stand coolly on the sidelines. Your participatory energy is needed to help fuel the fun. So Dickens dances at our backs rhetorically to rouse us into joining the festive community of his characters. He is then not only the author of the novel we are reading: he is also our insistently genial party host. Dickensian conviviality is not just what happens in the pages of his novels; it is a community event, bringing author, characters and readers into one big festivity.

I now want to move on to the role of laughter in this context, and to think about how it promotes conviviality in the core meaning of that word—'living together'. Laughter more generally conduces to community in various ways. Let me mention a couple: laughter as a social corrective, and laughter as social glue. Regarding laughter as a social corrective, the French theorist of laughter, Henri Bergson, notes its social purpose:

> a defect that is ridiculous, as soon as it feels itself to be so, endeavours to modify itself, or at least to appear as though it did. Were [a miser] to see us laugh at his miserliness, I do not say that he would get rid of it, but he would either show it less or show it differently. Indeed, it is in this sense

only that laughter 'corrects men's manners.' It makes us at once endeavour to appear what we ought to be, what some day we shall perhaps end in being.
....Laughter...pursues a utilitarian aim of general improvement.[7]

Laughter of this kind stigmatises eccentric behaviour and encourages a deviant's return to the tribal fold. It also marks out the laughers as those who belong to the same cultural community in finding certain kinds of eccentric behaviour ridiculous. So, on both counts, this contributes to the circumstances favourable to conviviality.

Secondly, laughter as social glue. Laughter and smiling are known to be primitive anthropological response-signals to disarm hostility, incite good-humoured sympathy, and encourage social play. The smile in our culture is a distinct signal, and can of course be used artificially and professionally as such, as in the so-called Pan Am or Botox smile, in which only the mouth smiles. There are obvious connections here with our theme of conviviality. All these are, as it were, obvious inducements to congenial group laughter. They bring laughter in to reinforce community: by infectious *bonhomie* exemplified in the Dingley Dell episode; by social correction through ridicule; and by smile and laughter signals to generate a social glue.

But Dickensian laughter also springs from calculated shock, in ways that might seem to run against the grain of conviviality. I would like to argue that this more abrasive and extravagant laughter ultimately, if rather obliquely, actually conduces to the creation of forms of conviviality. First, though, I want to discuss the mechanisms of laughter and its triggers. In particular, I want to concentrate on incongruity. Aristotle defines the comic, in chapter 5 of *The Poetics*, as a mistake or indecorousness that is not painful or destructive. Laughter can be detonated by the spectacle of abrupt violence that proves not to cause hurt. Someone falls on a banana skin; you laugh only when there's no serious injury. You would not laugh if someone moving slowly on crutches slipped and fell on a banana skin. It compounds misfortune, and erodes incongruity. But comic incongruity is a refreshing shock-collision of contraries. You *would* probably laugh if a pompous and self-satisfied politician slipped on a banana skin, spraining only his dignity. Dickens remarked how much he enjoyed this kind of spectacle in pantomime: 'it really was a comfortable thing to see all conventional dignity so outrageously set at naught'.[8] The pantomime pratfall brings into violent juxtaposition artificial dignity and coarse humiliation, and resolves itself in a levelling which harmlessly jolts one into laughter.

The shock of incongruity in this standard kind of example is usually a physical spectacle. It can also be a linguistic turn, as in a startling verbal ambiguity. W. C. Fields was once asked about his views on community provision for the young: 'Do you believe, sir, in clubs for young people?' 'Only when kindness fails'. This is humorous frame-shifting. You establish meaning in one frame, and carry the same material into a second frame where that meaning is abruptly subverted: slight shock and then a realisation of the pun. Laughter accompanies that ensuing resolution. Dickens's comic imagination feasts on particular versions of shock incongruity and its resolution. Wellerisms in *Pickwick Papers* are one-liner examples. Sometimes it's a simple pun from Sam: "'We'll have to rehearse that,' said the undertaker as the coffin fell out of the car". Sometimes the incongruity comes from a gratuitously shocking macabre analogy. The often-cited example is Dickens's recording of a memory of five still-born babies laid out funereally in a room, 'side by side, on a clean cloth on a chest of drawers; reminding me by a homely association, which I suspect their complexion to have assisted, of pigs' feet as they are usually displayed at a neat tripe-shop'.[9] The initial shock of such a gross association modulates into laughter as the imagination then consents, reluctantly, to the similarity between the two.

Laughter can be the outcome of shock, benign shock. It erupts in response to the playful flouting of expectations and upsetting of conventions, which has been called the Benign Violation theory. Abrupt incongruity, or rather the resolution of abrupt incongruity, is one such mechanism. First there is the shock of the collision of discrepant ideas, then the relief in perceiving resolution, relief that finds expression in laughter. One more example, of a different kind or degree, perhaps; and then I want to bring the implications of these examples to bear on the question of generating conviviality.

Here is a more delicately balanced drama of incongruities, from *Dombey and Son*, chapter 12. Little Paul Dombey is with Mr Toots, down at Brighton by the sea. Both characters, incidentally, are walking incongruities in themselves: Paul is a disconcertingly old-fashioned child, and Toots is a grown-up man with a childish simplicity. In this scene Paul, already fading slowly from life, is dreamily recalling a vision he had the previous night:

'It was a beautiful night. When I had listened to the water for a long time, I got up and looked out. There was a boat over there, in the full light of the moon; a boat with a sail.'

The child looked [at him] so steadfastly, and spoke so earnestly, that Mr. Toots, feeling himself called upon to say something about this boat, said, 'Smugglers.' […]

'A boat with a sail,' repeated Paul, 'in the full light of the moon. The sail like an arm, all silver. It went away into the distance, and what do you think it seemed to do as it moved with the waves?'

'Pitch,' said Mr. Toots.

'It seemed to beckon,' said the child, 'to beckon me to come!–There she is! There she is!'[10]

The scene is a gentle variation on the banana-skin joke. Paul's dreamy language of epiphany is incomprehensible to Mr Toots, who is nonetheless trying earnestly to help out with Paul's narrative. He comically literalises and materialises everything that for Paul is visionary, and threatens to ridicule the heightened mood. We the readers resolve the incongruity as intermittent humorous relief from the spiritual earnestness of Little Paul. That's an important function of humour, related to the relief theory. Immanuel Kant defined this kind of laughter as stimulated by 'the sudden transformation of a strained expectation into nothing'.[11] Dickens's contemporary, the philosopher Alexander Bain, put it like this: 'It is the *coerced* form of seriousness and solemnity, without the reality, that gives us that stiff position, from which a contact with triviality or vulgarity relieves us to our uproarious delight'.[12] Bathos and mock-heroics are familiar literary examples of this manipulated incongruity. The difference in the Dombey passage is that the comic incongruity does not *terminally* ridicule the child's earnest spirituality, (a) because we know Toots is not deliberately deflating it, and (b) because Paul's solemnity is natural, not '*coerced*'. Toots's daft interventions allow us just enough relief from the slightly grotesque precocious spirituality of Paul, without discrediting it with ridicule, and affectionately draws these two oddities into a touchingly close relationship.

In all these examples, semantic or dramatic, one pattern seems to be insistent: the shock of incongruity and then benign resolution, the reconciliation of disparities in various forms. So many of the comic strategies familiar to us, in Dickens and in general, depend on tensions and incongruities between initially irreconcilable binaries—comically juxtaposed: irony, bathos, burlesque, travesty. Burlesque is the comic elevation to epic status of its opposite—mean and trivial activity; travesty the coarse undermining of dignified activity; irony the use of words, with emphatic tone, to mean the opposite of what you really think. The basic chemistry of humour seems to need these confrontational polarities. In this context, remember Carlyle's definition of humour as 'inverse sublimity': 'True humour exalts into our affections what is below us, while sublimity draws down into our affections what is above us'. That model has obvious affinities with the binary foundations of laughter I've just discussed; it is a bringing together of apparent irreconcilables. The high and mighty are drawn down to our level; and the lowly are elevated from our potential scorn into our affections. 'True humour', says Carlyle, 'is not contempt, its essence is love'. 'True humour', in the Carlylean context, takes the conventional antitheses and reconciles them benignly.

Dickens's practice as a writer, and not just as a comic writer, depends on exploiting humorous incongruity, on trying out some risky chemistry experiments with potentially volatile combinations of material. He seems to relish entertaining incongruities—outlandish metaphorical analogies, clashing speech styles and registers, incompatible modes: 'the romantic side of familiar things', his declared practice of making 'fanciful photographs', or relishing the oxymoron in what he called the 'fantastic fidelity'[13] of his extravagant characterisations. He had to defend his practice on several occasions. One was in a letter to his friend and fellow novelist Bulwer Lytton. It is a well-known wry confession: 'I think it is my infirmity to fancy or perceive relations in things which are not apparent generally'.[14]

Forster in his biography of Dickens glossed this 'infirmity' eloquently. Let us consider the section where Forster introduces this:

> Five years before he died, a great and generous brother artist, Lord Lytton, amid much ungrudging praise of a work he was then publishing, asked him to consider, as to one part of it, if the modesties of art were not a little overpassed. [In his reply Dickens wrote] 'I think it is my infirmity to fancy or perceive relations in things which are not apparent generally'. [Forster then comments:] To perceive relations in things which are not apparent generally, is one of those exquisite properties of humour by which are discovered the affinities between the high and the low, the attractive and the repulsive, the rarest things and things of every day, which bring us all upon the level of a common humanity.[15]

This suggestive formulation echoes Carlyle's 'inverse sublimity', productive of a humour that issues in 'warm, tender fellow-feeling with all forms of existence'. More importantly for our purposes, it recognises in Dickens's distinctive brand of humour impulses which we associate both with his social sympathies and with his imaginative strategies. Dickens's art brings together ideas and people that cultural habit and social conformity have separated. His humorous imagination can shock us into recognition of hidden affinities. One writer on wit and humour, discussing original and striking comparisons in 1872, expressed this in a vivid analogy: 'it is as if a partition-wall in our intellect was suddenly blown out; two things formerly strange to one another have flashed together'.[16]

Two things formerly strange to one another have flashed together. In this sudden shock of conceptual affinities we have the germ of conviviality, in its core original meaning—a living together. One Dickensian mode of laughing conviviality is the Dingley Dell model of insistent bonhomie, with Dickens jigging rhetorically in support. Another is the benign fallout from extravagant juxtaposition and resolved incongruities when community is created between previously segregated entities. In an analogy with his crusading social programme for dissolving class hostilities, Dickens's humour, that explosively levelling device, promotes the jostling conviviality of ideas formerly separated and estranged.

NOTES

1. Charles Dickens, *The Pickwick Papers* (New Oxford Illustrated Dickens, Oxford University Press, 1948), 71.
2. Gerald Massey, 'American Humour,' *North British Review* 33 (November 1860), 462–463.
3. Thomas Carlyle, 'Jean Paul Friedrich Richter,' *Edinburgh Review* (1827); repr. in Thomas Carlyle, *Critical and Miscellaneous Essays* (Boston: James Munroe and company, 1838), I, 1–27.
4. Thomas Carlyle, 'Sartor Resartus,' in *The Works of Thomas Carlyle*, ed. Archibald MacMechan (Boston: Ginn and Company, 1896), 26.
5. Thomas Carlyle, 'Jean Paul Friedrich Richter,' *Edinburgh Review* (1827); repr. in Thomas Carlyle, *Critical and Miscellaneous Essays* (Boston: James Munroe and company, 1838), I, 1–27.
6. Mamie Dickens, *My Father As I Recall Him* (Westminster: Roxburghe Press, 1897), 31.

7. Henri Bergson, *Laughter: An Essay on the Meaning of the Comic*, trans. C. Brereton and F. Rothwell (Rockville Maryland: Arc Manor, 2008), 16–17.

8. Letter to Wilkie Collins, 4 April 1855, in *The Letters of Charles Dickens*, eds. M. House, G. Storey et al., Pilgrim Edition (Oxford: Oxford University Press, 1965–2002), 7: 585. Hereafter abbreviated to Pilgrim *Letters*.

9. Charles Dickens, 'Dullborough Town,' in *The Uncommercial Traveller*, ed. Daniel Tyler (Oxford: Oxford University Press, 2015), 118.

10. Charles Dickens, *Dombey and Son* (New Oxford Illustrated Dickens, Oxford University Press, 1950), 167–168.

11. Immanuel Kant, *Critique of Judgement*, trans. J. H. Bernard (London: Macmillan, 1914), 223.

12. Alexander Bain, *The Emotions and the Will* (London: John W. Parker and Son, 1859), 283.

13. Letter to Forster, ?midSeptember 1862, in Pilgrim *Letters*, 10: 126.

14. Letter to Edward Bulwer Lytton, ?12 November 1865, in Pilgrim *Letters*, 11: 113.

15. John Forster, *The Life of Charles Dickens*, ed. J. W. T. Ley (London: Cecil Palmer, 1928), 721.

16. Anon, 'Wit and Humour,' *British Quarterly Review*, 56 (July 1872), 43–49.

Works Cited

Anonymous, 'Wit and Humour.' *British Quarterly Review*, 56 (July 1872): 43–49.

Bain, Alexander. *The Emotions and the Will.* London: John W. Parker and Son, 1859.

Bergson, Henri. *Laughter: An Essay on the Meaning of the Comic.* Translated by C. Brereton & F. Rothwell. Rockville Maryland: Arc Manor, 2008.

Carlyle, Thomas. 'Jean Paul Friedrich Richter.' [Edinburgh Review, 1827]. Reprinted in *Thomas Carlyle, Critical and Miscellaneous Essays.* Boston: James Munroe and Company, 1838, vol.I, 1–27.

Carlyle, Thomas. *Sartor Resartus. The Works of Thomas Carlyle*, edited by Archibald MacMeehan. Boston: Ginn and Company, 1896.

Dickens, Charles. *Dombey and Son.* Oxford: Oxford University Press, 1950.

Dickens, Charles. 'Dullborough Town.' *The Uncommercial Traveller*, edited by Daniel Tyler. Oxford: Oxford University Press, 2015.

Dickens, Charles. *The Letters of Charles Dickens*, edited by M. House, G. Storey et al. Pilgrim Edition; Oxford: Oxford University Press, 1965–2002, vols.12.

Dickens, Charles. *The Pickwick Papers.* Oxford: Oxford University Press, 1948.

Dickens, Mamie. *My Father As I Recall Him*. Westminster: Roxburghe Press, 1897.

Forster, John. *The Life of Charles Dickens*, edited by J. W. T. Ley. London: Cecil Palmer, 1928.

Kant, Immanuel. *Critique of Judgement*. Translated by J. H. Bernard. London: Macmillan, 1914.

Massey, Gerald. 'American Humour.' *North British Review*, 33 (November 1860): 462–463.

Brutal Buffoonery and Clown Atrocity: Dickens's Pantomime Violence

Jonathan Buckmaster

[W]e screamed outright with laughter, when the funny man, in the after-piece, essaying to scale a first-floor front by means of a rope ladder, fell, ladder and all, to the ground.[1]

It seemed to me that the distinguishing mark of this type of the comic was violence. [...] And everything in this singular piece was played with [...] excess; it was a giddy round of hyperbole.[2]

In the epigraph that begins this chapter, Charles Dickens and George Augustus Sala jointly reflect on some 'curious and wonderful' first experiences in life: notable not only because they are so widely experienced, but also because they translate into vivid, indelible memories. As they dare the reader: 'Cast the stone as far into the river of Lethe as you will [and] the sluggish tide shall wash it back again, and, after playing duly with it on the sand, ever land it high and dry upon the beach'.[3] Such oblivion-proof youthful firsts include the first pair of trousers, first picture book, first love, first baby and first death. Among these is also the first visit to a play at a small country theatre, 'stupid, badly acted, badly got up', yet filling the child with admiration, the sorry band ringing

J. Buckmaster (✉)
University of Buckingham, Buckingham, UK

© The Author(s) 2020
L. Lee (ed.), *Victorian Comedy and Laughter*,
https://doi.org/10.1057/978-1-137-57882-2_3

philharmonic to his untrained ear, and the nourishment of oranges and sponge cake at the theatre, and after-midnight sandwiches once back home, affording strong sensory recollections. At the theatre, a subduedness was required for the sake of good manners, counterbalanced during the comic after-piece with the release of laughter.

These phenomenological firsts emerge as a heady mixture of sustenance and emotion, of people coming and going, of stimuli both good and bad, conjuring up an entire life cycle. Somewhere in this mix is the strange force of laughter, juxtaposed with convention, but also clearly signalled as a mock-transgression, something in fact licensed by the 'condonatory smiles' on a parent's face. Laughter is part of our initiation into the world, which is to say into our sensory existence with all its seductiveness, limitations and inherent violence. It is a double bind, both a norm and a violation, a creator of affiliations and excommunicator, soothing and violent, light and dark.

Laughter is thus a contradiction and a multitude. As the second quote, by poet Charles Baudelaire, states, it is frequently a hyperbole and excess. For him, what most differentiates English pantomime from its French counterpart is passion, in a dizzying combination of exaggeration and violence. In Baudelaire's view, Deburau's Pierrot, 'cet homme artificiel', is evocative of death, mysterious, pale and silent, both moon-like and serpent-like, 'straight and long as the gibbet', positioned outside or above life.[4] By contrast, the English clown's base and jubilant excesses are the life-essence of comedy, firmly located within life's material, everyday nature. This is a comic who can embody anything, high or low—a mighty tempest one second, an inanimate sack of potatoes the next. He is present and alive, larger than life even, in his conspicuous physicality and bestial insatiability for food and sex. More importantly, he also appears to be larger than death, seemingly indestructible no matter what may befall him. To this end, violence is indispensable. This is the 'comique féroce et très-féroce', or 'comic savagery', as close to absolute or pure comedy as possible. Its intensity is vertiginous, the laughter intoxicating, both 'terrible and irresistible'. For Baudelaire, then, violence is the essence of English pantomime, and pantomimic violence and slapstick clownery emerge as particularly apt illustrations of the familiarity between our laughter and the more obviously dark segments of existence, such as cruelty and death.

The two energetic responses to pantomime above encapsulate the physical and sensory impact of the form's violence on its spectator.

Dickens does not merely laugh, but 'screams' with laughter at the clown's fall from a significant height, while Baudelaire is made 'giddy' by the violence of the spectacle. Their visceral reactions are only partial translations of the energy created by the mime, attesting to the intensity of these exchanges. Slapstick routines were the mainspring of pantomime's central 'harlequinade' section, which was popularised and given its fullest expression by the great Joseph Grimaldi (1778–1837) during the Regency period, and remained a feature of pantomime until the latter part of the nineteenth century.

Despite such enduring popularity, this enactment of violence problematised the laughter of spectators, who grew increasingly aware of being simultaneously delighted and appalled, an effect registered in a range of contemporary responses spanning the sixty years after Grimaldi's retirement. A *Times* review of the pantomimes of Christmas 1823 excused Grimaldi's crimes in hyperbolic terms without a trace of discomfort: 'If he took up a red-hot poker to anybody, we could never interfere – though it had been to save our own father – and when he stole apples, we really doubted whether common honesty was not a kind of prejudice'.[5] The review emphasises the audience's shared affection for the clown to the extent that, in the unlikely event of the fictional and real worlds merging, their affiliations would still lie with the mischievous clown rather than 'their' father. This is about laughter's power to suspend rules, to question and disturb the status quo, and make us look at the world afresh. It locates the comic firmly outside mundane convention—in the ludic world, where everything is both possible and allowed. Fifteen years later, H. D. Miles similarly acknowledged a happy complicity with the clown's violent acts, asserting that 'Grimaldi was a household word; it was short for fun, whim, trick, and atrocity,— that is to say, clown atrocity, crimes that delight us'.[6] Such gleeful amorality is made possible by the very non-reality of the clown's world, and is further abetted by the ludic-comic mode that rules his world. In this account, while the clown possessed a litany of vices, being 'cruel, treacherous, unmanly, ungenerous [and] greedy [...] —yet for all this, multiplied up to murder, [...] we loved him, and rejoiced in his successes'.[7] Thus, it seems, the very outrageousness of the clown's actions exculpated him, leaving the spectators 'quite blind to the moral delinquency of Mons. Clown's habits'.[8]

However, from mid-nineteenth century onwards, this unqualified acceptance is increasingly tempered with a more self-conscious awareness that such violence may not be universally popular or even funny.

Jim Davis traces a shift across the period, 'from pantomime as a radical spectacle to pantomime as a more conservative force'.[9] Its focus shifted onto morality and providing family entertainment, becoming 'so strongly inter-linked with Victorian notions of childhood, childhood innocence and domesticity', that this necessitated a softening of the form, including a displacement of the Harlequinade.[10] At the same time as it became 'less adult', to echo Michael Booth, pantomime also 'grew simpler, less satiric, more cruel, more obvious comically and scenically, more ostentatiously moral and even instructional'.[11] The responses it elicited grew more complicated and ambiguous. Thus, in his *Comical Fellows* (1863), Andrew Halliday starts in the same vein as Miles, rhetorically pondering: 'Where is the witticism that can compete with sitting on a baby, and flattening it to the shape of a pancake?' In a shift away from Georgian sensibilities, however, he calls the clown 'dreadfully cruel, [...] forever burning Pantaloon with red-hot pokers, slapping him in the face, and shutting his head into boxes'. Still, he happily catalogues the cruelties, and exclaims 'how we enjoy it all!', sidestepping any introspection with the following proclamation: 'We will not stop to inquire why cruelty is so exquisitely funny; but it is exquisitely funny; nothing more so'.[12]

More ambivalence ensued, as Jacky Bratton (2010) demonstrates in her analysis of pantomime reviews in *Punch* from mid-century onwards. What emerges from these reviews is a shift in attitude towards old and new pantomime alike. It was now something both to 'relish' and to 'repudiate', to experience but to disapprove of and reject as 'violent, immoral and altogether vulgar'.[13] A review of the 1877 pantomime *Little Goody Two-Shoes* brings us full circle as it attempts to contain, rather than ignore, the contradictory feelings the harlequinade engenders. In describing it as 'a very silly and stupid piece of brutal buffoonery', it balances the dismissive with a more calculated and measured consideration of its effect, and, in its softened reworking of the 'clown atrocity' epithet, neatly bookends this general trajectory of Victorian comical taste from the robust and earthy to the gentle and decorous.[14] It is an apt illustration of the Victorians' complex relationship with slapstick, and the changing appeal of its visceral impact.

Building on Malcolm Andrews's discussion of comic violence in *Dickensian Laughter*, this chapter explores how Dickens evaluated this troubling laughter and how he sought to generate its effects in his work. Andrews finds in Dickens the same 'dizzy bewilderment', or 'giddy round of hyperbole' (*le vertige de l'hyperbole*), that Baudelaire sees in the English clown's performance. However, he notes a 'problematic difference' between live pantomime and Dickens's comical anecdotes, in that—unlike the novel reader—the pantomime spectator approaches the moment of violence 'prepared for its zanily playful mode'.[15] Consequently, prior to 'staging his comical performance', Dickens must artfully 'rouse his reader's sensibility' into an equivalent state, using violence even to 'seize his audience and warm them up quickly'.[16] In other words, readers must be 'lured into share this intoxication', whereas the author needs to 'break down [their] sober detachment', thus priming them for the madness of laughter.[17]

I will first expand on Andrews's thesis by demonstrating how Dickens's writing becomes an insulated space from where he can experiment with slapstick violence and move his reader both mentally (to become more receptive to Dickens's fanciful and comic sensibility) and physically (to enjoy the 'physiologically beneficial' 'kinetic energy' of their own laughter).[18] As Andrews points out, laughter is a 'violently tonic exercise' with the potential both to revitalise and to harm.[19] The key formula Dickens relies on to ensure that his readers laugh this invigorating laughter is '[v]iolence with safety',[20] a dynamic Dickens himself acknowledges as crucial. On the one hand, he writes, there is an 'audience of vulnerable spectators, liable to pain and sorrow', and on the other, 'the jocund world of pantomime', where 'every one [... is...] superior to all the accidents of life',[21] offering a welcome temporary respite from an otherwise perilous existence.

Secondly, by delineating how Dickens nurtures a place of safety for the laugher I will develop the notion of 'combined immunity-vulnerability' as defined by James R. Kincaid, whereby 'laughter provides a kind of immunity which may become a special kind of vulnerability'.[22] Spectators may laugh at a pie-in-the-face gag, but in the scenario of 'the custard pie containing sulphuric acid' everything changes.[23] For laughter to occur, then, we generally require the pain—or its target—not to be real. The binary between comfort and shock is fragile, unstable, and porous, and the more comfortable we are made to feel during the build-up, the more potent the shock when this comfort or our expectations are upturned. Thus, the 'combined immunity-vulnerability' effect 'makes us so open, even if just for an instant, to the deepest attacks'.[24] On the one hand, Dickens's choice of the public pantomimic mode as a method with which to work upon his private readers can be read as a manifestation of his desire to connect with them on a more physical, immediate level. On the other hand, by cultivating this connection within this mode, Dickens both inherits and harnesses the instability registered in the spectator responses quoted above. His slapstick violence therefore requires careful authorial management, yet, as in pantomime, it appears to be in continual opposition to control, positioning the reader in an uncomfortable and ambivalent state.

Bergson proposes that laughter emerges 'every time a person gives us the impression of being a thing',[25] and I will demonstrate how Dickens's use of culturally recognised tropes places his characters upon the permeable margin between things and people. Once there, they can be laughed at more comfortably, but may also maintain a semblance of humanity that makes that comfort provisional. In this way, Dickens's method draws on the aesthetic of the grotesque, defined by Michael Hollington as 'an essentially mixed or hybrid form, [...] its elements, in themselves heterogeneous, [...] combining in unstable, conflicting, paradoxical relationships'.[26] Dickens deploys this irresolution to enact a specific physical effect upon his readers, akin to the immediate experience of attending a live theatrical performance. The grotesque is an illuminating lens through which to view Dickensian laughter and violence, specifically the ambiguity of its effect on the reader, but also its kaleidoscopic potential for Dickens himself.

Here, Thomas Hood represents an important intersection between Dickens and Grimaldi. He was a friend of Dickens from 1840, and, in a creative symbiosis typical of the period, Dickens was both a reader of Hood's *Comic Annual* (1830–1839) and a contributor to *Hood's Magazine* (1844–1845). Hood, in turn, was an admirer of Grimaldi: his study wall carried the clown's portrait, and Grimaldi was the subject of one of Hood's *Odes and Addresses to Great People* (1825). Contemporary commentators also traced such affinities: in one article, H. F. Chorley felt it 'beseeming and proper' to move from a discussion of 'Boz' to Hood, while another called Hood 'the Grimaldi of literature'.[27]

Sara Lodge has extensively traced Hood's use of the grotesque body and the crosscurrents between Hood's work and the illegitimate theatre of Grimaldi's pantomime. Like Dickens and Cruikshank, she notes, Hood was attracted to the grotesque 'for its popular qualities', including 'its insistence on the public and physical body [and] its frequent violence'.[28] She further notes that Hood drew on the grotesque's unsettling ability to make the line between subject and object permeable, in a manner that implicates the viewer/reader within the work and 'threatens to reveal the reader as himself or herself grotesque'.[29] Hood adopted the grotesque as a site where violently subversive fantasies could be 'both relished and punished', and Dickens draws on these same elements in his recasting of pantomime violence as novelistic slapstick violence.[30]

John Carey alludes to Dickens's grotesque sensibility when he comments that 'he is able to see almost everything from two opposed points of view'.[31] In 'A Curious Dance Round a Curious Tree' (1852), which describes Dickens's Boxing Day visit to St Luke's Hospital for the Insane, we get a glimpse of his evaluation of comic violence. He rhetorically wonders why he should choose to visit this institution over going to see a pantomime, which he describes as a space where 'no affliction or calamity [...] leaves the least impression', where the only consequence of rehearsing reality is laughter. There, 'a man may tumble into the broken ice, or dive into the kitchen fire, and only be droller for the incident'.[32] Pantomime characters' superiority 'to all the accidents of life, though encountering them at every turn' is a mode of the grotesque body, whereby superhuman triumphs over corporeal limits stand for what Bakhtin calls the 'grandiose, exaggerated, immeasurable' body, connoting 'fertility, growth, and a brimming-over abundance'.[33] However, while Bakhtin sees this as a collective experience, enjoyed by 'a people, who are continually growing and renewed', Dickens seems to indicate that the audience are invested in pantomime violence as individuals.[34] He identifies the apparent invincibility of pantomime's participants as 'the secret (though many persons may not present it to themselves) of the general enjoyment which an audience of vulnerable spectators, liable to pain and sorrow, find in this class of entertainment'.[35] Despite terming this a 'general' enjoyment, then, this is not (only) the communal pleasure that Bakhtin posits, but something 'secret', that the audience 'may not present [...] to themselves'. Although this laughter occurs in a public space, its true underlying cause cannot be publicly acknowledged, lest it reveal the spectators' own private vulnerability, and so it becomes 'a kind of secret freemasonry, or even complicity with other laughers'.[36]

This dynamic becomes relevant in the context of the choice facing Dickens, between visiting a real and vulnerable suffering woman in St Luke's—a 'poor creature [...] driven mad by an infuriated ox in the streets'—and going to the theatre to watch a 'Pantomimic woman', one of those invulnerable performers who could have been 'gored to any extent by a Pantomimic ox, at any height of ferocity', but would leave the audience with 'the comforting assurance that she had rather enjoyed it than otherwise'.[37] The two settings are compared both for contrast and for similarity between the exaggerated actions of the asylum's inhabitant and the exuberant gestures of the comic actor. Opting for the morally commendable choice, Dickens visits St. Luke's rather than Covent Garden, with the wholly seasonal message that one should attend to the vulnerability of real people rather than vicariously enjoy the illusory invulnerability of fantasy figures. Yet, as Carey contends, 'savagery [has] to be there before Dickens' imagination is gripped'.[38] This thesis is borne out by the comparative force of the imagery in the passages describing pantomime, which is at least as compelling as his more wholesome conclusion. This dialectic between what is wholesome but possibly bland and what is dark and riotous extends from Dickens the novelist to his work.

The private enjoyment of violence that Dickens so relishes in the clown's performances is recreated from stage to page in a number of his works. As I shall demonstrate, the grotesque pantomimic mode enables him to enjoy the act in a gleeful Bakhtinian manner simultaneously with registering his discomfort. This seeming paradox of affect in fact aligns well with Dickens's work more generally, at the nexus of the private experience of reading and a shared, communal performance.

The principal component of the stage pantomimic mode that Dickens adopted was its perennial cultivation of the body as the primary mode of expression and primary site for the exploration of the grotesque. The stage clown used a range of strategies to assert the centrality of the corporeal, including expanding it through overconsumption and foregrounding it through innovative costume. Typically, the pantomimic body is 'grandiose' rather than diminished, 'continually growing' rather than destroyed, and 'immeasurable' rather than limited. Crucially, it is a target for blows, punches, slaps, burns and gunshots, which serve a particular symbolic purpose. As Bakhtin explains, the 'abuse and thrashing [to which the grotesque body is subjected] are equivalent to a change of costume, to a metamorphosis' which can simultaneously 'kill and regenerate, put an end to the old life and start the new'.[39] One way in which the pantomime clown enacts this transformation is through displays of superhuman indestructibility. For example, Baudelaire describes a clown's onstage guillotining as follows:

His head came away from his neck, a big white and red head, rolling down with a thump in front of the prompter's box and exposing the bleeding neck, split vertebrae and all the details of a piece of butcher's meat, just cut up for the shop window.[40]

The rich cascade of colour and sound, the minute detail and the metaphor of the butcher's meat emulate a report of a real execution. Suddenly, 'the truncated torso, driven by the irresistible monomania of thieving, got up, triumphantly filched its own head, like a ham or a bottle of wine, and [...] rammed it into its pocket!'[41] In sketching the scene for his readers, Baudelaire sets up and then violates their expectations, just as the clown does with his audience when his head becomes a stage prop, stashed away with the other stolen goods.

Of course, this apparent indestructibility was just choreographed illusion, and Dickens allows glimpses of this awareness to surface in his work when it suits his authorial purposes. What he is keen to stress in the *Memoirs of Joseph Grimaldi* (1838) is the physical pain to the clown, his actual vulnerability. He catalogues the multiple accidents and injuries suffered during the clown's career in order to foreground the fortitude of his character. In a rebuttal to the anti-theatrical views that regarded the profession as indolent, Dickens reads Grimaldi's participation in slapstick spectacles as representative of the 'anxieties, and hardships, and privations, and sorrows, which make the sum of most actors' lives'.[42] He weighed the effects of such mental and physical toils in the 'Stroller's Tale' of *The Pickwick Papers* (1836–1837), which describes the heavy toll paid by a clown for a lifetime of physical comedy, as well as in *Hard Times* (1854), when Sissy Jupe reminds that clowns 'bruise themselves very bad sometimes'.[43] More often, however, Dickens's acute awareness of the semiotic and affective potential of the invulnerability illusion makes him keen to maintain the illusion rather than dispel it and resolve the conflict.

1   COMIC VIOLENCE: CHARACTER-AS-THING AND CHARACTER-AS-CLOWN

In Dickens's opus, limbs and other body parts often become detachable or semi-autonomous appendages, like the mock-decapitation witnessed by Baudelaire. Thus, in *Oliver Twist* (1837–1839), Mr Grimwig threatens to eat his own head in a manifestation of comic by-play between the sober forces of the establishment represented by the nay-saying Grimwig and a human body seemingly uncontainable by the regular laws of biology.[44] One year later, the theme of physical dislocation continues in a spoof proposal in 'The Mudfog Papers' for 'an entirely new police force, composed entirely of automaton figures' who could 'walk about until knocked down like any real man'.[45] This is both about invincibility and about blurring the boundary between things and humans, where

> the great advantage would be, that a policeman's limbs might all be knocked off, and yet he would be in a condition to do duty next day. He might even give his evidence next morning with his head in his hand, and give it equally well.[46]

In Cruikshank's illustration, these automata carry their body parts with seeming indifference but look sufficiently human-like to represent 'something mechanical encrusted on the living'.[47] Other 'officers' are neatly stacked on the shelves, with two stacked upside down. Throughout Dickens's writing, we find this in-between domain populated by entities defying labels, convention and unity, fluidly yet rigidly crossing the boundary between the animate and inanimate, which is 'where [his] imagination is mostly engaged'.[48] He 'gives distinct and individual attention to each part of a body, and watches it moving as something apart from the mass, [thus contradicting] the accepted view of what constitutes a unity'.[49]

In *Barnaby Rudge* (1841), the legs of the Gordon rioter Sim Tappertit become detachable appendages. We are told that in Sim's small body 'there was locked up an ambitious and aspiring soul', cramped and chafing at its confinement. Originally, Sim fetishises his legs, as when he 'placed the fragment of a mirror on a low bench, and looked over his shoulder at so much of his legs as could be reflected in that small compass, with the greatest possible complacency and satisfaction'. 'Enraptured' by his legs 'to a degree amounting to enthusiasm', and always displaying them 'to the best advantage',[50] through his daily ritual of self-admiration Sim renders his legs objects separate to the rest of his body. When they become crushed in the violent press of the mob and are replaced with wooden ones, Sim continues to pompously assert his authority and threaten to 'correct his lady with a brush, or boot, or shoe'.[51] However, she can now check his hubris by removing his legs, puncturing his undeserved loftiness. While Kincaid calls these scenes 'the most truly obscene [...] anywhere in [Dickens's] novels',[52] they are simultaneously an affirmation of Sim's clownish indestructibility. Like the Mudfog policeman, he may be knocked down today, but will be ready for more tomorrow.

In *Our Mutual Friend* (1864–1865), Dickens again materialises and degrades the hypocritical *hauteur* of his comic villain with a wooden leg. Silas Wegg's detached leg is a comic prop in Mr Venus's hands, 'a sort of brown paper truncheon' that was 'bought […] in open contract' despite Wegg's wish that he might 'collect myself like a genteel person' and not be 'dispersed, a part of me here, and a part of me there'.[53] Wegg refers to his wandering leg as 'I' and 'me' in order to own it verbally, but this in fact provides it with a separate identity as the subject of the verbal tug-of-war between Venus and Wegg. As part of Dickens's fascination with the inanimate and 'characters which inhabit [a] hinterland between life and non-life',[54] such acts of physical disintegration represent a 'collapse of secure distinctions between subject and object, between that which acts and that which is acted upon',[55] and have a twofold effect. Firstly, as Andrews notes, they break down the symbolic armour of the individual ego and expose the vulnerable human beneath.[56] Furthermore, in foregrounding each body part as a component of the uncircumscribable grotesque body, these detachable members are a positive, levelling force. In Hood's poetry, for example, in works such as 'Tim Turpin: A Pathetic Ballad' (1826) and 'Miss Kilmansegg and Her Precious Leg' (1844), they generate a 'pre-rational, visceral reaction in its viewers that makes them conscious of their own existence as physical entities'.[57]

In a denial of biological laws, the clown is routinely able to cheat Death. In *The Old Curiosity Shop* (1840–1841), Daniel Quilp achieves this twice. In the first instance, recalling a prank performed by Grimaldi's father, he gleefully spies upon his own wake, held after he was assumed drowned, before surprising the assembled mourners by being very much alive. This symbolically mocks Death, as Quilp's 'belligerent life and honesty' achieves what Kincaid calls 'a victory over the ghouls' including the Brasses, who represent 'cold and artificial mourning'.[58] This both affirms the clown's immortality and punctures the social pretence of the assembled mourners.

Even when Death seems certain to claim Quilp at the end of the novel—this time, we witness his apparent drowning—Dickens hints that he may still be alive. Like the first memories from the opening quote, his body refuses to go away or be still as it becomes an 'ugly plaything' of the tide, which 'toyed and sported with its ghastly freight, now bruising it against the slimy piles, now hiding it in mud or long rank grass, now dragging it heavily over rough stones and gravel'. Dickens employs a ludic vocabulary as the malleable clown moves unpredictably in a simulacrum of pantomime's hostile environment, where everything is a potential pratfall or trap. Quilp's 'corpse' is finally washed into a swamp, yet retains the appearance of animation: his hair is 'stirred by the damp breeze [...] in a kind of mockery of death', and his clothes 'fluttered idly in the night wind'.[59] A final hint at Quilp's ability to 'rise' again is offered by the suggestively thrusting pillar depicted in Phiz's illustration of his 'dead' body. There, his small twisted body lies amidst the marsh-reeds, but is dwarfed by a central wooden post rising in a priapic manner from around Quilp's midriff, acting as another independent body part with a life of its own. If, following Carey, we view Quilp as 'an embodiment of [Dickens's] violence who could also express his black and anarchic laughter', it is little wonder that he would want to leave this death tantalisingly provisional.[60]

Another important pantomimic method Dickens uses to offset or contain the troubling nature of laughter is to situate violence within repetitive cycles, whereby any blow inflicted is sure to be revisited on the offender at a later point in an act of poetic justice. The clown's grotesque, indestructible body enabled him to participate fully in such cycles. He never exhibits any lasting effects from the blows received, however extreme, and stands up immediately, to be struck afresh or to kick 'downwards' at the vulnerable (typically children or the elderly) or at unpopular authority figures, such as magistrates and policemen.

In the 1806 pantomime *Harlequin Mother Goose*, the clown is shot by a 'sportsman' who emerges from a clock, but then assaults the landlord of 'A Country Inn' and has two crockery fights, before he is caught in 'a steel trap and spring gun', beaten like a clock bell in St. Dunstan's Church and chased by stinging bees.[61] As the to-and-fro of this lengthy ordeal suggests, the clown was both giver and receiver of violence, bringing carefully composed disruption to each scenario in, to use Andrews's phrase, 'choreographed symmetry'.[62]

Comic violence towards authority figures such as pantaloons or watchmen bears a radical, 'retributive' quality, whereby, as David Mayer explains, 'mutiny [is] made harmless and even pleasurable', and protest can occur 'without injurious consequences to the protester'.[63] Mayer contrasts retributive comedy with 'normative' comedy, which attempts to reassert 'the conservative position from which [it] operates' by prompting the audience to laugh at aberrations from social norms and thus publicly declare their 'allegiance to the norms'.[64] While normative comedy is directed against nonconformists, retributive comedy is directed against those who govern. This radical potential explains comedy's appeal to thinkers like Hazlitt and Hunt, but also to Dickens, who used panto-mime's model of retributive comedy to generate the communal laughter of 'the people' against 'authority' and divert attention from the trou-bling private laughter at the accompanying violence against such vulner-able targets as children. As mentioned earlier, the grotesque aesthetic supports the coexistence of such conflicting feelings, as the spectator can enjoy the violence and see it punished at the same time.

As a low-level representative of corrupt authority, the beadle was a perennial soft target for Grimaldi's pranks, and Dickens's first experiment with the more enduring comic butt. By turns, Bumble in *Oliver Twist* is an eager dispenser of 'parochial flagellation', then a victim, then a vigor-ous asserter of the male prerogative, and then finally victim again. The scene in which Mrs Bumble asserts her authority reads as a thoroughly pantomimic piece of slapstick. During the initial setup, Bumble upbraids her and revels in his own mischief through a highly theatrical, non-verbal performance:

> Mr Bumble took his hat from a peg; and putting it on, rather rakishly, on one side [...] thrust his hands into his pockets, and sauntered towards the door with much ease and waggishness depicted in his whole appearance.

Now Bumble has been puffed to his utmost level of *hauteur*, Dickens proceeds to deflate him. The first target is the sartorial symbol of his sup-posed authority, as he experiences 'the sudden flying off of his hat to the opposite end of the room', after which his wife assaults him: 'clasping him tight round the throat with one hand, [she] inflicted a shower of blows (dealt with singular vigour and dexterity) upon it with the other'. Dickens employs hyperbole in the double-handedness of the assault and the 'shower' of blows to heighten the attack beyond the credible bounds of reality. As a final comic *coup de grace*, Bumble succumbs to a carefully managed, stereotypical prank, as 'she pushed him over a chair, which was luckily well situated for the purpose'.[65] Although the author is the very person who 'situated' the prop, in this final subclause he attributes the comic mishap to the same ineffable laws governing pantomime, in a deliberate piece of comic misdirection.

But Bumble is not finished, and initiates the cycle again when he is discovered by Mrs Bumble berating the women in the workhouse laundry. Anxious to preserve her own authority, his wife 'caught up a bowl of soap-suds, and motioning him towards the door, ordered him instantly to depart, on pain of receiving the contents upon his portly person'.[66] This threat of soap-suds implicates Bumble in a pantomime 'slosh' scene, a messy routine whereby characters were doused in water or other liquids.

Bumble meets a fitting ending, and, although he does become a 'hen-pecked husband', Kincaid's broader argument that he 'can no longer be laughed at so easily'[67] because the novel has moved us away from 'comfortable laughter'[68] is less convincing. He suggests that we 'delight in Bumble's fall, but [...] are revolted at the extended details of his degradation', as Dickens exposes 'the potential darkness within us'.[69] However, embedding that degradation firmly within the pantomimic mode is what generates a powerful retributive laughter that overwhelms and obscures the darkly secret enjoyment of Bumble's normative comic violence against the workhouse boys.

Dickens's enclosure of Bumble within this hyperreal theatrical framework ensures that the beadle consistently comes across as a Bergsonian 'thing' or a clown, rather than as the representation of a real human being. Carey describes Dickens's major comic characters as figures who 'have no insides, or none we can confidently penetrate', and for whom life 'consists of physical proximity and mental distance'.[70] In the case of Bumble, Dickens's pantomimic mode is so forceful that even the briefest suggestion of Bumble shedding a tear for Oliver sounds 'an astonishingly false note'.[71] Bumble's position within the framework of retributive violence precludes us from feeling sympathy for him or from accessing any private, inner self at this moment, for to do so would offset the comedy Dickens extracts from his ultimate fall.

Dickens returns to this cycle in several of his early novels: in *Nicholas Nickleby* (1838–1839), we initially laugh guiltily at Squeers's cruelty to the boys in his charge, whether he is knocking boys down, or widening their mouths with the comically oversized brimstone-and-treacle spoon. This then transforms into more comfortable laughter when Squeers is beaten himself, a comfort prolonged by the impermanence of his injuries that means the cycle can quickly begin again. Nicholas's first revolt against Squeers begins in a melodramatic tone, as after their lofty exchanges, Squeers, 'in a violent outbreak of wrath, and with a cry like the howl of a wild beast', strikes Nicholas with his ruler, 'which raised up a bar of livid flesh as it was inflicted'. But Dickens cannot maintain this seriousness and it quickly shifts into the pantomimic mode as Squeers's family intervenes: 'Mrs Squeers, with many shrieks for aid, hung on to the tail of her partner's coat, and endeavoured to drag him from his infuriated adversary'. Similarly Fanny Squeers, 'after launching a shower of inkstands at the usher's head, beat Nicholas to her heart's content: animating herself at every blow with the recollection of his having refused her proffered love'.[72]

The deliberate choreography and stylised nature of this violence is made further apparent when Squeers is attacked again later. John Browdie elbows him

> with so much dexterity that the schoolmaster reeled and staggered back upon Ralph Nickleby, and being unable to recover his balance, knocked that gentleman off his chair, and stumbled heavily on him.[73]

This stage-managed chain reaction reduces participants to components within a comic machine, inanimate interlocking cogs rather than feeling people—and consequently more suitable targets for our laughter.

The cycle concludes with the revolt at Dotheboys Hall, which enacts a carnivalesque inversion against the entire Squeers family. Burlesquing Mrs Squeers's symbols of authority, one boy 'snatched off her cap and beaver-bonnet, put it on his own head, armed himself with the wooden spoon, and bade her, on pain of death, go down upon her knees and take a dose directly'. This performance of misrule escalates as she is forced to swallow the brimstone and treacle in front of 'a crowd of shouting tormentors', closing with a 'slosh' scene, when the bowl of liquor was 'rendered more than usually savoury by the immersion in the bowl of Master Wackford's head'.[74]

Seth Pecksniff in *Martin Chuzzlewit* (1843–1844) is a further example of the indestructible clown, repeatedly bouncing back from his blows and doggedly refusing to be beaten by pain. The violent acts directed against him are comic reminders of his materiality, and serve to undermine his false superiority. For Kincaid, they are presented within a 'new kind of humour [...] which finds laughter not in a denial of the pains of living but in an acceptance of them'.[75] While it is true that Pecksniff absorbs, diminishes and renders the novel's pervasive violence comical, the laughter directed towards him is as retributive as it is democratic. Although he is not physically violent like Bumble or Squeers, he is nonetheless a pompous, selfish hypocrite whom the audience are expected to dislike, and, like Squeers, he is dehumanised in order to make the violence against him more acceptable. He is repeatedly knocked over but springs back up again for more punishment in a markedly mechanical way, 'constantly diving down [...] and coming up again like the intelligent householder in Punch's show, who avoids being knocked on the head with a cudgel'.[76]

Pecksniff is implicated in a succession of pratfalls as his environment conspires against him. Early on, the wind outside his house 'slammed the front-door against Mr Pecksniff who was at that moment entering, with such violence, that in the twinkling of an eye he lay on his back at the bottom of the steps'. The actual blow is described with such imaginative verve that we are distanced from its true impact, as Pecksniff

> received, from a sharp angle in the bottom step but one, that sort of knock on the head which lights up, for the patient's entertainment, an imaginary general illumination of very bright short-sixes, [and] lay placidly staring at his own street-door.

More comic business unfolds almost immediately, as Pecksniff's daughter opens the door and peers out with her candle looking 'provokingly round him, and about him, and over him, and everywhere but at him', the anaphora giving the act a rigid, automatic feel. Dickens hyperbolically layers the incident with additional comical texture:

> Mr Pecksniff, being in the act of extinguishing the candles before mentioned pretty rapidly, and of reducing the number of brass knobs on his street-door from four or five hundred (which had previously been juggling of their own accord before his eyes in a very novel manner) to a dozen or so, might in one sense have been said to be coming round the corner, and just turning it.[77]

Dickens shrouds Pecksniff's concussion in comic obfuscation and a grotesque accumulation of comic effects, as suggested by the 'four or five hundred' brass knobs 'juggling' in front of his eyes. The wind moves on, 'weary of such trifling performances', but this is the first of many stage traps that Dickens sets for Pecksniff to stumble into.

Even at a significant dramatic moment within the narrative, when Pecksniff throws young Martin out of his house, Dickens the pantomimist cannot resist throwing a slapstick prop into the scene. In an echo of the Squeers-Nickleby confrontation, this scene opens melodramatically, as Pecksniff declares: 'Like all who know you, I renounce you!' The mode then switches abruptly:

> With what intention Martin made a stride forward at these words, it is impossible to say. It is enough to know that Tom Pinch caught him in his arms, and that at the same moment Mr Pecksniff stepped back so hastily, that he missed his footing, tumbled over a chair, and fell in a sitting posture on the ground; where he remained without an effort to get up again, with his head in a corner; perhaps considering it the safest place.

As with Bumble's falling over the chair, Dickens knowingly misdirects us here; only he would know what Martin's intention was, but frames it as a fortuitous accident. As Pecksniff sits on the floor 'with his head in an acute angle of the wainscot, and all the damage and detriment of an uncomfortable journey about him', he is 'not exactly a model of all that is prepossessing and dignified in man',[78] but instead resembles Bergson's surrogate for man's indignity, the clown.

Pecksniff's clownish position within the cycle of violence is relevant for his final exit from the novel. The cyclical pattern dictates that his retributive beating at the end of the narrative should be an expected and comical event with no serious or lasting consequences, providing a final sense of relief and gratification to the reader. Dickens frames it precisely in this manner. When old Martin strikes Pecksniff with his stick, with 'a well-directed nervous blow', he goes down 'as heavily and true as if the charge of a Life-Guardsman had tumbled him out of a saddle', a wholesome military image which validates the violent spectacle like the patriotic tar brought on at the end of Regency pantomimes to sing 'Rule Britannia'. Dickens then uses the audience within the scene to direct the audience outside the scene—the readers—on how to read the event. Pecksniff lies on the floor stunned, 'looking about him, with a disconcerted meekness in his face so enormously ridiculous, that neither Mark Tapley nor John Westlock could repress a smile',[79] even as they held back old Martin from striking again. This semi-covert expression of amusement represents another hint of Bergson's 'secret freemasonry' in Dickens's work. Completing the pattern, Pecksniff the automaton cannot be suppressed for long and so rises to make a dignified exit – only to be deflated again:

> With [a] sublime address Mr Pecksniff departed. But the effect of his
> departure was much impaired by his being immediately afterwards run
> against, and nearly knocked down by, a monstrously-excited little man in
> velveteen shorts and a very tall hat.[80]

He was obviously never meant to make a dignified exit. His 'sublime
address' is merely the setup for his final fall, and he exits Dickens's narrative just as he entered it, on a carefully composed slapstick note which
delicately balances comic incongruity: the 'sublime' versus 'monstrous'
excitement, the 'little man' versus 'a very tall hat'.

The trajectories of such figures as Bumble, Squeers and Pecksniff
betray Dickens's guilt at his enjoyment of the violence they dispense,
Carey contends. Because 'the great prophet of cosy, domestic virtue [...]
never seems to have quite reconciled himself to the fact that violence and
destruction were the most powerful stimulants to his imagination', he is
forced to 'tritely' punish his 'savages'.[81] Dickens and his readers can only
enjoy the violent acts of the clown because there is a conventional expectation that he will suffer himself, and rather than a worn-out, apologetic
afterthought, such treatment has a specific form and aesthetic heritage
within the popular mode of the pantomimic grotesque.

In this final section, I wish to suggest that, despite the implication
that cycles of crime and retribution resolve matters in a neat and satisfy-
ing pattern, the peculiar dynamic of such violence can in fact reveal the
generic threat that comedy poses. As C. L. Barber has outlined, festive,
Saturnalian comedy has a centripetal narrative drive towards resolution,
harmony and construction; in parallel to this, however, single episodes
of laughter move us centrifugally towards chaos, disorder and destruction.[82] In pantomime, the slapstick violence of the harlequinade serves
no narrative purpose and interrupts what little plot exists. While this had
little consequence onstage (during Grimaldi's career at least, spectators
went for the harlequinade above all else), such lengthy indulgences are
impractical and destabilising within a novel, even one granted the digressive licence of the serial form—and so it proved for Dickens.

My analysis of *Nicholas Nickleby* and *Martin Chuzzlewit* has already
noted examples of this impracticality, particularly exacerbated in loosely
plotted works such as *The Pickwick Papers* and *The Old Curiosity Shop*.
Kincaid could almost be describing the harlequinade when he locates
the latter in 'a madhouse world' in which, 'for all the travelling and
frantic rushing about that goes on, no one really moves anywhere or

finally escapes from the pursuers'.[83] This frantic inertia is partly caused by the contradictory motions of Dickens's comic writing, attempting, as Kincaid puts it, 'the restoration of order or equilibrium', but coming 'dangerously close to anarchy' due to the laughter generated by his contradictory 'desire to cleanse the existing order of absurdity and rigidity'.[84]

The pockets of harlequinade violence in *The Pickwick Papers* threaten the work's notional integrity. They are only momentary intrusions, but are no less striking for their seemingly casual or ephemeral nature. These include Sam Weller's digressive anecdotes and dark aphorisms, which make play of such subjects as domestic abuse:

> You know what the counsel said, Sammy, as defended the gen'lem'n as beat his wife with the poker, venever he got jolly. 'And arter all, my Lord,' says he, 'it's a amiable weakness.'[85]

and infanticide:

> 'Business first, pleasure arterwards,' as King Richard the Third said ven he stabbed the t'other king in the Tower, afore he smothered the babbies.[86]

These discomforting *tableaux* which burst in unannounced to cause ripples across the gentle waters of Samuel Pickwick's existence, like miniature grenades of grotesque disruption, counterpoise a 'higher' and more abstract ideal (the 'amiable weakness', 'business before pleasure') with its 'lower', material instantiation (beating with a poker, child suffocation). For Bakhtin, laughter 'degrades and materializes',[87] and this recasting of lofty *sententiae* as physical savagery both lowers the high and raises the low, leavening their difference so that the commonplace 'accidents of life' attain dignity, and gnomic philosophising attains practicality. Dickens's democratically grotesque comic sensibility once again relates things seemingly unrelated and incongruous, and as Forster notes, finds 'affinities between the high and the low, the attractive and the repulsive', which bring 'us all upon the level of a common humanity'.[88]

This is also the case in Sam's lengthier tales of dubious culinary practices. Writing of the pieman who uses cat meat (which he 'seasons [...] for beef-steak, weal, or kidney, 'cordin to the demand'[89]), Dickens humorously unites the act of eating pets with shrewd commercial acumen. In another story, the inventor of a sausage-making machine 'rashly converted his-self into sassages!', and is only found after a disgruntled customer discovers trouser buttons in his dinner, yoking cannibalism to sartorial domesticity.[90]

Sam's anecdotes are supplemented by Jingle's equally remarkable tales, whose disjointed style often reads like stage directions or a harlequinade's 'book of words':

> Terrible place – dangerous work – other day – five children – mother – tall lady, eating sandwiches – forgot the arch – crash – knock – children look round – mother's head off – sandwich in her hand – no head to put it in – head of a family off – shocking, shocking.[91]

Andrews notes how this stage-coach performance is a double fragmentation and dismemberment, in terms of its subject matter (the decapitated passenger, like Baudelaire's clown) and its form (fragmented, incomplete phrases). Like Sam's tales, it holds together the shocking and the mundane—a beheading witnessed by children and a coaching picnic—in comic incongruity. A final example of this technique is observable in *Dombey and Son* (1846–1848), when Major Bagstock recalls his tough military training at Sandhurst:

> We put each other to the torture there, Sir. We roasted the new fellows at a slow fire, and hung 'em out of a three pair of stairs window, with their heads downwards. Joseph Bagstock, Sir, was held out of window by the heels of his boots, for thirteen minutes by the college clock.[92]

Again the incongruity is swiftly foisted upon the reader. The Major's diction and the rich minor details (the window and college clock) are foregrounded and combined with the detailed description of the boys' torture in a way that diverts our attention from a pain that is only implied.

Obviously, slapstick is not the only form of violence that Dickens explores in his work, and he can use violence for more serious effects elsewhere, be it in his exhilarating and terrifying descriptions of rioting mobs or in landmark depictions of smaller-scale domestic violence like Sikes's treatment of Nancy.[93] However, the very different intentions behind his sustained use of comic violence are suggested in his correspondence with Mary Tayler. She wrote to Dickens, asking him to pen a new, more morally instructive, version of *Punch and Judy* in which 'the faces of Virtue and Innocence were presented oft to the popular eye [...] instead of the face of Vice'. Dickens declined, characterising both *Punch and Judy* and pantomime as 'extravagant reliefs from the realities of life which would lose [their] hold upon people if [they] were made moral and instructive'.[94] Such entertainments were, Dickens writes, 'quite harmless' in their influence, consisting of 'outrageous joke[s] which no-one [...] would think of regarding as an incentive to any course of action, or a model of any kind of conduct'.[95]

Despite the dismissal of comically violent spectacles as mere frivolities, the reader's laughter is clearly more complex than that—as Dickens himself knew. He draws this laughter out from its secret location and puts it centre stage, yet provides, to manage any potential discomfort, a double palliative for his readers, combining the communal laughter of a shared humanity with the retributive laughter of the oppressor brought low. As Carey asserts, '[r]iot, murder, savagery have to be there before Dickens' imagination is gripped'.[96] Dickens's depiction of slapstick violence is nonetheless as stylistically inventive and carefully constructed as his darker material, engaging directly with the problematic politics of slapstick to produce a brand of laughter predominantly radical in spirit and entirely in keeping with his engagement with popular forms of entertainment.

Notes

1. Charles Dickens and George Augustus Sala, 'First Fruits,' *Household Words*, May 15, 1852, 191.
2. Charles Baudelaire, 'Of the Essence of Laughter, and Generally of the Comic in the Plastic Arts,' in *Selected Writings on Art and Literature*, trans. P. E. Charvet (London: Penguin, 2006), 155–156.
3. Dickens and Sala, 'First Fruits,' 191.
4. Baudelaire, 'Essence of Laughter,' 155–156.
5. *The Times*, December 27, 1823, 3.
6. Henry Downes Miles, *The Life of Joseph Grimaldi: With Anecdotes of His Contemporaries* (London: Charles Harris, 1838), 192.
7. Ibid., 6–7.
8. Ibid., 6.
9. Jim Davis, *Victorian Pantomime—A Collection of Critical Essays* (London: Palgrave Macmillan, 2010), 9.
10. Ibid., 5.

11. Michael R. Booth, *English Plays of the Nineteenth Century. V. Pantomimes, Extravaganzas and Burlesques* (Oxford: Oxford University Press, 1976), 42–43.
12. Andrew Halliday, *Comical Fellows* (London: J. H. Thomson, 1863), 5–6.
13. Jacky Bratton, 'Pantomime and the Experienced Young Fellow,' in *Victorian Pantomime—A Collection of Critical Essays*, ed. Jim Davis (London: Palgrave Macmillan, 2010), 96.
14. *Illustrated Sporting and Dramatic News*, January 6, 1877, 365.
15. Malcolm Andrews, *Dickensian Laughter* (Oxford: Oxford University Press, 2013), 42.
16. Ibid., 42.
17. Ibid., 41–42.
18. Ibid., 42.
19. Ibid., 42.
20. Ibid., 44.
21. Charles Dickens and William Henry Wills, 'A Curious Dance Round A Curious Tree,' *Household Words* (1852).
22. James R. Kincaid, *Dickens and the Rhetoric of Laughter* (Oxford: Clarendon Press, 1971), 16.
23. Kincaid, *Rhetoric of Laughter*, 16.
24. Ibid., 16.
25. Henri Bergson, 'Laughter,' in *Comedy*, ed. Wylie Sypher (Baltimore: Johns Hopkins University Press, 1956), 97.
26. Michael Hollington, *Dickens and the Grotesque* (London and Sydney: Croon Helm, 1984), 1.
27. H. F. Chorley, '[Review of *National Tales*],' *London and Westminster Review*, no. 29 (April 1838): 119; [Review]; *London Magazine*, no. 16 (December 1827): 537.
28. Sara Lodge, *Thomas Hood and Nineteenth-Century Poetry: Work, Play, and Politics* (Manchester: Manchester University Press, 2007), 136.
29. Ibid., 106.
30. Ibid., 126.
31. John Carey, *The Violent Effigy—A Study of Dickens' Imagination* (London: Faber and Faber, 1973), 15.
32. Dickens and Wills, 'A Curious Dance,' 385–386.
33. Mikhail Bakhtin, *Rabelais and His World*, trans. Helene Iswolsky (Cambridge, MA: Massachusetts Institute of Technology, 1968), 19.
34. Bakhtin, *Rabelais*, 19.
35. Dickens and Wills, 'A Curious Dance,' 385–386.
36. Bergson, 'Laughter,' 64.
37. Dickens and Wills, 'A Curious Dance,' 385–386.
38. Carey, *Violent Effigy*, 29.

39. Bakhtin, *Rabelais*, 197, 205.
40. Baudelaire, 'Essence of Laughter.'
41. Ibid., 156–157.
42. *The Memoirs of Joseph Grimaldi*, ed. Charles Dickens, 2 vols. (London: Richard Bentley, 1838), I, 11.
43. Charles Dickens, *Hard Times*, ed. Fred Kaplan and Sylvère Monod (London and New York: Norton, 2001), 24.
44. Jonathan Buckmaster, 'Ten Thousand Million Delights,' in *Dickens and the Imagined Child*, ed. Peter Merchant and Catherine Waters (Farnham: Ashgate, 2015), 118–119.
45. Charles Dickens, 'Full Report Of the First Meeting of the Mudfog Association for the Advancement of Everything,' in *Dickens' Journalism: 'Sketches by Boz' and other early papers 1833–1839*, ed. Michael Slater (London: Dent, 1994), 545.
46. Dickens, 'Meeting of the Mudfog Association,' 545.
47. Bergson, 'Laughter,' 84.
48. Carey, *Violent Effigy*, 101.
49. Ibid., 96.
50. Charles Dickens, *Barnaby Rudge*, ed. Kathleen Tillotson (Oxford: Oxford University Press, 1982), 33, 34, 184.
51. Dickens, *Barnaby Rudge*, 630.
52. Kincaid, *Rhetoric of Laughter*, 129.
53. Charles Dickens, *Our Mutual Friend*, ed. E. Salter Davies (Oxford: Oxford University Press, 1981), 297, 82.
54. Carey, *Violent Effigy*, 90.
55. Lodge, *Thomas Hood*, 105.
56. Andrews, *Dickensian Laughter*, 102.
57. Lodge, *Thomas Hood*, 103.
58. Kincaid, *Rhetoric of Laughter*, 98.
59. Charles Dickens, *The Old Curiosity Shop*, ed. Elizabeth M. Brennan (Oxford: Clarendon Press, 1997), 528–529.
60. Carey, *Violent Effigy*, 24–25.
61. Thomas Dibdin, *Harlequin and Mother Goose, or, The Golden Egg!*, reprinted in Andrew McConnell Stott, *The Pantomime Life of Joseph Grimaldi* (Edinburgh: Canongate, 2009), 333–341.
62. Andrews, *Dickensian Laughter*, 48.
63. David Mayer, *Harlequin in His Element: The English Pantomime, 1806–1836* (Cambridge, MA: Harvard University Press, 1969), 56.
64. Mayer, *Harlequin in His Element*, 52.
65. Charles Dickens, *Oliver Twist*, ed. Fred Kaplan (London and New York: Norton, 1993), 241–242.
66. Ibid., 243.

67. Kincaid, *Rhetoric of Laughter*, 63.
68. Ibid., 68.
69. Ibid., 57.
70. Carey, *Violent Effigy*, 64–65.
71. Ibid., 68.
72. Charles Dickens, *Nicholas Nickleby*, ed. Arthur Waugh, Hugh Walpole, Walter Dexter and Thomas Hatton (Bloomsbury: Nonesuch Press, 1938), 156.
73. Ibid., 596.
74. Ibid., 830.
75. Kincaid, *Rhetoric of Laughter*, 135.
76. Charles Dickens, *Martin Chuzzlewit*, ed. Margaret Cardwell (Oxford: Clarendon Press, 1982), 491.
77. Dickens, *Martin Chuzzlewit*, 9.
78. Ibid., 211.
79. Ibid., 799.
80. Ibid., 808.
81. Carey, *Violent Effigy*, 16.
82. C. L. Barber, *Shakespeare's Festive Comedy: A Study of Dramatic Form and Its Relation to Social Custom* (Princeton, NJ: Princeton University Press, 1959).
83. Kincaid, *Rhetoric of Laughter*, 76.
84. Ibid., 14.
85. Charles Dickens, *The Pickwick Papers*, ed. James Kinsley (Oxford: Clarendon Press, 1986), 344.
86. Ibid., 371.
87. Bakhtin, *Rabelais*, 20.
88. John Forster, *The Life of Charles Dickens*, J. W. T. Ley (London: Cecil Palmer, 1928), 721.
89. Dickens, *Pickwick Papers*, 278.
90. Ibid., 464–465.
91. Ibid., 14.
92. Charles Dickens, *Dombey and Son*, ed. Alan Horsman (Oxford: Clarendon Press, 1974), 128.
93. See: Lisa Surridge, *Bleak Houses—Marital Violence in Victorian Fiction* (Athens, OH: Ohio University Press, 2005); Marlene Tromp, *The Private Rod: Marital Violence, Sensation, and the Law in Victorian Britain* (Charlottesville and London: University Press of Virginia, 2000).
94. Charles Dickens, 'Letter to Mary Tayler,' 6 November 1849, in *The Letters of Charles Dickens: 1847–1849*, ed. Graham Storey and K. J. Fielding (Oxford: Clarendon Press, 1980).
95. Ibid., 640.
96. Carey, *Violent Effigy*, 29.

Works Cited

Bakhtin, Mikhail. *Rabelais and His World.* Translated by Helene Iswolsky. Cambridge, MA: Massachusetts Institute of Technology, 1968.

Barber, Charles. *Shakespeare's Festive Comedy: A Study of Dramatic Form and its Relation to Social Custom.* Princeton, NJ: Princeton University Press, 1959.

Baudelaire, Charles. 'Of the Essence of Laughter, and generally of the Comic in the Plastic Arts.' In *Selected Writings on Art and Literature.* Translated by P. E. Charvet, 140–161. London: Penguin, 2006.

Bergson, Henri. 'Laughter.' In *Comedy*, edited by Wylie Sypher, 59–190. Baltimore: Johns Hopkins University Press, 1956.

Booth, Michael. *English Plays of the Nineteenth Century. V. Pantomimes, Extravaganzas and Burlesques.* Oxford: Oxford University Press, 1976.

Bratton, Jacky. 'Pantomime and the Experienced Young Fellow.' In *Victorian Pantomime: A Collection of Critical Essays*, edited by Jim Davis, 87–99. London: Palgrave Macmillan, 2010.

Buckmaster, Jonathan. 'Ten Thousand Million Delights.' In *Dickens and the Imagined Child*, edited by Peter Merchant and Catherine Waters, 111–130. Farnham: Ashgate, 2015.

Carey, John. *The Violent Effigy: A Study of Dickens's Imagination.* London: Faber, 1973.

Chorley, Henry. '[Review of *National Tales*].' *London and Westminster Review*, no. 29, April 1838.

Davis, Jim, ed. *Victorian Pantomime: A Collection of Critical Essays.* London: Palgrave Macmillan, 2010.

Dickens, Charles. *Barnaby Rudge*, edited by Kathleen Tillotson. Oxford: Oxford University Press, 1982.

Dickens, Charles. *Dombey and Son*, edited by Alan Horsman. Oxford: Clarendon Press, 1974.

Dickens, Charles. 'Full Report Of the First Meeting of the Mudfog Association for the Advancement of Everything.' In *Dickens' Journalism: 'Sketches by Boz' and Other Early Papers 1833–1839*, ed. Michael Slater. London: Dent, 1994.

Dickens, Charles. *Hard Times*, edited by Fred Kaplan and Sylvère Monod. London and New York: Norton, 2001.

Dickens, Charles. *The Letters of Charles Dickens: 1847–1849*, edited by Graham Storey and K. J. Fielding. Oxford: Clarendon Press, 1980.

Dickens, Charles. 'Lying Awake.' *Household Words.* October 30, 1852.

Dickens, Charles. *Martin Chuzzlewit*, edited by Margaret Cardwell. Oxford: Clarendon Press, 1982.

Dickens, Charles, ed. *The Memoirs of Joseph Grimaldi*, vols. 2. London: Richard Bentley, 1838.

Dickens, Charles. *Nicholas Nickleby*, edited by Arthur Waugh, Hugh Walpole, Walter Dexter and Thomas Hatton. Bloomsbury: Nonesuch Press, 1938.

Dickens, Charles. *The Old Curiosity Shop*, edited by Elizabeth M. Brennan. Oxford: Clarendon Press, 1997.

Dickens, Charles. *Oliver Twist*, edited by Fred Kaplan. London and New York: W. W. Norton and Company, 1993.

Dickens, Charles. *Our Mutual Friend*, edited by E. Salter Davies. Oxford: Oxford University Press, 1981.

Dickens, Charles. 'The Pantomime of Life.' In *Dickens's Journalism: 'Sketches by Boz' and Other Early Papers 1833–1839*, edited by Michael Slater, 530–551. London: Dent, 1994.

Dickens, Charles. *The Pickwick Papers*, edited by James Kinsley. Oxford: Clarendon Press, 1986.

Dickens, Charles and George Augustus Sala. "First Fruits." *Household Words*. May 15, 1852.

Dickens, Charles and William Henry Wills. "A Curious Dance Round A Curious Tree." *Household Words*. January 17, 1852.

Findlater, Richard. *Joe Grimaldi: His Life and Theatre*. Cambridge: Cambridge University Press, 1978.

Forster, John. *The Life of Charles Dickens*. Vols. 2, edited by A. J. Hoppe. London: Dent, 1966.

Halliday, Andrew. *Comical Fellows*. London: J. H. Thomson, 1863.

Hollington, Michael. *Dickens and the Grotesque*. London and Sydney: Croon Helm, 1984.

Kincaid, James. *Dickens and the Rhetoric of Laughter*. Oxford: Clarendon Press, 1971.

Lodge, Sara. *Thomas Hood and Nineteenth-Century Poetry: Work, Play, and Politics*. Manchester: Manchester University Press, 2007.

Mayer, David. *Harlequin in His Element: The English Pantomime, 1806–1836*. Cambridge, MA: Harvard University Press, 1969.

Miles, Henry Downes. *The Life of Joseph Grimaldi: With Anecdotes of His Contemporaries*. London: Charles Harris, 1838.

Robbins, Norman. *Slapstick and Sausages*. Devon: Trapdoor Publications, 2002.

Stott, Andrew McConnell. *The Pantomime Life of Joseph Grimaldi*. Edinburgh: Canongate, 2009.

Surridge, Lisa. *Bleak Houses: Marital Violence in Victorian Fiction*. Athens, OH: Ohio University Press, 2005.

Taylor, Millie. *British Pantomime Performance*. Bristol: Intellect Books, 2007.

Tromp, Marlene. *The Private Rod: Marital Violence, Sensation, and the Law in Victorian Britain*. Charlottesville and London: University Press of Virginia, 2000.

Edward Lear's Travels in Nonsense and Europe

Peter Swaab

'Nonsense writing' sounds like a negation of sense, but the genre is more accurately seen as part-sense or semi-sense—not entirely as an assault on meaning or a repudiation of it, but as an exploration of its dynamics.[1] Nonsense writing is a place where sense and absurdity meet, often on cordial terms. It negotiates between the sensible and the senseless, and explores the limits of where we can go with coherence. It expresses scepticism about the feasibility and usefulness of making ourselves meaningful but is also fascinated by the ways that we are impelled to do so. If one single person is responsible for this dubious idea of 'nonsense writing', it is Edward Lear , who in 1846 gave the title *A Book of Nonsense* to his first collection of limericks (as they would get called for mysterious reasons fifty years later). I think the term has fostered two exaggerated tendencies in readers and critics. One of these is defeatist and quasi-aesthetic, holding to an idea of nonsense for nonsense's sake, as though it were a fault of taste to attempt to speak sense of nonsense, it's strictly for the kids; Lear himself may have given a lead here, speaking of '"Nonsense", pure and absolute, having been my aim throughout'.[2] The other is more solemn, and sees nonsense as a version of philosophy,

P. Swaab (✉)
University College London, London, UK

© The Author(s) 2020
L. Lee (ed.), *Victorian Comedy and Laughter*,
https://doi.org/10.1057/978-1-137-57882-2_4

an attack of schemes of meaning, an essay in epistemology by other means.[3]

As against these hermetic positions, we could see nonsense writing as a messier and more hybrid genre, overlapping with various other socially inflected kinds of writing, among them parody,[4] satire, utopianism, mock-epic and travel writing. The last two are especially suggestive. Writing about Alexander Pope's use of the mock-epic, Emrys Jones described him as

> setting out to exploit the relationship between the two realms [the epic and the modern], but ending up by calling a new realm into being. And this new realm does not correspond either to the coherent imagined world of classical epic or to the actual world in which the poet and his readers live and which it is ostensibly the poet's intention to satirise. It is to some extent self-subsistent, intrinsically delightful, like the worlds of pastoral and romance.[5]

Or indeed like nonsense writing. Starting out to exploit the relation between sense and nonsense, it ends by calling a new realm into being, one that combines the freedom of fantasy and the acumen of satire. 'Realm' suggests how readily we can see the genre as itself a kind of place. Departing from our usual places and norms, nonsense poetry is always a poetry of departures, always therefore a kind of travel writing, and it frequently narrates quests and journeys. Likewise when we travel in the ordinary world, we can often stop making sense, especially if we don't speak the language. One reason for travelling is to get to a new place where things don't make sense in the usual way and nor do we, we too can feel and look strange and new. Such considerations mattered for Lear in all his writings—the neglected travel journals as well as the nonsense. He liked travelling and wrote about it with relish both as nonsense writer and travel writer, but he had also a divided sense of what his biographer, Vivien Noakes, called 'the life of a wanderer'.

1   QUESTIONS OF TRAVEL IN LEAR'S LIFE

In July 1859 Edward Lear wrote to his friend Chichester Fortescue: 'How I wish I had some settled aboad, at least until the last narrow box. —— // But if I settled myself I should go to Tobago the next day'.[6] Perhaps Lear misspelt 'aboad' as he did because his mind had unconsciously gone ahead to the following sentence, in which 'aboad' becomes abroad. Questions about abode and abroad occupied Lear throughout his life, and more especially in its second half when he wrote most of the poems for which he is remembered (his first nonsense song probably dated from 1865 when he was 53, so his were mostly poems of later middle age and beyond). He wanted a settled abode but he also wanted to be out and away, on the road, out to sea. He never reconciled these divided feelings, and we can see from the letter that he takes a fatalistic view of himself as a creature of contradiction. He expresses his urge to be on the move both as a creatively vital impulse and a self-thwarting constraint.

Struggling to reconcile the desire for mobility with the need for roots is a Wordsworthian and more generally a post-romantic predicament. Lear always felt both sides, the nesting and the questing urges, with unusual intensity. He often imagines, for instance, that staying in one place is like dying. The 'settled abroad' calls to mind 'the last narrow box'; the place where he is is the place where life isn't, so on he must go. In 1873 when he was a globetrotter of sixty-one he wrote that 'a sedentary life—after moving about as I have done ever since I was 24 years old, will infallibly finish me off SUDDINGLY'.[7] On New Year's Day 1870 we find him thinking about a life and a death of travelling when he writes to Chichester Fortescue that 'it is perhaps the best plan to run about continually like an Ant, and die simultaneous some day or other'.[8] It is as though the end of running about would be the end of life itself. He had a horror of stagnancy. 'I HATE LIFE unless I WORK ALWAYS',[9] he wrote to Fortescue in July 1870, with a violence of feeling that he would momentarily allow himself with his most trusted correspondents. Vivien Noakes tells us that 'Each year he copied into the front of his diary, "Always have 10 years' work mapped out before you, if you wish to be happy"'.[10] This resolve, renewed so punctually every year, expresses an intense fear of vacancy, as though unrelenting purpose were the precondition of happiness. It suggests reasons why Lear as artist and also letter-writer was an astonishingly hard worker even by Victorian standards.

And yet he was drawn too to the calm of inactivity. It features especially in his way of imagining domestic bliss, all passion at a distance. On Christmas Day 1871 he wrote 'I think of marrying some domestic hen-bird and then of building a nest in one of my own olive trees, where I should only descend at remote intervals during the rest of my life'.[11]

Will Mrs Henbird Lear be up the tree too? Probably, to judge from the charming drawing alongside the letter (Fig. 1). The marital idyll is touched by reclusiveness, descending to the world only at intervals. Marriage seems here to be a cure for the need to get out and about in the difficult world of others. The letter travels away from human contact and the human condition.

Elsewhere Lear again thinks himself into bird form as he thinks about earthly paradise:

> When shall we fold our wings, & list to what the inner spirit says—there is no joy but calm? [...] Perhaps in the next eggzistens you & I & Mylady may be able to sit for placid hours under a lotus tree a eating of ice creams & pelicanpie with our feet in a hazure coloured stream.[12]

This sounds like a mid-Victorian turn on an Islamic paradise, akin to Edward FitzGerald's *Rubáiyát of Omar Khayyám*, but replacing

Fig. 1 A nest in one of my own olive trees (*Later Letters of Edward Lear*, edited by Lady Strachey [London: T. Fisher Unwin, 1911], 122)

FitzGerald's 'Jug of Wine, a Loaf of Bread,—and Thou | Beside me singing in the Wilderness'[13] with a nonsense diet of ice creams and pelicanpie and Edward Lear as gooseberry. 'There is no joy but calm', he writes in this letter to Fortescue, alluding to Tennyson's "The Lotos-Eaters" (line 68), yet two days later he tells his diary that "on the whole as calm brings with it inevitable recollections & their pain, – it is perhaps better that calm should be as rarely found as it nowadays is".[14] Lear's dialogue of the mind with itself about 'calm' seems blankly but sustainably contradictory.

Lear had bad luck about where to live. Circumstances kept moving him on and away. The first time was as a child of four, with a temporary eviction from the family home in Holloway Road when his father's financial affairs were in crisis. Thereafter he was brought up mainly by his sister Ann, not his mother, and so the eviction entailed maternal loss as well as other estrangement. He grew to be at home with being unsettled. He liked staying at Knowsley Hall, where he resided for long periods in the 1830s, drawing the animals in Lord Stanley's menagerie and entertaining the children of the big house; but even here, writing to Fanny Coombe in 1837, he said that 'I shall always look back to it as the best home I have ever met with',[15] with a desolate implication that 'home' is something you 'meet with' rather than 'living in'. In later adult life, too, Lear's homes were temporary, on several occasions because of political upheavals in nineteenth-century Europe. In the late 1840s, he established a clientele and social position in Rome, but he was forced to relocate when the 1848 revolution arrived. In 1863 he had to leave Corfu at the time of its cession to Greece, after living there for seven years. In 1868 he left Cannes when the Franco-Prussian conflict made living elsewhere a safer option; and finally, once he was in that better option of San Remo, a new hotel was built, to his rage. It blocked his light, forcing him again to relocate.

These were all bad luck. So too were changes in his professional situation as an artist: the remunerative zoological work in which he was so astonishingly a master at a young age proved too much of a strain on his eyes, so he said. He turned from this established expertise, which might have been pursued at English zoological collections, to landscape painting, which entailed a life of travel. Lear chose to go to remote regions of Europe and sometimes beyond, and to live by the market for paintings depicting inaccessible lands. He made lithographs to illustrate the four volumes of journals he published between 1846 and 1870, recording travels in Italy, Greece and Albania, Calabria and Corsica. Of his many unpublished journals, selections from the ones he wrote in India, Crete and Sicily have since been published.[16] One further factor was his health. English winters were bad for his lungs. He told his sister Ann that he was 'regarding my EXILE, as a medicinal & necessary remedy'[17] for his ill health in the coldest months. This was mainly to help with his asthma, but the arduous walking he undertook for his landscape painting had the big secondary health benefit of keeping his epilepsy at bay better than any other treatment. Beyond all these plausible reasons, however, there is a sense in which Lear's unsettled relation to place was elected; it suited him, or parts of him. Adam Phillips has suggested that 'his endless restlessness and travels' may have been partly driven by 'a fear of the dependence he craved and was deprived of as a child, and needed to master'.[18] From October 1854 'he would belong nowhere', as Vivien Noakes puts it,[19] dividing his time between England in summer and continental Europe at other seasons. He might have chosen to see this as a success, the best of two worlds, like one of the migratory birds he had drawn, sensibly dividing its time seasonally; but Lear was a Victorian pessimist, and preferred a darker perspective.

2   'MOVE ABOUT CONTINUALLY AND NEVER STAND STILL'[20]

The contradiction between staying put and moving on finds comic expression even in Lear's earliest nonsense writing. His early children's poems were mainly limericks and a series of verse alphabets; he made around twenty of these, of which the first surviving one dates from about 1846. They were mostly for children he knew, as in this instance from an alphabet made for Gertrude Lushington (Fig. 2).

> A was an ant
> Who seldom stood still
> And who made a small house
> In the side of a hill.
>
>   a!
>
>   Nice little ant![21]

Fig. 2 A was an ant
(*Nonsense Songs, Stories, Botany, and Alphabets* [London: Robert John Bush, 1871], n.p.)

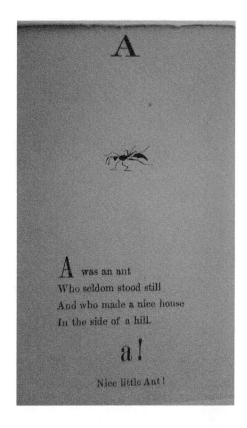

A teeny enough poem, the Ant's story is a success story. Like the ant in the letter from 1870 he may 'run about continually'—but he does not 'die simultaneous'. You might reasonably expect a 'but' in the third line—though restless the creature still wants a home—but there is no contradiction here; the ant has got together the wish to move about and to make himself somewhere to stay. Later in the same alphabet we meet a less fortunate M (Fig. 3).

> M was a Mouse
> With a very long tail
> But he never went out
> In the rain or the hail.
>   m!
> Poor little mouse![22]

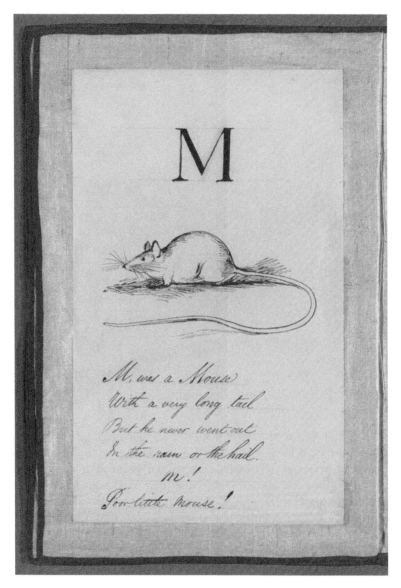

Fig. 3 M was a Mouse (Edward Lear drawing for 'M was a Mouse' from 'An original nonsense alphabet made for Miss Lushington,' ca. 1865. MS Typ 55.3. Image courtesy of the Houghton Library, Harvard University, Cambridge, MA. Web: https://iiif.lib.harvard.edu/manifests/view/drs:51101168$14i)

Why is he 'poor'? It seems perfectly sensible to stay in when the weather's bad. Perhaps the reason lies in his inordinate tail, which in Lear's original drawing looks self-corralling; he can never get away from his own enclosure, he can *never* get out from himself. The alphabets only have space to be small fanciful little pieces, but even these casually bring up the dichotomies about travel that Lear is interested in.

Lear's published limericks span 25 years or so from the two-volume *Book of Nonsense* in 1846, when he was in his early thirties, to *More Nonsense* in 1872, when he was sixty. Though brief, they are not trifling; deep matters are contained, in both senses, by the laconic form. I find them increasingly fascinating and occasionally haunting, as a series of tight little portraits of the human creature, seen as compulsive, appetitive, a prisoner of the self each happens inexplicably to be, subject to luck in a chancy world, the luck of their environment and of what they rhyme with.

He published 216 limericks and the number is raised to 270 by the further ones Vivien Noakes included in the 2001 edition of *The Complete Verse and Other Nonsense*. The form has elements of formula. All but one of the 270 start with that barest of indicators 'There was a' (sometimes 'There was an'), and 228 follow this with 'old' (118 old men, 102 old persons, 6 old ladies, one old sailor, and one old Derry).[23] After 'There was a' and 'old' the next most frequent component of the limericks is the word 'of'. In 199 out of the 270, a person is a person 'of' a place, in only eight cases not being returned to that place-name in the last line. For the published limericks the proportion is even higher, with 172 'of' protagonists out of 216 in all, with only five of these not returning to the place-name. It is often a given of the limericks that people want to leave the place they're 'of', but the 'of' makes that problematic in that the last line inexorably returns them back where they started. Some have disliked this circularity in the form. Adam Mars-Jones, for instance, reviewing Noakes's edition, complained that 'The limerick as Lear practised it (though he never used the word), ending with a repeated rhyme, is an oddly unsatisfying literary form—it's like a bicycle with stabilisers'.[24] His terms are suggestive even if we disagree. We might for instance take one step back and say that the limericks are *about* being odd and unsatisfied, which isn't the same as being odd and unsatisfying; the inbuilt bathos and self-enclosure of the form is expressive and apt. Or that they turn on a tussle between dynamism and stability, with again an aptness in the form.

Secondly, Mars-Jones calls the limerick a 'literary form', but it is important that in Lear it is a hybrid literary-and-visual one. All the published limericks comprise a drawing above the text. Since Holbrook Jackson's hugely reprinted 1947 edition of the *Complete Nonsense* (Faber and Faber), the limericks have tended because of the economics of publishing to be reproduced in a format that reduces the original size and proportion of the image. The early editions are scaled differently (see Figs. 4, 5, 8 and 9); the image predominates, as it does not later on with the drawings accompanying Lear's longer poems. The effect is to give us a picture with a caption rather than a story with a sketch. Moreover, the text and image often diverge and sometimes clash, one being a small narrative, the other a snapshot of one of its moments—almost always a moment recording the outing and not the state of having returned.[25]

In several limericks nonsense is both a poetry of departures and a poetry of returns.

> There was a Young Lady of Sweden ,
> Who went by the slow train to Weedon;

Fig. 4   There was a young lady of Sweden (*A Book of Nonsense* [London: Frederick Warne and Co, 1846; eighteenth edition, 1866], 100)

When they cried, 'Weedon Station!' she made no observation,
But thought she should go back to Sweden.[26]

This lady has her private purposes, inexplicable but satisfactorily carried through, with time enough on the slow train out to decide she should go back. We see her doing just that in the drawing, which must in this case take place after the poem ends. We are inclined to support her decision from the words because of the shapeliness of the chiasmus (Sweden Weedon, Weedon Sweden) and the sense to the ear at least that Weedon has nothing to offer that Sweden doesn't, it just lacks an 's'; and from the drawing because the perspective leads us away with her into the distance and we can just make out her tranquil smile in the window of the back carriage. Going there and then going back again may be a perfectly sensible or a perfectly absurd venture, depending on the context and your point of view.

The Lady of Sweden goes back to Sweden, but some of Lear's other journeys seem to be one-way (Fig. 5).

There was an old person of Ems, who casually fell in the Thames;
And when he was found they said he was drowned,
That unlucky old person of Ems.
107

Fig. 5 There was an old person of Ems (*A Book of Nonsense* [eighteenth edition, 1866], 107)

> There was an Old Person of Ems ,
> Who casually fell in the Thames;
> And when he was found, they said he was drowned,
> That unlucky Old Person of Ems.[27]

We hear that this Old Person of Ems 'casually fell into the Thames', which makes etymological sense, but what we *see* in the drawing makes it look other than casual. It seems like a voluntary dive into what his glassy eyes, cross-hatched frock-coat and finny tails suggest may be somewhere he can belong. 'They said' he was drowned, but though he's gone to join the fishes he doesn't look at all drowned. Nor does he look 'unlucky', but instead happily integrated into a new element. One of the fish nuzzles him, and they all cluster round, the chubby one, the pointy one, and the two with a more pesco-normative shape, together making one of the interspecies familial groups of the nonsense world. Remarkably, this Old Person still has his pipe, which makes him look self-hooked in some variation of the usual conventions of fishing. He might be his own merman.

In 1879 Lear wrote in his diary that 'it was decreed I was not to be human', one of his most stricken utterances.[28] Nonsenses such as these are dreams of metamorphosis. In them, he imagines ways of not being human but being still a happy creature. He follows here in the line of a number of famous Romantic narratives which feel the pull of the non-human world, Goethe's 'Der Fischer ' and 'Erlkönig', for instance, or Heine's 'Die Lorelei ', transposing their romantic supernaturalism into a cooler mode of comic fantasy. He follows too in the line of poetic narratives which take inspired leave of dry land for perilously fluid sites of lakes and waterfalls, such as Wordsworth's 'Idiot Boy' and 'Blind Highland Boy'.

As with the Person of Ems, Lear's other limericks often show his human protagonists taking partial leave of the human world. Most often they consort with the world of birds (Fig. 6).

> There was a Young Lady whose bonnet,
> Came untied when the birds sate upon it;
> But she said, 'I don't care! all the birds in the air
> Are welcome to sit on my bonnet!'[29]

Of the twenty-eight Young Lady figures this one is the most amply and securely maternal. Her bonnet is loose but doesn't look likely to fall off

There was a Young Lady whose bonnet,   came untied when the birds sate upon it;
But she said, " I don't care !   all the birds in the air
Are welcome to sit on my bonnet !"
5

Fig. 6   There was a Young Lady whose bonnet (*A Book of Nonsense* [London: Frederick Warne and Co, third enlarged edition, 1861], 5)

even if the big duck lands there, her pose is tiptoe but not precarious, and she has avian-friendly features, with fingers like webbed feet and dress frills like bird quills. She's altogether blissed out, and Lear's little poems wonder if you're likeliest to feel blissful when you're out of the human element.

Like his fondness for animal–human encounters, Lear's limerick conventions were influenced by his work as a zoological artist.[30] The limericks resemble the descriptions of animals in nineteenth-century zoology: they name the creature, then specify its habitat, then record its chief behaviour in relation to an environment. And indeed the descriptions of creatures in books with Lear's illustrations sometimes sound like they come from the world of the limerick. The 'Egyptian Neophron', for instance, of which there was one example only taken in England:

It appears that the example alluded to was killed near Kilve in Somersetshire, in the month of October 1825, and is now in the possession of the Reverend A. Matthew of the same place. When first discovered, it was feeding upon the body of a dead sheep, with the flesh of which it was so gorged,

Fig. 7   Ramphastas Toco (John Gould, *A Monograph of the Ramphastidae, or Family of Toucans* [1834])

as to be either incapable of flight, or, at all events, unwilling to exert itself sufficiently to effect its escape; it was therefore shot with little difficulty.[31]

Or take the magnificent 'Ramphastos Toco', the toucan later famous in adverts for Guinness (Fig. 7):

> it is but thinly dispersed, and according to the information afforded me by my friend Dr. Such, is extremely shy, and not procured without consider-able difficulty, keeping to the tops of the highest trees, and exercising the utmost wariness and caution. [...] it is said to be extremely partial to the banana.[32]

The world of ornithology supplied Lear with such nonsense-friendly names as 'Dr Wagler' as well as Dr Such. He worked also on illustrat-ing turtles—they feature in two of his alphabets and 'The Courtship of the Yonghy-Bonghy-Bò'[33]—and they too sometimes bridge the worlds of zoology and nonsense. Here is Trionyx Gangetus, the snapping turtle:

> Woe betide the limb, however, which comes in reach of the infuriated ani-mal! I saw the top of one man's toe bitten clean off by a trionyx plagyry which was being staked; as these animals are both active and ferocious, it is always advisable to set a bullet through their brain as soon as possible. So tenacious of life, however, are these creatures, that their heads bite vigor-ously after being completely dissevered from their bodies.[34]

It is not difficult to imagine connections between these little life stories of far-fetched, colourful, endangered creatures, with their weird, dubious and various ways, and the narratives of remarkable fauna in the nonsense writings.

The new world of zoos and menageries brought creatures together in ways that may have stimulated Lear's imagination. A drawing from the mid-1830s included in the Houghton Library exhibition 'The Natural History of Edward Lear' shows 'an eastern Gray Kangaroo and Geese from Knowsley Hall'.[35] The Kangaroo is surrounded by five geese, one of them placed on the drawing just next to his big hind paws, nearer on the paper than they would ever be in life. Perhaps Lear remembered their proximity thirty years later in what was probably the earliest of his nonsense songs, 'The Duck and the Kangaroo'.[36] Bringing creatures unprecedentedly together is something nonsense writing can do, and it was also something in the original 1825 'Prospectus' of the Zoological Society of London where Lear worked as a precocious teenager. This announced an aim 'to introduce ... new varieties, breeds or races of liv-ing Animals', bringing for instance dodgy foreign marsupials to sturdy

British wildfowl.[37] The very Victorian activities of global exploration and scientific classification suggest a structure and analogue for the discoveries of the nonsense world, and also at times a parodiable target for it, in Lear's botanies and alphabets as well as in his narrative poems. (With Lewis Carroll, born a generation later, the no less Victorian activity of philology is the chief suspect.)

Travel in many of the limericks is a wondrous adventure to the beyond and sometimes back again. But some of the other limericks present failures of travel, showing experiments in having your life well-arranged to a fault. Settledness, tranquillity, serenity threaten to become terminal sulks. Here are three limericks in which the protagonists take up residence reclusively on high, away from the danger of others, secured in a self-allegiance which is both the triumph and nightmare of the limerick figures.[38]

> There was an old Person of Philae ,
> Whose conduct was scroobious and wily;
> He rushed up a Palm, when the weather was calm,
> And observed all the ruins of Philae.

> There was a Young Lady of Portugal,
> Whose ideas were excessively nautical;
> She climbed up a tree, to examine the sea,
> But declared she would never leave Portugal.

> There was an Old Person of Bar ,
> Who passed all her life in a jar,
> Which she painted pea-green, to appear more serene,
> That placid Old Person of Bar.[39]

The Old Person of Bar may be as wisely foolish as Diogenes, but Portugal and Philae seem moody and misanthropic. Such nightmares of stasis and hinterlands of desperation are normal to Lear, and they can be a prompt to the nonsensical travelling he imagines as a remedy for the status quo (Fig. 8).

> There was an Old Man whose despair
> Induced him to purchase a hare;
> Whereon one fine day, he rode wholly away,
> Which partly assuaged his despair.[40]

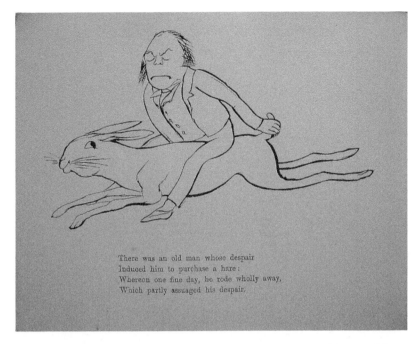

There was an old man whose despair
Induced him to purchase a hare ;
Whereon one fine day, he rode wholly away,
Which partly assuaged his despair.

Fig. 8   There was an old man whose despair (*More Nonsense, Pictures, Rhymes, Botany, Etc.* [London: Robert John Bush, 1872], n.p.)

Sometimes the limerick despairers do away with themselves (like those from New York, Cape Horn and Tartary) but here despair prompts a project that turns out quite well.[41] This Old Man buys a hare, and it's an instance of retail as therapy. The magic of 'away' makes things better. However, it is not completely better, in that though he rides 'wholly away' this only 'partly assuaged' his despair—and 'assuaging' as against 'dispelling', for instance, already carries a sense of partiality.[42] He may be elsewhere but he is still himself. The drawing gives an imperfect match between the oddly masked eyes of the man and the considerate backward glance of the hare, looking back to him and also looking after him it seems, a rather nicer animal perhaps than he has any right to expect.

A final limerick voyager also seems to be going 'wholly away' (Fig. 9).

There was an Old Person of Grange ,
Whose manners were scroobious and strange;

There was an old person of Grange,
Whose manners were scroobious and strange;
He sailed to St. Blubb, in a waterproof tub,
That aquatic old person of Grange.

Fig. 9   There was an old person of Grange (*More Nonsense, Pictures, Rhymes, Botany, Etc.* [London: Robert John Bush, 1872], n.p.)

> He sailed to St Blubb, in a waterproof tub,
> That aquatic Old person of Grange.

He probably comes from Grange because Lear's imagination was haunted by Tennyson's poetry, and above all, to judge from his repeated allusions to the poem, by 'Mariana', with its Shakespearean epigraph 'Mariana in the moated grange'.[43] Tennyson was always the poet who counted most to Lear; he worked for decades on an illustrated selection of Tennyson and he also set a number of the laureate's poems to music, to some acclaim. Tennyson stimulated his serio-comic vein; Lear's 'Mr and Mrs Discobbolos' takes up from Tennyson's 'St Simeon Stylites', for instance, and his great autobiographical poem 'Some Incidents in the Life of my Uncle Arly' imagines his own life to a metrical tune modelled on Tennyson's 'The Lady of Shallott'. In relation to travel Lear is more compelled by Mariana, static in her 'moated grange', than for instance by Tennyson's Ulysses who 'cannot cease from travel' or his 'Lotos-Eaters' whose travels lead to the cessation of activity. In this limerick the Person of Grange may be heading for St Blubb because of a memory of Mariana's terminal weeping; the refrain line 'She said,"I am aweary, aweary' modulates passionately in Tennyson's final stanza to 'She wept, "I am aweary, aweary'.[44]

Although the Person of Grange's fishy eyes and finny thumbs again align human life with its setting in animal nature, he seems unreachably off in his own world. He embarks into the world of the 'scroobious', Lear's favourite invented nonce-word (we saw it also in the Philae limerick), the sign that this is a world of his own words as well as the usual stock. The tub is waterproof, but as his legs are outside it that seems beside the point. It's hard to see how he gets to St. Blubb: he has no sail, though he himself is like one. Moreover, the boat is facing right to left whereas the words go left to right, making us doubt his sense of direction. But the story tells us that he does arrive and the fish look like his escort, his pilot fish. On the epic seas of nonsense you don't have to be sensible to get places.

3   QUESTIONS OF TRAVEL IN THE NONSENSE SONGS
     AND JOURNALS OF A LANDSCAPE PAINTER

This is something we also know at more length from such poems as 'The Jumblies ' and Carroll's *The Hunting of the Snark*. The Jumblies go to sea in a sieve, but they do arrive. With a dramatic and musical modulation each stanza switches into a present tense for its chant-like refrain: 'Far and few, far and few, | Are the lands where the Jumblies live'.[45] The poem starts in the past—'They went to sea in a sieve'—but the present tense brings the Jumblies and their lands nearer to us. However, the refrain also keeps them 'far' at a distance, so it is simultaneously what grammarians call 'proximal' (in time) and 'distal' (in place). The phrase 'far and few' is a play on 'few and far between', but there is something strange about it. Far is usually a relational term; a place can be far *away* from you or far *off* or even far *out*, but not just far; Tobago may be far but not if you live in Trinidad. But the lands where the Jumblies live are 'far', just like that, and they remain far at the end of every verse. The place that not only can but must remain permanently 'far' is the horizon, which is always unreachable, like the destination of nonsense. Its way of being forever inaccessible can suggest affinities with lost love, as for the stricken Dong with the Luminous Nose 'Ever keeping his weary eyes on | That pea-green sail on the far horizon'.[46] Lear was repeatedly drawn to the word 'far', with its evocation of a distance between nonsense and sense. 'The Daddy Long-legs and the Fly', for example, find a little boat, 'And off they sailed among the waves, | Far, and far away'.[47] They go not just 'far' but 'far away', as if actively and rather fiercely repudiating the unfriendly world they leave behind and its insectophobic ways. And they go not 'across' the waves but among them, as though the waves were companionable encouragers of the getaway. 'Affection was miles away', Auden wrote in his sonnet on Lear.[48] The sites of nonsense tend to be miles away, far off yet also real enough for anyone who accepts the invitation to imaginative travel offered by the genre.

That doubleness is reflected in further layers of uncertainty within 'The Jumblies '. Should we think of 'the lands where the Jumblies live' as the place they set out from or the one they sail to, the cautious world of home or the sublime land of adventure? And who for that matter are the Jumblies themselves? Is it only the brave voyagers who deserve the name of Jumblies or does the group include also the risk-averse friends at the start? The poem keeps an amiable and undivisive silence about these possible lines of division. It manages to bring together in a spirit of celebration the stay-at-homes, who are like adults, and the voyagers, who are like children.

Lewis Carroll's great nonsense poem, *The Hunting of the Snark*, contrasts in many ways with Lear's. His crew members are hierarchical, professional, imperial, loquacious and liable to kill each other, whereas Lear's are anarchic, non-verbal and united by impulse. But Carroll's is another poem linking absurdity with courage; here the courage is to do what they dutifully must do, not as with the Jumblies what they recklessly want to. Following the map in Carroll, like steering by sieve in Lear, is a nonsensical undertaking.

> ... the crew were much pleased when they found it to be
> A map they could all understand.

> 'What's the good of Mercator's North Poles and Equators,
>   Tropics, Zones, and Meridian Lines?'
> So the Bellman would cry: and the crew would reply
>   'They are merely conventional signs!

Other maps are such shapes, with their islands and capes!
  But we've got our brave Captain to thank'
(So the crew would protest) 'that he's bought *us* the best –
  A perfect and absolute blank!'[49]

The tone of social satisfaction is purely Carrollian, with absurdity having decorums and pecking orders of its own, and the brave captain thanked for supplying a veritable Moby-Dick of a white map.

Travel has figured variously in this discussion as escape from stasis, alleviation of grief, existential impulse, adventure, fun. It may also be a site of romance. Lear's poem, which never tells us whether the Jumblies are boys or girls, children or adults, has much of the lure of romanticism, but none of the complications of sex that are common elsewhere in the literature of exotic travel. Hence in part the lightness of 'The Jumblies'. Elsewhere his nonsense world is full of allegories of frustrated and some-times rapturous love. If his loving families are unpredictably matched (the Person of Ems with his fishes, for instance, and the Young Lady with the bonnet and the birds of the air), then so too are his loving couples. The famous cross-species couples include 'The Owl and the Pussy-cat' and 'The Duck and the Kangaroo' and 'The Daddy Long-Legs and the Fly'; other couples who go off together come from the world of kitch-enalia, 'The Nutcrackers and the Sugar-tongs' and 'The Table and the Chair'.

Lear himself never married, though he often considered it, and the biographical evidence, though still disputed, points strongly to his being gay. He showed far greater intensity of feeling towards the men who meant most to him, above all Franklin Lushington, than the women, including those with whom he contemplated marriage. I have argued elsewhere that his poems are so frankly about social non-conformity and romantic love that there is no great discovery in seeing them as part of a history of queer writing.[50] The experience of unrequited love in Lear's own life suggests a shape for his stories and a context for the outsider-liness which fired his imagination, and they can give us respect for the mettle of the nonsense songs. Lear imagines for us and for himself a world where extraordinary intimacies can flourish, but always within the boundaries of the self-consciously fantastical genre, and sometimes within limits evoked by the nonsense narratives themselves. He locates the idea of fulfilled love in a world of nonsense and he also makes absurdity into the true and proper element of desire. Travelling until you are at a remove from the ordinary world is integral to his imagining of loving relationships.

Some of Lear's nonsenses seem to voice an impatience with their own creation of fantasy. His ambivalence about change of place can sometimes be heard in dark hints or grumbles within his own nonsense stories. In the last stanza of 'The Duck and the Kangaroo', 'away they went with a hop and a bound, | And they hopped the whole world three times round'.[51] That sounds sprightly and energised, but how would a fourth time round be? Or a fortieth? Even a child might eventually weary of repetition. Mr Daddy Long-legs and Mr Floppy Fly arrive at the end of their voyage at the 'great Gromboolian plain': 'And there they play for evermore | At battlecock and shuttledore'.[52] For evermore? Is that a happy ending? As Lear's contemporary Baudelaire asked in his poem 'Le Voyage', 'Et puis, et puis encore?'[53] In T. S. Eliot's *Sweeney Agonistes* South Seas romance turns both deathly and murderous and, as Doris and Sweeney agree, not interesting.

> *Doris*: I'd be bored.
> *Sweeney*: You'd be bored.[54]

Some of Lear's travel writings also bring death and ennui into their voyagings. His first prose narrative, 'The History of the Seven Families of the Lake Pipple-Popple', sends forty-nine children tearfully out on their voyages and meticulously kills off the lot of them; the surviving predators jump into pickling bottles and donate themselves to the museum of Tosh, 'for the perpetual benefit of the pusillanimous public'.[55] We might even wonder about the Owl and the Pussy-cat; how long can the dancing by the light of the moon go on? In Lear's unfinished sequel poem, written in 1885, the offspring say 'We made a happy home and there we pass our obvious days'.[56] The far-fetched places of nonsense do not always impress their maker; they can become obvious too.

Lear's travel journals remain little known. They are vivid and appealing books, full of Pickwickian English humour, exquisite landscape description, pioneering cultural anthropology, and an interesting union of religious sensibility with fierce anti-clericalism. 'In an age that abounded in travel writers and travel painters', Susan Hyman argues, 'he was both, leaving a visual and verbal record of foreign lands that was unique in his own time and possibly unequalled in any other'[57]—a high but not an implausible claim. His journals deserve far more attention than they have yet received. I have space here only to suggest that many of their most vivid moments are reflexive and cast a light on Lear's sense of the wonder and nonsense of travel.

In his excursions of the 1840s to the Abruzzi, Calabria and Albania, Lear is frequently the first Englishman that local people have met. Misconceptions follow. In Calabria in August 1847 he is greeted in puzzlement though hospitably at the monastery where he is spending the night:

> 'Why had we come to such a solitary place? No foreigner had ever done so before!' The hospitable father asked a world of questions, and made many comments upon us and upon England in general, for the benefit of his fellow-recluses. 'England', said he, 'is a very small place, although thickly inhabited. It is altogether about the third part of the size of the city of Rome. The people are a sort of Christians, though not exactly so. Their priests, and even their bishops, marry, which is incomprehensible, and most ridiculous. The whole place is divided into two equal parts by an arm of the sea, under which there is a great tunnel, so that it is all like one piece of dry land. *Ah – che celebre tunnel!*'[58]

Who is the absurd one here? Each is an object of energetic wonderment to the other. Lear as a polite guest is not heard to remonstrate and is somewhat at a disadvantage; as narrator, however, he has the advantage. But the good temper survives and even flourishes across cultural misunderstanding and beyond competition.

The Albanian journal includes another exchange where the differences do not get the last word.

> We halted at the *khan* of Episkopì, close to a little stream full of capital watercresses which I began to gather and eat with some bread and cheese, an act which provoked the Epirote bystanders of the village to ecstatic laughter and curiosity [...] One brought a thistle, a second a collection of sticks and wood, a third some grass; a fourth presented me with a fat grasshopper – the whole scene was acted amid shouts of laughter, in which I joined as loudly as any. We parted amazingly good friends, and the wits of Episkopì will long remember the Frank who fed on weeds out of the water.[59]

This meeting is structured like a limerick, with Lear as the oddball. He sees himself from both sides, as the discerning Englishman with a horticultural eye for 'capital watercresses', but also as the strange ruminant transplanted from home, feeding on weeds. Englishman and Albanians part 'amazingly good friends' indeed, with the idea that amazement is a healthy state in which to meet life. They become friends not in a conventional traveller's way by learning to understand each other's ways—and not via the explorations of history and archaeology and textiles which the journals also include—but from shouts of laughter, from exulting in their differences. The world of difference is the condition of friendship.

Lear's first travel book, *Illustrated Excursions in Italy* (1846), includes another meeting focused on contrasts around what people choose to eat.

> August 13th, 1843. The cool valley of Antrodoco is in deep shade till late in the morning. I was sauntering by the brawling river, when a little boy passed me carrying a dead fox. 'It is delightful food (*cibo squisito*)', said he, 'either boiled or roast'; –said I, 'I wish you joy'.[60]

And that's the whole of this beautifully shaped and enigmatic meeting. Separated by age and nationality, the two people pass in a changeless landscape, exchanging information and good will, never to meet again. The little translated phrase in italics makes us conscious of how much has not been translated, and how differently 'delightful food' and 'joy' may be understood in different languages and places. Is it much or little to wish somebody joy, a mere courtesy or something heartfelt? It feels like much here.

Lear's narrator is a reticent figure, but some of the encounters open out onto his sense of his own life and identity. In Calabria he is quizzed by a Baron who is utterly mystified to see Lear drawing the landscape and asks him what he can possibly be doing.

> 'Signore Baron,' said I, when I had done my sketch, 'we have no towns in our country so beautifully situated as Gioiosa!'
> '*Ma* – perchè?' quoth he.
> I walked a little way, and paused to observe the bee-eaters*, which were flitting through the air above me, and under the spreading oak branches.
> '*Per l'amor del Cielo, cosa guardate? Cosa mai osservate?*' said the Baron.
> 'I am looking at those beautiful blue birds.'
> 'Perchè? perchè? perchè?'
> 'Because they are so very pretty, and because we have none like them in England.'

'*Ma* perchè? perchè?'
It was evident that do or say what I would, some mystery was connected with each action and word [...]
                                    *Merops Apiaster. [Lear's footnote][61]

The Baron brings about a certain vertiginousness when he keeps asking
'why', like an unappeasable child. Lear dramatises first his own composure but then his discomfiture, with the mannerly 'Signore Baron' and
'said I' disappearing as the dialogue goes on. The footnote denoting the
bee-eaters as 'Merops Apiaster' is intriguing. To whom is it addressed?
Presumably not to the Baron, but to the reader or even to himself, as if
his knowing the Latin name of the bird explained his presence there. In a
way it does so; it signals his zoological knowhow and cultural credentials.
It is as if the challenge of the Baron's questioning prompts this unusual
gesture of self-authentication in Lear. But his replies are entirely unsatis-
factory to the Baron, who thinks him very likely a spy and continues to
find his actions as a travelling artist beyond the intelligible.
   A final passage, from the journal for the following day (20 August
1847), also turns also on Lear's discovery of a point of view from which
he appears entirely strange.

> At dinner-time, good old Don Giovanni Rosa amused and delighted us
> by his lively simplicity and good breeding. He had only once in his long
> life (he was 82) been as far as Gerace, but never beyond. 'Why should I
> go?' said he; 'if, when I die, as I shall ere long, I find Paradise like Cánalo,
> I shall be well pleased. To me "*Cánalo mio*" has always seemed like
> Paradise—*sempre mi sembra Paradiso, niente mi manca*'. Considering that
> the good old man's Paradise is cut off by heavy snow four months in the
> year from any external communication with the country round, and that
> it is altogether (however attractive to artists) about as little a convenient
> place as may well be imagined—the contented mind of Don Giovanni was
> equally novel and estimable.[62]

Don Giovanni is much less exasperating than the Baron, but he poses
another challenge to how the Landscape Painter leads his own life. Don
Giovanni is always rooted, Edward Lear always wandering. However,
the contrast is not pushed into a disagreement or a comparison of ethical value beyond the pacific word 'estimable'. From one point of view
that may be disappointing. The conclusion here—that Don Giovanni's
contentment was 'novel and estimable'—is blandly expressed; Lear does

not argue the point. From another point of view, though, the narrator's courteous reticence suggests distinctive attributes of Lear's journals; they are zestful, observant, appreciative, curious narratives, never self-preoccupied. Lear is a generously curious observer who takes pleasure in the world being wide and not always being what he expects or can easily deal with. Like the nonsense writings, the travel journals are explorations of different perspectives on things, different assumptions about where in the world to stay and what to want from it.

NOTES

1. Critical literature on nonsense writing begins with some focused and suggestive essays, including notably G. K. Chesterton, 'A Defence of Nonsense,' in *The Defendant* (London: R. Brimley Johnson, 1901), 42–50; Aldous Huxley, 'Edward Lear,' in *On the Margin* (London: Chatto and Windus, 1923), 167–172; William Empson, 'Alice in Wonderland: the Child as Swain,' in *Some Versions of Pastoral* (London: Chatto and Windus, 1935), 253–298; George Orwell, 'Nonsense Poetry,' *Tribune*, 21 December 1945, reprinted in *The Collected Essays, Journalism and Letters of George Orwell* (Harmondsworth: Penguin, 1970), iv, 64–68; T. S. Eliot, 'From Poe to Valéry' (1948), in *To Criticize the Critic and Other Essays* (London: Faber and Faber, 1965), 27–42. Influential full-length studies begin with Elizabeth Sewell, *The Field of Nonsense* (London: Chatto & Windus, 1952), and continue with Susan Stewart, *Nonsense: Aspects of Intertextuality in Folklore and Literature* (Baltimore: Johns Hopkins University Press, 1979); Jean-Jacques Lecercle, *Philosophy of Nonsense. The Intuitions of Victorian Nonsense Literature* (London: Routledge, 1994); an important anthology, *The Chatto Book of Nonsense Poetry*, ed. Hugh Haughton (London: Chatto & Windus, 1988). See also *Edward Lear and the Play of Poetry*, ed. James Williams and Matthew Bevis (Oxford: Oxford University Press, 2016).
2. 'Introduction' to *More Nonsense, Pictures, Rhymes, Botany, Etc.* (London: Robert John Bush, 1872), vi. James Williams discusses 'nonsense for nonsense's sake' in *Nineteenth-Century Nonsense Writing and the Later Work of James Joyce* (Ph.D. thesis, University of Cambridge, 2008), 8–13, citing instances from Carolyn Wells, 'The Senses of Nonsense,' *Scribner's Magazine* 29 (1901): 239, and Emile Cammaerts, *The Poetry of Nonsense* (London: Routledge, 1925), 7.
3. The relationship between philosophy and nonsense literature is most fully considered in Jean-Jacques Lecercle, *The Philosophy of Nonsense*.

4. Compare T. S. Eliot on Lear in 'The Music of Poetry' (1942): 'His non-sense is not vacuity of sense: it is a parody of sense, and that is the sense of it' (*On Poetry and Poets* [London: Faber and Faber, 1957], 29).
5. Emrys Jones, 'Pope and Dulness,' *Proceedings of the British Academy* 54 (1970): 240–241.
6. *Letters of Edward Lear*, ed. Lady Strachey (London: T. Fisher Unwin, 1907), 141.
7. To Lady Waldegrave, 6 July 1873; cited in Vivien Noakes, *Edward Lear: The Life of a Wanderer* (fourth edition, revised and extended, Stroud: Alan Sutton, 2004), 224.
8. *Later Letters of Edward Lear*, ed. Lady Strachey (London: T. Fisher Unwin, 1911), 93.
9. *Edward Lear: Selected Letters*, ed. Vivien Noakes (Oxford: Oxford University Press, 1990), 222.
10. *The Life of a Wanderer*, 249.
11. *Later Letters* dated, 121–122; to Fortescue.
12. The full letter, 16 August 1869, is in *Later Letters*, 87–89. I cite the excerpt from *The Life of a Wanderer*, 204, as it more closely reproduces Lear's spelling and punctuation.
13. *The Rubáiyát of Omar Khayyám* (fourth edition, 1879); from stanza 12.
14. *The Life of a Wanderer*, 204; citing Lear's diary for 18 June 1869.
15. *The Life of a Wanderer*, 39; letter to Fanny Coombe, 8 July 1837.
16. *Illustrated Excursions in Italy* (2 volumes, 1846); *Journals of a Landscape Painter in Albania, &c* (1851); *Journals of a Landscape Painter in Southern Calabria, &c.* (1852); *Journal of a Landscape Painter in Corsica* (1870). Excerpts from these are included in *'Over the Land and Over the Sea': Selected Nonsense and Travel Writings*, ed. Peter Swaab (Manchester: Carcanet Press, 2005). See also *Lear in Sicily*, with an introduction by Granville Proby (1938), *Edward Lear: The Cretan Journal*, ed. Rowena Fowler (1984) and *Edward Lear's Indian Journal*, ed. Ray Murphy (1953).
17. *The Life of a Wanderer*, 106; to Ann Lear, 21 December 1853.
18. 'Edward Lear's Contribution to British Psychoanalysis,' in *Edward Lear and the Play of Poetry*, 340.
19. *The Life of a Wanderer*, 110.
20. *Letters of Edward Lear*, 136; to Fortescue, 1 May 1859.
21. *Nonsense Songs, Stories, Botany, and Alphabets* (London: Robert John Bush, 1871), n.p.
22. Edward Lear's drawing for 'M was a Mouse' from 'An original nonsense alphabet made for Miss Lushington,' ca. 1865. MS Typ 55.3. Image courtesy of the Houghton Library, Harvard University, Cambridge, MA. Web: https://iiif.lib.harvard.edu/manifests/view/drs:51101168$14i.

23. The remainder are made up of 28 young ladies, 2 others, 10 young persons and 4 who are introduced in other ways. The exception is 'There lived a small puppy at Narkunder'.

24. *The Guardian*, 11 November 2001.

25. See for instance the Young Lady of Dorking, the Old Man of Dundee, the old person of Shields, and the Old Person of Bree in *Complete Verse*, 96, 100, 119, 337.

26. *Edward Lear: The Complete Verse and Other Nonsense*, ed. Vivien Noakes (Penguin Classics: London, 2001), 89. This essay will cite the text and punctuation used by Noakes, who follows Holbrook Jackson and most later editors in using the four-line version of the limericks. However, the drawings used for the Lady of Sweden, the Person of Ems and the 'Young Lady whose bonnet' show the three-line format that Lear used in *The Book of Nonsense* (1846) but not in his later collections, where the limericks have four lines. For another returning venturer see p. 335 of the *Complete Verse*, the Old Man of Dunluce, who went out to sea on a goose: 'When he'd gone out a mile, he observ'd with a smile, | "It is time to return to Dunluce."'

27. *Complete Verse*, 104.

28. *The Life of a Wanderer*, 187; citing the diary for 20 October 1879. The fuller context laments his childlessness, when he takes leave of some visitors, 'wishing, as I left them that I had sons or daughters. But it was decreed I was not be human'.

29. *Complete Verse*, 159. For a richly suggestive discussion of Lear and birds see Matthew Bevis, 'Edward Lear's Lines of Flight,' *Journal of the British Academy* 1 (2013): 31–69.

30. This paragraph and the next draw on my introduction to Edward Lear, *'Over the Land and Over the Sea': Selected Nonsense and Travel Writings* (Manchester: Carcanet Press, 2005), x–xi.

31. *'Over the Land and Over the Sea'*, 344–345; extract from John Gould, *The Birds of Europe* (1837).

32. *'Over the Land and Over the Sea'*, 344; extract and image from John Gould, *A Monograph of the Ramphastidae, or Family of Toucans* (1834).

33. *Complete Verse*, 266, 326–327, 489.

34. *'Over the Land and Over the Sea'*, 348; extract from *Tortoises, Terrapins and Turtles* (1872), illustrated by Lear in about 1836.

35. See 'The Natural History of Edward Lear: Exhibition Catalog,' *Harvard Library Bulletin* 22, no. 2–3 (Summer–Fall 2011): 125–159 (p. 145).

36. *Complete Verse*, 207–209 and note on p. 500.

37. Cited in Robert McCracken Peck, 'The Natural History of Edward Lear,' *Harvard Library Bulletin* 22, no. 2–3 (Summer–Fall 2011): 6; see also Robert McCracken Peck, *The Natural History of Edward Lear* (Boston: David R. Godine, 2016).

38. On self-sufficiency in Lear see also Peter Swaab, '"Some Think Him ...
    Queer": Loners and Love in Edward Lear,' in *Edward Lear and the Play
    of Poetry*, 96–107.
39. *Complete Verse*, 167, 163, 358.
40. *Complete Verse*, 329.
41. *Complete Verse*, 100, 97, 77.
42. Compare the 'old man whose despair, | Induced him to purchase a bear; |
    [...] Which rather assuaged his despair' (*Complete Verse*, 113).
43. *Complete Verse*, 329. For other echoes of 'Mariana' see *The Life of a
    Wanderer*, 261, 292, *Complete Verse*, 458, 548, *Selected Letters*, 117.
    For Lear and Tennyson see Ruth Pitman, *Edward Lear's Tennyson*
    (Manchester: Carcanet Press, 1988), 35–38. Lear and Tennyson
    are also discussed in Richard Cronin, 'Edward Lear and Tennyson's
    Nonsense,' in *Tennyson Among the Poets: Bicentenary Essays*, ed. Robert
    Douglas-Fairhurst and Seamus Perry (Oxford: Oxford University Press,
    2009), 259–275, and in two pieces by Anna Barton, 'Delirious Bulldogs
    and Nasty Crockery: Tennyson as Nonsense Poet,' *Victorian Poetry* 47,
    no. 1 (2009): 313–330, and 'The Sense and Weariness of Nonsense,' in
    Edward Lear and the Play of Poetry, 243–259.
44. The OED lists the first use of 'blub' as short for 'blubber' from Austin
    Dobson in 1866: 'Bob privately confessed to me that he always felt
    inclined to "blub" over those whipper-tunes.' The quotation marks
    round 'blub' suggest that it is a new usage; Lear's limerick was published
    six years later.
45. *Complete Verse*, 254.
46. Ibid., 423; the poem includes a reprise of the refrain from 'The Jumblies '
    (lines 36–39).
47. *Complete Verse*, 248.
48. 'Edward Lear,' line 7, in W. H. Auden, *The English Auden: Poems, Essays
    and Dramatic Writings 1927–1939*, ed. Edward Mendelson (London:
    Faber and Faber, 1977), 239.
49. *The Hunting of the Snark: An Agony in Eight Fits*, introduced by Martin
    Gardner (London: Penguin Classics, 1995), 55–56.
50. Peter Swaab, '"Some think him ... queer": Loners and Love in Edward
    Lear,' in *Edward Lear and the Play of Poetry*, 89–114; on the biographical
    contentions about Lear's sexuality, 89–96.
51. *Complete Verse*, 209.
52. Ibid., 248.
53. 'And then, and then what?'; Charles Baudelaire, *Oeuvres Complètes*
    (Bibliothèque de la Pléiade. Paris: Gallimard, 1975), 135. The half-line is
    the entirety of Section V of the poem.

54. *The Poems of T. S. Eliot: Volume I, Collected and Uncollected Poems*, ed. Christopher Ricks and Jim McCue (London: Faber and Faber, 2015), 122.
55. *Complete Verse*, 206.
56. Ibid., 541.
57. *Edward Lear in the Levant: Travels in Albania, Greece and Turkey in Europe, 1848–1849*, ed. Susan Hyman (London: John Murray, 1988), 10.
58. *Journals of a Landscape Painter in Southern Calabria, Etc.* (1852); in 'Over the Land and Over the Sea', 249–250.
59. *Journals of a Landscape Painter in Albania, Etc.* (1851); in 'Over the Land and Over the Sea', 223.
60. 'Over the Land and Over the Sea', 140.
61. *Journals of a Landscape Painter in Southern Calabria*; in 'Over the Land and Over the Sea', 259.
62. *Journals of a Landscape Painter in Southern Calabria*; in 'Over the Land and Over the Sea', 262.

Works Cited

Baudelaire, Charles. *Oeuvres Complètes*. Paris: Gallimard (Bibliothèque de la Pléiade), 1975.
Bevis, Matthew. 'Edward Lear's Lines of Flight'. *Journal of the British Academy* 1 (2013): 31–69.
Eliot, T. S. 'The Music of Poetry' (1942). In *On Poetry and Poets*. London: Faber and Faber, 1957.
Gardner, Martin, ed. *The Hunting of the Snark: An Agony in Eight Fits* (Lewis Carroll). London: Penguin Classics, 1996.
Hyman, Susan, ed. *Edward Lear in the Levant: Travels in Albania, Greece and Turkey in Europe, 1848–1849*. London: John Murray, 1988.
Jones, Emrys. 'Pope and Dulness', *Proceedings of the British Academy* 54 (1970): 231–263.
Karlin, Daniel, ed. *The Rubáiyát of Omar Khayyám* (Edward FitzGerald). Oxford: Oxford University Press, 2009.
Lear, Edward. *A Book of Nonsense*. London: Frederick Warne and Co, 1846; eighteenth edition, 1866.
Lear, Edward. *Nonsense Songs, Stories, Botany, and Alphabets*. London: Robert John Bush, 1871.
Lear, Edward. *More Nonsense, Pictures, Rhymes, Botany, Etc*. London: Robert John Bush, 1872.
Mars-Jones, Adam. *Review of Edward Lear: The Complete Verse and Other Nonsense*, edited by Vivien Noakes. *The Guardian*, 11 November, 2001.

Mendelson, Edward. *The English Auden: Poems, Essays and Dramatic Writings 1927–1939*. London: Faber and Faber, 1977.

Noakes, Vivien, ed. *Edward Lear: Selected Letters*. Oxford: Oxford University Press, 1990.

Noakes, Vivien, ed. *Edward Lear: The Complete Verse and Other Nonsense*. London: Penguin Classics, 2001.

Noakes, Vivien. *Edward Lear: The Life of a Wanderer* (fourth edition, revised and extended). Stroud: Alan Sutton, 2004.

Peck, Robert McCracken. 'The Natural History of Edward Lear: Exhibition Catalog'. *Harvard Library Bulletin* 22 (2011): 125–159.

Peck, Robert McCracken. *The Natural History of Edward Lear*. Boston: David R. Godine, 2016.

Phillips, Adam. 'Edward Lear's Contribution to British Psychoanalysis'. In *Edward Lear and the Play of Poetry*, edited by James Williams and Matthew Bevis, 339–46. Oxford: Oxford University Press, 2016.

Ricks, Christopher and Jim McCue, eds. *The Poems of T. S. Eliot: Volume I, Collected and Uncollected Poems*. London: Faber and Faber, 2015.

Strachey, Lady, ed. *Letters of Edward Lear*. London: T. Fisher Unwin, 1907.

Strachey, Lady, ed. *Later Letters of Edward Lear*. London: T. Fisher Unwin, 1911.

Swaab, Peter, ed. *'Over the Land and Over the Sea': Selected Nonsense and Travel Writings of Edward Lear*. Manchester: Carcanet Press, 2005.

Swaab, Peter. '"Some think him … queer": Loners and Love in Edward Lear'. In *Edward Lear and the Play of Poetry*, edited by James Williams and Matthew Bevis, 89–114. Oxford: Oxford University Press, 2016.

Williams, James and Matthew Bevis, eds. *Edward Lear and the Play of Poetry*. Oxford: Oxford University Press, 2016.

Jokes

'Capital Company': Writing and Telling Jokes in Victorian Britain

Bob Nicholson

1   THE JOKE COPYRIGHT PROTECTIVE COMPANY

On 25 January 1845, the *Lancaster Gazette* published an article calling for the immediate formation of a 'Joke Copyright Protective Company'. The urgent need for its foundation was made plain in the article's opening paragraph:

> It has been the custom of certain individuals frequently encountered in society (who are desirous of being called 'droll dogs', 'smart fellows', 'capital company', 'funny creatures', 'agreeable rattlers', 'wags', and similar appellations) to maintain their reputations by pilfering the jokes of other people, and thus trade on false capital [...] [This] appropriation [has] arrived at such a pitch that no legitimate wit dares make a joke for fear of its being directly taken up.[1]

In order to protect the rights of 'true jokers', the article proposed a series of rules and procedures by which all jests would henceforth be valued and licenced for retelling. Firstly, the worth of a joke would be

B. Nicholson (✉)
Department of English, History and Creative Writing,
Edge Hill University, Ormskirk, UK

© The Author(s) 2020   109
L. Lee (ed.), *Victorian Comedy and Laughter*,
https://doi.org/10.1057/978-1-137-57882-2_5

determined by 'delivering it to the Clown at Astley's [Circus] to say in the ring' and then measuring the levels of applause and laughter bestowed upon it by his audience. With this valuation in place, the 'use of a joke for an evening [would] be fixed at half a crown, if the utterer [took] credit of it to himself'. If the would-be-wag was willing to attribute the jest to its original author—'Markwell told me a devilish good thing' or 'Carter made me laugh very much the other day'—then the price would be dropped to a shilling. The 'writers of pantomimes and burlesque extravaganzas' would be permitted to hire jokes on the same terms, but would receive a discount for bulk orders. Magazine editors and 'writers of newspaper paragraphs' were warned against any attempt to circumvent this system by attributing new jokes to historical figures and celebrated wits such as 'Sydney Smith, Sam Rogers, Sir Peter Laurie, and others, when the smart things have evidently never been said by those gentlemen'. For those who failed to heed these warnings, the penalties would be severe. If a jest was 'damaged by too frequent use', 'impaired in the telling', or 'kept beyond the evening' then the culprit would be compelled to compensate its 'original manufacturer' by repaying the full value of the joke. If caught, an 'utterer of a forged joke, or an old one in a new shape' would be 'directly prohibited from telling another for some time'. Finally, if they were summarily convicted, then the worst offenders would be 'sentenced to see Hamlet performed three times at Covent-garden Theatre'.

The whole proposal, of course, was itself a joke. Unfortunately for the proprietors of the Covent Garden Theatre, the Company's rules were never enforced, and the copyright status of jokes remains ambiguous and contentious to this day. But if these rules had been implemented, the editors of the period's newspapers would have been punished often enough to have known Hamlet by heart. Columns of jokes, jests, puns, witticisms and humorous anecdotes were a staple feature of the press during the 1840s.[2] As *Blackwoods* observed in 1848, the country was now being subjected to a 'torrent of facetiæ, a surfeit of slang and puns'.[3] They confidently predicted that this trend would be short-lived. 'The truth is, the funny style has been overdone, the supply of jokers has exceeded the demand for jokes until the word "comic" resounds unpleasantly upon the public tympanum'. They could not have been more wrong. For the remainder of the nineteenth century and beyond, joke columns were a staple feature of the press. They could be found in almost every kind of periodical, but were particularly prevalent in mass-market weekly papers such as *Lloyds*, popular magazines like *Tit-Bits* and *Answers*, the weekend editions of provincial newspapers, and in dedicated comic papers such as *Punch*, *Fun* and *Illustrated Chips*.

While some editors conscientiously purchased jokes directly from authors, many 'pilfered' their gags from other sources and printed them without compensation or even attribution to the 'true jokers' who origin-ated them. Indeed, the *Lancaster Gazette* obtained its piece on joke copyright in precisely this fashion. It appeared on the back page of the paper in a column titled 'Selected Anecdotes, &c', which was com-posed of miscellaneous paragraphs clipped from other periodicals. That week's instalment included a characteristically eclectic range of extracts: a paragraph of political satire and a couple of social jokes attributed to *Punch*; a witty remark supposedly made by 'the late Dr. Mason' that had been bouncing around the provincial press for the past few months; an unattributed, and almost certainly spurious, anecdote concerning Louis Philippe's exile in America; a pithy paragraph clipped from the *Illuminated Magazine* about the wonders of shopping in London; a piece of Scottish dialect humour supplied by the *Dumfries Herald* and an incongruous extract from the *Gardener's Chronicle* on the reproductive habits of a parasitic insect.[4]

The piece on joke copyright was clipped from *The Great Gun*—a short-lived comic weekly that enjoyed a brief, but spirited, rivalry with *Punch*.[5] Like most comic periodicals, its jokes were widely reprinted by the daily and weekly press; it is possible, therefore, that the paper's remarks about the need to address joke piracy were not entirely in jest. The *Lancaster Gazette* generously included an attribution alongside its reprint of the extract, but it is extremely unlikely that they paid the *Great Gun* a fee for 'hiring' its gag. Nor, for that matter, did the paper demon-strate any awareness of the irony involved in reprinting a joke about cop-yright without securing the owner's permission. This kind of reprinting was deeply embedded in the day-to-day practices of Victorian journalism and, despite occasional complaints from the 'owners' of pirated material, it does not seem to have been regarded by the majority of editors, or their readers, as an objectionable form of plagiarism.[6] In fact, while the comic press may have taken exception to such widespread and shameless acts of piracy, the unfettered circulation and reinvention of jests was a vital part of business. As this chapter explores, reprinting and retelling jokes was central, not just to the workings of nineteenth-century newspa-per humour, but to a broader Victorian culture of joke-telling.

While the 'Joke Copyright Protective Company' was nothing more than the whimsical invention of a comic paper, the ideas underpinning its proposals provide a useful framework with which to begin unpacking the place of jokes in Victorian culture and society. Firstly, the humour of the *Great Gun's* wheeze rested primarily on the assumed absurdity of applying a rigorous system of copyright protection to something as ephemeral, frivolous and valueless as a joke. Two years earlier, the passage of *The Copyright Act 1842* had bolstered the rights of the authors of 'books' and 'dramatic pieces', and thereby reaffirmed the principle (amidst heated opposition from some elements of the publishing trade) that works of this nature could be owned and controlled.[7] While it was evidently considered plausible for Dickens to seek the protection of the law in order to curtail the pirating of his stories, the idea of extending similar protections to a single pun or a comic one-liner was assumed, in the *Great Gun's* article at least, to be inherently ridiculous.

This distinction prompts us to consider the uncertain place of jokes and joke-writers in the Victorian literary marketplace, and to question whether these texts could ever be 'owned' in the same way as a novel or play. This, in turn, leads us to even thornier questions about the origins of Victorian jokes. Who was responsible for creating jokes in this period? How did they go about performing this work? And, most importantly of all, why did they devote their energies to producing jokes in the first place? The pathway to answering these questions is again illuminated by the regulations of the 'Joke Copyright Protective Company', which highlight the different social and cultural contexts in which jests circulated. According to the Company's terms for hiring out a joke, the same gag might be used in: (1) print culture such as newspapers, magazines, periodicals, and books; (2) commercial performances such as circuses, burlesques, pantomimes and later music halls and (3) the informal oral culture of day-to-day conversation, as well as the semi-performative quips of 'droll dogs' at dinner parties. In the absence of enforceable copyright regulation, jokes flowed freely across oral, print, and performance cultures; they were, as this chapter demonstrates, circulated and continually refashioned through the dynamic interplay of conversation, correspondence, performance and publication. In short, if we are ever to make sense of the role that jokes and joking played in Victorian culture and society, then we need to look at the page and the stage and everywhere in between.

2   An Anonymous Calling

The core principle behind the 'Joke Copyright Protective Company' was that 'henceforth every joke be considered the property of the manufacturer'.[8] This assertion of ownership is central to any system of copyright, but neatly sidesteps what would have been the chief difficulties in establishing a system of copyright over jokes—identifying their authors. This problem is not unique to jokes; similar difficulties attend the attribution of more substantial literary and journalistic texts. But jokes are particularly slippery, and their production has always been resistant to conventional models of authorship.

It is easy to imagine the novelist seated at a desk, quill in hand, engaged in the solitary production of a new manuscript, or the artist standing in concentration at their easel. Indeed, representations of this creative 'brain work' circulated very widely in Victorian culture. The period's portrait painters and caricaturists, for instance, routinely positioned authors at writing tables or in front of bookcases, even if these scenes of romanticised authorial labour needed to be artificially manufactured. For example, a widely circulated caricature of Dickens depicted him seated at a desk with, as he himself put it, 'pen in hand, tapping his forehead to knock out an idea'.[9] The *deliberate* nature of Dickens' authorial work is made apparent. He sits in a dedicated workspace and expends mental energy in order to manufacture a literary product—it is, plainly, hard work. While his level of individual celebrity was clearly extreme, the *visibility* of literary authors was universal; even the most uncelebrated novelist would expect to see their name printed on a book cover. Some genres of writing, such as journalism, featured a greater volume of unsigned work. While this might have obscured the identity of *individual* authors, the *profession* of journalism was still visible in nineteenth-century culture and society; journalists appeared as characters in novels and plays, wandered the streets with notebooks in hand, recorded their profession in the census and worked inside office buildings with their paper's name emblazoned on the front. Even the most disreputable kind of reporting was understood to have been *deliberately written by somebody* and the insults levelled at penny-a-liners only served to recognise their professional existence.

Professional joke-writers were less fortunate. An article published in 1899 by the *Hampshire Telegraph* neatly captured the distinction between joke-writing and more recognised forms of authorship. It featured an imagined conversation between a professional humourist and a 'favoured short-story writer'.[10] The latter complains about the amount of attention he receives—'This makes the third request for my autograph this month...'—and speculates that his companion probably 'escaped a good many of these petitions'. The humourist confesses that this was 'quite true' and that:

> The professional joke-writer is never interviewed by a reporter of any of the great newspapers, and the public is therefore never informed of his inner life, what he eats, what time he rises in the morning, what are his pets, who are his favourite authors, and of the way in which he writes his jokes. When he happens to run down to Brighton for a day the papers neglect to state that "Mr Scribbler, the popular joke-writer, is stopping at such-and-such an hotel." Nor do we receive many letters from would-be joke writers complimenting us upon our beautiful ideas and faultless literary style, and incidentally enclosing a bunch of their own manuscripts [...]. That is one of the rewards of the joke-writer for adopting his anonymous calling.[11]

While this exchange is fictional, the distinction drawn between anonymous joke-writing and more recognised forms of literary work is quickly reinforced by browsing the rest of the *Hampshire Telegraph*. On the very same page, we find a short story called 'Molly's Fortunes', which was credited to the novelist Clara Mulholland.[12] By contrast, the next page featured a typical humour column titled, 'Unassorted Fun', and none of the eleven jokes contained within it were attributed to an author.[13]

Having established the anonymity of his calling, the fictional joke-writer went on to reveal the inner workings of his profession. 'Joke writing is much like any other line of literary work', he explained:

> The more you work at it, the easier it becomes. After a person has originated one thousand jokes, it is not a great effort to write a certain number, say twenty or twenty-five, at a sitting. A joke-writing friend of mine once wrote forty jokes in, I think, an hour, on a wager; though it is hardly likely that the majority of them would have proved saleable.

The process of writing a joke, he continued, begins with 'concentrating [one's] mind' on a recent event and then attempting to find a humorous 'line':

Take the recent snowstorms. I at once think with pity of the sad plight in which it put the suburbanite. My sympathy is easily aroused in his behalf, for I am a suburbanite myself […] The servant girl and her brief stay in the suburbs are subjects which Londoners ever accept as highly humorous. The snowstorm can easily be imagined to have upset the best-laid plans of many a suburban cook, and, as a result you jot down a joke.

If this kind of inspiration was not immediately forthcoming, then the professional joke-writer would fall back on his 'standard list of tramp, actor, freak, and other joke characters', or take 'one of our classical joke lines' and use it as a foundation to invent a new batch of saleable jests. In order to maximise productivity, the nucleus of a good joke might be repeated in several different guises, each designed to match the 'requirements and literary atmosphere' of a specific newspaper or magazine. When this 'process of manufacture' was complete, jokes would be written on little slips of paper and sent to editors for consideration. The *Hampshire Telegraph's* article offers limited insights into this part of the process, but similar articles about professional joke-writers in America suggest that a humourist would typically send work 'first to the paper that pays the highest price [*approximately $2*], and then in regular order from weekly to weekly, until he has exhausted the list and gotten down to where they pay as little as fifteen cents a joke'.[14] Once a joke was sold, its writer ceased to have any claim on it; his name would never be printed alongside it, and he would assert no future ownership. Their labour was complete and the 'remainder of the day may be spent at golf or yachting'.[15]

While it is unlikely that joke-writing actually supported such a leisured lifestyle, the *Hampshire Telegraph's* account makes it clear that it was a viable line of literary work. Indeed, the daily process of writing original material and sending it off to editors would have been recognisable to freelance journalists, essayists, poets, artists and writers of popular fiction. And yet, the existence of a professional joke market was almost entirely invisible to readers. While some gifted humourists managed to gain recognition—usually by publishing or editing more substantial comic texts—those who wrote merely short 'squibs' were known only to their editor. While readers digested a fresh batch of jokes each time they picked up a weekly newspaper, the writers of the jests were encountered only fleetingly. Contemporary articles sometimes provided insights into the profession, but these were uncommon. Even with the help of

large-scale digital archives, I have located only four—and three of these
were focused on the American market.

Jokes themselves also provided occasional reminders of their authors'
existence:

> **Parkrow:** "I write jokes for a living."
> **Pennibs:** "Is that a boast or an appeal for charity?"[16]
>
> - - -
>
> **She:** "What a sad-looking fellow you just bowed to; he must have
> experienced some severe affliction."
> **He:** "Poor fellow. He has, indeed. He is forced to write jokes for the
> funny papers to get a living."[17]
>
> - - -
>
> **Joke Writer (boastfully):** "Creating a joke and polishing it ready for
> publication is no light job, I can tell you. You'd laugh if you could
> see the rough draft of some of my jokes."
> **Candid Friend:** "Better send in the rough draft after this, if that's the
> case. I never heard of any one laughing at any of your jokes after
> they were finished."[18]
>
> - - -
>
> **The Editor:** "I see that they have at last deciphered the Hittite hiero-
> glyphics, supposed to be 4000 years old."
> **The Joke Writer:** "Really? I hope there are none of my jokes among
> them."[19]

Each of these gags mined a similar seam of self-deprecating humour that
cast joke-writing as low-brow. The stock jest usually hinged on the idea
that a joke-writer's material was either old or unfunny. However, their
humour also stems from the novelty of joke-writing as a profession; the
idea that humour could be produced in such mercenary ways was funny
in itself. But these representations were uncommon. The people who
supplied comic papers with gags might have been chained to their writing tables, manufacturing a daily supply of new jokes to make a living,
but broader Victorian conceptions of joking rarely imagined it taking
place in this way.

3   On the Origins of Jokes

In his monumental *History of Punch* (1895), the art critic and historian Marion H. Spielmann devoted an entire chapter to the 'origin, pedigree, and appropriation' of the magazine's jokes.[20] 'To trace the history of much of *Punch's* original humour would', he conceded, 'hardly be desirable, even if it were possible. But there are many examples of it which, while essentially original to *Punch*, have yet sprung from circumstances independent of it'. Spielmann highlights several examples and traces them back to what he claims to be their origins. It is impossible to verify the accuracy of his work, but he seems to have gone to remarkable lengths to unearth some of the jokes' true authors. In one case, he claims to have secured the assistance of the Post Office to track down a lady from the North of England who, nearly half a century earlier, was rumoured to have submitted a popular joke offering 'Advice To Persons About to Marry – Don't'.[21] He eventually discovered her in a remote village, only to find that she was 'quite innocent of the credit of *Punch's* Monumental Cynicism'.[22]

Spielmann also 'cross-examined' and corresponded with many of the magazine's surviving writers and artists—as well as those who knew them—and appears to have had access to documents that have since been destroyed. Most tellingly, F. C. Burnand, who joined *Punch* in 1863 and went on to become its fourth editor in 1880, described Spielmann's book as 'wonderfully accurate' and used it as an *aide-memoir* when writing his own reminiscences.[23] This is not to say that it should be accepted without question. As Patrick Leary points out, Spielmann's history of *Punch* is remarkably detailed, but it is also sentimental, reverential and nostalgic. The author claims not to have succumbed to the blindness of 'hero-worship', but his affection for the magazine, and his respect for the men who worked on its staff, seems to have led him to smooth over some of the 'bitter conflicts and violent prejudices that marked both private and public aspects of the magazine's history'.[24] Nevertheless, his account gives a rare glimpse into how jokes might have circulated in Victorian Britain and the pathways of transmission that he traces between print, performance and oral culture highlight the complexity and ambiguity of Victorian joke authorship.

One of Spielmann's most striking examples concerns a joke about a miserly Scotsman who returns early from a trip to London, explaining that he found the city 'so awfu' extravagant that he hadna been in it more than a few hours "*when bang went saxpence!*"[25] It was published in *Punch* and illustrated by Charles Keene, one of the magazine's longest serving and most celebrated cartoonists.[26] It went on to become one of his most enduringly successful jests; the phrase 'bang went saxpence' entered common parlance and was still circulating more than a century later. Under the terms of the joke copyright company, Keene might have made a small fortune from it, were it not for the fact that he was not the joke's true author. In fact, Spielmann claims, 'the reader will be interested to learn that this expression [...] did really issue from the lips of a visitor from the neighbourhood of Glasgow'.[27] The identity of the outraged Glaswegian remains a mystery, but his complaints were overheard by Sir John Gilbert, the celebrated watercolour artist and illustrator. It was Gilbert who transformed this overheard quip into an amusing anecdote that could later be shared with friends. The origins of this joke were by no means unusual. Spielmann highlights several other jests from *Punch* that were supposedly based on real incidents that their 'authors' observed in streets and restaurants, or overheard on the omnibus. While he concedes that 'many of *Punch's* jokes [were] deliberately manufactured', he nevertheless stresses that a 'vast number' were 'improved from actual incidents' or 'used with but slight textual editing, just as they occurred'.[28]

Jokes, in this observational model of authorship, were not deliberately *written* or *manufactured*, but accidentally *encountered*, *captured* and *adapted*. There are echoes here of Baudelaire's *flâneur*, of would-be jokers strolling casually through life, subjecting the environment and the unsuspecting people around them to a hidden, humour-seeking gaze.

Even when these encounters were entirely accidental, the agency and interpretative powers of the observer were privileged; the perpetrator of the incident or remark might easily remain ignorant of having 'manufactured' a joke. Indeed, Spielmann relates just such an incident. It apparently took place in the house of the prominent printer and publisher Andrew White Tuer. When a new maidservant was asked to name the profession of her previous employer, she responded that 'he kept a Vicarage'. Her employers considered it amusing to refer to a reverend's spiritual calling with the same language that would ordinarily be used to describe a trade. Tuer, who was fond of jokes and sent them into *Punch* 'almost as regularly as the weekly paper', duly forwarded the story to George du Maurier, the magazine's leading cartoonist.[29] When the cartoon was published in *Punch*:

the legend was read out to the maid, and it was explained to her that it was *her* joke. She showed no enthusiasm, not even appreciation; but on seeing the others laugh, she said, with perfect gravity, yet still with hopeful perseverance, "Well, I must try and make some more!"[30]

There are powerful class dynamics at work here. The maid is incapable of seeing the joke or her role in creating it. The fact that the caption was 'read out' suggests that she may have been illiterate, or at least that Tuer and his family felt the need to mediate between her and the complexities of the printed jest. Her employers rather condescendingly informed her that this was '*her* joke', though of course their laughter was entirely at her expense. And so, a working-class woman's unconscious gaffe was transformed into a recognisable (and publishable) joke by the wit of an educated male observer.

Of course, this is not to suggest that women and working-class Victorians were incapable of conceiving, recognising and telling jokes. As Louise Wingrove's chapter in this volume demonstrates, music-hall serio-comediennes like Bessie Bellwood demonstrated ample comic talent in their onstage patter, as well as quick-wittedness in their unscripted responses to hecklers. Nevertheless, the culture of joking that fed into *Punch* was embedded in a male, middle-class, literary sphere; the world of the private gentleman's club, the public school and the suburban villa. Accordingly, 'punching down' was a common feature, in which readers evidently liked to snigger at jokes inspired by the peculiar manners of those beneath them.

These examples represent one model of Victorian joke creation—the 'observational' approach. As we have seen, the agency in this process rests firmly with the *conscious observer*, rather than the *unconscious perpetrator*. But there were other ways in which jokes could be manufactured and disseminated. The editors of jest books and joke columns often attributed their anecdotes to celebrities, historical figures and famous wits. This style of joke-writing was particularly prevalent in the eighteenth-century and was found most notably in *Joe Miller's Jests* (1739)—an assortment of humorous anecdotes originally compiled by the dramatist John Motley.[31] Most of the stories were told in connection with well-known personages, and started with phrases like: 'When the Duke of Ormond was young...'; 'A certain author was telling Dr Sewell...'; 'When Rablais, the greatest Drole in France, lay on his death bed...'; 'A Soldier was bragging before Julius Caesar...'; or 'Somebody asked Lord Bacon what he thought of poets...'. *Joe Miller* was regularly revisited by publishers who edited and expanded its original stock of jests in response to shifting tastes until, by the 1830s, it was home to more than 1500 comic anecdotes.

New publications, such as Tom Hood's *Book of Modern English Anecdotes* (1872), adopted the same formula and expanded the canon to include witticisms from Douglas Jerrold, Thackeray and Sydney Smith. A typical anecdote showcased the famously quick wit of the editor's own father:

> The late Thomas Hood, driving in the country one day, observed a notice beside a fence, "Beware the Dog." There not being any signs of a dog, Hood wrote on the board, "Ware be the Dog?"[32]

Like most anecdotes of this kind, the story was not drawn from the published writings of the wit in question. Instead, the humorous incident was, once again, captured and mediated by an unknown observer. This time, however, the power dynamic between the *recorder* of a joke and its *perpetrator* was different. Unlike the Glaswegian and the housemaid, Hood deliberately made the joke in order to demonstrate wit. While the jest's re-teller might enjoy the benefits of sharing it, credit for the joke is demonstrably given to its original creator.

A truly great wit, of course, would have no need to record his quips. As the *Hampshire Advertiser* observed of Douglas Jerrold: '[he] did not write his best jokes; he cast them forth in the course of conversation, and forgot them as soon as they were launched'.[33] Jokes, in this model, were supposed to be generated spontaneously; their piquancy rested on the instinctive demonstration of wit. This goes some way to explain why some Victorian commentators were resistant to the idea of jokes as a product of deliberate authorial labour. In a remarkably po-faced article titled 'A Plea for Seriousness', an essayist for the *Atlantic Monthly* took aim at the 'dismal jocosity' of 'newspaper facetiæ' and argued that:

> If people take comfort in exchanging such pleasantries among themselves, well and good, but to see them in print recalls Macaulay's outburst – "A wise man might talk folly like this by his fireside, but that any human being, having made such a joke, should write it down, copy it out,

transmit it to the printer, correct the proof, and send it forth to the world, is enough to make us ashamed of our species."[34]

Viewed in this context, the deliberate work of professional joke-writers was evidently beyond the pale.

The circulation of historical anecdotes and 'old chestnuts' worked against the professional reputation of modern joke-writers in other ways too. The original *Joe Miller* was often referred to by Victorian commentators as a kind of comedy canon; the primordial ooze from which all jokes evolved. Indeed, it was routinely referenced by critics who sought to characterise the work of modern comics as derivative and inferior. In an 1882 article written in praise of American humour, the *Leeds Mercury* argued that imported Yankee jests were 'refreshing to the jaded brain that is accustomed to wade through the flavourless, six-water-grog kind of wit of the English comic journals; where, if the laboured joke is dissected, it is found to be but a new corpus built upon the skeleton of an old Joe Miller'.[35]

Other essayists adopted a less dismissive tone, but took pleasure in tracing 'the antiquity of jests' back to Hierocles, Alexander the Great, and other ancient sources. 'A merry jest about a preacher or a player or a physician', observed one typical example, 'is reincarnated in every generation. It is like royalty, it never dies'.[36] It was difficult therefore to manufacture a *new* joke. As an 1837 article in *Bentley's Miscellany* put it:

> The diamond is precious from its scarcity, and, for the same reason, a new thought is beyond all price. Unluckily for us moderns, the ages who came before us have seized upon all the best thoughts, and it is but rarely indeed that we can stumble upon a new one [...] This is especially the case with regard to jokes; all the best of them are as old as the hills. On rare occasions some commanding genius astonishes the world by a new joke; but this is an event – the event of the year in which the grand thing is uttered.[37]

The author recalled how he briefly laboured under the rapturous impression that he had invented a new joke, only to discover (during a hallucinatory conversation with a dancing champagne bottle) that 'his' jest was more than thirty centuries old. Jokes were eternal; they could not be *created*, only *revived*.

4   THE CIRCULATION OF JOKES

The creation of a joke—whether at a Victorian dinner party or an ancient Roman feast—was only the start. As the article in *Bentley's* explained, a good joke then began to circulate:

> Hardly has it seen the light ere it passes with the utmost celerity from mouth to mouth; it makes the tour of all the tables in the kingdom, and is reproduced in newspapers and magazines, until no corner of the land has been unhonoured and ungladdened by its presence.[38]

The circulation of jokes depended on the interplay of oral and print culture. By way of example, let us return to Spielmann's account of the Scotsman and his sixpence. Sometime after Sir John Gilbert overheard the Glaswegian's complaints, he told the story to his friend, and fellow artist, Myles Birket Foster. This particular conversation took place in the galleries of the Royal Water Colour Society, but the informal exchange of jokes happened across a wide range of other social situations and locations. Middle-class men like Gilbert and Birket Foster would have met in conversation at dinner parties, clubs, taverns, theatres, coffee-houses, omnibuses and offices.

While most of this oral culture has now been lost to historians, some traces remain that show the place of jokes in Victorian conversation. The most notable examples come from the 'table-talk' that took place at *Punch*'s weekly dinner meetings; a vibrant oral culture of debate, gossip and joking that has been skilfully reconstructed by the historian Patrick Leary.[39] A diary kept by Henry Silver—one of *Punch*'s regular contributors—recorded the conversations and quips made by the magazine's staff. While some portions of this conversation found their way into *Punch*'s next issue, it is clear that many jokes were performed simply to amuse the company. At a typical gathering in 1859, political debate about the merits of Disraeli's reform bill was abruptly redirected when 'apropos of nothing in particular, Shirley Brooks interject[ed] with a joke: "If you put your head between your legs, what planet do you see? Uranus."'[40] Thackeray was reportedly consumed with laughter and proceeded to crack a joke about his own problems with urethral stricture. These men clearly took pleasure in making one another laugh, and there was an inevitable degree of competitive one-upmanship. Most of the jokes cracked around the table—particularly those based on such bawdy subjects—never appeared in the magazine. Indeed, when Spielmann drew upon Silver's diary to describe the same evening, he replaced the Uranus gag with a more respectable pun and omitted Thackeray's follow-up.[41] The policing of *Punch's* table-talk serves as an important reminder that the boundaries between print and oral culture were not always permeable; some jokes were too risqué to be transferred from the pub to the page.[42]

The table-talk of *Punch* offers a uniquely detailed glimpse at the oral culture of middle-class men, but it is hardly surprising that the staff of a comic magazine liked to exchange jokes. There is, however, ample evidence to suggest that jokes were routinely performed at more ordinary gatherings. Dinner parties were particularly associated with the sharing of jests and humorous anecdotes. Before he discovered the antiquated nature of his joke, the writer for *Bentley's* observed that:

> If I had been a diner-out, I might have provided myself with dinners for two years upon the strength of it; but I was contented with the honour, and left the profit to the smaller wits, who, by a process well known to themselves, contrive to extract venison out of jests, and champagne out of puns.[43]

Jokes acted as a literal form of capital; a conversational currency that could be exchanged for a good evening of food and drink. Here we might begin to understand the frustration felt by 'legitimate wits' at the people who stole their jokes and 'thus traded on false capital'.

The production and performance of dinner party jokes was comically explored by Charles Allston Collins in a short story for the Christmas edition of *All The Year Round* in 1865.[44] It features a professional joke-writer who makes a living by selling comic riddles and conundrums to the comic press. The first half of the story focuses on the author's 'bewildering' method for devising new jokes, which involved reading the dictionary in a state of intense concentration and then unpacking the comic potential of every word that seemed 'in the slightest degree promising'.[45] Here, once again, the authorial labour of *deliberate* joke writing was cast as something of a novelty. The resulting jokes could be 'disposed' by selling them to comic periodicals, but Collins' protagonist soon discovered a 'Private as well as a Public sale for the productions of the epigrammatic artist'.[46] He recalls being approached by a gentleman who 'liked dining-out above all things' but 'had not a particle of humour in his composition'.[47] In order to sustain his 'precarious reputation' as 'a sayer of good things', this gentleman offered to pay handsomely for a regular and exclusive supply of jokes and comic stories. For a while, this arrangement proved fruitful for both parties, except for occasions when the humourless purchaser mangled a punchline and returned 'in state of high indignation' to complain that it had fallen 'as flat as ditch-water' and embarrassed him at the table.[48] However, the story ends with a set piece in which the joke-writer accidentally supplies two rival gentlemen with the same riddle and then recounts the toe-curling moment when they each attempted to claim it as their own at the same social gathering. It is hard to determine whether this private market for dinner party jokes really existed, or indeed if the broader joke-writing experiences recounted in Collins' article were autobiographical. It is certainly possible that he sold riddles alongside the more substantial journalistic, literary and artistic projects for which he is credited. However, even if the specific details in the story were invented, they nevertheless capture the place and the power of joking within this culture of Victorian sociability.

The gentlemen in Collins' story were prepared to pay a handsome price to obtain original jokes, but if this private market did exist then it must surely have been a small one. Fresh jests were highly prized, but the continual recirculation of well-worn jokes and anecdotes was evidently in wider operation. Indeed, one of the period's jest books was subtitled 'A Manual of Table-Talk'; an implicit invitation to share jokes with company, or else to refine one's own joke-telling technique by studying notable examples.[49] Similarly, a pocket-sized book of imported American minstrel show, *Jokelets* (1901), described itself as a:

> valuable volume for professionals, socials, clubmen, literary societies, parlour amusements, parties and lodges; and, with its freedom from vulgarity, a book for private concerts and family entertainments of all sorts.[50]

In such cases, printed jokes begin to look more like scripts; texts to be performed in conversation with family and friends, or in the semi-formal context of a more organised programme of entertainment. Indeed, titles such as *Pearson's Humorous Reciter* (1903) and *Tit-Bits Monster Recitation Book* (1899) made this kind of performative function explicit and often included practical advice on the correct posture and diction to use when reciting an extract before an audience. Such texts remind us that Victorian comedy was not just performed in theatres, circuses, music halls and other professional spaces. Dinner tables, parlour rooms, railway carriages and schoolyards all acted as stages.

Jokelets made a telling distinction between the performance of jokes in homosocial male environments, such as clubs and literary societies, and mixed-sex gatherings like private concerts and family entertainments. 'Vulgar' jokes might be shared with men in the pub or the lodge, but were not suitable for respectable female ears. The scatological table-talk of Shirley Brooks and Thackeray, so dutifully airbrushed by Spielmann, was clearly not for mixed company. This is an enduring aspect of joke culture across many societies. In her study of modern Dutch attitudes to joke-telling, Giselinde Kuipers found that it was considered a predominantly male activity:

> Jokes, my respondents assured me again and again, are part of a 'man's world': the pub, the harbor, the soccer club, the billiard club and 'boys' nights out'. Joke tellers told their jokes mainly to other men, heard them from other men and preferred masculine company as the ambience for these activities. Most men also thought that you had to be 'careful' with jokes if women were around [...] Half of those interviewed expressed the opinion that it wasn't appropriate for women to tell jokes at any time [...] [Or that] women *cannot* tell jokes.[51]

Such opinions were in wide circulation during the nineteenth-century. For example, when the *Dundee Evening Telegraph* printed a short article about Miss Anne Partlan—a professional female joke-writer from New York—they made reference to 'the old theory that women have no sense of humour' and reassured readers that 'in appearance she [was] extremely modest, with a charming friendliness of manner, and [was] not in the least the 'new woman', as each gesture and accent [was] distinctly feminine'.[52] It was surprising, in other words, that such a masculine pursuit should leave her womanly charms intact.

We should not be too quick however to exclude women from the Victorian culture of joke-telling. *Punch's* ledgers reveal hundreds of contributions from women writers. Indeed, Spielmann informs us that a pair of women played a part in the circulation of *Punch's* 'bang went saxpence' joke. Having heard the anecdote from Sir John Gilbert, Birkett Foster 'tried the effect of the joke on two ladies whom he accompanied into Bond Street to take tea'. The two ladies apparently 'exploded with laughter'. In Spielmann's narrative, Birkett Foster was motivated by a desire to field-test a promising new joke. However, heterosocial joke-telling sometimes had more romantic motives. Indeed, Spielmann reveals that some men were in the practice of pretending to be *Punch* contributors and then using this 'borrowed reputation' 'to ingratiate [themselves] with the fair and trusting sex'.[53] Matrimonial adverts— such as those published in the comic weekly *Ally Sloper's Half Holiday*— routinely described their authors as 'jolly' (as well as things like 'thoroughly domesticated') and often expressed a preference for jolliness in prospective partners.[54] This term encompassed a great deal more than simply joke-telling, but it indicates that the possession of a good sense of humour was perceived as an attractive quality by members of both sexes.[55]

Having successfully performed the 'saxpence' joke over tea in Bond Street, Birkett Foster 'concluded that it was good enough for his friend [Charles] Keene, to whom he thereupon sent it'.[56] Spielmann's narrative does not make the method of transmission clear, though it seems that the joke was sent via letter—the first time it had been rendered in writing. Keene saw potential in the jest, sketched an appropriate cartoon, and published the result in *Punch* with no hint of its origins. The practice of sending material like this to *Punch* was evidently very common. Keene was reportedly 'in receipt of a great number of jokes' from Birkett Foster, Andrew Tuer and an artist from Newcastle named Joseph Crawhall.[57] Similarly, George du Maurier received the 'benevolent assistance' of 'non-professional wits', such as Canon Alfred Ainger, and stored their suggestions in vases called 'joke pots'.[58] Whenever:

> a moment arrived in which he had to scratch his head for a subject, he would dip his hand, or rather his arm, into this lottery, and fish up one contribution after another, until he found one that might be regarded as a prize ticket.[59]

While many of these jests were supplied by friends, Spielmann suggests that the act of sending jokes to *Punch* was a 'national practice'. Of course, most of these contributions were never used; Spielmann estimated less than one per cent. Of the authors that passed muster, few received any pecuniary reward. Joke-writers were, according to Spielmann, 'disinterested persons, usually seeking neither pay nor recognition'.[60]

Punch was not the only publication to garner jokes from readers. The editors of rival comic weeklies, such as *Fun* and *Judy*, probably received similar contributions. Some editors openly encouraged submissions. For example, during the final decades of the nineteenth century, several popular newspapers and magazines began inviting readers to enter regular joke competitions. In 1887, the *Dundee Weekly News* announced its version in the following manner:

> Every day in almost every place in Scotland a good joke is 'perpetrated' by somebody. With a view to amuse our Readers and catch these ready witticisms and ludicrous sayings, and preserve them in a permanent form, we have pleasure in announcing that we shall give a PRIZE of 2s 6d every week for the Best Original SCOTCH JOKE from any Town or Village in Scotland.[61]

The paper exhibited a familiar resistance to the idea of jokes being written. Instead, its desire to 'capture' and 'preserve' specimens of 'Scotch' wit is reminiscent of the jest-book's aim to immortalise the ephemeral quips of celebrated wits, though the newspaper's open invitation to readers suggests a more demotic approach. The competition was a runaway success and appeared each week for several years. In 1889 the paper sent a compilation of these jests, tellingly entitled 'Jokes for the People, by the People', to Gladstone and other celebrities.[62] It was, the former Prime Minister replied, 'an acceptable supplement to the well-known work of Dean Ramsay'.[63] This was hardly effusive praise, but the *Weekly News* proudly printed the 'Grand Old Man's' tepid endorsement at the top of their joke column for weeks after his letter had been received.

The success of the *Dundee Weekly News'* competition sparked many imitators. Indeed, the *Sheffield Weekly Telegraph* and the *Belfast Telegraph* were both so enamoured that they plagiarised the idea and the wording used to announce it.[64] The following year, the *Hull Weekly News* raised the stakes and took out an advert on the front page of *The Athenaeum*, challenging 'Jokists in all parts of the country' to compete for a five shilling prize.[65] These competitions were particularly popular in the provincial press, where the publication of locally flavoured jokes sat comfortably alongside dialect literature, poetry, sports reports and other expressions of regional identity. However, nationally circulating publications also invited readers to submit jokes in the hope of earning a prize. *Illustrated Chips*—a popular comic weekly published by Alfred Harmsworth—introduced its own version of the competition in the 1890s. It informed readers that 'all [they needed] do is to make, beg, or borrow a joke' and then send it to the paper's London office.[66] This process is strikingly similar to that used by the professional joke-writers discussed earlier. Indeed, *Illustrated Chips* even advertised its competition as a way for readers 'to increase [their] income'. However, these hints at professionalism were misleading; while the paper published jokes sent in by readers, only the winner and runners-up were paid, and few were successful more than once. The competition mimicked the *process* of professional joke-writing, but not its *scale*.

In addition to receiving a few shillings as prizemoney, winners saw their name and address published in the paper—a notable departure from the anonymity expected of *Punch* contributors and freelance joke-writers. Tracing this information in the 1891 and 1901 censuses provides a rare glimpse into the location, age, gender and socio-economic background of amateur joke-tellers. A comprehensive survey is beyond the scope of this chapter, but the broad picture is worth noting. Of the 75 competition winners who could be located in the census, ten were female. This sub-group included a sixteen-year-old schoolgirl, an eighteen-year-old housewife, a 22-year-old 'shawl fringer', an unmarried, thirty-year-old post office clerk, and a 48-year-old widow living on her own means. The professions of male winners were equally varied and included schoolboys, unskilled workers like casual labourers, pitmen and warehousemen, skilled workers like glass blowers and cabinet makers, lower-middle-class clerks, school teachers and one station master. Most were unmarried and in their teens or early twenties—a reflection of *Illustrated Chips'* adolescent target audience—but roughly a quarter were twenty-five or older. Winners came from across the country, but were particularly centred in the industrial heartlands of Lancashire and Yorkshire. All of these amateur joke-writers were far removed from the rarefied world of London clubland, or the friendship networks of artists, writers, and printers that supplied *Punch*. Their jokes circulated in workplaces, schoolyards, pubs, offices and homes. While the *Punch* brotherhood had a diligent diarist to record their table-talk, this more pervasive, popular culture of joke-telling went largely unchronicled. Indeed, the comparative ephemerality of working-class joke culture may help to explain the provincial press' mission to preserve these jests 'in a permanent form'; the runaway success of these competitions suggests that readers valued home-grown jokes that reflected their neighbourhoods and experiences. There is a great deal more work to be done to recover the place of joking in these working-class Victorian communities.

5   JOKE REPRINTING

Throughout this chapter we have tracked four ways in which jokes were created and then published in the Victorian press: (1) the deliberate literary work of professional joke-writers; (2) the observation and retelling of amusing incidents among friendship networks; (3) the resurrection and refashioning of ostensibly historical anecdotes and (4) the direct contribution of readers, sometimes solicited via competitions. It would be a mistake, however, to assume that the printed text marked the end of a joke's journey. The easiest way for a Victorian editor to find jokes was to clip them from rival publications. Within hours of the 'saxpence' joke appearing in *Punch*, the editors of provincial papers in Sheffield, Edinburgh, Huddersfield, Cardiff, Lancaster, Halifax and Reading had all poached it. While this jest enjoyed a particularly warm reception, the reprinting of jokes from *Punch* was part of the weekly rhythm of Victorian journalism. Just like Parliament and the police court, the comic press could be relied upon to supply regular content. For example, Fig. 1 charts the reprinting of twenty jokes, all of which appeared in a typical issue of *Punch* from 4 October 1884. While the paper was printed with a Saturday date, it was actually published on the preceding Wednesday. First to pillage its pages were Wednesday's evening papers, who were quick to emphasise that these jokes had been freshly caught from 'This Morning's Comic Papers'. On Thursday and Friday, a couple of daily newspapers made selections, but the most extensive reprinting took place at the weekend. Each Saturday and Sunday, *Punch* was raided by the editors of mass-market weeklies such as *Lloyd's* and *Reynolds's*, and by their provincial rivals. The feast continued into the following week when latecomers, such as the *Leighton Buzzard Observer*, finally made selections. On Wednesday, a new issue of *Punch* appeared and the process began anew.

It is tempting to dismiss these rhythmic reprintings as nothing more than a thoughtless form of 'scissors-and-paste' journalism. However, each of the papers represented in Fig. 1 chose different jokes and printed them in different order. Some, like the *Hampshire Telegraph*, gleefully clipped as many as eleven jokes from *Punch*; others, like the *Essex*

		Lawn Tennis – George du Maurier [Token from Cartoon]	Distinguished Amateurs – George du Maurier [Token from Cartoon]	All the Difference [Token from Cartoon]	Ruling the Waves? – Charles Keene [Token from Cartoon]	Ruling the Waves? – John Tenniel [Token from Cartoon]	Cowper's Task – Edwin James Milliken	Autumn Leaves – Edwin James Milliken	Shakspeare – Edwin James Milliken	The Managers... – Edwin James Milliken	Police Intelligence... – Edwin James Milliken	A Question of an Answer – Edwin James Milliken	Macbeth in Midlothian – Edwin James Milliken	Ruling the Waves (poem) – Edwin James Milliken	Caution on Cards – F. C. Burnand & Percival Leigh	Look at Home – F. C. Burnand & Percival Leigh	Ex Voto – F. C. Burnand	On Court Herbert... – F. C. Burnand	Bad for the Bullock – Joseph Ashby-Sterry	Loaves & Learning – Joseph Ashby-Sterry	New City Edition – Unattributed	Motto for a Theatre... – Unattributed
1 Oct 1884	'This Morning's Comic Papers' Evening Telegraph [Dundee]	2	2	1	1	7			6	5	3	4						3				
	'To-day's Comic Papers' The Citizen [Gloucester]	1	6	6	6																6	
	'Cream of the Comic Papers' Edinburgh Evening News	5	2	3	3		5		4											3	5	
	'Pickings from Comic Papers' Derby Daily Telegraph	1	2	5	5	3		4	6													
	'Current Humour' York Herald	1	2	4	4	3	7	6							4	11	10		11	2		1
2 Oct 1884	'Extracts from the Comic Papers' Huddersfield Daily Chronicle	1						3														
3 Oct 1884	'Varieties' Exeter and Plymouth Gazette	2						4					4									
	'John Bull's Jokes' Hampshire Telegraph & Sussex	9	10				2	3	1							7						
	'From Punch' Manchester Times	8	9				3	4	5	5									7			
	[Untitled Miscellany] Essex Standard						1	1														
	'Comic Clippings' York Herald	1	2				1		1						3							
	'Pickings from Punch' Gloucester Journal	4	7					2			6											
	'Facts and Facetiae' Reading Mercury	1	2				2	2														
	'Pickings from Punch' Sheffield Independent	5	7				4	5	1													
	[Untitled Column Filler] Bury Free Press						1	1														
4 Oct 1884	'Cuttings from Comic Papers' Wrexham Advertiser	3	4	1			3				5						6	2				3
	'Selections of Wit and Humour' Huddersfield Chronicle	5	6				1	2							3	7	6		7			
	'Pickings from Punch' Sheffield and Rotherham	5	7				2										6					
	'Comic and Gossip Papers' The Bucks Herald	1	2	6			2			3					3							
	'Jokes and Jokers' North Wales Chronicle	5	3	2	2	4								4								3
	'The Comic Papers' Warminster & Westbury Journal	6	7	5	5	3	1	1				1			4	3						5
	'Extracts from the Comic Papers' Manchester Courier	1	2	1			5	2		3												
	'Odd Bits' Leeds Times						5	1		5					4	3						
5 Oct 1884	'Scraps from the Comic Papers' Reynolds's Newspaper	1	1			2												2				
	'Cuttings from the Comics' Lloyd's Weekly Newspaper						3															
7 Oct 1884	'Cuttings from Comic Papers' Leighton Buzzard Observer	1					3		4						1			2			2	

Fig. 1 The reprinting of jokes from *Punch*, 4 October 1884. Shaded squares indicate the presence of a particular joke in a specific paper. The numbers inside each shaded box indicate the sequences in which jokes were printed by these papers

Standard and the *North Wales Chronicle*, restricted themselves to only one. It seems that the sub-editors responsible for compiling the columns were critically assessing the material. Their decisions may have been informed by the amount of column-inches available, but the quality and relevance of a jest were surely factors in determining its recirculation. On one particularly fallow week, the *Worcester Chronicle* informed its readers that *Punch* was 'decidedly dull' and reprinted only three of its jokes. Truly popular jests transcended the weekly cycle depicted in Fig. 1 and continued to be reprinted in newspapers, magazines, and books for years to come. This kind of reprinting allowed some jokes to 'go viral' and travel the world. A gag written in New York might, within a few months, appear in newspapers throughout the English-speaking world.[67] Similarly, while *Punch* was often teased by the American press for being hopelessly unfunny, jokes from the paper circulated widely on the other side of the Atlantic, and some editors even printed crude reproductions of the paper's cartoons.[68]

This vibrant, transnational culture of joke-reprinting was allowed to exist precisely because an institution like the Joke Copyright Protective Company was never founded. While copyright law theoretically protected the content of periodicals, reprinting was deeply embedded in the period's journalistic practices and few papers sought legal protection from it. According to Spielmann, *Punch* made occasional attempts to curtail the activities of domestic pirates. In 1891 they obtained an injunction against the *Ludgate Monthly* after it reprinted one of du Maurier's cartoons without permission or attribution. In 1872, a similar attempt to stop John Camden Hotten from using *Punch's* cartoons in his *Story of the Life of Napoleon* resulted in 'a farthing damages', after which 'Hotten went on publishing his book just as if nothing had occurred'.[69] As well as attempting to curtail the theft of its cartoons, *Punch* also took measures to protect lengthier comic stories and essays. In 1845, for example, the magazine went to court in order to prevent what Spielmann terms the 'Rape of Mrs Caudle whose 'curtain lectures' were widely reprinted in the provincial press. But these recourses to the law were rare, and never seem to have been used in defence of the short, textual jokes that were reprinted so extensively in newspapers and magazines.

There are several ways that we might explain this. Firstly, it is possible that *Punch* saw little monetary value in retaining control over single jokes. Jerrold quickly republished *Mrs Caudle's Curtain Lectures* in book form; a decision that might explain *Punch's* unusually keen defence of their copyright in this case. The cartoons of Leech, Keene and du Maurier also possessed considerable resale value, though their chief purpose seems to have been attracting and retaining the magazine's readership. As the paper's critics often pointed out, the skill and reputation of *Punch's* artists did much to mask the defective quality of its jokes. Newspapers routinely reprinted the captions underneath *Punch's* cartoons with heedless impunity—the 'saxpence' joke being an example—but, when the *Ludgate Monthly* plagiarised a cartoon, they were dragged into court. This hierarchy found its clearest expression in *Punch's* own ledgers, where weekly contributions were recorded and attributed to particular writers. Comic stories, articles and scraps of verse were listed in full, while the majority of standalone jokes, puns, captions and other column-fillers were left unrecorded. Secondly, it is possible that *Punch* recognised the promotional benefits of allowing jests to flow freely through the press. Just as *The Times'* reputation for newsgathering was bolstered by the constant reprinting of its reports, so the large-scale plagiarism of *Punch's* work helped to establish it as the period's Joker of Record. By the 1890s, mass-market weeklies like *Lloyd's Weekly News* boasted circulations in excess of one million, and so a caption clipped from one of *Punch's* cartoons and reprinted in this paper might reach more than ten times the audience of the original. *Punch*, in other words, was 'read' by millions each week, most of whom never saw the paper.

Finally, however, it is possible that *Punch* adopted a relaxed attitude to copyright because its contributors did not believe that jokes could be owned. As this chapter has explored, Victorian conceptions of joke-telling resisted the dominant modes of production that characterised other literary genres. Jokes were supposed to be *observed, recorded, revived* or *caught*; they were not meant to be *written*. According to some commentators, new jokes could not be created at all; they were passed down from one generation to the next, continually revived from an ancient original. After its moment of conception—or resurrection—a joke would flow freely between oral, print, and performance culture. It might be retold around dinner tables in return for a plate of venison, shared with a friend while strolling an art gallery, performed at a family concert, written on a postcard and submitted to a joke competition or printed in newspapers from London to New York. At various stages of its life, it might be attributed to different wits, but the connection between a joke and its author was easily invented and even more easily severed.

This was the precarious environment in which professional joke-writers attempted to make a living, spending their days 'turning out jokes as other men would turn out chair-leg'.[70] These 'Unknown Men' may well have been some of the period's most widely read authors, though no one, apart from editors, knew their name. Once their fee was paid, their ownership of a joke ended; newspapers, circus clowns, joke book editors, music-hall comedians, politicians and thousands of other 'droll dogs' might now claim it as their own. None of which should lead us to the conclusion that the Victorians did not value jests; indeed, the pervasive and near-uncontrollable circulation of jokes suggests the opposite. By the end of the nineteenth century, joking was so firmly established in Victorian popular culture that jests were inescapable. 'If I were asked what has been the most striking characteristics of British wit and humour during the past century', observed the *Pall Mall Magazine* in 1901, 'I think I should answer, it is the way in which they have spread [...] There was a time when a man could avoid [jokes] if he would [...] But nowadays one is never quite safe'.[71]

NOTES

1. Anon., 'The Joke Copyright Protective Company,' *Lancaster Gazette*, 25 January 1845, 4.
2. A brief word on terminology. In her study of modern cultures of Dutch joke telling, the sociologist Giselinda Kuipers defines the joke in a relatively narrow terms: a 'tightly standardized' and historically specific genre of humour that draws on familiar set-ups (knock-knock, a man walks into a bar, etc... and compositions (e.g. the thrice repeated event), features recognisable characters and settings (mothers-in-law, lawyers, dumb blondes, etc.), and always ends in a punchline. She distinguishes jokes from the early-modern genre of 'jests', which encompassed a more eclectic range of humorous stories, witticisms, anecdotes, and incidents. While this historical distinction is worth noting, the Victorians often used the terms 'jokes' and 'jests' interchangeably—nineteenth-century newspaper columns headed 'JOKES', for example, routinely included material that would not fit with Kuiper's relatively narrow definition of the genre. Moreover, in reference to oral culture, the words 'jesting' and 'joking' were also used to describe humorous conversational interjections, witty quips and practical jokes, as well as the tightly-structured, punchline-driven stories described by Kuiper. Accordingly, this chapter uses the terms 'jests', 'jokes' and 'gags' in a relatively loose fashion to

describe a short text, or discrete passage of speech, delivered with the primary intention of exciting laughter—in most cases, a single moment of laughter released at the joke's denouement. The form and genre of specific jokes (puns, conversations, comic definitions, anecdotes, conundrums, verse, etc.) will be signalled whenever appropriate. See: Giselinde Kuipers, *Good Humor, Bad Taste: A Sociology of the Joke* (New York: Mouton de Gruyter, 2006), 28–31.

3. Anon., 'Satires and Caricatures of the Eighteenth Century,' *Blackwood's Edinburgh Magazine,* November 1848, 543–556, (543).

4. Anon., 'Selected Anecdotes, &c,' *Lancaster Gazette,* 25 January 1845, 4.

5. See: Donald J. Gray, 'A List of Comic Periodicals Published in Great Britain, 1800–1900,' *Victorian Periodicals Newsletter,* no. 15 (1972): 2–39; M. H. Spielmann, 'The Rivals of Punch,' *The National Review,* July 1895, 654–666, (657).

6. A great deal of work has recently been undertaken on historical practices of reprinting. See, for example: Meredith L. McGill, *American Literature and the Culture of Reprinting, 1834–1853* (Philadelphia: University of Pennsylvania Press, 2003); Catherine Feely, '"What Say You to Free Trade in Literature?" The Thief and the Politics of Piracy in the 1830s,' *Journal of Victorian Culture* 19, no. 4 (2014): 497–506; Bob Nicholson, 'You Kick the Bucket; We Do The Rest!: Jokes at the Culture of Reprinting in the Transatlantic Press,' *Journal of Victorian Culture* 17, no. 3 (2012): 273–286; M. H. Beals, 'Musings on a Multimodal Analysis of Scissors-and-Paste Journalism (Parts 1–4), <mhbeals.com> [accessed 14 May 2018]; David A Smith, Ryan Cordell and Abby Mullen, 'Computational Methods for Uncovering Reprinted Texts in Antebellum Newspapers,' *American Literary History* 27, no. 3 (2015): E1–E15; Stephen Pigeon, 'Steal It, Change It, Print It: Transatlantic Scissors-and-Paste Journalism in the Ladies Treasury, 1857–1895,' *Journal of Victorian Culture* 22, no. 1 (2017): 24–39.

7. See: Catherine Seville, *Literary Copyright Reform in Early Victorian England: The Framing of the 1842 Copyright Act* (Cambridge: Cambridge University Press, 1999).

8. Anon., 'The Joke Copyright Protective Company.'

9. Malcolm Andrews, *Charles Dickens and His Performing Selves* (Oxford: Oxford University Press, 2007), 161.

10. Anon., 'In a Joke Factory,' *Hampshire Telegraph,* 22 April 1899, 10.

11. Ibid.

12. Clara Mulholland, 'Molly's Fortunes,' *Hampshire Telegraph,* 22 April 1899, 10.

13. Anon., 'Unassorted Fun,' *Hampshire Telegraph,* 22 April 1899, 11. The paper also contained a column of 'Clippings from the Comics', whose

jokes were attributed to specific publications such as *Punch*, *Fun*, and *Judy*—most of the individuals who produced these jokes, however, remain invisible even in the original publications.

14. Anon., 'The Business of Joke-Making,' *Derry Journal*, 6 March 1895, 2. See also: 'Men Who Write Jokes,' *Newcastle Weekly Courant*, 16 June 1894, 2; Thomas L Masson, 'How I Write 50,000 Jokes,' in *Our American Humorists*, ed. Thomas L. Masson (New York: Moffat, Yard and Company, 1922), 432–448; Daniel Wickberg, *The Senses of Humor: Self and Laughter in Modern America* (Ithaca: Cornell University Press, 1998), ch. 4.
15. Anon., 'In a Joke Factory.'
16. Anon., 'Motley,' *Bristol Mercury*, 28 November 1896, 1.
17. Anon., 'Grains of Gall,' *Hampshire Telegraph*, 21 July 1888, 12.
18. Anon., 'Wit and Humour,' *Cardiff Times*, 23 January 1897, 3.
19. Anon., 'Stories of the Sanctum,' *Hartlepool Northern Daily Mail*, 23 June 1894, 2.
20. M. H. Spielmann, *The History of Punch* (London: Cassell & Company, 1895), 138–167.
21. The joke appeared in: 'Worthy of Attention,' *Punch Almanac*, 1845, 1.
22. Spielmann, *History*, 142.
23. F. C. Burnand, 'Punch Notes—II,' *The Pall Mall Magazine*, July 1899, 326–338, (326).
24. Patrick Leary, *The Punch Brotherhood: Table Talk and Print Culture in Mid-Victorian London* (London: British Library, 2010), 2–3.
25. Spielmann, *History*, 140.
26. Charles Keene, 'Thrift,' *Punch*, 5 December 1868, 235.
27. Spielmann, History, 140.
28. Ibid., 143.
29. Ibid., 147.
30. Ibid., 147.
31. John Motley, ed., *Joe Miller's Jests or, the Wits Vade-Mecum* (London: T. Read, 1739).
32. Tom Hood, ed., *The Book of Modern English Anecdotes, Humour, Wit and Wisdom* (London: Routledge, 1872), 51.
33. Anon., 'New Publications,' *Hampshire Advertiser*, 8 May 1858, 4.
34. Sarah Butler Wister, 'A Plea For Seriousness,' *Atlantic Monthly*, May 1892, 625–630, (628).
35. Anon., 'Imported Humour,' *Leeds Mercury*, 29 April 1882, 1.
36. Brander Matthews, 'On the Antiquity of Jests,' *Longman's Magazine*, February 1885, 432–442, (433).
37. Anon., 'The Autobiography of a Good Joke,' *Bentley's Miscellany*, July 1837, 354–359, (354).

38. Ibid.
39. Leary, *The Punch Brotherhood.*
40. Ibid., 38.
41. Spielmann, History, 69.
42. This presents a familiar problem for historians. While dirty jokes rarely appeared in mainstream Victorian jest books and newspaper columns, it is likely that they circulated in conversation—not universally, perhaps, but within locations, communities and friendship groups where vulgar talk was acceptable. But we are compelled, for the most part, to build our understanding of Victorian joke-telling upon jests that were deemed respectable enough to print. Sources such as Silver's diary, and the bawdy facetiae published in privately circulated pornographic magazines like *The Pearl* (1879–1880), offer tantalising glimpses into the existence of vulgar jokes and the oral persistence of scatological and sexual themes that loomed so large in eighteenth-century humour.
43. Anon., 'The Autobiography of a Good Joke,' 354.
44. Charles Allston Collins, 'To Be Taken At The Dinner Table,' *Doctor Marigold's Prescriptions; Being the Christmas Number of All the Year Round* (1865): 15–20.
45. Ibid., 16.
46. Ibid., 17.
47. Ibid.
48. Ibid., 18.
49. Anon., *The Book of Humour, Wit, and Wisdom: A Manual of Table-Talk* (London: Routledge, 1867).
50. Lawrence Brough and John R. Kemble, eds., *Jokelets, Being the Merry Book of the Moore & Burgess Minstrels* (London: Saxon & Co., 1901).
51. Giselinde Kuipers, *Good Humor, Bad Taste*, 44–45.
52. Anon., 'Notes—Mainly Personal,' *Dundee Evening Telegraph*, 14 January 1898, 3. This article incorrectly names her 'Ann Partian'.
53. Spielmann, *History*, 146.
54. A column of matrimonial advertisements appeared in *Ally Sloper's Half Holiday* each week from May 1886 to June 1891.
55. For more on this, see: Wickberg, *The Senses of Humor.*
56. Spielmann, *History*, 140.
57. Ibid., 147.
58. Ibid., 147.
59. Anon., 'Du Maurier's "Joke Pots",' *London Journal*, 15 October 1904, 353.
60. Spielmann, *History*, 139.
61. Anon., 'Half-A-Crown Every Week for a Joke,' *Dundee Weekly News*, 19 February 1887, 2.

62. Anon, 'Our Joke Competition,' *Dundee Weekly News.*
63. Anon., 'Mr Gladstone and the Jokes,' *Dundee Weekly News*, 21 September 1889, 6.
64. Anon., 'Imitation The Sincerest Flattery,' *Dundee Courier*, 19 November 1887, 3; Anon., 'Half-A-Crown Every Week For A Joke,' *Belfast Telegraph*, 24 November 1887, 1.
65. *The Athenaeum*, 21 January 1888, 1.
66. For a typical instalment, see: 'Jokes By Our Readers,' *Illustrated Chips*, 23 March 1895, 6.
67. See: Bob Nicholson, 'You Kick the Bucket; We Do The Rest!'
68. See: *Pacific Commercial Advertiser*, 23 December 1884, 4.
69. Spielmann, *History*, 151–152.
70. Spielmann, *History*, 138.
71. Walter Emanuel, 'A Note on British Wit and Humour,' *Pall Mall Magazine*, July 1901, 421–423, (421).

WORKS CITED

Andrews, Malcolm. *Charles Dickens and His Performing Selves*. Oxford: Oxford University Press, 2007.

Anonymous. 'Advertisement.' *The Athenaeum*. January 21, 1888.

Anonymous. 'Du Maurier's "Joke Pots."' *London Journal*. October 15, 1904.

Anonymous. 'Grains of Gall.' *Hampshire Telegraph*. July 21, 1888.

Anonymous. 'Half-a-Crown Every Week for a Joke.' *Belfast Telegraph*. November 24, 1887.

Anonymous. 'Half-a-Crown Every Week for a Joke.' *Dundee Weekly News*. February 19, 1887.

Anonymous. 'Imitation the Sincerest Flattery.' *Dundee Courier*. November 19, 1887.

Anonymous. 'Imported Humour.' *Leeds Mercury*. April 29, 1882.

Anonymous. 'In a Joke Factory.' *Hampshire Telegraph*. April 22, 1899.

Anonymous. 'Jokes by our Readers.' *Illustrated Chips*. March 23, 1895.

Anonymous. 'Men Who Write Jokes.' *Newcastle Weekly Courant*. June 16, 1894.

Anonymous. 'Motley.' *Bristol Mercury*. November 28, 1896.

Anonymous. 'Mr Gladstone and the Jokes.' *Dundee Weekly News*. September 21, 1889.

Anonymous. 'New Publications.' *Hampshire Advertiser*. May 8, 1858.

Anonymous. 'Notes—Mainly Personal.' *Dundee Evening Telegraph*. January 14, 1898.

Anonymous. 'Satires and Caricatures of the Eighteenth Century.' *Blackwood's Edinburgh Magazine*. November 1848.

Anonymous. 'Selected Anecdotes, &c.' *Lancaster Gazette*. January 25, 1845.

Anonymous. 'Stories of the Sanctum.' *Hartlepool Northern Daily Mail.* June 23, 1894.

Anonymous. 'The Autobiography of a Good Joke.' *Bentley's Miscellany.* July 1837.

Anonymous. 'The Business of Joke-Making.' *Derry Journal.* March 6, 1895.

Anonymous. 'The Joke Copyright Protective Company.' *Lancaster Gazette.* January 25, 1845

Anonymous. 'Unassorted Fun.' *Hampshire Telegraph.* April 22, 1899.

Anonymous. 'Wit and Humour.' *Cardiff Times.* January 23, 1897.

Anonymous. 'Worthy of Attention.' *Punch Almanac.* 1845.

Anonymous. *The Book of Humour, Wit, and Wisdom: A Manual of Table-Talk.* London: Routledge, 1867.

Beals, M. H. 'Musings on a Multimodal Analysis of Scissors-and-Paste Journalism (Parts 1–4).' Accessed May 14, 2018. https://www.mhbeals.com.

Brough, Lawrence, and John R. Kemble, eds. *Jokelets, Being the Merry Book of the Moore & Burgess Minstrels.* London: Saxon & Co., 1901.

Burnand, F. C. 'Punch Notes—II.' *The Pall Mall Magazine.* July 1899.

Collins, Charles Allston. 'To Be Taken at the Dinner Table.' *Doctor Marigold's Prescriptions; Being the Christmas Number of all the Year Round.* December 1865.

Emanuel, Walter. 'A Note on British Wit and Humour.' *Pall Mall Magazine.* July, 1901.

Feely, Catherine. '"What Say You to Free Trade in Literature?" The Thief and the Politics of Piracy in the 1830s.' *Journal of Victorian Culture* 19, no. 4 (2014): 497–506.

Gray, Donald J. 'A List of Comic Periodicals Published in Great Britain, 1800–1900.' *Victorian Periodicals Newsletter,* no. 15 (1972): 2–39.

Hood, Tom, ed. *The Book of Modern English Anecdotes, Humour, Wit and Wisdom.* London: Routledge, 1872.

Keene, Charles. 'Thrift.' *Punch.* December 5, 1868.

Kuipers, Giselinde. *Good Humor, Bad Taste: A Sociology of the Joke.* New York: Mouton de Gruyter, 2006.

Leary, Patrick. *The Punch Brotherhood: Table Talk and Print Culture in Mid-Victorian London.* London: British Library, 2010.

Masson, Thomas L. 'How I Wrote 50,000 Jokes.' *Our American Humorists,* 432–448. New York: Moffat, Yard & Company, 1922.

Matthews, Brander. 'On the Antiquity of Jests.' *Longman's Magazine.* February, 1885.

McGill, Meredith L. *American Literature and the Culture of Reprinting, 1834–1853.* Philadelphia: University of Pennsylvania Press, 2003.

Motley, John, ed. *Joe Miller's Jests or, the Wits Vade-Mecum.* London: T. Read, 1739.

Mulholland, Clara. 'Molly's Fortunes.' *Hampshire Telegraph*. April 22, 1899.

Nicholson, Bob. 'You Kick the Bucket; We Do The Rest!: Jokes at the Culture of Reprinting in the Transatlantic Press.' *Journal of Victorian Culture* 17, no. 3 (2012): 273–286.

Pigeon, Stephen. 'Steal It, Change It, Print It: Transatlantic Scissors-and-Paste Journalism in the Ladies Treasury, 1857–1895.' *Journal of Victorian Culture* 22, no. 1 (2017): 24–39.

Seville, Catherine. *Literary Copyright Reform in Early Victorian England: The Framing of the 1842 Copyright Act*. Cambridge: Cambridge University Press, 1999.

Smith, David A., Ryan Cordell, and Abby Mullen. 'Computational Methods for Uncovering Reprinted Texts in Antebellum Newspapers.' *American Literary History* 27, no. 3 (2015): 1–15.

Spielmann, M. H. 'The Rivals of Punch.' *The National Review*. July 1895.

Spielmann, M. H. *The History of Punch*. London: Cassell & Company, 1895.

Wickberg, Daniel. *The Senses of Humor: Self and Laughter in Modern America*. Ithaca: Cornell University Press, 1998.

Wister, Sarah Butler. 'A Plea for Seriousness.' *Atlantic Monthly*. May 1892.

George Eliot's Jokes

Louise Lee

1   *MIDDLEMARCH* & 'AMUSING TACTICS'

In one of the more excruciating moments in the life of *Middlemarch*'s beleaguered scholar Edward Casaubon, he is prescribed—after the first of two heart strokes that will eventually kill him—what is cheerfully called, 'amusing tactics'. Like another famous, and real life, thinker of the nineteenth century, Charles Darwin, Casaubon is told he must 'unbend' his mind to avoid further recurrences of his physical malaise.[1] Enforced levity, however, is a source of considerable misery and distress to Casaubon: he treats the proposed new health regime like a prison sentence, dolefully and questioningly commenting to his doctor Tertius Lydgate: 'In short, you recommend me to anticipate the arrival of my second childhood [...] These things [...] would be to me such relaxation as tow-picking is to prisoners in a house of correction'.[2] Casaubon's sufferings are further compounded by an unlooked-for, but nonetheless enthusiastic, paean to the importance of 'light things' given by his wife's uncle, Mr Brooke:

> 'Yes, yes,' said Mr. Brooke. 'Get Dorothea to play backgammon with you in the evenings. And shuttlecock, now—I don't know a finer game than

---

L. Lee (✉)
Department of English and Creative Writing,
University of Roehampton, London, UK

© The Author(s) 2020
L. Lee (ed.), *Victorian Comedy and Laughter*,
https://doi.org/10.1057/978-1-137-57882-2_6

shuttlecock for the daytime. I remember it all the fashion. To be sure, your eyes might not stand that, Casaubon. But you must unbend, you know. Why, you might take to some light study: conchology, now: I always think that must be a light study. Or get Dorothea to read you light things, Smollett—*Roderick Random, Humphrey Clinker*: they are a little broad, but she may read anything now she's married, you know. I remember they made me laugh uncommonly—there's a droll bit about a postilion's breeches. We have no such humour now. I have gone through all these things, but they might be rather new to you.'

'As new as eating thistles,' would have been an answer to represent Mr. Casaubon's feelings. But he only bowed resignedly, with due respect to his wife's uncle, and observed that doubtless the works he mentioned had 'served as a resource to a certain order of minds.'

'[...] But I recommend you to talk to Mrs. Casaubon. She is clever enough for anything, is my niece. Tell her, her husband wants liveliness, diversion: put her on amusing tactics'.[3]

While 'lightness' may not be the pre-eminent texture of *Middlemarch*, nor indeed a quality cherished by Casaubon, what Mr Brooke wheezily calls 'liveliness' and 'diversion' are certainly not in short supply in the novel's earlier books—as many Victorian readers commented during their serial publication. Henry James, for example, observed in slightly condemnatory tone in 1873, a tendency to 'make light of the serious elements of the story and to sacrifice them to the more trivial ones'.[4] Eliot's friend Barbara Bodichon, meanwhile, observed in a letter of December 1871 (admittedly, on the way to a more anxious comment about Dorothea Brooke's marital fate): 'I hear people say it is so witty amusing and lively [...]'.[5] A *Spectator* essay of the following year entitled 'The Humour of Middlemarch' observed an 'attitude[...] directly creative' in its 'zest[ful]' treatment of 'the ludicrous'; one which could depict the mental 'haze' and 'slip-shod good nature' of Mr Brooke, but which was 'enhanced by the contrast' with other characters' 'startling abruptness and trenchant wit'. The same essay, noted in slightly more disconcerted mode, the narrator's 'many sharp sayings' and 'fascinating and irritating sarcasms' which made 'the reader a little afraid of his author'—but which it was 'impossible not to look forward to, and backward, at'.[6]

Today, very few critics focus on the humour, or indeed the wit, of *Middlemarch* as explicit capacities of the text, or as subjects of serious academic enquiry. One who has, however, is Elizabeth Deeds Ermarth, who observes a 'chronic risibility' and an 'extra margin for amusement in the [novel's] narrative language'.[7] In this essay, I want to explore this 'extra margin for amusement' in *Middlemarch*, and in Eliot's broader aesthetic project, to consider 'amusing tactics' as a means through which to reread her work. While acknowledging that 'tactics' may represent a necessarily more localised approach than a strategy, my argument pursues humour and wit, both distinctive but also swiftly changing categories in Victorian culture, as both complication and counterpoint to what I propose is a pervasive current narrative about Eliot's realism—one which increasingly, and temperamentally, associates it with seriousness. To be clear: it is not that I am suggesting twenty-first-century critics are averse to thinking about humour or wit in Eliot's novels, it is just that most regard these as the *least* interesting aspects of her work; or rather, as in Casaubon's comment to Mr Brooke above, as 'resource[s] to a certain order of minds'. According to the current state of the discipline, then, it is better to be a critical Casaubon than a Brooke.

My argument here aims to address a lacuna in current responses to Eliot's novels that may be motivated by conscious, or unconscious, agelastic (or laughter-fearing) tendencies. In the first part, I challenge a key exponent of this approach—Franco Moretti—particularly his account in 'Serious Century' of the cultural work of the realist 'filler' in generating apparently seamless, steady and bourgeois values—contrasting it to Eliot's own stated preference for the disturbance of such easy and apparent 'truths'.[8] Building on this idea of unsettling conventional predictability as a heightened form of attention-creation in her work, I introduce Eliot's forgotten essay on laughter, 'German Wit: Heinrich Heine' (1856), drawing on Daniel Wickberg's work on the Victorian 'sense of humour' as a new and privileged form of interiority; and, incongruity as *that* educated and urbane sense of humour, disrupting the monism of seriousness, and other 'closed' fictional forms (like caricature and sentimentality).[9]

In the final two sections, taking up Eliot's insights in 'German Wit', I map out a two-stage theory of Eliot's novelised laughter—incongruous realism—arguing that understanding how wit and humour (or 'descending' and 'sympathetic incongruity') operates, grants a new apprehension of the 'real' in her novels but also posits—through Eliot's long-standing enthusiasm for the jokes of the highly controversial and iconoclastic

Heine—an alternative account of her relation, as both culture-maker and culture-breaker, to bourgeois conventionality; and to the constantly shifting and co-creative relation between author, readers and narrators.[10]

2   THE PROBLEM WITH MORETTI'S 'SERIOUSNESS': FILLERS VERSUS IMPOSTORS

Seriousness is apparently *everywhere* in the Victorian realist novel—not just in the big moments—but the small ones. Indeed, it is at the level of what Moretti calls (following Roland Barthes) the realist 'filler' where much of the ideological labour is done, providing reassuring cues to readers about their everyday existence while subtly inculcating them with sober values. The filler, as Moretti wryly argues, is the 'only narrative invention of the entire [nineteenth] century'—the fuzzy in-between bit of the action of a plot—proffering epistemological comforts akin to physical ones.[11] Fillers are plump, soft-power ideological tools for creating sombre professionalism[12]:

> Incessant in quiet action, this is how fillers work [...] small things become significant, without ceasing to be 'small'; they become *narrative*, without ceasing to be *everyday*. The diffusion of fillers turns the novel into a 'calm passion' [...] a process that begins in the economy and in the administration [...] [This produces] a world of few surprises, fewer adventures, and no miracles at all. They are a great bourgeois invention, not because they bring into the novel trade, or industry, or other bourgeois 'realities' (which they don't), but because through them the logic of rationalization pervades *the very rhythm of the novel.*[13]

What's attractive about this argument, is, of course, that it's partly true, but considering it's about seriousness, it also rests on an extended and unstated joke that whatever philosophic complexity might be imputed to the realist novel, it is actually immersed in a kind of bland poetics of middle management. The debunking animus of Moretti's quasi-burlesque can be further viewed by the attention he pays, at a granular level, to clusters of what he calls (following Raymond Williams) 'keywords' in realist texts which are 'clues to bourgeois values': words such as 'efficiency,' 'useful' and 'influence'.[14] If, as J. Hillis Miller has observed, 'text' etymologically means 'woven thing', the way that Moretti constructs realism here is with all the fibres moving one way: '[i]ncessant in quiet action'.[15]

The problem about Moretti's interpretation, though, as a number of critics have already observed, is its implicit Foucauldian undertow.[16] The rationalising rhythm relies on the notion of the disciplined body (and text), lulled, smoothed, cantilevered even, into regularity; internally taking on, at the scene of domestic reading, the administrative and productive rhythms of external Victorian existence: those connected to factory life, to Bradshaw's railway timetable, and to, even, administrative committee rooms. Moretti's imagined reader is ensconced in what he calls a 'morphospace' where the 'history of *literature*' intersects with 'literary history (as part of the) history of *society*' [...].[17] But while the emphasis on the realist bibliophile as a systematised subject is convincing, historically, it is also somewhat anti-intuitive: for it elides their status as a credible, fleshly body, experiencing all kinds of affective states from sympathy, excitement, amusement, sadness, hope, even erotic arousal, to more negative emotions, such as feeling uncomfortable, embarrassed or just being bored.

As Gillian Beer, and theorists of affective realism like Nicholas Dames, Rae Greiner, Harry E. Shaw and Rachel Ablow have shown, Victorian novelists often sought to cause their readers, in the words of Beer, to 'laugh and weep [...] rictus and wetness', and even, at times, 'to be physically disarranged by the reading experience'.[18] This 'disarrangement' occurs, *pace* Moretti, within a certain amount of social regulation that must be assumed if one is going to attempt to actually *read* a Victorian novel, rather than throw it on the fire for warmth, or use it as a weapon against potential assailants, but, surely, one of the singular pleasures of perusing just such a work, is its 'disarranging' faculties, amid synchronised comfort, which, often, as Beer suggests, 'confirm[s] experience by appeal to the physical [...]'.[19]

In Eliot's work, this physical disarrangement is often coterminous with an epistemological one, so that instead of 'smoothing' readers into any one particular ideological position, her narrators aim at piquing the attention, not via a well-tempered realist idiolect, but rather by provoking a reassessment of previous expectations—through varying degrees of upturn and surprise. In this, Caroline Levine's recent discussion of realism is particularly suggestive, arguing an aesthetic '*in* motion' and '*of* motion' in which realist authors perpetually 'innovate' and rewrite previous versions of their own and others' conventions, delivering what Levine calls, through the thinking of Roman Jakobson, the 'shock' of the real.[20] In Eliot's unpublished 1868 essay, for example, 'Notes on Form in Art', she proposes consciously adopting a looked-for amnesia, cleaving oneself of all knowledge, authority, or opinion about a particular subject or word, in order to see it with new eyes:

> Abstract words and phrases which have an excellent genealogy are apt to live a little too much on their reputation and even to sink into dangerous impostors that should be made to show how they get their living. For this reason, it is often good to consider an old subject as if nothing had yet been said about it; to suspend one's attention even to revered authorities and simply ask what in the present state of our knowledge are the facts which can with any congruity be tied together [...].[21]

The professionalising ethic that Moretti talks about is only mentioned in ironised terms here (ideas and concepts are made to 'show how they get their living') but the important function is routing out 'dangerous impostors': precisely those words and phrases or 'clues to bourgeois values', that, in Moretti's narrative, are stealthily doing realism's bidding.[22] Contra Moretti, then, the literary micro-event I am proposing in regard to Eliot's realism, is not incrementally and teleologically building to one unified, utilitarian and Gradgrindian way of reading, but rather, inducing various degrees of surprise, 'suspending attention' and 'making strange': the purpose of which is to disconnect, briefly, in order to reconnect, with a new or enhanced focus. This is a form of vision that requires looking afresh at the world (*for realism was young once!*); but one that is also liberated, or de-bugged, from previous orthodoxies and/or idealisms. *Interruption*, then, rather than a 'rhythm of continuity' is the root to Eliot's apprehension of the real, and this is an important concept for thinking about her forgotten essay on laughter.

3   Sensing Eliot's Humour & the Falling-*up* of Victorian Joke Culture

And this brings me to what is singularly—and strikingly—absent from Moretti's depiction of realism: the operations of wit and humour. Indeed, he doesn't merely pass over these categories but actively discounts them as meaningful; deploying one of the *OED*'s definitions of seriousness as being 'in opposition to amusement or pleasure-seeking'.[23] The effect of this *aporia* is to risk reprising a rather commonplace, and indeed, outmoded assumption about the Victorians (as dour-faced

Mutton-chops reading with watch-chains and fob in hand), but also about realism itself, particularly in regard to Eliot. But I want to use Moretti's argument as a discursive prompt to retroactively fit humour back into the narrative of Eliotian realism, acknowledging that Moretti's standpoint represents a fairly dominant view in Victorian studies—but importantly, not the only one.

My method in the following sections rests on considering what versions of the 'real' are suggested by indicatively humorous—rather than serious—'fillers' from Eliot's novels, but also, to use this as a means to engage with her distinctive and ground-breaking ideas about Victorian laughter. This involves excavating from a state of critical and cultural ossification, her essay 'German Wit: Heinrich Heine', a work which—in two major and important critical Eliot companions in the past twenty years—received no more than a name-check in over fifty essays exceeding seven hundred pages.[24]

One of the reasons, among many, why Eliot's work on laughter has languished in such deep and untroubled levels of critical obscurity is because of a perceived (though not actual) disconnect between its pithy introductory *aperçus* on the state of Victorian wit and humour in the 1850s, and the way it is followed by apparently laudatory passages concerning the relatively unknown German Romantic writer Heine, that savour of biographical rather than analytical interest. I propose, however, that the essay fulsomely deserves reappraisal, firstly, because it posits a distinctively new view of laughter in relation to the real—which vociferously, and satirically, departs from early Victorian lachrymose and Carlylean versions—but because it also pursues, in the second, and substantial, part of the essay, a clearly demonstrable (but unnamed) physiological theory of wit, which allies itself to twentieth-century iterations of the form—particularly the joke. In this regard, 'German Wit' anticipates, and problematises, both Herbert Spencer's 1860 treatise 'The Physiology of Laughter', and also Sigmund Freud's *The Joke and Its Relation to the Unconscious* (1905).[25]

But before getting to this, I want to continue to 'disturb' the underlying assumption of Moretti's argument: which is that humour is an enemy to seriousness, drawing on Daniel Wickberg's important critical renovation, *The Senses of Humor: Self and Laughter in Modern America*. For Wickberg proposes, contrarily, that what is distinctive about Victorian humour, particularly, is its ability to absorb, rather than deflect, the 'bourgeois values of sympathy, benevolence and

democratic universalism'.[26] While the 1800s began with the passion-
ate inwardness of evangelical seriousness, rendered even as an *erotics* in
E. P. Thompson's famous account of the 'Sabbath orgasms' and 'psychic
masturbation' of outdoor revival meetings, Wickberg charts an accu-
mulative shift through the generations of the nineteenth century which
sees 'the sense of humour' increasingly imbued with the complexity that
had previously been attributed to seriousness.[27] As he shows, the phrase
'sense of humour'—today, an emptied-out cliché of lonely hearts columns and internet dating sites—has a peculiarly Victorian provenance,
being first coined in the 1840s.[28] Yet it connoted the ability not only
to see life and people through an amused (and often kindly) gaze, but
also—in an apotheosis of sympathetic looking—to enjoy seeing oneself as
the *target* of a witticism.

Wickberg calls this capacity 'self-objectification'[29] and it requires a
generous and wide-ranging emotional repertoire, often something akin
to transliterated Christian humility, invested with such a sense of new
possibilities that, at the beginning of the twentieth century, Thomas
Hardy imagined that the 'sense of humour' might end all wars, with 'the
growth of the introspective facility in mankind [...and...] their power of
putting themselves in another's place [...] and taking a point of view that
is not their own'.[30] An indicator of the sense of humour's shifting status in *Middlemarch* is that some of the most amused self-mockers (or
'*self-objectifiers*') are Church of England vicars, who not only regard their
secularity as fodder for a good joke, but also habitually foreground their
faults as part of a reflexive comic self-deprecation. This is a condition
that connotes not moral slovenliness—but rather the opposite—a resistance to the kind of self-preening pieties that are evident elsewhere in the
novel, where 'celestial intimacies seem[...] not to improve [...] domestic
manners'. Lydgate observes, for example, in Rev. Camden Farebrother,
a 'sweet-tempered, ready-witted, frank' nature; one that is in evidence
when he pre-emptively reminds Lydgate of his gambling habits (rather
than all his many virtuous causes) and pardons Lydgate in advance for
not backing his bid to become Middlemarch's new hospital chaplain.[31]

In a novel haunted by the spectre of humourlessness, as much as it is
interleaved with scenes of wise-cracking asides, neither is presented as a
measure of how to be; yet seriousness, per se, often leads to an asocial
or antisocial monism, while a sense of humour (though not named as
such in the novel) allows for a world vision that sees multiple perspectives, and is as un-touchy about personal indignities as it is about

subjective foibles: a mildness that is *crucially* extended to the faults of others. When asked, for example, to pontificate on the rightness of the ageing Rector of Lowick, Casaubon, as a suitor for the blooming young Dorothea, Rev. Humphrey Cadwallader resists condemnation—even amid an atmosphere of high comic licence:

> 'Casaubon is as good as most of us. He is a scholarly clergyman and creditable to the cloth. Some Radical fellow speechifying at Middlemarch said Casaubon was the learned straw-chopping incumbent, and Freke was the brick-and-mortar incumbent, and I was the angling incumbent. And upon my word, I don't see that one is worse or better than the other.' [...] His conscience was large and easy, like the rest of him: it did only what it could do without any trouble.[32]

This 'easiness' is corporeally realised, too, for one of the chief aspects of Cadwallader is his outsized but ungainly physicality (another source for his cheerful self-abasement) but this is decidedly not accompanied by what Sianne Ngai calls 'ugly *feelings*': those ignoble small-scale resentments which have no cathartic outlet.[33] Indeed, Cadwallader's genial self-objectification—a magnanimity that derives from a spirit both holy *and* comic—corresponds with what Wickberg depicts as a wider 'transformation [in...] humoral thought' that occurs from the second half of the nineteenth century and relies on:

> [A] deep interiority capable of perceiving incongruities and a capacity for infinite adaptation to the circumstances of social life. [The sense of humour] is one of the fundamental traits of personhood characterized by accommodation between psychological and social modes of seeing [...], [a] continuity of meaning [...] from the 1870s to the present [that] suggests [...]both 'character' and 'personality' are comprehended as a relationship between expansive and contractive modes of being [...][34]

This emphasis on humour's newly 'expansive modes' in Victorian 1870s modernity makes way for a different account of Eliot's realism, specifically in its effect on characterology and the real, one that can be approached left-handedly by unpacking a comparatively minor moment (another filler) involving Cadwallader from the infamous 'Christian Carnivora' funeral scene. Here, he is viewed from an upper window at Lowick Manor, leading mercantile-minded mourners (described as 'strange animals [...] bent on a limited store which each would have liked to get the most of') proceeding towards the site of miser Peter Featherstone's burial. Looking downwards at this vista from on high, the reverend's wife, Middlemarch's resident quipper-in-chief Elinor Cadwallader, expostulates to others watching with her (including Dorothea, Mr Brooke, Casaubon, Sir James and Celia): 'Those dark, purple-faced people are an excellent foil. Dear me, they are like a set of jugs! Do look at Humphrey: one might fancy him an ugly archangel towering above them in his white surplice'.[35]

Although this tableau may give weight to Christopher Lane's claim of latent and occasional enmity in Eliot's work,[36] clearly, there is a distinction to be made between two varieties of unsightliness: that of the good-humoured Cadwallader (the 'ugly archangel towering above'), who would have enjoyed his wife's marital jibe if he'd have heard it—and who, is here, architectonically realised as ethically elevated, in socially *expansive* rather than contractive mode—and the acquisitive mourners ('the purple-faced [...] jugs'), who, in their non-smiling poverty of purpose resemble the living corpses invoked by George Meredith in his 1877 essay 'On the Idea of Comedy and of the Uses of the Comic Spirit', where 'non-laughers' are depicted as 'dead bodies which if you prick them do not bleed'.[37] For Cadwallader's sense of humour, or self-objectification, like Meredith's comic spirit, has the potency to break beyond the bounds of the self, beyond the material, delivering insights freed from self-absorption and egotism, and invested with an emotional perspective—a comic objectivity—that is both commensurate and proportional. By the end of the century, this falling-*up* of the 'sense of humour', and of joke culture more generally, is enshrined in G. K. Chesterton's work of Christian apologetics, *Orthodoxy* (1908):

> Seriousness is not a virtue. It would be a heresy, but a much more sensible heresy, to say that seriousness is a vice. It is really a natural trend to lapse into taking one's self gravely, because it is the easiest thing to do. It is much easier to write a good *Times* leading article than a good joke in *Punch*. For solemnity flows out of men naturally; but laughter is a leap. It is easy to be heavy: hard to be light. Satan fell by the force of gravity.[38]

The assumption that laughter is the more difficult process, and that the Satanic descent is associated with a kind of cumbrous, even venal, over-thinking follows on from a succession of aerial images in notable works, like Meredith's, on comedy and humour in the 1870s onwards, in which both take flight, 'leaping' from weighted earth-bound and quotidian concerns to an airborne quest for a broader and more all-seeing perspective; one that is often disconnected from the amoral paraphernalia of the Victorian world.[39]

Yet while the nightmare scene of bourgeois materialism in the Christian Carnivora filler reveals what *Middlemarch*'s narrator calls the 'pathetic hopefulness' of barely repressed appetite; on the other hand, the depiction of Cadwallader's self-amused but sacerdotal ugliness operates *against* what Aaron Matz has called the 'fetishization of surface' inherent in nineteenth-century realism.[40] Matz addresses what he sees as an apparent contradiction in Eliot's *oeuvre* which is that despite an inclusive and sympathetic identification with ordinary everyday life, there is also, a competing, and more *irruptive*, mode of looking in her novels which he calls 'ocular intelligence'. This draws on a form of 'judgment' where if we acknowledge that 'things [are to be seen] with an amplified and even exceptional clairvoyance', this same 'insight does not just stop at [...] superficies [...]'. It is, he maintains, 'precisely the heightened power of vision that can lead to disparagement'.[41] As evidence of this condition in *Middlemarch*, he cites the narrative treatment of Casaubon, whose hairy facial moles are talked about by Celia on a number of occasions, but also—more revealingly, according to Matz—are 'a subject of *great interest* [my italics] to the author'.[42] It is worth revisiting the scene where Celia and Dorothea are discussing them:

> When the two girls were in the drawing-room alone, Celia said –
> 'How very ugly Mr Casaubon is!'
> 'Celia! He is one of the most distinguished-looking men I ever saw. He is remarkably like the portrait of Locke. He has the same deep eye-sockets.'
> 'Had Locke those two white moles with hairs on them?'
> 'Oh I dare say! when people of a certain sort looked at him,' said Dorothea, walking away a little.
> 'Mr Casaubon is so sallow.'
> 'All the better. I suppose you admire a man with the complexion of a *cochon de lait*.'[43]

Apart from signalling the only, and somewhat uncomfortable, occasion in *Middlemarch* where Dorothea makes a joke (and, at someone else's expense—in this case, Sir James's)—the surprise is, by Matz's summation, that Celia's observations, practical-minded and unimaginative though they may be, turn out to be true. Matz concludes: 'In the end [...]Celia [...] is right. Eliot is not teaching us here the error of judging someone on the basis of his skin: she is indicating a repulsive personality, to be revealed gradually, by a repulsive complexion which can be detected immediately'.[44] I disagree with Matz here that Casaubon is either presented—or *revealed*—as a 'repulsive personality', for this judgement belongs to the Manichean repertoire of satire, with its sharp ethical polarities.

It is noteworthy, however, that many of Eliot's stated ideas about aesthetics in the 1850s are realised through disrupting and repudiating such apparently inauthentic—and *static*—modes; ones which induce what Juliet John calls, via the work of Robert B. Heilman, a 'reassuring monopathy' or a sense of characterological 'wholeness' and 'singleness of feeling'.[45] In this regard, G. H. Lewes memorably commented that the opposite of realism is 'not Idealism', but 'Falsism', and realism is often theorised by Eliot in the 1850s as a negative space between what she regards as affectively flat fictional forms: it is a *false*-first genre.[46] Her famous indictment of Charles Dickens, in 'The Natural History of German Life' (1856), for example, praised the 'precious salt of his humour' but critiqued the 'transcendent [...] unreality' of his characters' interiority,[47] while her review of Julia Kavanagh's novel *Rachel Gray*, published in the same year, speculates about the possibilities of writing between these two starkly knowable oppositions: '[There] is really a new sphere for a great artist who can paint from close observation, and who is neither a caricaturist nor a rose-colour sentimentalist'.[48]

Reading the scene above with Dorothea and Celia through this prism, it is clear *both* views of Casaubon are skewed: Celia's visual caricature (too much externality) versus Dorothea's not-exactly 'rose-colour sentimentalism' but certainly, sepia-hued idealism (too much interiority). In the rest of this essay, I depart from both accounts by Moretti and Matz and demarcate a form of reading—and indeed a kind of reader—that operates as a *via media* between unchanging and finite fictional forms, imbricated, as Dames suggests, in the act of Victorian novel-reading as 'process rather than [...] structure', and motivated not only by sympathy but, '*delicious* sympathy'.[49] This serio-comic emotion is provoked, or brought into being, by the humorous rather than serious activity of incongruity, which provides the central affective and aesthetic mechanism in 'German Wit', and promotes small or large conundrums in the text that require intellectual and affective resolutions from readers—often working backwards through narrative events during the act of reading and rereading itself. Michael Billig has suggested that the rise of intellectual and philosophical interest in incongruity in the nineteenth century signals the challenge of rationalism by 'sensuous emotion', which anticipates the psychoanalysis of Freud.[50] But incongruity, I propose, in Eliot's work, operates in a different way joining a radical predilection for exposure and *éclaircissement* that posits a continuous unsettling of idealism or 'falsism' with a new or surprise apprehension of the real or '*a* real'. Incongruity obtrudes, sometimes mildly and sometimes 'shockingly', on the reader's previous expectations while the 'real' produced here belongs not to a solid thing-bound world—suggested by the description of the superfluous barometer in Barthes's 'reality effect', or even by the 'wainscoted parlour' that Fred Vincy rides towards at the end of *Middlemarch*—but to the realm of *labile*, rather than unchanging, forms of attention, perception and thought that are constantly assimilating and reassimilating during the act of turning—and returning—Eliot's pages.[51]

4   ELIOT'S TICKLISH BITS: SYMPATHETIC AND DESCENDING INCONGRUITY

In delineating incongruous realism, then, I propose a reality *affect* arising from a shifting exchange of meaning-making between author, narrator and reader engendered by incongruity.[52] This proceeds from the baseline presupposition, as suggested by *Middlemarch*'s narrator, that 'the real' cannot be ordinarily retrieved in the everyday—or *recognised*—because the self is too habitually insulated by delusion; or too 'well wadded with stupidity'.[53] But incongruity, either as a comic, aesthetic or philosophic technique—and all three aspects were discussed widely in the nineteenth century by Immanuel Kant, Charles Darwin, Arthur Schopenhauer, Herbert Spencer, Søren Kierkegaard and S. T. Coleridge,[54] among others—disturbs the 'real', or a previously un-apprehended version of it, *into* being, becoming glimpsable in moments, when conventional expectation is thwarted, broken or redirected towards a different or unusual focus; or when there is a conflict of emotional registers (often, though not always, resulting, in laughter) which depicts the unresolvable exigencies of sympathy and analysis. While paradigmatic work has been done on the structuring device of analogy in Eliot's work, incongruity operates in a different way.[55]

Like analogy, incongruity is a mode of perception, a way of disclosing the narrative world, and also a means (albeit one that relies on antithesis rather than synthesis) of comparing characters and themes, but unlike the hypothetical reaching-towards of analogy, incongruity registers itself first as a *rupture* to pre-existing meaning-making, one that is often corporeally realised, either through *actual* laughter—or through varying degrees of suspended, redirected or what Mikhail Bakhtin calls 'muffled' or 'reduced laughter'.[56]

Casaubon is a significant character for beginning to understand how incongruous realism works—both aesthetically and comedically—for he is the prompt for one of the most well-known and spectacular reversals in all of Eliot's writing which occurs at the beginning of *Middlemarch*'s famous Chapter Twenty-Nine. Here, the story performs a narrative bait-and-switch with the words: 'One morning some weeks after her arrival at Lowick, Dorothea—but why always Dorothea? Was her point of view the only possible one with regard to this marriage?' This dramatic, and indeed, *dramatised*, volte face curtails an apparently more orthodox impulse to talk about the heroine, rebutting the novel's own self-indicted interest in Dorothea, but also, through the breakage of the narrative's rhythm, (its 'reassuring monopathy') we are granted new access to Casaubon's interior world, a form of depth perception that, unlike the emotional repertoire of melodrama or caricature, does not show him to be either ineffably good, or ineffably bad, but rather 'spiritually a-hungered like the rest of us'.[57] The critical language normally used to describe such a move is 'ironic reversal' but this instance demonstrates one of the key effects of incongruity, which is that it posits an affective or intellectual puzzle (or both) which requires some work on the part of the reader to 'resolve' it.

As Alan Partington describes, incongruity does not necessarily need to be amusing to produce its effects: 'If the process of [...] connection is a *collision* then humour will ensue, if a *fusion*, intellectual understanding, if a *confrontation*, an aesthetic experience'.[58] And while the excursus above is not meant to be funny, it *does* engage with humour, albeit at a distance, because we are left puzzling over what feels like a piece of story-telling legerdemain from a narrator, who up until now has appeared to participate in—or at least act as amused bystander to—repeated outbreaks of virtually Saturnalian cheerfulness among the characters on the subject of Casaubon's pedantry or his assumed humourlessness: from his conjectured ability, as an infant, to make academic abstracts out of nursery rhymes ('Hop O' My Thumb'), to the assuredness that were his blood to be put under a microscope, it would yield not red corpuscles, but 'semicolons and parentheses'—and to the assertion that should these same blood-lines be analysed genealogically, they would yield 'family quarterings [as] three cuttle-fish sable and a commentator rampant'.[59]

In these 'lighter' moments, incongruity's natural register is revealed as educated urbanity, one of the reasons (among many) why, by the 1850s, it was accepted as the dominant form of humour in Victorian Britain.[60] Situational rather than directly *ad hominem*, incongruity's playfully heterogeneous and unusual splicing of ideas or emotions sidestepped—to some extent—the blunter, more direct cruelties of Aristotelian or Hobbesian superiority theories, relying on ingenuity and creativity rather than the 'sudden glory' of exultation at another's frailty or weakness.[61] Through this comic mode, as Wickberg suggests, the Victorians 'de-fanged laughter'—softening it and making it 'less threatening'—largely through an act of diversion, but one which also leads you back, with new insights, to the original subject under discussion.[62] Sydney Smith described in *Elementary Sketches of Moral Philosophy* (1849), incongruity's central features as the innovative mixing of disparate things or events—as the 'conjunction of objects and circumstances not usually combined'—while William Hazlitt called it 'the jostling of one feeling against another'.[63]

'Jostling' is a helpful word to understand Eliot's forms of incongruity, because her humour, wit and her realism often involve competing affective impulses which are equally compelling: in regard to Casaubon, we might say, provisionally, at least, that these are *pathos* and *schadenfreude*, but this will change. For another effect of incongruity is that its resolution induces a state that—following the recent work of Alfie Bown—and repurposing a concept from Freudian trauma theory, can be called its *afterwardsness*.[64] This is a form of retroactive memory that involves repeatedly revisiting, or rereading, earlier events in the light of a most recent rupture or experience (in the case of Casaubon this is both comic *and* aesthetic) and reinterpreting it in the light of this new prolapse in meaning-making. This is a move which produces new insights, attentiveness and even internal transformations.[65] And, in this regard, there is an extent to which Chapter Twenty-Nine's afterwardsness reproduces *all* readers as Casaubon: for the earlier laughter at his expense is revealed to be only half the story. As Lauren Berlant suggests, the 'comic is motivated by the pressure of humorlessness' but it also rests on what she calls the 'wishful' notion that this temperamental incapacity is '*over there*'. By not seeing or anticipating the narrative reversal, we encounter what Berlant calls the 'relational rigor mortis' that lies at the heart of humourlessness, experiencing in ourselves its 'fundamental intractability'.[66] This is a reconfiguration of sovereignty that enmeshes both reader and character.[67] The joke may be on us, then, but in tracing out this rather sobering outcome or punch-line above, I am in danger of reprising an all-too familiar twenty-first-century critical manoeuvre in regard to Eliot, which is to imply that her *oeuvre*, like Casaubon himself, is constitutionally sombre, after all.

Instead, though, I want to link the shifting resolutions of Eliot's incongruities here to Mikhail Bakhtin's insights regarding the changing cultural status of the author and narrator implicated in such quasi-comedic acts of contrast and observation. In *Problems of Dostoevsky's Poetics* (1965), he notes a paradigm shift away from the openly festive laughter of the Renaissance to the muted modes of the nineteenth-century novel: 'Under certain conditions and in certain genres [...] laughter can be reduced', he suggests, but adds the intriguing qualifier that it is 'a form-shaping ideology' so potent that despite being 'muffled down to the minimum', it continues to leave 'the track left by laughter in the structure of represented reality, but the laughter itself we do not hear'.[68]

It may seem, admittedly, a little anti-intuitive to attempt to apply a 'laughter track' to Eliot's novels—even modified by the claim of its operating *in absentia* in the production of what Bakhtin calls the 'culture of the weekday'[69]—but it is tantalisingly, even *surprisingly*, in evidence from her earliest work, including the famous Dutch painters scene from *Adam Bede*'s Chapter Seventeen, presaged *again* by an interruption ('In Which the Story Pauses a Little'), and where, as with *Middlemarch*'s Chapter Twenty-Nine, the mechanism for submerged or reduced laughter rests on Partington's 'aesthetic' incongruity, staged as part of the narrator's direct appeal to the reader:

> It is for this rare, precious quality of truthfulness that I delight in many Dutch paintings, which lofty-minded people despise. I find a source of delicious sympathy in these faithful pictures of a monotonous homely existence, which has been the fate of so many more among my fellow-mortals

than a life of pomp or of absolute indigence, of tragic suffering, or of world-stirring actions. I turn, without shrinking, from cloud-borne angels, from prophets, sibyls, and heroic warriors, to an old woman bending over her flower-pot, or eating her solitary dinner, while the noonday light, softened perhaps by a screen of leaves, falls on her mob-cap, and just touches the rim of her spinning wheel, and her stone jug, and all those cheap common things which are the precious necessaries of life to her [...].[70]

Under different circumstances, the vertiginous descent from triumphant power and grandeur ('cloud-borne angels' and 'heroic warriors') to the homely and quotidian (a solitary old woman quietly eating dinner) might well provoke a particularly heartless cackle of superiority but largely through the efforts of the narrator, this is withheld—and creatively transmuted—to 'discover' a new sense of the world that is made more prescient, more urgent, not in spite of the antithesis, but *because* of it.[71] Incongruity, here, can be seen as the ghost in the machine of Eliot's sympathy, softening scorn into something more humane, while, through the bi-focal authorial position that dwells in the humdrum but also looks beyond it, imports *agon* and drama to the everyday.

Significantly though, the energy for seeing such new points of view is not coming from what Schopenhauer calls the 'rigid determinateness' of seriousness but rather from teetering towards laughter and then, by a Bakhtinian authorial swerve, 'muffling it' and redirecting it, to see not one viewpoint, but potentially, many.[72] In one of the very few works to consider incongruity in art and science, *The Act of Creation* (1964), Arthur Koestler notes:

[The effect of incongruity] consists in shifts of attention to aspects previously ignored; in seeing appearances in a new light; in discovering new relations and correspondences between motif and medium [...] the emotive potentials of the matrices participating [in the aesthetic experience] should provide a hint, however tentative or teasing, of some hidden reality in the play of forms and colours.[73]

The 'shifts of attention' involve the teasing-out of 'hidden realities' as part of incongruity's after-effects but what is also intriguing about the scene is how it talks to Bakhtin's construction of the nineteenth-century author's *new* role as mediator between the lived and novelistic worlds:

[T]he most important—one could say, the decisive—expression of reduced laughter is to be found in the ultimate position of the author. This position excludes all one-sided or dogmatic seriousness and does not permit any single point of view, any polar extreme of life or of thought, to be absolutized. All one-sided seriousness (of life and thought), all one-sided pathos is handed over to the heroes, but the author who causes them all to collide in the 'great dialogue' of the novel, leaves that dialogue open and puts no finalizing period at the end.[74]

The 'caus[ing] [...] to collide in the "great dialogue" of the novel' is incongruity's central activity, but it also suggests why the narrator here is *not* disappearing into the background—into what Moretti calls (in another iteration of his conditions of seriousness) 'objective impersonality'—but rather coming to the fore as an affective, and by implication, embodied mediator of reduced laughter: sounding the 'laughter track' that we do not hear.[75] For we might think the intervention of the narrator regarding the old woman is asking for a kind of goody-goody renunciation of enjoyment or a dutiful earnestness (through the cessation of spontaneous laughter), but the scene rather draws on a feeling, that, as James Kincaid suggests, is the 'central emotion of comedy', and, I argue, of Eliot's sympathy: *delight*.[76]

Indeed, delight is hidden in plain sight in the passage above, for it is not only 'sympathy' but '*delicious* sympathy' that is invoked by the narrator, with the proclamation of 'I delight' conveying not only a response to an imagined visual picture but also something more internalised, sensuous and experiential. 'Delight' is defined by the *OED*, as a 'pleasure, joy, or gratification felt in a high degree', and it is a word, and indeed a state, that appears frequently in Eliot's early works.[77,78] 'Delight' and 'delicious sympathy' transitively imply new relations to the subject-object world; ones that carry with them sympathetic pleasure at other selves; but also convey, as in the Dutch painters passage, a dreamed utopian sense of what Dames calls 'oneness'—a sensuous and sensual co-mingling between author and reader.[79] Although Dames's original definition of 'oneness' is pre-eminently a conservative one, noting the assumed ideological unity between Victorian literary critics and their readers, Eliot's here is more radically *looked-for*, enticing the reader through 'delight' as a yearned-for 'participatory emotion'—as Koestler calls it—one that is premised on the possibility of shared pleasure rather than self-denial.[80]

But a reasonable objection to what has so far been described is that withheld or reduced laughter (rather than *actual* laughter) produced by aesthetic incongruity is just what we might *expect* of Eliot's realism—with 'delicious sympathy' merely being an over-determined version of Moretti's 'seriousness' only dressed up in its glad-rags to look less glum. And certainly, such scenes above *could* count, in Moretti's terms, as the self-controlled and controlling animus of 'the bourgeoisie on its way to being the ruling class' in a definitional act that involves an 'irrevocable detachment from the "carnivalesque" of the labouring classes'.[81]

Yet while Moretti is right—this *isn't* the carnivalesque—it is undoubtedly *something*—and not what he demarcates as another condition of seriousness: 'something dark, cold, impassable, silent, heavy [...]'.[82] Besides, the besetting fallacy that *Middlemarch* exposes, or at the very least complicates, is that 'seriousness' *begets* seriousness or attention; for in the thwarted inanition of Casaubon, with his 'formal measured address delivered with the usual sing-song', there resides an abidingly false assumption of a synthesis with the world beyond the self.[83] As Schopenhauer suggests, the 'serious man is convinced he thinks the things as they are, and that they are as he thinks them' but this 'can never exactly fit the subtle nuances and manifold modifications of actual reality'.[84] In *Middlemarch*, then, seriousness may even be style over substance.

For the final two parts of this essay, I want to draw on the ideas expounded in 'German Wit' to explore the comic structures of sympathetic and descending incongruity in Eliot's work—both of which correspond to Victorian definitions of humour and wit respectively—but which also *recalibrate* these terms in ways that are taken up later by twentieth and twenty-first-century thinkers. Both forms deliver specifically literary ways of 'knowing': firstly, by engendering sympathy and attention towards characters through the emotion of 'delight'; and secondly, and also more controversially in the case of Eliot's wit—or descending incongruity—through the *sudden* breakage of that very same sympathetic, sublime, or poeticised thinking in the spirit of comic facing and exposure to the 'real'. Here, through the prism of intertextual and anonymous quotation, it is possible to recover a decidedly alternative, *darker* (even, at times, 'shocking') Eliot, who celebrates the short form of the joke—as well as the long-form of the novel—and who grants it space within a coherent (though unnamed) system of laughter that anticipates, though differs from, both Spencer's 1860 and Freud's 1905 theories.

It is perhaps worth noting, at this point, that despite a monolithic reputation for what George Levine has called Eliot's 'high seriousness'— the reason he attributes to the modernists' rejection of her—comedy and laughter were decidedly part of both her public and private appeal in mid-Victorian Britain, and indeed, throughout her career.[85] Juliette Atkinson has recently observed that it is 'striking' given 'later representations [of Eliot] as a moralist' how 'important humour was in securing her popularity'.[86] Again and again, critics praised her comicality, and did so explicitly in terms of its capacity to render the everyday. An unsigned review of *Adam Bede* asserted it was 'humorous with [...] truth, not of exaggeration',[87] while Dickens, perhaps the most guilty exponent of just such hyperbole, was generosity itself about *Scenes of Clerical Life* (1857), writing of the 'exquisite truth and delicacy, both of the humour and the pathos of these stories'.[88] Meanwhile, E. S. Dallas pronounced *Adam Bede*'s Mrs Poyser a 'firstling of the author's mind', as 'glorious' as Dickens's own 'firstling' Sam Weller in *Pickwick Papers*[89]; while in 1872, an anonymous reviewer in *The Spectator* made the audacious claim (to modern eyes at least) that Eliot's legacy was specifically a comic one:

> [...] George Eliot is the only woman of our time whose writings would be remembered for humour alone, or whose sayings, just now collected into a volume by themselves, are at all likely, like Shakespeare's sayings, to pass into the substance of the language.[90]

Within her intimate circles, too, Eliot was celebrated for her ability to induce not just amused smiles, but outright hilarity. G. H. Lewes professed himself to be in a 'perpetual gurgle of laughter all the while' on rereading the first book of *Middlemarch*,[91] while Eliot's publisher John Blackwood reported of the early scenes of the same novel: 'I found myself pausing upon nearly every page to laugh and think over something equally happy in thought and expression. There is a perfect wealth of thought and fun and then it is real life'.[92]

To many twenty-first-century critics, Blackwood's yoking of 'thought and fun' in the same sentence—specifically in reference to Eliot, *and* to *Middlemarch*—might induce a wince, perhaps an actual *groan*, of critical embarrassment, even froideur. But Eliot herself covers similar terrain with unabashed enthusiasm—and decidedly effusive alliteration—when she describes in 'German Wit', what she calls 'that wonderful and *delicious* mixture of *fun, fancy, philosophy, and feeling*' [my italics] which rests upon 'the *sympathetic* [italics in the original] presentation of incongruous elements in human nature and life,' which constitutes 'modern' humour'.[93] Yet both Eliot's and Blackwood's account of simultaneously laughing and thinking—and also, in Blackwood's case, 'pausing'—replicates Koestler's description of the *comic* effects of incongruity:

> It is the sudden clash [or delightful mental jolt] between [...] two mutually exclusive codes of rules—or associative contexts [...] which produces the comic effect. It compels us to perceive the situation in two self-consistent but incompatible frames of reference at the same time; it makes us function simultaneously on two different wavelengths.[94]

The 'delightful mental jolt' comprises part of the 'delicious mixture' that in Eliot's fiction combines 'philosophy' with the impedimenta of daily life (or 'fun')—and attending to these structures, and what's more, resisting the urge to transform sympathetic incongruity's often domesticated minutiae into the global stakes of irony, grants new insights into her worldview; and new ways to texturise our understanding of her realism.

To explore this further, I want to go to some decidedly down-home instances of comic incongruity—the first, though, *not* from Eliot—but from a historical contemporary who, like her, is often more directly associated with irony: Kierkegaard. As John Lippitt suggests, Kierkegaard was also, like Eliot, interested in forms of thinking that punctured the ideal, and this often involves the epistemological coming-down-to-earth of incongruity—about which he wrote in some detail. In a joke about Hegelian thinkers, for example, his character Anti-Climacus tells the story of a philosopher who has built a '"huge building"' like a palace—a 'magnificent system of thought'—yet actually lives '"in a shed alongside it, or in a doghouse, or at best the janitor's quarters"'.[95] The splicing of grandiloquence and the unassumingly quotidian is replicated but also amplified in a much smaller-scale Kierkegaardian example from an extended multi-page footnote on incongruity in his *Concluding Unscientific Postscript* (1846)—and is good preparation for thinking how 'sympathetic incongruity' works in Eliot. Here, he quotes a 'comic' instance of a four-year-old saying 'patronisingly' to a child of three-and-a-half, 'Come now, my little lamb'.[96] To resolve the incongruity, to 'fix' the joke, it is necessary to recall what it was like to be that four-year-old for whom an age difference of six months was felt to be virtually generational—but also to have witnessed, as an adult watching the behaviour of children, such benignly magisterial, and in Eliot's terms, 'delightful' acts of condescension. The understanding required here is worth lingering on: Koestler's 'functioning simultaneously' on two different levels operates but also insinuates the reader in the gentler effect of incongruity already described—its afterwardsness.

The retroactivity, on this occasion, involves reaching back through half-remembered images, drawing on a lived past or what Freud calls 'mnemic traces' where a 'memory [once] touched [...] springs into life again and shows itself cathected with excitation'.[97] In 'The Reader as Author', Gillian Beer suggests a similar revivification and reanimation, particularly in regard to the haptic memories of childhood, but also more generally:

> We each import landscapes from our own particular repertoire of places; we endow the characters with faces and bodies from the range of our particular awareness – and all this despite, or alongside, any indications offered by the author. To that degree any fiction or memoir is composed jointly by writer and reader. The reader's childhood in particular provides places, sounds, scents, haptic images, that bury themselves deep in the author's text and are released by that one reader alone.[98]

Victorian realism, and indeed Eliot's realism—in particular—is one of *the* gateway genres for this kind of readerly activity: stirred, prompted, benignly 'shocked' and *cathected* into acts of co-authoring. Two examples from Eliot's rich archive of similar moments reveal a series of narrative strategies that challenge and entice readers to 'enter' the world of her characters. The first concerns the depiction of the enduring miller's wife Mrs Tulliver in *The Mill on the Floss* (1860) as a 'patriarchal goldfish':

> Mrs Tulliver had lived thirteen years with her husband, yet she retained in all the freshness of her early married life, a facility of saying things that drove him in the opposite direction to the one she desired. Some minds are wonderful for keeping their bloom in this way, as a patriarchal goldfish apparently retains to the last its youthful illusion that it can swim in a straight line beyond the encircling glass. Mrs Tulliver was an amiable fish of this kind, and after running her head against the same resisting medium for thirteen years would go at it again today with undulled alacrity.[99]

The incongruous splicing of a threatening and all-pervasive ideology with a small, docile, and significantly silent, household pet produces Koestler's 'delightful mental jolt' but also avoids the charge of merely cruel characterisation by its determinedly bi-focal purview. The comedy, as with the micro-world of Kierkegaard's four-year-old, requires, in Beer's terms, 'importing' haptic childhood memories that layer the sense-world physicality of a goldfish's movements (sashaying through water and apparently self-referentially enjoying its own sense of fluidity) onto Mrs Tulliver's innocuous pride at her household management skills and neat Dodson features—and also, more pertinently, her chronic and unconquerable state of maritally induced infantilism.

But it is on the limitations of Mrs Tulliver's ability to comprehend herself, and others, that we can see how the unprepossessing image of the goldfish bowl works as a textual model for how sympathetic incongruity operates to *build* the nuances of character—rather than obviating them—and how this differs from other contemporaneous models of humour. The image of the fishly nose repeatedly banging itself ('with undulled alacrity') against the 'resisting medium' of the bowl might suggest the kind of concussed consciousness or self-ignorance that both Henri Bergson and Freud suggest is the secret of the comic[100]—and which led G. H. Lewes to complain about Dickens's characters that they were like 'frogs whose brains have been taken out',[101] having no plausible insides or motivation; a point also made by John Carey, who memorably commented about *Oliver Twist*'s incompetently venal beadle Mr Bumble that he is an 'innocent' as great as Oliver himself.[102] Here, the 'resisting medium' is both the comic and novelistic form, and the critical issue is the perennial one of how to depict, and indeed understand, a consciousness not one's own. In this respect, comedy represents both an opportunity to open up subjectivity, but also a danger of shutting it down—through such devices as condensation, abstraction and caricature.

The passage above, however, is more contingent and speculative, asking the reader to hold at least two characterological frames at the same time; looking inside-out to 'experience meaning', as Rae Greiner calls it, as part of an insider laughter track of sympathetic 'felt-ness' which allows for an appreciation of Mrs Tulliver's sense of having her existence seemingly confirmed through her highly circumscribed movements: believing they amount to autonomy ('swimming in a straight line'), but also perceiving, as an outsider looking in, that her sphere of influence is,

of course, pitifully minuscule, and, the goldfish bowl has an owner.[103]
Harry E. Shaw has commented that the issue of apparent transparency
has been a critical bugbear for realist authors charged with naïve forms of
representation (though not perhaps Eliot) but here sympathetic incongruity engenders neither vilification nor idealisation, but an experiential and intellectual understanding of what Greiner calls the 'historically
embedded mentalities of others'; one that imbricates both humour and
sympathy.[104]

The second scene of sympathetic incongruity (which also
includes examples of Eliot's wit) comes from the Larchers auction in
Middlemarch, a novel which, as Moretti drolly suggests, is *choc*-full of
fillers, and 'serious' iterations of this narrative anodyne (where 'background, conquer[s] the foreground') are implicated, *indirectly* at least, in
an important question that he discusses about nineteenth-century realism: 'How did the everyday manage to become interesting?'[105] Moretti's
answer to this (which he, himself, considers 'strange') is, as parsed earlier,
perplexingly a-textual at times, in that he suggests that the filler induces
a state of *not*-boredom (rather, implicitly, than *overt* pleasure) and is
informed by the meta-conditions of the Victorian world (the move to
objectivity, improvement and professionalism). Like 'good manners',
he suggests, fillers are strategies of containment: designed to keep the
'"narrativity" of life under control'.[106]

Yet attention paid to the comic activity of fillers in *Middlemarch* sees
not so much a stabilising and consolidation of the bourgeois project but,
at times, a radical imaginative dismantling. For while, in theory, at least,
the Larchers auction might be construed as the *locus classicus* of Victorian
realism, involving the re-sale of fungible, domestic things (or 'portable
property') in transition in the public sphere—thereby reprising one of the
conditions of Moretti's seriousness that he calls 'sublimated commercial
honesty'—the following exchange sees 'business' rapidly move from the
mercantile to the threatened epistemological.[107] It sees interest shift from
an apparent consolidation of 'value' to a consideration of subjective vulnerability, in a discussion among Middlemarch townsfolk about the sale of
a large steel fire-fender with a conspicuously sharp edge:

> 'It's not a thing I would put in *my* drawing-room', said Mrs Mawmsey,
> audibly, for the warning of the rash husband. 'I wonder *at* Mrs Larcher.
> Every blessed child's head that fell against it would be cut in two. The
> edge is like a knife'.

'Quite true', rejoined Mr Trumbull, quickly, 'and most uncommonly useful to have a fender at hand that will cut, if you have a leather shoetie or a bit of string that wants cutting and no knife at hand: many a man has been left hanging because there was no knife to cut him down. Gentlemen, here's a fender that if you had the misfortune to hang your-selves would cut you down in no time—with astonishing celerity—four-and-sixpence—five—five and sixpence—an appropriate thing for a spare bedroom where there was a four-poster and a guest a little out of his mind—six shillings—thank you, Mr Clintup—going at six shillings—going—gone!' The auctioneer's glance, which had been searching round him with a preternatural susceptibility to all signs of bidding, here dropped on the paper before him, and his voice too dropped into a tone of indiffer-ent despatch as he said, 'Mr Clintup. Be handy, Joseph'.

'It was worth six shillings to have a fender you could always tell that joke on', said Mr Clintup, laughing low and apologetically to his next neighbour. He was a diffident though distinguished nurseryman, and feared that the audience might regard his bid as a foolish one.[108]

The vitality and humour of this encounter arises initially from the jux-taposition of two worlds that hardly seem to know each other: between practical-minded and common-sense domesticity contrasted with vary-ing degrees of suicidal despair. It begins with Mrs Mawmsey's opening salvo—her 'warning' to the 'rash husband'—in doughtily matriarchal tones, that a fire-fender as keen as a blade will not be allowed congress with hearth and home, regardless of the fanciful, big-house imaginings of any deluded *pater familias*. This prompts a brief but intense form of affective contagion between her and the auctioneer Trumbull—a *comic* bidding war—that also becomes a conjured fight (and flight) to the death, in which the fire-fender is summoned variously as baby-maimer, as terrifying penal instrument of the state, and as conduit to the next life, while this litany of possible dire domestic consequences (from decapitated infants to momentarily despondent and self-im-molating house guests) is only brought to a close by the nurseryman Clintup's rather meek and rueful joke—nervously made to pre-empt the criticism of his neighbours. The imaginative hyperbole here appears positively Dickensian, rather than from the pages of Eliot. Indeed, W. M. Thackeray once complained about Dickens's prose that things 'waken into ludicrous life,' where even a kettle '"dribbles like an idiot"' and '"leans forward as if drunk"'.[109] But the fire-fender proves resolutely resistant to such animist constructions or Dickensian grotesquery, remaining implacably itself—*deadpan* even.

Yet, like realism, the fire-fender's apparent sturdy, stolid, weightiness, its 'overwhelming immediacy', is narratively productive, for around it, hover the multiple conflictual energies of characters' perceptions and inner lives ('reality affects') with the humour produced by its silent unreadability.[110] And here, incongruity interacts with another dominant mode of Eliotian narration—that of free indirect discourse—moving fluently in and out of the thought-worlds of characters, melding first and third-person voice, with the most fertile point of incongruity arising at what Freud calls the 'thick of it' where subjectivity collides— sometimes mildly, sometimes dramatically—with the outside world.[111] As such, what has been demarcated as the privileged position of the omniscient narrator—who, in Moretti's terms is recessed but nonetheless obliquely powerful—might be reconfigured here, not as a wielder of a pseudo-scientific narrative speculum who can penetrate consciousness to produce cool-headed and abstracted forms of judgement—but instead, as a rather more humane archivist of characters' thoughts, fleshly imaginings, daydreams and dreads: a figure who can aggregate and synthesise such multiple expressions into a composite of brief but quasi-comedic intensities.[112]

It is part of the realist narrative, as Shaw suggests, to create the *desire* for transparency, but these moments are short-lived, nonetheless sympathetic incongruity ('amusing tactics') opens up small apertures in the text, generating speculation rather than controlling and deadening it, as readers retroactively begin to immerse themselves in the scene's 'story space' to resolve a series of localised (*micro* rather than macro) narrative conundrums.[113] We might conjecture, then, that Mrs Mawmsey embodies an excessive kind of domestic introversion that constructs anything beyond her own front doorstep as a threat of inordinate proportions; or conversely, that Trumbull is attempting to divert the panic from what is (plainly) a murderously life-threatening fire-fender by appealing specifically to the derring-do and bravado of the masculine contingent of his audience; or that the mild-mannered and 'careful' Clintup, in apparently 'foolishly' winning the fender, disregards (or, alternatively, believes utterly in) its dismembering capacities—but is won over by Trumbull's images of swaggering, Byronic masculinity.[114] None, or all, of these readings might be true, or have elements of truth, but the scene is poised between many possibilities. Somewhere amid these contingencies may be the 'real' or *a* real; but then incongruous realism is not linear nor even-handed—nor given the imprimatur of finality.

The auction scene concludes with a joke about a joke (about hanging yourself) but I want to linger on the tropes of height and suspension because they suggest why wit and humour are good to think with in Eliot's novels. For there are two structures at work here: the first is, as we have seen, the horizontal, companionable humour of sympathetic incongruity that treats characters with a kind of familial intimacy and intricacy, and is an example of the readerly and authorial practice that Greiner calls '"going along with" others'.[115] Going along, *laughing* along, this is convivial, inclusive humour. There is also, however, an upward momentum in the auction scene—comically catastrophised—towards unknown and unthinkable futures, which dramatises characters' attempts to reach beyond their everyday worlds, beyond their own Socratic limits; as part of what Shaw calls the realist urge to 'pierce beyond the veil of the familiar [...]'.[116] This vertiginous, but *otherly,* energy, transporting into the scene what is unexpected, *un*-obvious or not conventional, is also replicated in Eliot's own description of the joke in 'German Wit', which she suggests—unlike humour—often arises from *above* or beyond polite everyday bourgeois culture, and significantly *before* moral sympathies are engaged, sometimes producing dramatic physiological effects. For while humour leaves us 'masters of ourselves', Eliot suggests, wit takes you by force, removing your self-control and *amour-propre*:

> Probably the reason why high culture demands more complete harmony with its moral sympathies in humour than in wit, is that humour is in its nature more prolix—that it has not the direct and irresistible force of wit. *Wit is an electric shock, which takes us by violence, quite independently of our predominant mental disposition*; [my italics] but humour approaches us more deliberately and leaves us masters of ourselves.[117]

The idea of 'wit' using the body as a lightning rod for an attractive, novel, or even a licentious or 'shocking' idea (a metaphor she also uses to connote sexual attraction) allows for a new way of approaching the real in Eliot's work.[118] For unlike other debates in Victorian culture, such as those surrounding sensation fiction, or pornography, the temporary suspension, even 'violation' of the moral and the rational self, produced by the short form of wit, or the joke (and I use these terms interchangeably) does not represent a threatening or anxiety-producing subjective degradation to Eliot, but rather as she argues, '*reasoning raised to a higher power*' (italics in the original). In a further elaboration of this potent state of *post*-laughter in 'German Wit', she describes the end result of a joke, particularly one of Heine's, as leading to 'just thought'. This is not '*merely* thought', but rather the opposite, a near-Platonic state of retroactivity (stronger than that produced by sympathetic incongruity), where the be-laughed self, in the aftermath of the unexpected 'shock' of wit, conjures new calculations of the real, as potential resolutions to the revelations created by the joke.[119]

Critics have historically had a problem with Eliot and wit *specifically*— as opposed to the apparently more warmly inclusive humour—because it appears inimical to sympathy. Eileen Gillooly, for example, suggests, in an important psychoanalytic account, that Eliot privileges humour over wit as 'the morally dominant partner' because to do otherwise would mean taking 'unconscious pleasure' in the pain inflicted on wit's targets, rather than sympathising with its victims.[120] But this is to see wit, or the joke, predominantly as an anti-personnel weapon—rather than, as it is in Eliot's work, a truth-seeking device that resists what she calls the 'vulgarity of exclusiveness' and the sugariness of sentimentality.[121] For Eliot is no sensibility writer issuing precious pieties from her literary pulpit: *all* her characters are potentially subject to wit, and also to *her* wit, as part of the democratic everybody-ness of her fictive world—and also her often tireless appetite for comically facing what the narrator of *Daniel Deronda* (1876) calls, 'the hard, unaccommodating Actual, which has never consulted our taste and is entirely unselect'.[122]

Two brief examples from *Middlemarch*—and about two of the novel's notable idealists—begin to illustrate this phenomenon. About Will Ladislaw, as editor of the town's campaigning newspaper, *The Pioneer*, one of the townsmen Mr Hawley, says (with more than a measure of xenophobic suspicion about Ladislaw's radical and continental connections): 'He'll begin with flourishing about *The Rights of Man* and end with murdering a wench. That's the style'. Meanwhile, one of the members of Middlemarch's new fever hospital board, Mr Standish, says about Lydgate's pioneering medical practices: 'If you [would] like him to try experiments on your hospital patients, and kill a few people for charity, I have no objection'.[123] These jokes are not represented as all-encompassing truths but there might be a *filigree* of truth in both— and it is this recognition of the real or *a* real (what Koestler calls 'hidden realities') that renders their comic impact, unexpectedly cutting through the epistemological insulation that separates high ideals from the less pure actuality; for Ladislaw begins the novel quixotic and shiftless, while the nature of Lydgate's medical ambitions, are, at times, not fully quantifiable, even to himself. These insights can be rejected or accepted by the reader but they wage war on easy and finite truths and untruths—and are perpetually subject to reconfiguration and renegotiation.

But, as with the examples about Lydgate and Ladislaw above, it is also a particular aspect of Eliot's jokes, that they do *not* desert sympathy (laughter is not here the Bergsonian temporary 'anaesthesia of the heart')[124] but dramatise the often irreconcilable exigencies between caring and insight, between the 'prolixity' of moral sympathy and the brevity of new and unanticipated thoughts. This structure is central to many of Eliot's jokes—and, as we will see, those she admires in Heine. The affective and cognitive dissonance caused by a 'shocking' or unexpected interruption is also limned in Herbert Spencer's account of 'descending incongruity' theorised in 1860. In the following scene, he describes the conclusion of a painful love story at a theatre, when suddenly a goat ambles indifferently onto the stage and starts sniffing the actors:

> Take a case. You are sitting in a theatre [...] Some climax has been reached which has aroused your sympathies [...] a reconciliation between the hero and heroine, after long and painful misunderstanding. The feelings excited by this scene are not of a kind from which you seek relief; but are, on the contrary, a grateful relief from the more or less painful feelings with which you have witnessed the previous estrangement. Add to which, that the sentiments these fictitious personages have for the moment inspired you with, are certainly not such as would lead you to rejoice in any indignity offered to them; but rather, such as would make you resent the indignity. And now, while you are contemplating the reconciliation with a pleasurable sympathy, there appears from behind the scenes a tame goat, which, having stared round at the audience, walks up to the lovers and sniffs at them. You cannot help joining in the laughter which greets this *contretemps.*[125]

What is essential here to cause the roar of laughter is the audience's *full* emotional absorption in the scene, as the goat appears at a moment of 'aroused [...] sympathies'. But the audience doesn't *stop* caring about the lovers but oscillates between the apparently irreconcilable antitheses of the dénouement of a poignant love story but *also* Koestler's 'shift of attention' caused by the goat incongruously treating the lovers like other animals—and smelling them—rendering new apprehensions of the real (anthropocentrism versus creatureliness) which might be discarded or accepted. It is a similar irresolution and alternation between compassion and thinking which is at the heart of one of Eliot's funniest—and also most mordant—jokes from *Adam Bede*. It arises during a good-natured and evenly matched gendered knockabout between the no-nonsense farmer's wife, Mrs Poyser, and the self-styled (but not entirely convincing) woman-hater and local schoolteacher Bartle Massey:

> 'Ah!' said Bartle sneeringly, 'the women are quick enough—they're quick enough. They know the rights of a story before they hear it, and can tell a man what his thoughts are before he knows 'em himself.'
>
> 'Like enough,' said Mrs. Poyser, 'for the men are mostly so slow, their thoughts overrun 'em, an' they can only catch 'em by the tail. I can count a stocking-top while a man's getting's tongue ready; an' when he outs wi' his speech at last, there's little broth to be made on't. It's your dead chicks take the longest hatchin.'[126]

In 'dead chicks take the longest hatchin'' what is being held up to the light is what Mrs Poyser constructs as the self-flattering belief that all words that fall from male lips will naturally be authoritative and full of élan (when, actually, elsewhere in the novel, she says that 'it's a small joke sets men laughing when they sit a-staring at one another with a pipe i' their mouths'.)[127] But here, the laughter is caused by multiple descending incongruities, for 'dead chicks' cuts apparently invulnerable and 'big' masculine discourse to size firstly by comparing it to something endangered and delicate, and then in a further incongruous layering, equating the joyful excitement of waiting for the fluffy and albumen-covered creature to falteringly emerge from an egg (*a new life!*) to the melancholy sadness of finding it stillborn; and then again, in another level of meaning-making, splicing that dolefulness with the exuberant anticipation of waiting for a really good *bon mot* to fly combined with the disappointment of finding that, in Mrs Poyser's terms, it's a dud. It is partly the inappropriateness of the comparisons here that is funny—dead chicks and failed wit shouldn't be coupled together—but a strange new sense of aptness is produced, that after reflection, invigorates the commonplace, and through surprise, renders an amplification of the real while inducing the Spencerian 'roar' of descending incongruity.

5   Suspending George Eliot, 'Saving' Rosamond

It is this similar capacity for intense and subtly wrought emotion—but also comically unexpected twists and turns—that Eliot admires in Heine's work, leaving his readers, and implicitly, *Eliot herself*, rocking with amusement. Heine can, she asserts:

> [S]hake us with laughter at his overflowing fun, or give us a piquant sensation of surprise by the ingenuity of his transitions from the lofty to the ludicrous. This last power is not indeed essentially poetical; but only a poet [...] can poise our emotion and expectation at such a height as to give effect to the sudden fall.[128]

Heine's jokes—like Eliot's dead chicks—don't desert sympathy, but splice it with a puncturing contrast of interrupted lyricism that renders new understandings while avoiding the conventionality of how-true moralisms. This is suggested in 'German Wit', where Eliot quotes an autobiographical passage from Heine's *Reisebilder* or 'Travel Pictures' (1826–31) in which he recalls visiting a grave of a childhood friend, William, whose death he inadvertently caused, when his cat fell into the river Düssel. Heine remembers how he calls out:

> 'William, fetch out the kitten that has just fallen in'—and merrily he went down on to the plank which lay across the brook, snatched the kitten out of the water, but fell in himself, and was dragged out dripping and dead. *The kitten lived to a good old age.*[129]

The descending incongruity between the boy's tragically short life and the kitten's great age—the central point of the joke—does not turn William into an object of ridicule, however, but posits, in retrospective analysis, a reflection (Eliot's 'just thought') on human thwarted-ness; while the image of William being dragged out of the river 'dripping and dead' comically displaces the tears cried out on his behalf beyond the predictable literary schmaltz while still retaining (indeed *adding* to) the pathos of the scene. It is the universe's cruelty, rather than the author's, that is again rendered by Heine in another passage quoted in 'German Wit', where he recalls, with fondness, but also a discomforted sense of awe, the intellectual and spiritual earnestness of his former school-master—the 'knowing old Canon'—from the Franciscan Monastery where he was tutored, who is stricken with illness:

> [W]hat an object he looked when I last saw him! *He was made up of nothing but mind and plasters*, and nevertheless studied day and night, as if he were alarmed lest the worms should find an idea too little in his head.[130]

Here, the descent from the ideal of the 'mind' is pitted against the frail mortality of injured physicality, being covered in bandages, and layered with the somewhat more bleakly funny—and also rather more 'shocking' in Eliot's terms—incongruity of a brain crammed with knowledge being subject to a particularly ghastly subterranean version of peer review by anthropomorphic worms. The democracy of common fates is implied in another quoted scene in 'German Wit' where Heine describes a moment in 'a little hospital at Cracow' where cancer patients tear off each others' blankets, and laugh at each others' tumours, which Eliot describes as 'Dantesque'.[131] Nothing *quite* so gruelling appears in Eliot's novels, but there are clear genealogies between Heine and Eliot. For example, in *The Mill on the Floss*, the lachrymose Aunt Pullet is upbraided by one of her sisters for crying about a dying neighbour—even when she knows she will not inherit her money—and comforts herself thus:

> It was not everybody who could afford to cry so much about their neighbours who had left them nothing; but Mrs Pullet had married a gentleman farmer, and had leisure and money to carry her crying and everything else to the highest pitch of respectability.[132]

What such jokes show is the *risk* of the real in Eliot's work, and its ability to cut right at the heart of bourgeois cosiness, and self-comforting rationalisations.

* * *

Given then the anonymous intertextual choices made by Marian Evans, the journalist, in 1856, it is something of a descending incongruity itself that the writer who would become George Eliot—the iconic novelist of Victorian sympathy—should be such an admirer of an iconoclastic wit recently described as the 'most controversial figure in modern German literature'.[133] Embroiled in at least two major literary scandals in the 1830s and the 1840s, Heine spent many of his final years as a cultural exile in Paris, with Friedrich Nietzsche, later in the century, counting himself as one of Heine's most ardent devotees.[134] Indeed, in a further unexpected twist, it is Nietzsche, who famously in *Twilight of the Idols* (1889) condescendingly referred to 'the moralising little woman *à la* Eliot' but also praised Heine in *Ecce Homo* (1908) as the 'divine malice without which I am incapable of conceiving perfection'.[135] As the narrator of *Daniel Deronda* asserts, 'a difference of taste in jokes is a great strain on the affections'.[136] But the opposite might also be true.

It would be difficult to make a case, however, for Eliot as a secret Nietzschean nihilist, but it is also useful to know what kinds of humour she was rejecting in 'German Wit' in order to celebrate what she calls the *'esprit'* of Heine.[137] And while, as Dames has shown, Eliot has been perennially associated with duration and long-form, as part of her seriousness, in 'German Wit' she inveighs against a particular type of long-winded humour, which she links to Carlyle's favoured German comic writer, Jean Paul Richter.[138] Indeed, what is often overlooked about 'German Wit' is how it begins with a pretty wholesale denouncement of Richter as 'unendurable to many readers and frequently tiresome to all'. But Richter's humour, which at one point, involves the Moon frisking with the Earth, was deemed too other-worldly by Eliot to be engaging: 'All [Richter's] subtlety is reserved for the region of metaphysics [...] but the presence of more or less tobacco-smoke in the air he breathes is imperceptible to him'.[139] Eliot is making a plea here for wit and humour to be considered as part of the real—a pretty uncontroversial stance perhaps—but it is the *terms* of Eliot's 'real' that are noteworthy. For Heine is the most quoted literary writer in Freud's *The Joke*, but in that work, he appears merely understatedly sardonic—a sayer of modish quips—but it takes Eliot's essay to truly realise the nature of his subversion.[140]

But then Freud's concept of joke-work differs to Eliot's, for he, like Spencer, is a 'relief theorist'—a peculiarly Victorian invention—and posits a temporary lifting of the prohibition against transgressive thoughts as a protection from harm to the psychic self.[141] But although the joke structure of 'descending incongruity' is common to Freud, Spencer *and* Eliot, the outcome is different in Eliot's work: hers is an *un*-relief theory of laughter. For only by constantly testing the real can sympathy and understanding be arrived at—not as a starting point but an end point—and this requires a continual process of effacement (rather than 'saving') of the self that cuts against 'well wadded [...] stupidity' and internal insulation. This is not a dire process though—touch a 'true' nerve and Eliot is 'shaking' with amusement as part of a comic erotics of the real—[142] but there is also a provisionality and mobility to Eliot's thinking; what Jeanie Thomas has called the 'leniency of the comic vision'.[143] Indeed, Eliot recommends that a 'friendly penknife' is required to expurgate the more shocking aspects of Heine's work for the 'immature mind'.[144] But behind the leniency, there is also a remorseless scepticism about the 'sympathy ready-made' that Eliot describes in 'The Natural History of German Life'.[145] When in *Middlemarch*, Dorothea vows to 'save' Rosamond, after witnessing what may or may not be a flirtation with Ladislaw, whom Dorothea loves, she spends a night of turmoil, lying on the 'bare floor' as the 'night gr[e]w cold around her'.[146] Spencer suggests that the opposite of 'descending incongruity' is 'ascending incongruity' in which a small moment works in the reverse way to the relief of laughter—and leads to 'awe' and 'wonder'.[147] Wit, in Eliot's work, is also connected to the real in this way. Laugh first, then think—and then act—might be a motto for Eliot, in a way that Freud's verbalisms are not. But to do so means moving beyond conventional or trite thinking—and Eliot's jokes are a part of this.

NOTES

1. See Charles Darwin and Paul H. Barrett. *Charles Darwin's Notebooks 1836–1844* (Cambridge: Cambridge University Press, 1987), 539–541.
2. George Eliot, *Middlemarch* (Hertfordshire: Wordsworth Editions, 1994), 237–238.
3. Ibid., 237.
4. Henry James, unsigned review, *Galaxy* 15 (March 1873): 424–428.
5. Barbara Bodichon, 'Letter to George Eliot,' 10 December 1871, in George Eliot, *The George Eliot Letters*, 9 vols., ed. Gordon S. Haight (New Haven and London: Yale University Press, 1954–1978), IX, 32–33.
6. R. H. Hutton, 'The Humour of *Middlemarch*,' *The Spectator*, December 14, 1872, 182–183.
7. Elizabeth Deeds Ermarth, 'Negotiating Middlemarch' in Karen Chase, ed. *Middlemarch in the 21st Century* (Oxford: Oxford University Press, 2006), 110.
8. Franco Moretti, 'Serious Century,' in *The Novel: History, Geography, and Culture, vol. 1*, ed. Franco Moretti (Princeton, NJ: Princeton University Press, 2006), 367–381.

9. Daniel Wickberg, *The Senses of Humor: Self and Laughter in Modern America* (Ithaca NY: Cornell University Press, 1998). George Eliot, 'German Wit: Heinrich Heine,' *Westminster Review* 65 (January 1856): 1–33.

10. The essay on Heine for the *Westminster Review* was one of a number that Eliot wrote on Heine in the late 1840s and the 1850s. See also, Sol Liptzin, 'Heine, the Continuator of Goethe: A Mid-Victorian Legend,' *The Journal of English and Germanic Philology* 43, no. 3 (July 1944): 317–325; Rosemary Ashton, *The German Idea: Four Writers and the Reception of German Thought 1800–1860* (London: Libris, 1994).

11. Franco Moretti, *The Bourgeois: Between History and Literature* (London: Verso Books, 2013), 79.

12. See Moretti, *The Bourgeois*, 81. Roland Barthes, 'Introduction to the Structural Analysis of Narratives,' in *Barthes: Selected Writings*, ed. Susan Sontag (Glasgow: Fontana Press, 1983), 266.

13. Moretti, *The Bourgeois*, 82. Italics in original.

14. Moretti, *The Bourgeois*, 171, 35, 39, 120.

15. As Moretti observes, this is from Walter Bagehot's *The English Constitution* (1867). See Moretti, The *Bourgeois*, 82; J. Hillis-Miller, 'Optic and Semiotic in *Middlemarch*,' in *The Worlds of Victorian Fiction*, ed. Jerome Hamilton Buckley (Cambridge, MA: Harvard University Press, 1975), 128.

16. Luke Davies, 'The Way of the World: Franco Moretti, The Bourgeois: Between History and Literature,' *Review 31*. http://review31.co.uk/article/view/158/the-way-of-the-world. Accessed Jan 20, 2020. For a differing account of Moretti and Foucauldian thinking, see John Plotz, 'Review of *The Bourgeois: Between History and Literature* by Franco Moretti,' Victorian Studies 56, no. 4 (Summer 2014): 734–736.

17. Moretti, *The Bourgeois*, 14, n. 27.

18. Gillian Beer, *Darwin's Plots* (Cambridge: Cambridge University Press, 1983), 41.

19. Ibid., 41.

20. Caroline Levine, 'Victorian Realism,' in *The Cambridge Companion to the Victorian Novel*, ed. Deirdre David (Cambridge: Cambridge University Press, 2012), 87–88.

21. George Eliot, 'Notes on Form in Art,' in *George Eliot: Selected Essays, Poems and Other Writings*, ed. A. S. Byatt (London: Penguin, 2005), 231.

22. Ibid., 232. See Moretti on 'the rhythm of continuity' in *The Bourgeois*, 51.

23. Moretti, *The Bourgeois*, 72.

24. George Levine and Nancy Henry, eds., *The Cambridge Companion to George Eliot* (Cambridge: Cambridge University Press, 2019); Amanda

Anderson and Harry E. Shaw, eds., *A Companion to George Eliot* (Hoboken, NJ: Wiley, 2016).

25. Sigmund Freud, *The Joke And Its Relation to the Unconscious*, trans. Joyce Crick (London: Penguin, 2003). Herbert Spencer, 'The Physiology of Laughter,' *Macmillan's Magazine* 1 (March 1860): 395–402.

26. Wickberg, *The Senses of Humor*, 172.

27. E. P. Thompson, *The Making of the English Working Class* (London: Pelican Books, 1963), 368–369.

28. Wickberg, *The Senses of Humor*, 80.

29. Ibid., 101.

30. Martin Ray, *Thomas Hardy Remembered* (London: Routledge, 2017), 35. See also Anna West's discussion of this assertion by Hardy about the 'sense of humour,' in West, *Thomas Hardy and Animals* (Cambridge: Cambridge University Press, 2017), 189 n.91, 109.

31. Eliot, *Middlemarch*, 147.

32. Ibid., 58.

33. Sianne Ngai, *Ugly Feelings* (Cambridge, MA: Harvard University Press, 2005).

34. Wickberg, *The Senses of Humor*, 9.

35. Eliot, *Middlemarch*, 269.

36. See Chapter Four, 'George Eliot and Enmity' in Christopher Lane, *Hatred & Civility: The Antisocial Life in Victorian England* (New York: Columbia University Press, 2004).

37. George Meredith. 'On the Idea of Comedy, and of the Uses of the Comic Spirit.' *New Quarterly Magazine* 8 (January–July 1877): 2.

38. G. K. Chesterton, *Orthodoxy* (New York: Lane, 1909), 222.

39. See also Leslie Stephen, 'Humour,' *Cornhill Magazine* 33 (March 1876): 318–326. I am indebted to Wickberg's discussion of Stephen's essay in *The Senses of Humor*, 84.

40. Eliot, *Middlemarch*, 272. Aaron Matz, *Satire in an Age of Realism* (Cambridge: Cambridge University Press, 2010), 14.

41. Matz, *Satire in an Age of Realism*, 14–15.

42. Ibid., 7.

43. Eliot, *Middlemarch*, 16.

44. Matz, *Satire in an Age of Realism*, 7.

45. Juliet John, *Dickens's Villains: Melodrama, Character, Popular Culture* (Oxford: Oxford University Press, 2003), 110, 27. I say 'apparently inauthentic' modes, because as Matz rightly points out, it is not that these do not tell a story about the 'real' but rather access it through other means. See Matz, *Satire in an Age of Realism*, chapter five.

46. G. H. Lewes, qtd. in Alice Kaminsky, 'George Eliot, George Henry Lewes, and the Novel,' *PMLA* 70, no. 5 (December 1955), 1001.

47. George Eliot, 'The Natural History of German Life,' *Westminster Review* 66 (July 1856): 55.

48. George Eliot, 'Rachel Gray,' *Leader*, 7 January 5, 1856, 19.

49. Nicholas Dames, *The Physiology of the Novel: Reading, Neural Science and the Form of Victorian Fiction* (Oxford: Oxford University Press, 2007), 11. George Eliot, *Adam Bede* (Hertfordshire: Wordsworth, 1997), 153.

50. Michael Billig, *Laughter and Ridicule: Towards a Social Critique of Humour* (New York: Sage, 2005), 83.

51. Eliot, *Middlemarch*, 685.

52. See Roland Barthes, 'The Reality Effect,' in *The Rustle of Language*, trans. Richard Howard, ed. François Wahl (Berkeley: University of California Press, 1989), 141–148.

53. Eliot, *Middlemarch*, 161–162.

54. I discuss all these thinkers in Louise Lee, 'Charles Darwin's "Scientific Wit": Incongruity, Species Fixity & the Nonsense of Looking' in Martin Priestman and Louise Lee, eds., 'Evolution and Literature: The Two Darwins,' *Romanticism on the Net* 66–67, no. 8 (2016): 1–36.

55. See Beer, *Darwin's Plots*, chapter three; Devin Griffiths, *The Age of Analogy* (Baltimore: Johns Hopkins University Press, 2016).

56. Mikhail Bakhtin, *Problems of Dostoevsky's Poetics*, trans. Caryl Emerson (Minneapolis, MN: University of Minnesota Press, 1984), 164.

57. Eliot, *Middlemarch*, 230.

58. Cited in Malcolm Andrews, *Dickensian Laughter* (Oxford: Oxford University Press, 2013), 80. Alan Partington, *The Linguistics of Laughter: A Corpus-Assisted Study of Laughter Talk* (New York: Routledge, 2006), 25.

59. Eliot, *Middlemarch*, 58; 46.

60. Wickberg, *The Senses of Humor*, 56.

61. Thomas Hobbes, *Leviathan* (Peterborough, ON: Broadview Press, 2002), 45.

62. Wickberg, *The Senses of Humor*, 56, 172.

63. Sydney Smith, *Elementary Sketches of Moral Philosophy* (London: Spottiswoodes and Shaw, 1849), 136; William Hazlitt, 'On Wit and Humour,' in *Lectures on the English Comic Writers* (New York: Russell & Russell, 1969), 4.

64. See Alfie Bown, *In the Event of Laughter: Psychoanalysis, Literature and Comedy* (New York: Bloomsbury, 2018), 1–6. Bown's ingenious application of Freud's concept of *nachträglichkeit*, and what Jean Laplanche in the 20th century termed 'après-coup,' to laughter theory, suggests new ways to think about comedy in relation to both experience and time. *Afterwardsness* has the greatest cultural potency, though, I suggest, when considered specifically in terms of the puzzle-solving aspects of incongruity.

65. It is noteworthy that another work of 1871, Lewis Carroll's *Through the Looking-Glass* is saturated with incongruities, and requires what the White Queen calls 'living backwards.' See *Through the Looking-Glass* (London: Macmillan & Co., 1872), chapter five.

66. Lauren Berlant, 'Humorlessness (Three Monologues and a Hairpiece),' *Critical Inquiry* 43 (Winter 2017): 308.

67. See Berlant's discussion of sovereignty: 308–310.

68. Bakhtin, *Problems of Dostoevsky's Poetics*, 164. See also John Bruns's discussion of 'form-shaping ideology' in *Loopholes: Reading Comically* (New Brunswick and London: Transaction Publishers, 2009), chapter three.

69. Mikhail Bakhtin, 'From Notes Made in 1970–71,' in *Speech Genres and Other Late Essays*, trans. Vern W. McGee, eds. Caryl Emerson and Michael Holquist (Austin, TX: University of Texas Press, 1986), 135.

70. Eliot, *Adam Bede*, 153.

71. See n.73 on Koestler and the 'discoveries' of incongruity/bisociation.

72. Arthur Schopenhauer, *The World as Will and Presentation* Vol. I, trans. Richard E. Aquila (New York: Pearson Longman, 2008), 93–94.

73. Arthur Koestler, *The Act of Creation* (London: Hutchinson and Company, 1964), 392. The term Koestler uses for incongruity is 'bisociation,' which, in a humorous context, rests on 'perceiving a situation or event in two habitually incompatible associative contexts.' (See *The Act of Creation*, 95.) But, like Partington's concept of 'aesthetic incongruity,' bisociation has wider applications in art and science, particularly in breaking through clichéd or formulaic thinking: delivering what Koestler calls the 'originality of genius' (392).

74. Bakhtin, *Dostoevsky's Poetics*, 165.

75. Moretti, *The Bourgeois*, 89.

76. James Kincaid, *Dickens and the Rhetoric of Laughter* (Oxford: Oxford University Press, 1971), 74.

77. 'delight, n.,' OED Online, June 2019, Oxford University Press. https:// www.oed.com/view/Entry/49382?rskey=20qfXM= (accessed July 16, 2019).

78. See uses of 'delight' in George Eliot, *Scenes of Clerical Life* (Hertfordshire: Wordsworth Editions, 2007), 4; Eliot, *Adam Bede*, 134.

79. Nicholas Dames, 'On Not Close Reading: The Prolonged Excerpt as Victorian Critical Protocol,' in *The Feeling of Reading: Affective Experience & Victorian Literature*, ed. Rachel Ablow (Ann Arbor, MI: University of Michigan Press, 2010), 18.

80. Koestler, *Act of Creation*, 299.

81. Moretti, *The Bourgeois*, 74.

82. Moretti, *The Bourgeois*, 74.

83. Eliot, *Middlemarch*, 349.

84. Schopenhauer, *Will and Presentation*, 94. Also, A. Schopenhauer, *The World as Will and Idea: Vol. II*, trans. R. B. Haldane and J. Kemp (Boston: Ticknor and Company, 1887), 280. The latter quotation concerns what Schopenhauer scathingly calls 'pedantry.'
85. George Levine, 'Introduction: George Eliot and the Art of Realism,' in *The Cambridge Companion to George Eliot*, ed. George Levine (Cambridge: Cambridge University Press, 2001), 8.
86. Juliette Atkinson, 'Critical Responses: to 1900,' in *George Eliot in Context*, ed. Margaret Harris (Cambridge: Cambridge University Press, 2013), 66.
87. Anonymous, 'Unsigned Review,' *Saturday Review*, 26 February 1859, vii, 250–251.
88. Eliot, *Letters*, II, 423.
89. E. S. Dallas, 'Adam Bede,' *The Times*, April 12, 1859, 5.
90. Anonymous, 'The Wit and Wisdom of George Eliot,' *The Spectator*, 13 January 1872, 43.
91. Eliot, *Letters*, V, 195.
92. Ibid., 199. For some useful Victorian responses to Eliot's humour, see Mark Irvine, 'Mrs (Polly) Lewes's Comic *Middlemarch*,' *George Eliot–George Henry Lewes Studies*, no. 34/35 (September 1998): 28–47.
93. Eliot, 'German Wit,' 3.
94. See Arthur Koestler, 'Joking Apart,' in *Bricks to Babel: Selected Writings with Comments by the Author* (London: Hutchinson, 1980), 328. I am indebted to Malcolm Andrews's excellent discussion of incongruity in *Dickensian Laughter*, 77–98.
95. Quoted in John Lippitt, 'Humor and Irony in the *Postscript*,' in *Kierkegaard's 'Concluding Unscientific Postscript': A Critical Guide*, ed. Rick Anthony Furtak (Cambridge: Cambridge University Press, 2010), 163.
96. Søren Kierkegaard. *Concluding Unscientific Postscript to the Philosophical Crumbs*, ed. and trans. Alastair Hannay (Cambridge: Cambridge University Press, 2009), 432n. See also Lippitt, 'Humor and Irony in the *Postscript*,' 151.
97. Sigmund Freud, *The Standard Edition of the Complete Psychological Works of Sigmund Freud, Volume V: The Interpretation of Dreams (Second Part) and On Dreams*, ed. and trans. James Strachey (London: Vintage, 2001), 578. Freud's account is of traumatic recall. For broader applications of 'mnemic traces,' see Cristina Alberini, ed. *Memory Reconsolidation* (London: Academic Press, 2013), chapter fourteen.
98. Gillian Beer, 'The Reader as Author,' *Authorship* 3, no. 1 (April 2014): 2.
99. George Eliot, *The Mill on the Floss* (Hertfordshire: Wordsworth Editions, 1995), 66.
100. Henri Bergson, *Laughter: An Essay on the Meaning of the Comic*, trans. Cloudesley Brereton and Fred Rothwell (Rockville Maryland: Arc

Manor, 2008), 13–14; see also Freud, *The Joke and Its Relation to the Unconscious*, chapter seven.
101. G. H. Lewes, 'Dickens in Relation to Criticism,' *Fortnightly Review* 11, no. 62 (February 1872): 148.
102. John Carey, *Here Comes Dickens: The Imagination of a Novelist* (Ann Arbor, MI: University of Michigan Press, 1974), 68.
103. Rae Greiner, *Sympathetic Realism in Nineteenth-Century British Fiction* (Baltimore: Johns Hopkins University Press, 2012), 24. Greiner is summarizing an argument here that appears in Harry E. Shaw, *Narrating Reality: Austen, Scott, Eliot* (Ithaca, NY: Cornell University Press, 1999), xi–xii.
104. Shaw, *Narrating Reality*, 14, 38–89; Greiner, *Sympathetic Realism*, 28.
105. The question was Thomas Mann's. See Moretti, *The Bourgeois*, 78–79.
106. Ibid., 79, 72.
107. See John Plotz, *Portable Property: Victorian Culture on the Move* (Princeton, NJ: Princeton University Press, 2008), 1–23; Moretti, *The Bourgeois*, 87.
108. Eliot, *Middlemarch*, 498.
109. See Gordon N. Ray, ed., *Thackeray's Contributions to the Morning Chronicle* (Urbana: University of Illinois Press, 1955), 90.
110. Shaw, *Narrating Reality*, 51. As Shaw explains, such 'immediacy stands in contrast to normal narrative texture.'
111. Quoted in Joyce Crick, 'Translator's Preface,' in Freud, *The Joke and Its Relation to the Unconscious*, xxix.
112. Moretti, *The Bourgeois*, 99.
113. Shaw, *Narrating Reality*, 51, 38–63. Shaw's point is specifically about ethical transparency.
114. See also Kate Flint, 'The Materiality of Middlemarch,' in *Middlemarch in the Twenty-First Century*, ed. Karen Chase (Oxford: Oxford University Press, 2006), 73.
115. The phrase is originally Adam Smith's. See Greiner, *Sympathetic Realism*, 15–49.
116. Shaw, *Narrating Reality*, 51.
117. Eliot, 'German Wit,' 3.
118. See the 'electric' imagery between Maggie Tulliver and Stephen Guest, in *The Mill on the Floss*, Book Six, chapter eleven.
119. Eliot, 'German Wit,' 3, 7.
120. Eileen Gillooly, *Smile of Discontent: Humor, Gender and Nineteenth-Century British Fiction* (Chicago: Chicago University Press, 1999), 166.
121. Eliot, 'Natural History of German Life,' 54.

122. George Eliot, *Daniel Deronda* (Hertfordshire: Wordsworth Editions, 1996), 314.

123. Eliot, *Middlemarch*, 295, 76.

124. Bergson, *Laughter*, 11.

125. Spencer, 'The Physiology of Laughter,' 399.

126. Eliot, *Adam Bede*, 452.

127. Ibid., 413.

128. Eliot, 'German Wit,' 28.

129. Ibid., 8–9. Italics in original.

130. Ibid., Italics in original.

131. Ibid., 31.

132. Eliot, *Mill on the Floss*, 51.

133. Ruth Wisse, *No Joke: Making Jewish Humor* (Princeton, NJ: Princeton University Press, 2015), 35.

134. See Jeffrey L. Sammons, *Heinrich Heine: A Modern Biography* (Princeton, NJ: Princeton University Press, 1979), parts V & VI.

135. Friedrich Nietzsche, *Twilight of the Idols*, trans. and ed. Duncan Large (Oxford: Oxford University Press, 1998), 45; Friedrich Nietzsche, *Ecce Homo: How to Become What You Are*, trans. and ed. Duncan Large (Oxford: Oxford University Press, 2009), 25. The other key figure of the mid-Victorian period who wrote on Heine was Matthew Arnold. See Arnold, 'Heinrich Heine,' *Cornhill Magazine*, 8 (1862): 233–249.

136. Eliot, *Daniel Deronda*, 134. The original quote is parenthesised.

137. Eliot, 'German Wit,' 6. Italics in the original.

138. See Dames, *The Physiology of the Novel*, chapter three.

139. See Thomas Carlyle, 'Jean Paul Friedrich Richter,' *Critical and Miscellaneous Essays Collected and Republished* (New York: Alden, 1885) 18. Also, Eliot, 'German Wit,' 4–5.

140. See discussions of Heine on the following pages in Freud, *The Joke*: 6–7, 11–15, 19, 29, 30, 31, 33, 39–40, 42–43, 45, 66–68, 74–76, 87, 111, 137–140, 142, 206.

141. Ibid., 223, 228.

142. See N. 118.

143. Jeanie Thomas, *Reading Middlemarch: Reclaiming the Middle Distance* (Michigan: Umi Research Press, 1987), 70.

144. Eliot, 'German Wit,' 7.

145. Eliot, 'Natural History of German Life,' 54.

146. Eliot, *Middlemarch*, 646–647.

147. Spencer, 'Physiology of Laughter,' 400–401.

WORKS CITED

Alberini, Cristina, ed. *Memory Reconsolidation*. London: Academic Press, 2013.

Anderson, Amanda, and Harry E. Shaw, eds. *A Companion to George Eliot*. Hoboken, NJ: John Wiley and Sons, 2016.

Andrews, Malcolm. *Dickensian Laughter*. Oxford: Oxford University Press, 2013.

Anonymous. 'The Wit and Wisdom of George Eliot.' *The Spectator*, January 13, 1872.

Anonymous. 'Unsigned Review.' *Saturday Review*, February 26, 1859.

Atkinson, Juliette. 'Critical Responses: to 1900.' In *George Eliot in Context*, edited by Margaret Harris, 65–73. Cambridge: Cambridge University Press, 2013.

Bakhtin, Mikhail. 'From Notes Made in 1970–71.' In *Speech Genres and Other Late Essays*. Translated by Vern W. McGee, edited by Caryl Emerson and Michael Holquist, 132–158. Austin, TX: University of Texas Press, 1986.

Bakhtin, Mikhail. *Problems of Dostoevsky's Poetics*. Translated by Caryl Emerson. Minneapolis, MN: University of Minnesota Press, 1984.

Barthes, Roland. 'The Reality Effect.' In *The Rustle of Language*. Translated by Richard Howard, edited by François Wahl, 141–148. Berkeley: University of California Press, 1989.

Beer, Gillian. 'The Reader as Author.' *Authorship* 3, no. 1 (April 2014): 1–9.

Beer, Gillian. *Darwin's Plots: Evolutionary Narrative in Darwin, George Eliot and Nineteenth-Century Fiction*. Cambridge: Cambridge University Press, 1983.

Bergson, Henri. *Laughter: An Essay on the Meaning of the Comic*. Translated by C. Brereton and F. Rothwell. Rockville Maryland: Arc Manor, 2008.

Berlant, Lauren. 'Humorlessness (Three Monologues and a Hairpiece).' *Critical Inquiry* 43 (Winter 2017): 305–340.

Billig, Michael. *Laughter and Ridicule: Towards a Social Critique of Humour*. New York: Sage, 2005.

Bown, Alfie. *In the Event of Laughter: Psychoanalysis, Literature and Comedy*. New York: Bloomsbury, 2018.

Carey, John. *Here Comes Dickens: The Imagination of a Novelist*. Ann Arbor, MI: University of Michigan Press, 1974.

Carlyle, Thomas. 'Jean Paul Friedrich Richter.' *Critical and Miscellaneous Essays Collected and Republished*. New York: Alden, 1885.

Carroll, David. *George Eliot: The Critical Heritage*. London: Routledge, 2000.

Chesterton, G. K. *Orthodoxy*. New York: Lane, 1909.

Dallas, E. S. 'Adam Bede.' *The Times*, April 12, 1859.

Dames, Nicholas. *The Physiology of the Novel: Neural Science and the Form of Victorian Fiction*. Oxford: Oxford University Press, 2007.

Dames, Nicholas. 'On Not Close Reading: The Prolonged Excerpt as Victorian Critical Protocol.' In *The Feeling of Reading: Affective Experience and Victorian Literature*, edited by Rachel Ablow, 11–26. Ann Arbor, MI: University of Michigan Press, 2010.

Darwin, Charles and Paul H. Barrett. *Charles Darwin's Notebooks 1836–1844*. Cambridge: Cambridge University Press, 1987.

Davies, Luke. 'The Way of the World: Franco Moretti, The Bourgeois: Between History and Literature.' *Review 31*. http://review31.co.uk/article/view/158/the-way-of-the-world (accessed January 20, 2020).

'delight, n.' OED Online. June 2019. Oxford University Press. https://www.oed.com/view/Entry/49382?rskey=20qfXM&result= (accessed July 16, 2019).

Eliot, George. *The George Eliot Letters*, 9 vols., Edited by Gordon S. Haight. New Haven and London: Yale University Press, 1954–1978.

Eliot, George. 'German Wit: Heinrich Heine.' *Westminster Review* 65 (January 1856): 1–33

Eliot, George. 'Notes on Form in Art.' In *George Eliot: Selected Essays, Poems and Other Writings*, edited by A. S. Byatt, 231–239. London: Penguin, 2005.

Eliot, George. 'Rachel Gray.' *Leader*, 7 (January 5, 1856).

Eliot, George. 'The Natural History of German Life.' *Westminster Review* 66 (July 1856): 51–79.

Eliot, George. *Adam Bede*, 1859. Hertfordshire: Wordsworth Editions, 1997.

Eliot, George. *Daniel Deronda*, 1876. Hertfordshire: Wordsworth Editions, 1996.

Eliot, George. *Middlemarch*, 1871–2. Hertfordshire: Wordsworth Editions, 1994.

Eliot, George. *Scenes of Clerical Life*, 1857. Hertfordshire: Wordsworth Editions, 2007

Eliot, George. *The Mill on the Floss*, 1860. Hertfordshire: Wordsworth Editions, 1995

Ermarth, Elizabeth Deeds. 'Negotiating Middlemarch.' In *Middlemarch in the 21st Century*, edited by Karen Chase, 107–132. Oxford: Oxford University Press, 2006.

Flint, Kate. 'The Materiality of Middlemarch.' In *Middlemarch in the Twenty-First Century*, edited by Karen Chase, 65–86. Oxford: Oxford University Press, 2006.

Freud, Sigmund. *The Joke and Its Relation to the Unconscious*. Translated by Joyce Crick. London: Penguin, 2003.

Freud, Sigmund. *The Standard Edition of the Complete Psychological Works of Sigmund Freud, Volume V: The Interpretation of Dreams (Second Part) and On Dreams*, edited and translated by James Strachey. London: Vintage, 2001.

Furtak, Rick Anthony, ed. *Kierkegaard's 'Concluding Unscientific Postscript': A Critical Guide*. Cambridge: Cambridge University Press, 2010.

Gillooly, Eileen. *Smile of Discontent: Humor, Gender, and Nineteenth-Century British Fiction.* Chicago: University of Chicago Press, 1999.

Greiner, Rae. *Sympathetic Realism in Nineteenth-Century British Fiction.* Baltimore: Johns Hopkins University Press, 2012.

Griffiths, Devin. *The Age of Analogy.* Baltimore: Johns Hopkins University Press, 2016.

Hazlitt, William. 'On Wit and Humour.' In *Lectures on the English Comic Writers.* New York: Russell & Russell, 1969.

Hillis-Miller, J. 'Optic and Semiotic in Middlemarch.' In *The Worlds of Victorian Fiction*, edited by Jerome Hamilton Buckley, 125–148. Cambridge, MA: Harvard University Press, 1975.

Hobbes, Thomas. *Leviathan*, 1651. Peterborough, Canada: Broadview Press, 2002.

Hutton, R. H. 'The Humour of Middlemarch.' *The Spectator*, December 14, 1872.

Irvine, Mark. 'Mrs (Polly) Lewes's Comic Middlemarch.' *George Eliot–George Henry Lewes Studies*, no. 34/35 (September 1998): 28–47.

James, Henry. Unsigned Review. *Galaxy* 15 (March 1873): 424–428.

John, Juliet. *Dickens's Villains: Melodrama, Character, Popular Culture.* Oxford: Oxford University Press, 2003.

Kaminsky, Alice. 'George Eliot, George Henry Lewes, and the Novel.' *PMLA* 70, no. 5 (December 1955): 997–1013.

Kierkegaard, Søren. *Concluding Unscientific Postscript to the Philosophical Crumbs*, edited and translated by Alastair Hannay. Cambridge: Cambridge University Press, 2009.

Kincaid, James. *Dickens and the Rhetoric of Laughter.* Oxford: Oxford University Press, 1971.

Koestler, Arthur. 'Joking Apart.' In *Bricks to Babel: Selected Writings with Comments by the Author*, 321–343. London: Hutchinson, 1982.

Koestler, Arthur. *The Act of Creation.* London: Hutchinson and Company, 1964.

Lane, Christopher. *Hatred & Civility: The Antisocial Life in Victorian England.* New York: Columbia University Press, 2004.

Levine, Caroline. 'Victorian Realism.' In *The Cambridge Companion to the Victorian Novel*, edited by Deirdre David, 84–106. Cambridge: Cambridge University Press, 2012.

Levine, George. 'Introduction: George Eliot and the Art of Realism.' In *The Cambridge Companion to George Eliot*, edited by George Levine, 1–19. Cambridge: Cambridge University Press, 2001.

Lewes, G. H. 'Dickens in Relation to Criticism.' *Fortnightly Review* 11, no. 62 (February 1872): 141–154.

Lippitt, John. 'Humor and Irony in the Postscript.' In *Kierkegaard's 'Concluding Unscientific Postscript': A Critical Guide*, edited by Rick Anthony Furtak. Cambridge: Cambridge University Press, 2010.

Matz, Aaron. *Satire in an Age of Realism*. Cambridge: Cambridge University Press, 2010.

Meredith, George. 'On the Idea of Comedy, and of the Uses of the Comic Spirit.' *New Quarterly Magazine* 8 (January–July 1877): 1–40.

Moretti, Franco. 'Serious Century.' In *The Novel: History, Geography, and Culture*, vol. 1, edited by Franco Moretti, 365–400. Princeton, NJ: Princeton University Press, 2006.

Moretti, Franco. *The Bourgeois: Between History and Literature*. London: Verso Books, 2013.

Ngai, Sianne. *Ugly Feelings*. Cambridge, MA: Harvard University Press, 2005.

Nietzsche, Friedrich. *Ecce Homo: How to Become What You Are*. Translated and edited by Duncan Large. Oxford: Oxford University Press, 2009.

Nietzsche, Friedrich. *Twilight of the Idols*. Translated and edited by Duncan Large. Oxford: Oxford University Press, 2008.

Pater, Walter. 'Charles Lamb.' In *Appreciations: With an Essay on Style*. London: Macmillan & Co., 1889.

Plotz, John. 'Review of *The Bourgeois: Between History and Literature* by Franco Moretti.' *Victorian Studies* 56, no. 4 (Summer 2014): 734–736.

Plotz, John. *Portable Property: Victorian Culture on the Move*. Princeton: Princeton University Press, 2008.

Ray, Gordon N. ed. *Thackeray's Contributions to the Morning Chronicle*. Urbana: University of Illinois Press, 1955.

Ray, Martin. *Thomas Hardy Remembered*. London: Routledge, 2017.

Sammons, Jeffrey L. *Heinrich Heine: A Modern Biography*. Princeton NJ: Princeton University Press, 1979.

Schopenhauer, Arthur. *The World as Will and Presentation, Vol. I*. Translated by Richard E. Aquila. London: Routledge, 2016.

Schopenhauer, Arthur. *The World as Will and Idea: Vol. II*. Translated by R. B. Haldane and J. Kemp, Boston: Ticknor and Company, 1887.

Shaw, Harry E. *Narrating Reality: Austen, Scott, Eliot*. Ithaca, NY: Cornell University Press, 1999.

Smith, Sydney. *Elementary Sketches of Moral Philosophy*. London: Spottiswoodes and Shaw, 1849.

Spencer, Herbert. 'The Physiology of Laughter.' *Macmillan's Magazine* 1 (March 1860): 395–402.

Stephen, Leslie. 'Humour.' *Cornhill Magazine* 33 (March 1876): 318–326.

Thompson, E. P. *The Making of the English Working Class*. London: Pelican Books, 1963.

West, Anna. *Thomas Hardy and Animals*. Cambridge: Cambridge University Press, 2017.

Wickberg, Daniel. *The Senses of Humor: Self and Laughter in Modern America*. Ithaca, NY: Cornell University Press, 1998.

Wisse, Ruth. *No Joke: Making Jewish Humor*. Princeton, NJ: Princeton University Press, 2015.

The Game of Words: A Victorian Clown's Gag-Book and Circus Performance

Ann Featherstone

Even in its eighteenth-century infancy, the Victorian circus always included a funny man or clown. He is visible in some of the earliest depictions of Astley's Riding School on Westminster Bridge Road, a colourful, grotesque figure, poised for action in the ring, or running alongside the equestrian performer. Dressed in a highly decorated white suit and with a white face, the clown encouraged an audience's admiration for the skills they were enjoying by imitating the equestrian or the acrobat—and failing—while also covering up any shortcomings and faulty timing in the programme, keeping 'the ball rolling and the audience in good humour'.[1]

Throughout the nineteenth century, the circus clown managed the audience, and from this difficult position developed a varied repertoire of verbal as well as physical tricks. Alongside his ability as proficient equestrian, acrobat or balancer (like Les Dawson on the piano or Tommy Cooper as a magician, a performer must be an adept in order to play the fool), the clown worked on his personal relationship with the circus audience through material which connected with them. They might be parodies of melodrama or Shakespeare, stump speeches on topics close to

A. Featherstone (✉)
University of Manchester, Manchester, UK

© The Author(s) 2020
L. Lee (ed.), *Victorian Comedy and Laughter*,
https://doi.org/10.1057/978-1-137-57882-2_7

an audience's heart, elaborate monologues, reworkings of familiar songs, short gags and backchat, all expertly delivered within the close confines of the circus ring. As an indignant circus clown wrote in response to being called 'an annoyance and a bore':

> A Circus Clown is expected to vault, ride in saddle, hold balloons and ban-
> ners, ride comic ponies, act combats and play parts in pieces, practice every
> day, and are the worst paid men in the Profession.[2]

Why this clown (and many others) was so abused forms a sidelight to this essay since it has as much to do with the content of the clown's material as the audience's response to it. Throughout the nineteenth century, the clown was the target of attacks in newspapers (and perhaps at the performance also) from critical spectators who complained of the 'stale, flat and unprofitable' quality of the material. The responsibility of the clown, it was claimed, was to take ownership of his material, ensuring that it was topical, humorous and original and, above all, that old jokes were not repeated ad nauseam:

> Why are the same old wearisome jokes and time belaboured jests repeated
> year after year? ... If [clowns] have not the ability themselves can they not
> get some one to write them something original? Or, barring this, why
> don't they read the comic and American papers?[3]

It was a moot point, although commentators on the other side of the fence, often with a more sentimental regard for the circus, saw the clown's 'old favourites' as part of the safe and predictable circus expe-rience; clowns reliably represented those softer, unchanging, innocent emotions connected with the family and childhood. Perhaps everyone wanted the personal experience of seeing 'a little grandson [laughing] immoderately at the grimace of the clown', and even if they failed to appreciate the clown's performance, at least could leave the circus with a feeling of superiority.[4]

Material for their ring performance was surely accumulated by the many hundreds of clowns who populated the travelling and permanent English circuses, although whether or not they routinely wrote it down is unknowable. The clown's gag-book in any form, however, is as rare as hen's teeth, so there is every possibility that the gag-books belong-ing to Thomas Lawrence (1818–1896) are a unique survival.[5] During the time he was professionally active as a circus clown, between c.1865 and c.1873, he kept a personal record of his material in two hand-written notebooks. One is clearly a working copy, battered and well-used, with pages clipped, torn and some missing. The other notebook, which formed the basis for the material in *The Victorian Clown*,[6] repeated some of that material and was clearly a 'best' or master copy. Lawrence seems to have been in the process of transferring material from the first to the second book, rewriting it in a better hand, correcting some of the spelling errors and generally sharpening it. These wheezes are often revised versions of the originals, which suggests that Lawrence, during the ten or so years when he worked as a circus clown, modified and developed his material through performance.[7] But not every wheeze was transferred; the master copy is shorter than the working copy and there are blank pages. Perhaps he had not finished transferring the material before he became the proprietor of a portable theatre (in 1873) when he no longer needed the gag-book. Perhaps he decided that some of the material needed more work or had been unsuccessful in the ring and did not warrant a place in the master copy. Given, then, that this master copy is reproduced in its entirety in *The Victorian Clown*, this article will explore some of the material from the working copy which Lawrence chose to leave out of his master copy, and use it to illustrate the types of wheezes, their subjects and treatment, and their position as performance texts in the circus ring.

Lawrence did not organise the material in either notebook; very short wheezes sit alongside much longer recitations, burlesques and parodies. Content and layout suggest that Lawrence only ever intended the first notebook to be his working material, and I picture it, perhaps left in a familiar, safe place just inside the ring doors of the circus where he could consult it during the performance, turning the pages quickly to remind himself of a particular wheeze. It was 'hys boke' and he knew it well, hence its apparent disorder and the physical evidence of being well-used.

But at a distance of over 150 years, some imagination is required to appreciate how this material was performed and received. Its place was embedded in the extraordinary phenomenon of the Victorian circus which, after the mid-century, was still focused upon the equestrians—horses galloping, dancing, performing intricate steps, acting—but with additional acrobatic, balancing and strength acts, assembled in a seamless performance without breaks. Although the clown certainly had his own 'spot' or two, where a long, elaborate piece might be performed (a mute two-hander on a tightrope, perhaps, or an extended and intricate wheeze on a particular theme), the clown was ever-present in or near the ring to provide the connective tissue to the show. He was always on hand to cover the exits and entrances, the inevitable delays and breaks in the performance while performers (human and animal) caught their breath. Perfection in execution, for example, was aspired to but was not a given. Thus a trick on a horse or a complex somersault might take two or three attempts before it was accomplished and between those attempts were pauses which must be filled. Circuses were proud of their bands which might provide a *continuo*, but it was the clown's responsibility to 'mind the gap' of an indeterminate duration. The clown's input was not, then, a performance that could be planned to the letter, thus improvisational and ad-libbing skills were necessary. With one eye on the ring doors, watching for the re-entrance of the equestrian, or with an ear to the ringmaster for a cue to 'wind up', the clown selected from his repertoire of wheezes, ranging from old gags, sketches and songs, to parodies of melodrama or Shakespeare, for something to fit the moment and suit the audience.

The old short wheezes, often termed 'Sayings', were clearly best suited to a brief fill-in between acts or in the pauses:

> The height of nonsense is kissing an old Woman when there's a young one close by.
> Don't I look like a descendent of the seasons – my father was a season – he was a bumbailiff, he often used to seize.
> Why are the ladies the biggest thieves in the world they crib their babies, they bone their stays and they steel their petticoats.[8]

Both of Lawrence's gag-books have pages of these utilitarian wheezes reflecting the themes which populate his material: relationships, women, money troubles, trades, the fragility of life. Framed as a pun, which lies at the heart of these and many of Lawrence's wheezes, they sit awkwardly on the page, and thus only really come alive in the delivery. But there are no directions for performance: since he owned the material, Lawrence would not have needed any. Doubtless he instinctively or over years of practice (learning on the job as Victorian clowns did) demonstrated the advice given to Peter Paterson when he first became a clown. 'Just gag it', he was told by Chirper the ringmaster, 'and by a little physical exertion an immense deal of fun may be made out of nothing'.[9] Gagging—a term which often meant ad-libbing—suggests energetic performance, verbally and physically, using the circus ring and the clown's proximity to the audience. Often key to his energetic play-fulness was the ring fence, that substantial barrier, perhaps three or four feet high and two feet wide, which separated the pit from the arena and onto which the clown might leap and run around. The physical distance between ring, ring fence and the pit audience was so small it is hardly surprising that the clown and other performers often took advantage of that intimacy to approach spectators, even sitting with them or shaking hands. Proximity meant that nothing was lost on the audience. Indeed, 'Sayings' such as, 'Is that lady a relation of yours—because she is very much like you—with this little difference, she is graceful and you are dis-graceful' exploited it, allowing the clown to raise a smile and endear him-self by complementing the lady and mildly insulting the gentleman.

This was probably an old wheeze, the kind that audiences had heard before, and it was the material for which the clown was criticised (and quite harshly) for its lack of novelty. But those 'miserable old jokes', brought out quickly to cover a pause while the ring was cleared, also had a mild if sentimental appeal.[10] For the clown, old wheezes must have come swiftly to hand or mind, were accumulated from the ready sup-ply within the circus company; Tom Lawrence's gag-book acknowledges material given to him by 'George Nice', the strongman, and Mr Chirper recommended Peter Paterson to apply to the ringmaster who 'has all the old standard ones ready cut and dry'.[11]

The ring clown worked closely with all his professional colleagues, rehearsing with the equestrians and acrobats so that he was familiar with their tricks and could swiftly 'fill in' when required, and burlesque their skills when they left the ring. But his most intimate relationship was with his fellow clowns and, most importantly, the ringmaster. Many of the wheezes in the gag-books involve the clown working directly with ring-master, the archetypal authority figure and straight man, as in the open-ing of the wheeze Lawrence calls 'Man of Property':

> Don't you push against me – you did – (Bus pushing against ringmaster) you are not the Queen Victoria, nor you are not the Board of Works, nor you can't do everything, you can't lift a railway tunnel on a toasting fork, nor you can't pay a debt of 7 shillings with 2 s 6d, nor you haven't got

all the money in the world – well I have and sixpence more – I have more money than I know what to do with – yes I have – <u>bad Half Crowns</u> I don't know what to do with them, I'll let you know I am a Lord – (<u>Lord who</u>) The Lord knows who for I don't.[12]

Here the 'get in' or opening is an often-used complaint against the ringmaster with accompanying physical business: they push each other around. Lawrence uses the shorthand dash, often found in nineteenth-century printed dramas, for the second speaker's reply and the pause that might accompany, and it is only when he needs a very specific reply does he give it in full, in parentheses and frequently underlined (<u>Lord who</u>). The success of this kind of exchange depended upon the relationship between the clown and the ringmaster. Often this was presented in the form of a servant-master relationship, since the ringmaster was frequently the owner of the circus, but it is recognisable also as the basis for many double acts, with the ringmaster playing the middle-class man in charge to the clown's 'working-class underling, more goofy than glamorous'.[13]

The immediate reality of the ring underpins the interactions between Lawrence's clown and members of the circus company. Physical business evolves from the situation in the ring, whether running against the ringmaster in slapstick, or more contrived scenes such as the 'Buss. For Tight Rope' where two clowns parody the skills of other circus performers.[14] Here Clown Joe, acting as clown to the rope during the real act that precedes this piece, is joined by Clown Tom (Lawrence) to silently burlesque the rope dancing act. Neither speak, although according to Lawrence's instructions 'The clowns can whistle to each other as though talking'.[15] It is a protracted wheeze, with Tom in the lead and Clown Joe the foil, relying upon their real rope skills to throw into relief the skills of the departed rope act.

Interaction with the audience is a given throughout the clown's performance, including response to the audience's applause, laughter and participation. The 'Sayings' (above) depend upon the clown directing his performance to specific members of the audience. Certainly much humour and goodwill might be derived from a playful and benign relationship between clown and audience, one in which the clown was known by name and eagerly anticipated and enjoyed. Interaction is frequently written into Tom Lawrence's wheezes, with dashes or parentheses representing the response or action of the participant, as in another collection of 'Sayings', where the clown appears to be addressing an individual in the audience. Here dashes represent both names (which can be varied and thus made local) and responses:

> Is that – What the young – son of the old – Well I am very glad to see you (shakes Hands) and how is the missus – Well I am very glad to see you (Hands) and how is the little ones – Well I am very glad to see you (Hands) and are you quite well – Well I am very glad to see you (Hands) and are you doing pretty well – Well I am glad to see you (Hands) let me see where did I see you last – so it was Well I am very glad to see you (Hands) (Ring master – and why are you so glad to see him) Because he is the man that stole my umbrella.[16]

The repeated action—shaking hands—and the phrase—'Well I am very glad to see you'—are benign and inoffensive, unlikely to cause pain or distress, and is given so politely that the participant, willing or not, would probably not have refused the clown's outstretched hand. It is this repetition in the context of the wheeze that sets up the audience to anticipate the pay-off and it is the ringmaster who asks the question that is in everyone's mind—'why are you so glad to see him?' Typically, the punch-line is at once bathetic—'Because he is the man that stole my umbrella'—and deals a closing comic blow: there is nowhere for this wheeze to go after it and there is nothing more for the clown to do. Success relies, to a large extent, on the complicity of the audience member (it seems unlikely to have been another clown) who, though he is not required to do anything other than shake hands, must invest, however reluctantly, in the progress of the wheeze.

But perhaps Lawrence's audience member was a plant. Certainly, the Shakespearean clown, W. F. Wallett (1806–1892), made use of personal acquaintances in the audience to add a local flavour to his performance. In his autobiography he refers to a quarrel in the ring with another clown who threatened to knock his teeth out.[17] Wallett, knowing that a 'swell dentist' called Mann was sitting in the audience, retorted: 'You may be the man that can knock my teeth out, but you are not the Mann that can put them in again'.[18]

Wallett's autobiographical claims to settling scores in the ring, while doubtless included to build that superior impression he always wanted to create, is still indicative of the power that the clown holds. That licence to amuse, even if he offended, though distant from its Elizabethan roots, was taken seriously by talking clowns like Wallett and served to establish the reputation of a man not to be trifled with but who, at the same time, expected to have the audience's sympathy. Wallett relates the story of the man who visited the circus nightly and constantly cried 'Variety!' whenever the clowns entered, presumably as an ironic comment on the indifferent quality of their wheezes. Irritated by this and seeing him in the audience, seated between two prostitutes, Wallett took his revenge. 'Ladies and gentlemen', he said, 'you have heard that fellow for upwards of a hundred times tonight bawling out "Variety"'. This man, he continued, is married with children and yet 'he comes here tonight with two of the commonest women of the town' and that is what he calls 'variety'.[19]

Elsewhere, Wallett got the better of an annoying heckler by using information fed to him from the audience (he was sitting on the ring fence getting whispered gossip from them) to reveal unsavoury details of the heckler's private life to the man's discomfort and the audience's, perhaps uneasy, delight.[20] But as contemporary comedians have said, getting the better of the heckler is a delicate manoeuvre which doesn't always pay-off. Ted Ray's response to a heckler shouting: 'When are you going to say something funny?' was 'When you get a little more intelligence to understand it!' which echoes Wallett's more acerbic retorts. While Wallett doesn't describe the audience's response to his put-downs, Ray reports that his comeback backfired and that 'the interruption had upset the audience. I had lost them'. Bruce Forsyth, on the other hand, eating the chips thrown at him at the Wood Green Empire and commenting 'Too much vinegar and not enough salt', reclaimed an openly hostile crowd.[21]

Awkward members of the audience and willing participants in the hands of a skilled clown could establish a powerful dynamic from which uncomfortable humour or mild amusement might be derived. Specific members of the audience might be thus targeted for ridicule but also for more benign purposes. In his autobiography, circus clown James Frowde wrote about the handsome young American equestrian James Hernandez and how he, Frowde, effected an introduction between Hernandez and a very pretty girl seated in the front of the pit. Turning somersaults, striking a pose, and then leaping onto the ring fence to enchant the pretty girl and amuse the audience, the equestrian and the clown between them made her a feature of the act.[22] That she was flattered and willing seems indisputable according to Frowde's account.

Complaints were rarely made about a clown's 'fooling' where he overstepped his professional limits at the expense of a single member of an audience and alienated others. But this did occur in Edinburgh at Cooke's Circus when Clown Ernest was accused of embarrassing a lady occupant of the pit. While it illustrates the risks involved, it also highlights the careful professional judgement that needed to be exercised when involving unprepared participants, and the unpredictable perceptions of other members of the audience. 'Ladies are usually considered fit subjects for the "mirth producing" emanations of the clown', wrote a complainant to the local newspaper, 'their discomfiture having a seemingly pleasing effect upon the audience'. So much is clear from some of Tom Lawrence's wheezes and 'get ins' in which he singles out a woman for a compliment; women were soft targets, the potential butt of a mild joke and unlikely to retaliate. But Clown Ernest had targeted 'a respectable old lady', had left the ring and sat beside her to say in a loud voice: 'This is the woman that had three sons'.[23] This was a seemingly innocuous reference to a well-known nursery rhyme:

> There was an old woman had three sons,
> Jerry, and James, and John:
> Jerry was hung, James was drowned,
> John was lost and never was found,
> And there was an end of the three sons,
> Jerry, and James, and John![24]

But Clown Ernest could not have predicted the lady's response: she was so embarrassed that she hid her face. Whether this was simply because she had been singled out, or the implications of the nursery rhyme—that she had produced three sons, had thus been married or at least engaged in sexual activity—or some local or topical reason that we cannot know of, is unclear. But Clown Ernest was sufficiently moved to protect his professional reputation and make a response in writing to the newspaper. What he says comes as something of a surprise; he claims that the 'respectable old lady' was in fact a 'plant', had been 'spoken to and arranged with prior to commencing the evening's entertainment'. Indeed, he goes on to say, most clowns, including himself 'manage their jokes in this way' by seeking permission first from their victims. He even claims that he receives letters from strangers who tell him that they will be in the audience and what they will wear and begging him to target them, 'knowing ... that a little innocent joke perpetrated by the clown is not meant for an instant'.[25]

Of course, Clown Ernest may have been desperately wriggling to get out of a very awkward situation, but the incident points up the complexity of the relationship between the clown and his audience. Those unspecified, ad-libbed moments of intimacy, prefaced by a wink or a rush to the ring face, blowing kisses and kissing hands, are not noted in Lawrence's gag-books, but they were clearly present, the physical asides which fuelled the spoken humour. And although the gag-books reveal few direct addresses to individuals, the material as a whole is suggestive of a very close understanding with the audience. Lawrence occasionally adopts a persona—a love-sick simpleton, for example—but mostly he is himself and engages in a direct exchange of beliefs and prejudices with his audience with whom, in the majority, he anticipates a social affinity. It is around the themes which all will understand—love, courtship, marriage, women, work, poverty, food and drink, soldiers, railways, time and others—that he builds a mildly radical but not outwardly political body of wheezes.

In reflecting the attitude of the times and the prejudices of the audience, this is nowhere more clear than in his attitude towards women. The wheeze entitled 'A Woman in Distress' is typical:

> I saw a Poor Woman in the churchyard sitting on a gravestone crying as though her heart would break and curiosity prompted me to ask her what was the matter, and she seemed so struck down by grief that she could not answer ...[26] However after a good deal of Persuasion she told that she was mourning of the loss of her Husband, and of course I tried to comfort her as much as I could and I said Dry your Eyes and let us Hope he is gone to a Better Place. Ho she said it's all very well for you to talk, But there lays 30 bob a Week and a Bundle of Chips every Saturday Night.[27]

The set-up establishes the sentimental scene of the clown coming across the grieving widow, Lawrence taking his time to prepare the ground, in particular the severity of her grief as she sits at her husband's graveside. The matter of fact narrative in which the clown's sympathy is expressed serves to increase the audience's anticipation of the pay-off, which comes in the form of a frequently used device—the bathetic 'crusher', here privileging rank materialism (money and chips) over love and fond remembrance. The wheeze reminds men what women really think of them and how little they are valued.

The reverse, expressed in the majority of the wheezes in the gag-book, is an unremitting hostility towards women, entirely in keeping with similar traits in popular culture.[28] Wheezes depend upon old tropes such as the length of women's tongues (they talk too much, too vacuously, too indiscreetly, always with the suspicion that they are insulting men) and women's appearance. Though the object of the clown's adoration in the circus ring was the beautiful equestrienne, in his wheezes his pleasure is to elaborate on women's physical ugliness, as in the 'Blacksmith's Daughter':

> She was a Blacksmiths Daughter mild and meek
> With Tinpot Head, and Hot Iron cheek
> She'd Fiery Eyes, and rasp like Tongue
> And the Hair on her Head like Horsenails Hung.
> She'd a mouth like a vice, and cold chisel teeth
> Compass legs, and sledge Hammer Feet
> Her Hands were like Pincers, she'd Hob nail Toes
> She'd a Blow Bellows Face and a Anvil Nose.[29]

Here the clown compares the blacksmith's daughter's body parts to various hard and hideous items from the smithy in an inverted love-song, mocking rather than celebrating the body of the beloved. Its humour might be grotesque, even playful, but it does not disguise an undercurrent of violence. Lawrence copied this wheeze into the second gag-book, adding another piece to make a more solid—and overtly misogynistic—conclusion. This tail-piece involves physical business in the ring:

> She was an uncommon sort of girl there was a neatness in her style of dress, did you notice her Bonnet – wasn't it a little duck – I gave her that; then her Boots did you see them – I gave her them; and her Jacket did you take notice of that: - wasn't it a beauty – I gave her that; and her Eyes; you must have noticed them. Yes they were black. I gave her them! Buss: squares at ringmaster.

The pay-off, built from the mounting repetition of 'I gave her that' (spoken by Tom and emphasised by the underlining), is the confirmation of violent intent and the relish in it, culminating, as though reaching a climax, in the offer to fight the ringmaster.[30] In another wheeze, titled

'Good and Bad Job', Lawrence tops and tails it with, once again, unkind, grotesque observations on his sweetheart's appearance, and a get-out where he congratulates himself on burning his wife in a house-fire:

> You never saw my sweetheart – she was a nice Creature only she'd got but one eye (Blinded) then she'd got no nose (Snuff) only got one arm (search) then she got a wooden leg (let her out) 2000 lb (good Job) that was a Bad Job because I Bought sheep and they died of the rot (Bad) no that was a good Job. I sold the skins for more money than I gave for the carcases (G) no that was a Bad Job because I took a Public House and stocked it well with Beer and the Thunder turned all the ale sour (Bad) no that was a good Job because I sold the vinegar at 10d Per Quart so I made 6d Per Quart extra profit (good) no that was a Bad Job for I Bought a row of Houses with the money and they were all Burnt to the ground (Bad) no that was a good Job for I Insured them for 9 times the value and when the Houses were Burnt my Wife was Burnt with them so I got clear of the Lot at one Hit.

This is a curious wheeze, a two-hander, requiring carefully timed responses of either the ringmaster or another clown, those responses quickly becoming predictable (good followed by bad); it is quite conceivable that the audience is encouraged to join in, perhaps shouting them out as the pattern is established. But it is not a very clever wheeze, nor particularly funny on the page, a strange mash of misogyny, audience participation and commentary on the ups and downs of commercial life—buying a public house where thunder turns the ale to vinegar which is sold at a profit, buying a row of houses only to have them burn down but making a profit from the insurance. And getting rid of his wife to boot. There are no belly-laughs here but, performed at a lick with 'plenty of gag', it may have been successful, though, significantly, Lawrence does not include it in his master copy.

Another topic which matches that of women, is found in what might be termed the broad compass of everyday life, from trades and their working hours, to tiredness, food and accidents. 'Good and Bad Job' (above) allowed Lawrence to develop or curtail the extended conceit depending, as always, on the requirements of the ring performance; it is a wheeze that has a punch-line which, with a little manipulation, can be inserted anywhere. Wheezes such as 'Trades' (another variant on the extended conceit which appears frequently in the gag-book) allows him to play with puns. It begins:

I have always been unlucky nothing seems to Prosper with me. Once I got a Situation to carry two Boards. I was a Walking Sandwich I had Jenny Lind in front and Holloways Ointment up my Back, a shilling a week and my <u>Board.</u> Then I turned Barber, but they Didn't rush to the <u>Pole</u> I had to live on the <u>Hair,</u> and I found it a close <u>shave</u> to do that, then I turned Pawnbroker, I took a Partner, he <u>Pledged</u> his Word but – he never <u>Redeemed</u> it, one day he Bolted, and left me nothing but the three <u>balls</u> and the <u>run</u> of the spout, which was not the <u>Ticket.</u> So I left that and turned <u>Baker</u> that Being a <u>flowery</u> Business. I went in a <u>Buster</u> and tho I sold a <u>Cottage</u> for twopence they Didn't call me a <u>Brick</u> so I made a <u>turno-ver</u> and <u>Peel'd</u> out – before I was Quite <u>Baked.</u>

This wheeze (which continues for another 300 words) elaborates on a set of puns based on the jargon of various trades from barbering to carpentering. Once again, on the page, it is difficult to see how it might work *as a whole*; it is much too long and rather tedious. But broken down into smaller sections it was probably clever enough, and certainly would be one of those wheezes which Lawrence might have brought out if he had an indeterminate amount of time to fill since, without the necessity for a punch-line, he could wind it up it at any point. A similar function might be ascribed to the wheeze Lawrence cues at the end of 'Trades'—'Then I turned newsvendor, so that I could sit behind my very own counter (<u>and crack the newspaper Wheeze)</u>':

That's the Way to Bring up your Children, tough and Hardy. Bring them up like nails, not only that you can Drive them through the World but you may clench them on the other side. I Hardly know What to Bring my children [to]. I know What I should like to be if I had my Time to come again – I should like to be a London News Vendor – why I could set Behind my own Counter and Read the <u>Daily and Weekly News</u> that Would Put me in Possession of the <u>News of the World</u> I could Snap my Fingers at the <u>Times</u> Study the <u>Stars,</u> morning and evening that would make me an <u>Observer</u> I could <u>Chronicle</u> the Events of the Week, and in this <u>Sporting Life</u> I could Play with <u>Toby</u> Kiss <u>Judy</u> and <u>Weekly Advertiser</u> in the <u>World we Live in</u> the <u>Globe</u> Would yield me its Choicest Blessing which would raise me to such a <u>Standard</u> in this <u>Era</u> of life that I could <u>Daily Telegraph</u> to my Friends abroad to take <u>Punch</u> with me <u>Once a Week</u> and be Happy <u>All the Year Round.</u>[31]

A shorter wheeze (with an introductory riff on, perhaps, the children or young performers leaving the ring) and a sharper one than 'Trades' and, working on the audience's familiarity with not simply the newspapers but with the conceit itself and the in-built pauses (as the audience digests the pun), this has the potential to be performed in its entirety with pace, energy and 'gag'.

The wheezes in Lawrence's gag-book are a reminder that what is noted down is not necessarily what is performed, particularly in terms of totality. These are not precious objects in the sense of being speeches, but are working materials which had to be flexible enough to be terminated on cue. But like the 'Newspaper wheeze' above, there are wheezes which seem to be written as a contained piece. 'With Balloons' is a physical wheeze using balloons (those paper hoops through which equestrians and acrobats jumped) as props. The physical 'business' is here underlined by Lawrence:

> Are these Balloons, they look like overgrown Pancakes. Did you ever study astronomy – it's firmly Believed that the Globe Works on its own axis – if the axis was to Break Down, What Would become of you and me.
> <u>Bus with Balloons. Makes 7 Holes with finger</u>
> those are the seven sisters. <u>Tears a long hole</u>
> that is the Equator or Equinoctial line
> <u>another long hole</u> that's the comet with a long tail
> <u>puts arm through and strikes ringmaster</u> thats the north pole <u>puts Head through</u> and that's the man in the moon.[32]

This, like many of the wheezes in the first gag-book, seems to be a work in progress, with Lawrence perhaps envisioning the performance rather than recording it. The detail of the physical business is suggestive of the former which allows the physicality of the performance to carry a rather indifferent wheeze forward and it speaks to that facility of the talking clown to match erudition and learning with buffoonery. Its humour lies almost entirely in its performance, the clown interacting with the audience, the balloons and, of course, the pay-off with the ringmaster who, as usual, is the recipient of the clown's violence. The final thrust has the clown putting his head through the balloon as 'the man in the moon' with, we might speculate, an attendant funny face, and recalling gurning collars and similar practices throughout the country.[33]

Lawrence's gag-book also contains samples of what he calls 'poietry', verses which cover the themes reflected elsewhere. Some are substantial pieces (hardly wheezes) running to four or five verses, carefully set out and perhaps copied from a printed source. Others demonstrate knowledge of material which is bent and shaped to suit the circus ring. So 'Old Dog Tray' (an incomplete 'poim') is a somewhat weak parody of Stephen Foster's sentimental verses (published around 1853) on the speaker's attachment to his faithful dog. In Foster's poem and song, the speaker reflects on the mute love and sympathy of Old Tray now that, in old age, he finds friends and loved ones dead and he is alone. The sentimental attachment to Old Tray is celebrated in the chorus which runs:

> Old dog Tray's ever faithful,
> Grief cannot drive him away,
> He's gentle, he is kind;
> I'll never, never find
> A better friend than old dog Tray.[34]

Lawrence's poem—he may have sung it, since it was also a popular Christy Minstrel piece—gives the original a burlesque twist: Old Dog Tray is now 'departed', a victim of the introduction, in 1796, of a Dog Tax: five shillings on sporting dogs and three shillings on the rest. By 1812, it had quadrupled and was seen for what it really was—a source of government revenue. Over the years, many animals were killed when their owners could not afford the tax and this is the fate of Poor Dog Tray:

> A story I will tell, of a Friend who loved me Well
> Alas he's gone and long Passed away
> When his sand of life was run
> I lost my greatest chum
> The company of Poor Dog Tray
>
> Old Dog Tray was ever Faithful
> Grief came upon him one Fine Day
> For the Governmental Acts
> Would insist upon the Tax
> Which Prov'd Fatal to my Poor Dog Tray.
>
> He was very Fond of rats
> And a mortal foe to Cats
> We were more like Brothers than I care to say
> But twelve shillings every Year
> For his Company was dear
> So I parted with my Old Dog Tray

Old Dog Tray would eat a Plateful
Bears could not Drive him away
They Bore him from my sight
Which overcame me Quite
Faithful Friend was old Dog Tray[35]

An example of the continuum between oral and printed song culture, the circus, music hall and theatre, as well as street performance (Christy Minstrels were discovered on street corners), Lawrence makes a lovely job of de-sentimentalising Foster's original while retaining that fond attachment of the man to his faithful hound. And given that it was conceivably situated in the midst of equestrian and acrobatic demonstrations, it provided an emotional antidote to the physical pieces in the circus programme.

Lawrence's gag-books, then, offer a unique insight into the humour and performance of the Victorian circus clown, challenging the notion that he was the clichéd red-nosed, white-trousered harmless buffoon, appealing to small children and old men nostalgically revisiting their childhood. Lawrence's wheezes are specific and concrete and resist generalisations and sentimentality. They capture moments of popular culture which echo minstrelsy, melodrama and music hall, and demonstrate how the verbose conceit and the self-conscious pun, so popular in Victorian print, might be realised with 'side', edge and gender hostility, in the repertoire and wheezes of the circus clown.

NOTES

1. Peter Paterson, *Glimpses of Real Life as Seen in the Theatrical World and in Bohemia: Being the Confessions of Peter Paterson, a Strolling Comedian.* (Edinburgh: William P. Nimmo, 1864), 115.
2. *The Era*, 11 February 1866.
3. *The Era*, 4 August 1883.
4. *Western Mail*, 26 January 1880.
5. Generously donated to Royal Holloway, University of London by Lawrence's descendant, the late Paul Newman, I am grateful to be able to reproduce some of the material from Tom Lawrence's gag-books in this article.
6. Jacky Bratton and Ann Featherstone, *The Victorian Clown* (Cambridge: Cambridge University Press, 2006).

7. The wheeze (often spelt 'weaze' or 'weese' by Tom Lawrence) was the individual unit of the clown's performance, variously brief gags, sketches, songs and speeches.
8. In transcribing the wheezes from the first gag, I have corrected Lawrence's irregular spelling but have retained all punctuation (or lack of it), underlining, dashes, and parentheses.
9. Paterson, *Glimpses of Real Life*, 115.
10. *Morning Post*, 29 May 1862.
11. Paterson, *Glimpses of Real Life*, 113.
12. This and all following quotations of wheezes, poems, etc. are from Tom Lawrence's gag-book, which is now held in the archives by the library at Royal Holloway, University of London.
13. Oliver Double, *Britain Had Talent: A History of Variety Theatre* (Basingstoke: Palgrave Macmillan, 2012), 117.
14. Bratton and Featherstone, *The Victorian Clown*, 180–181.
15. Ibid., 181.
16. See note 12.
17. W. F. Wallett, *The Public Life of W. F Wallett, the Queen's Jester: An Autobiography Of Forty Years' Professional Experience & Travels in the United Kingdom, the United States of America (inc. California), Canada, South America, Mexico, the West Indies*, etc., ed. John Luntley (London and Derby: Bemrose & Sons, 1884). It is difficult to know whether Wallett embroidered the incident in a very typical self-aggrandising way, or if this was an actual, un-orchestrated quarrel. He was a notoriously difficult man.
18. Ibid., 55.
19. Ibid., 58.
20. Ibid., 149–150.
21. Double, *Britain Had Talent*, 134, 135.
22. Bratton and Featherstone, *The Victorian Clown*, 120.
23. *Edinburgh Evening News*, 31 December 1881.
24. See note 12.
25. Ibid., 2 January 1882.
26. There are 3 dots here in Lawrence's gag-book. They do not indicate an omission, but it is difficult to say what they mean, unless it is a pause (which Lawrence usually indicates by a dash) of a moment for Lawrence's business, perhaps burlesquing the woman's grief.
27. See note 12.
28. There are many examples, ranging from music hall songs, such as Dan Leno's 'I'm Waiting for Him Tonight' in which a battered wife itemises the injuries she received at the hands of her brutish husband, to Punch's violent treatment of Judy, to literary examples such as newspapers like

Tit-Bits and the *Illustrated Police News* where women are frequently objectified, often with titillating intent.

29. See note 12.

30. Comedy which relishes violence towards women and takes as its subject rape and brutality, has come under scrutiny recently. In 2012, the undiminishing popularity of jokes about rape and domestic violence told at the Edinburgh Festival ('I was waiting for my girlfriend to come round. Because I'd hit her really hard') prompted an article in the *Guardian* by Tanya Gold, in which she suggested that this attitude 'normalises and diminishes' the problem: 'if it is easy to laugh about, it is hard to take seriously. Accessed April 28 2016, http://www.theguardian.com/commentisfree/2012/aug/17/heard-one-about-rape-funny-now.   See also Simon Dickie, 'Rape Jokes and the Law,' in *Cruelty and Laughter: Forgotten Comic Literature and the Unsentimental Eighteenth Century* (Chicago: University of Chicago Press, 2011).

31. See note 12.

32. Lawrence has a number of wheezes concerned with astronomy and recent or famous astronomical events such as Donati's comet (1858) which was visible for months and the solar storm or Carrington event (1859) which disabled telegraph communications around the world. There was no solar eclipse visible from United Kingdom during the nineteenth century, but a total eclipse in 1860 was widely reported.

33. The clown certainly incorporated gurning into his performance: seventeenth-century woodcuts show Merry Andrews at Bartholomew Fair standing knock-kneed and with their tongues hanging out. A reviewer in 1880 saw a clown of similar appearance, who 'twists his tongue out at the corners of his mouth, and walks with his knees together' (*Western Mail*, 26 January 1880).

34. Accessed 29 April 2016, http://www.love-poems.me.uk/foster_old_dog_tray.htm.

35. Ibid.

Works Cited

Morning Post.

The Era.

The Guardian.

Western Mail.

Bratton, Jacky, and Ann Featherstone. *The Victorian Clown.* Cambridge: Cambridge University Press, 2006.

Double, Oliver. *Britain Had Talent: A History of Variety Theatre.* London: Palgrave Macmillan, 2012.

Foster, Stephen. 'Old Dog Tray.' Accessed April 29, 2016. http://www.love-po-ems.me.uk/foster_old_dog_tray.htm.

Paterson, Peter. *Glimpses of Real Life as Seen in the Theatrical World and in Bohemia: Being the Confessions of Peter Paterson, a Strolling Comedian.* Edinburgh: William P. Nimmo, 1864.

Wallet, W. F. *The Public Life of W. F. Wallett, the Queen's Jester: An Autobiography of Forty Years' Professional Experience & Travels in the United Kingdom, the United States of America (inc. California), Canada, South America, Mexico, the West Indies, etc.*, edited by John Luntley. London and Derby: Bemrose & Sons, 1884.

'Sassin' Back': Victorian Serio-Comediennes and Their Audiences

Louise Wingrove

In 1892, Jerome K. Jerome watched in slightly bemused awe as one of the nation's beloved music-hall stars, Bessie Bellwood, known popularly as 'Our Bessie', chastised a heckler from her audience:

> She announced her intention of 'wiping down the 'bloomin' 'all' with him, and making it respectable; and, metaphorically speaking, that is what she did. Her tongue hit him between the eyes and knocked him down and trampled him. It curled round and round him like a whip, and then it uncurled and wound the other way. It seized him by the scruff of his neck, and tossed him up into the air, and caught him as he descended, and flung him to the ground, and rolled him on it. It played around him like forked lightning, and blinded him. It danced and shrieked about him like a host of whirling fiends, and he tried to remember a prayer and could not. It touched him lightly on the sole of his foot and the crown of his head, and his hair stood up straight, and his limbs grew stiff. The people sitting near him drew away, not feeling it safe to be near, and left him alone, surrounded by space, and language.[1]

L. Wingrove (✉)
Bristol, UK

© The Author(s) 2020   207
L. Lee (ed.), *Victorian Comedy and Laughter*,
https://doi.org/10.1057/978-1-137-57882-2_8

Apart from the comedienne's pronouncement of intention, few other glimpses are proffered by Jerome of the actual verbal retort, or of the performer herself. Instead, he describes the rampageous tongue lashing about in all its metonymical glory. Somewhat paradoxically cursing to make the venue respectable, Bellwood not only decrees her power but also knowingly winks at and punctures the discourse of respectability, and claims intimacy between herself and the rest of the audience. Suddenly, Bellwood is her tongue running amok, a powerful weapon at first, then an autonomous warrior ruthlessly playing with the overwhelmed recipient. The tongue, or Bellwood, or is it her language, intent yet uncontrollable, turns the heckler into an object, performing a dozen different physical actions on him as if he were a mere plaything, helpless, weightless, and inconsequential. Suddenly, it is no longer an autonomy but a multiplicity, many uncanny, malevolent tongues acting in unison. The all-out assault, physical then fiendish, isolates the heckler as it escalates from violent to demonic to intangibly malicious, converting the space around him, as well as the heckler himself (the upstanding hair), in a Gothic but comically rendered caricature of shock.

Even before fully assuming her character, Bellwood thus reveals herself as herself to the (originally unwelcoming) audience, giving them a preview of her craft, and letting them witness 'the joins in the performance'.[2] She singles out the coal-heaver leading the booing and hissing for her retaliation, engaging him in a slanging match and defeating him completely, with Jerome comparing their duel to that between the lamb and the eagle. While Jerome assures us the singer displayed formidable linguistic and cultural competence, by leaving out Bellwood's actual replies to the heckler he facilitates the mythopoeia of it. Did the punishment fit the crime? In this prime example of 'volatile exchanges across the footlights',[3] the transgressor is left isolated, as nearby audience members draw away to escape this breath-taking, shiver-inducing threat. He is surrounded by the space they leave behind, an alarming vacancy filled with fear and language. Bellwood, however, suddenly faces universal approbation, also upright and breathless.

The above is punitive patter, with an effect on everyone present, the forlorn barracker a reminder to others of the comic performer's potency. Patter refers to 'the changing mélange of jokes and topical allusions interposed between verses [... where] social content appeared most markedly'.[4] It is part of the overall 'communal circuitry'[5] between performer and her audience, an intense exchange of affect that can be both a rupture in the performance and its climax, here resulting in a demonic apotheosis of the comedienne. In the space of just under six minutes, Bellwood's response transformed the audience's indifference, even hostility, into standing ovation and cheering. Her badinage was 'sometimes smart, [...] sometimes vulgar', enjoying 'a licence that would be permitted to no performer today'.[6]

Originally merely marginal accompaniment serving to bookend music-hall songs, patter contributed to the rhythm of the music hall, alongside the rhythms provided by the band and other performers' turns. It grew in stage prominence throughout the nineteenth century, heralding its later transformation into stand-up. It was sometimes longer than the songs it punctuated, while in many cases the songs were 'merely the quickest way of getting to [the] patter'.[7] Part of the performative dynamic between audience or stage partner and comedian, it was named in part after Charles Matthews' character, Captain Patter, in the 1838 play 'Patter versus Clatter'. The word's etymology is suggestive, denoting non-standard language designed to exclude outsiders (in line with Bailey's discussion of 'knowingness'), to grab attention and to sell. Yet, even at its most intense, patter connotes a lightness, rhythm, and speed, while its relationship to meaning and articulation is ambivalent. While originally patter might have conjured up an urbane, masculine, strolling force, I consider this form of apparently non-rehearsed and unscripted style of talk within the repertoire of a still under-researched phenomenon of the late Victorian period, the serio-comedienne, who reorients patter to her own requirements, strengths and repertoires.

The music-hall serio-comedienne was a performer whose act comprised a mixture of comic and serious songs and impromptu interactions. Where earlier reviews and advertising had used terms like 'characteristique vocalist' and 'impressionist', now 'serio-comic' and 'serio-comedienne' gained popularity. However, reviews continued to use 'comedienne' and 'low comic', largely to indicate that the humour on offer was not considered respectable. Thematically, serio-comediennes' repertoire ranged from scathing satire and politics to reflections on everyday life and love, providing music hall with its 'most distinctive idiom'.[8] It was so versatile that Beerbohm wrote that 'there is not one peculiarity of our race, good or bad, that is not well illustrated in the Music Halls'.[9] In terms of performance, serious actresses were frequently perceived via a sculptural metaphor, as Victorian-stage Galateas, beautiful, composed, and immaculate, not least because of lacking subjectivity and agency.[10] Comic actresses, on the other hand, while not free from objectification and negotiations of patriarchy, were—by dint of the comic mode or the illegitimacy of the stages they occupied—afforded more liberty and independence. This is clear from the assertive manner in which Bellwood handled her heckler. There, it is her very humanity—her passion and lived experiences comprising her social and linguistic competence—that wins over the audience. In an atmosphere where women's stage performance was still a contentious domain, and the spectacle they offered a transgressive defying of the norms, Bellwood's assertive handling of her heckler can be viewed as pre-theoretically proto-feminist, 'a form of cultural and professional practice'.[11]

Through the late nineteenth-century, the demand for the entertainment provided by serio-comediennes increased, seeing the number of London performers more than triple between 1868 and 1878, from 117 to 384.[12] This increase implies not only that the stage was a 'viable and growing trade for women',[13] but also that there was a surge in the popularity of this style of performance. Female performers could earn as much as male ones, depending primarily on box-office appeal, but there were extreme differences between individual female performers in terms of wages. Some (a minority) could earn others' annual salary in a week, or increase their own earnings tenfold in the space of only a few years.[14] On average, however, stage performers' annual earnings actually placed them firmly with the female labourers, not the middle class.[15] Their social respectability was continually questioned, even at peak popularity, yet their work gave them independence, liberty and opportunities denied many Victorian women. Their work transformed the material conditions of the Victorian stage, and augmented and complicated its layering messages.

New modes of expression and new domains were becoming available to women both on and off the stage, owing to social developments such as gender shifts in the workforce during the industrialisation. Audiences were growing more versatile towards the end of the century, but there were still considerable differences between halls in this respect. While there was some controversy about women's presence in the halls, working women actually had an established presence in the free and easy, music hall's predecessor.[16] Continually negotiating spectacle and femininity, women performers and audience members alike were also negotiating assertiveness and claim to other traditionally male domains, like humour. As Susan Glenn notes, there was a 'dynamic tension between women's desire (on as well as off the stage) to use theatrical spectacle as a vehicle for achieving greater voice in culture and politics, and theatre's countervailing urge to turn female spectacle into a symbolic expression of male mastery'.[17]

Just as complex as the dynamic between music hall and gender was the relationship between its comedy and class. Mostly working-class comedians reflected back life to a mixed audience. While 'holding up a mirror', as Dickens asserted in his 1860 essay, music hall also helped strengthen and create a specific sense of national, class, and gender identity, along the constantly shifting lines dividing and uniting its audiences. As Beerbohm writes, this mirror 'distorts life exactly as the public likes to see it distorted'.[18] It is doubtless that music hall was, at times at least, 'the exact and joyous result of the public's own taste'.[19] It was complex enough to contain multiple dichotomies, and, with women in the audience, both writers and performers had to take their tastes and needs into account, address their concerns and make sure their experience was a pleasurable one as well.

One way in which music-hall engaged its diverse audiences was via a concept paradigmatically described by Peter Bailey as 'knowingness'. Departing from Stedman Jones, who sees in popular entertainment a 'culture of consolation', a form of compensation for one's lack of socio-economic power, Bailey suggests instead (or additionally) focusing on 'cultures of competence' or empowerment.[20] What constituted this competence was a shared knowingness about the world, a continually updated navigation system so one wouldn't get lost—or would find one's place in the first place—in the increasingly complex urban world. Viewed by some middle-class critics as an 'objectionable' feature of music hall, it also served as a verbal and non-verbal shorthand, a metalanguage for the stars to engage with their public.[21] Revealing alliances, and including some while excluding others, participation in such exchanges confirmed or created a sense of identity and helped transform, however fleetingly, the 'volatile collectivity'[22] that was a music-hall crowd into a distinctive, identifiable entity. Particularly skillful or captivating performance could achieve this, but so could the efficient handling of a heckler, as in the anecdote about Bellwood. Knowingness about the everyday, city life, encroaching institutional authority, and sexuality in particular, was particularly powerful. This was no merely 'theoretical' expertise, but a dynamic, performative competence, 'the living out of this knowledge'.[23]

As a ground-up form of cultural authority in Bailey's account, know-ingness takes on a particular resonance that is both experiential *and* per-formed. It is transmuted further in the hands of Bellwood, and another contemporary comedienne prominent on this newly influential scene, Jenny Hill. Like Bellwood, Hill developed a persona as 'a strong minded female speaking her mind about men',[24] as well as about everyday life, which resonated with her female audience. In October 1885, Hill took to the stage of the Gaiety Theatre, Newcastle. The thirty-six-year-old from London had already built a reputation across the country as 'the vital spark', a reference both to her extremely energetic performance style and to her diminutive stature. Reviews and advertising consistently comment on her ability to entertain enormous audiences, resulting in repeated requests for encores and standing ovations. A reviewer in the *Gaiety* described her reception thus:

> Not until after singing five songs, the last of which was in response to an encore, and appearing twice before the curtain to excuse herself, amidst deafening cries for 'The Bookmaker,' did she manage to tear herself from the audience, when a burly fellow in the pit shouted 'Nivvor mind, we'll hev innuthor tannor's worth th'morrow neet'. Jenny is not a mere song-stress; she is a true, accomplished, and thoughtful comedienne. So does she act the characters she impersonates, that she makes a little drama of every song she sings, and teaches a moral.[25]

This description of the audience's enthusiastic, insatiable even, reaction to Hill provides only a hint of the fame and adoration that a music-hall serio-comedienne could enjoy. The performer-audience relationship relied largely on perceived authenticity and community, as echoed in T. S. Eliot's 1922 romanticised depiction of Marie Lloyd. Here he paints singers as representative not only of their own class (or gender), but of Englishness more generally, 'the true curators of their culture'[26]:

> In the music-hall comedians they find the expression and dignity of their own lives; and this is not found in the most elaborate and expensive revue. ... The working man who went to the music-hall and saw Marie Lloyd and joined in the chorus was himself performing part of the act; he was engaged in that collaboration of the audience with the artist which is nec-essary in all art and most obviously in dramatic art.[27]

Unpredictable and more unruly than Lloyd, Bellwood frequently featured in the press for her involvement in court cases for non-payment of fines and assault. Yet it was her very fallibility that seemed to hold the keys to her success, as she connected with her audiences through what one reviewer termed 'sassin' back'.[28] Whether scripted or seemingly spontaneous, music-hall exchanges held special pleasures for their audiences, male and female, in their live, collaborative nature. The unruly crowds required an unruly, strong-willed performer to call an audience into being, as Bailey reminds us above. To 'sass' as Bellwood does is to reply or speak to someone impertinently, to answer back, and derives from the Latin *salsus*, or *salsa*—feminine for *salted*. It connotes vigour and spirit, but also provocation and conceit, all energies that were welcome in the music hall. In an era of industrialisation and commodification, buyers, sellers and consumers occupied the hall. This meant that '[t]he music hall performer could count on the active engagement of an audience well practiced not only in being hailed but in hailing back, for the language of the street and market-place that informed the exchanges with the audience was very much one of give as well as take'.[29] Here, sass also connotes an indomitable, specifically female spirit, talking back, fighting back, and raising her voice, and in this sense the off-the-cuff, feisty extemporising that is sass is political.

Sass also connotes independence and self-reliance, characteristics open to radically different interpretations when applied to men and women. It is interesting, as Bratton writes of Hill's legacy, that:

> The music-hall myth-makers present her in a way which has transformed success, wealth and independence into a story of suffering and pathos more suitable to her gender, while mediation by reporters and the publishers of sheet music has disguised her performances so effectively that we find it difficult to discover what they contained that so pleased her working-class female admirers.[30]

Thus, contemporary media often emphasised Bellwood's and Hill's humble beginnings over their successes, possibly in an effort to assuage the anxieties associated with working-class women's upward mobility. Success itself was sometimes recast as failure, and 'interviews usually dwelled on the unhappiness which accompanied the performer's financial success as well as their inability to manage money sensibly'.[31] In other instances, the financial dimension was foregrounded and even exaggerated, boosting circulation but also reinforcing class boundaries by painting working-class performers as (solely) money-driven.[32] While the 'sass' was commodified to an extent, and Bellwood and Hill both highly paid stars, this was not mere 'fall' into capitalism that is often foregrounded in descriptions of working-class music-hall performers. Rather (or additionally), it was a condition of professionalism, celebrated and validated by the working class themselves, and by female audiences in particular.

1   WORKING WOMEN: THE MULTIVOCAL EFFECT OF A FEMALE AUDIENCE

In a music hall in Johannesburg in 1894, Hill, by then already in poor health, declared: 'Ladies and gentlemen,—Oh, but there aren't any ladies! Oh, yes; there's one up there. It seems so peculiar—nothing but men. It's not a bit like at home, where women always go to the music hall and seem to appreciate you more than the men do'.[33] Clearly, popular with both genders, with the quote from the 'burly fellow' in Newcastle and the huge successes generally suggesting wide appeal, serio-comediennes had a special rapport with their female audiences. The performer and her performance were commodities, but also vehicles of women's liberation as they gave their class- and gender-inflected interpretations of reality.

While working-class women already had a tradition of mobility, out of financial necessity, middle-class women's independence was gradually increasing through the nineteenth century, with the help of West End shopping and East End charity, and a 'new urban female style of "being at home" in the city'.[34] From the 1870s, music-hall management began to actively encourage the presence of women in the audience, hoping this would provide evidence of their new levels of respectability. Indeed, having women both in the audience and on the stage 'transformed the atmosphere of the halls, forcefully contributing to their multivocal effect'.[35] This in turn generated more demand and enthusiasm for these performers, potentially explaining the increase in numbers not only of performers but also of managers and impresarios. As Glenn remarks, 'the increasing visibility of members of their own sex in the theatrical profession [...] did more than offer the promise of employment: it provided an influential public space for experimenting with new, and sometimes controversial, forms of female self-expression'.[36] Female performers gave loud expression to female excess and autonomy, celebrated female identity and served as agents of shifting gender relations.

Attention paid to the frequency with which particular themes appeared in Hill's and Bellwood's careers, respectively shows that, although Hill and Bellwood performed over a similar time period and in similar venues, their repertoires often contrasted, with Bellwood performing a large amount of innuendo-based material, and Hill focusing on political and coster girl personations. What is continually at the forefront of both repertoires, however, is the focus on women—and working women in particular. Music hall was replete with accounts of henpecked husbands, tyrannical or martyr-like wives, and children outnumbering them both, sex, violence, alcohol, financial hardship and fidelity concerns, vice and virtue, and increasingly women venturing into traditionally male domains, like financial independence, humour, seduction or the drunken spree. Reflecting women's lives and their experiences of London street life resonated strongly with the mixed audiences, the positive feedback and demand presumably informing the serio-comedienne's repertoire. Reviewers described how there was 'an intense vitality and irresistible élan about Miss Hill's acting that would carry any audience, and her inimitable comic power has long ago secured her a first place in the delineation of characters taken from street life',[37] resulting in copious amounts of encores and applause. At the Cambridge music hall in 1885, following her personation of 'Arry, a penny swell, the audience appreciation was so intense that:

> Again and again it burst forth, roars of eager acclamation echoing back from the roof of the hall, and Miss Hill was recalled no less than three times. Even then, the audience were not satisfied, and with a deep-mouthed cheer they again summoned the fair singer, who this time appeared in a walking dress; and then, like the growl of a wild animal balked off its prey, the encores died sullenly away.[38]

This description of the request for an encore as something uncanny, the summoning of a spirit or hungry anticipation of prey, recalls Bellwood's handling of the heckler. Music hall thus emerges as a space that can forge a unison collective out of an unruly crowd seemingly marked by irreconcilable differences, but also a place where anything is possible and the everyday is celebrated.

Like Hill, Bellwood was consistently praised for realistic 'sketches of [characters] in the lower ranks of life',[39] with her songs depicting Whitechapel life a hit in Edinburgh.[40] Thus, accurate or detailed reflections of street life appeared to be a sure way of securing encores and audience appreciation. In *The Victorian City*, Judith Flanders reminds readers that '[t]he streets of London in the nineteenth-century were, in many cases, the same ones we walk today. But not only did they look different, their purpose was different; they were used differently. It is that use, that idea of purpose, that needs to be recaptured'.[41] Flanders considers London itself to be a 'pantomime and a masquerade',[42] and indeed it is possible to view the city as a performance, continual transformation its only constancy, with the street sellers (particularly costermongers), shoppers, entertainers, as well as members of all classes co-existing performing themselves to themselves. Observed and presented accurately, street life thus translated seamlessly into observational comedy. Certainly, the volatile and porous relations of gender, class and nation of late nineteenth century provided comediennes with a wealth of material. Music-hall songs served as a celebration of the city, as 'the ultimate space of liberty for all, though details as to what constituted liberty were a bit sketchy'.[43]

We find one example of Hill's observational comedy, as well as insight into her creative process, in the *Gal at the Coffee Shop* character. Dressed in an old apron over old petticoats, with no overly corseted chest to draw in the figure, Hill's personation attempted to depict an identifiable, not caricatured, worker.

What is missing most from our understanding of these texts is the performance itself—the non-verbal and paralinguistic so central to storytelling and to humour. The lyrics and score survive in some instances, as do some general descriptions of the style of performance, but we have no record of what Barthes calls the particular "grain" or materiality of the voice, and only occasional printed and presumably bowdlerised snatches of the "spoken" or patter which the comique would have slipped in between verses'.[44] Reliance on sheet music and subjective sources like memoires necessarily decontextualises and skews our understanding of these performances. This is partly the reason why these performers' legacy in comedy and gender history have largely been forgotten, and it is a challenge to pinpoint and reimagine their appeal.

There are few descriptions of Hill's physical demarcations for this character, and no notes of any catch phrases; however, reviews do describe how the character let 'her hearers into coffee-shop secrets relating to flights of "doorsteps" (slices of bread and butter) and "two-eyed steaks" (the harmless necessary kipper)'.[45] She was also described as 'an authority on appetites [...] relating, in her own inimitable style, an anecdote, the hero of which could demolish fourteen rashers of bacon at breakfast time'.[46] Other reviews described her serving, cleaning and chucking out, giving her a strong and powerful, almost masculine image. As the personation contained observational humour relating to customers' eating habits, part of the character's appeal appears to be her ability to reflect everyday life. It is estimated that as early as 1840 there were two thousand coffee shops in London, each serving up to nine hundred customers daily.[47]

Hill reflected both the consumers and the working girls back to themselves. When performing in New York in 1893, she posed as the *Gal at the Coffee Shop* for the photographer Sarony. In a later interview Hill remarked that the character was an 'absolutely faithful production [...] of a girl who waited in a Shoreditch eating house. The author and [Hill] went down day after day to study her'.[48] These comments, along with her assertion that she bought second-hand clothes from the East End in order to appear authentic in her other characterisations and her claims that she learnt 'the cellar Flap' from girls on Hampstead Heath as there was 'no dancing master who could teach her',[49] cement Hill's own creative process and role as social observer. Her success, in conjunction with her process of observation and close mimicry, indicate that this observational style and reflection appealed to and captivated her audiences.

2   'AND THEY ALL SHOUTED "WHAT CHEER 'RIA"': THE REFLEXIVE COSTERMONGER

In 1887, three years after Bellwood introduced the song into her repertoire, a reviewer reflected on the fact that Bellwood suffered 'from the popularity of her "What Cheer, 'Ria?" ditty, for she [had] become so completely associated with that particular line of comic singing that music-hall audiences would be only too pleased if she would go on repeating her success in that direction ad infinitum'.[50] The character of the costermonger, or street seller of fruit, vegetables and fish from a cart, was integral to both Hill's and Bellwood's repertoires, the personation clearly allowing for the employment of comic devices that a large proportion of the audience could enjoy. Bellwood's rendition of ''Ria' 'elicited applause which [...] made the walls of the building tremble',[51] and she was 'cheered again and again, pelted with bouquets, and recalled to sing "What cheer, 'Ria"'.[52]

Some costers sold from the same, stationary stall, others did rounds varying from two to ten miles.[53] In the 1840s, journalist and social commentator Henry Mayhew was particularly interested in the costermonger 'sub-culture',[54] dedicating considerable portion of his writing in *London Labour and the London Poor* to them in 1849. Mayhew also interviewed costers on their leisure time and they emerge as avid music-hall audience members. Describing the gallery of the Victoria Theatre, aside from its noise and the crush of people, Mayhew states that 'the gallery consists mainly of costermongers. Young girls, too, are very plentiful'.[55] A costermonger reveals to him in one discussion that for 'a song to take hold of us [it] must have a good chorus',[56] supported by Mayhew's own observation that 'the grand hit of the evening is always when a song is sung to which the entire gallery can join in chorus'.[57]

Sing-alongs were a distinctive and much loved aspect of music-hall entertainment, serving to create a convivial atmosphere that united an audience and provided them with a feeling of ownership over the material, the venue and the performer. A long-standing tradition in Britain, sing-along was most popular in the eighteenth and nineteenth centuries, but survives in contemporary leisure as well. Recent research by Pawley and Müllensiefen confirms and expands on the various functions of leisure sing-along behaviour. They list '[b]onding socially, expressing identity, and attracting a mate',[58] improving emotional well-being and exploring one's playful vitality. Singing along can improve the overall experience of music, which is inherently reliant on the body. Most importantly, it benefits the individual through enhancing his or her feelings of belonging and solidarity, achieving 'both the arousal and synchronization of audience members'.[59]

The unison of singing along creates an enjoyable collective, but audience knowingness also affords collective pleasure. When singing along, audience members could signal their knowledge of the song, performer or character. On a purely practical level it also helped amplify the song, allowing it to reach the highest areas of the venue long before amplification devices, and ensured that audience focus was on the performer rather than friends and drinks. Thus, singing along had an important part to play in terms of involving and controlling an audience, but also as acts which stood in dialogue with the comediennes, signalling approval and signifying success.

What Cheer 'Ria(1884–1885) was a storytelling song that showed Bellwood performing in character as costermonger 'Ria, who, following a financial windfall, buys a new dress and a ticket for the stalls at her local music hall. She is then challenged for her behaviour and embarrassed by her friends, music-hall management and partner, and resolves never to try to be a 'toff' again. The narrative appears to provide a warning to those considering breaking with established social hierarchies. The song begins:

> I am a girl what's a-doing wery well in the wegitable line
> And as I'd saved a bob or two I thought I'd cut a shine;
> So I goes and buys some toggery, these ere wery clothes you see,
> And with the money I had left I thought I'd cut a spree:
> So I goes into a Music Hall, where I'd often been afore,
> I don't go in the gallery, but on the bottom floor;
> I sits down by the chairman and I calls for a pot of stout,
> My pals in the gallery, spotted me and they all commenced to shout:
>
> *CHORUS*
> What Cheer 'Ria! Ria's on the job,
> What Cheer 'Ria! Did you speculate a bob?
> Oh Ria she's a toff and she looks immensikoff
> And they all shouted "What cheer 'Ria!"

Her dress torn and feeling mortified, in the final spoken word passage she says:

> You don't catch me going chucking money away, trying to be a toff any more, The way they served me wasn't so wery polite. They brought the 'Chucker out' and he said 'Come on 'Ria, you've been kicking up a pretty row, he says Come on outside, I says Shan't! shan't!! there you are! Shan't! He took hold of me and handled me out just as though I'd been a sack o' taters. When I got outside, my young man was outside, so he says Serves you right Ria! You shouldn't try to be a lady,'cause it don't suit yer, Just then my pals were coming out of the gallery and they all commenced shouting –

The song and patter allow for multiple interpretations. Prima facie, 'Ria is made an example of and taught that to step out of the norm and remove herself from her circle is not acceptable. On this reading, *'Ria* can be seen as describing an inflexible class system, with social hierarchies that cannot be disturbed and a culture of consolation to compensate for social and economic impotence.[60] Given the coster girl's decision to reassume her place in the hierarchy at the end, *Ria* reads as propaganda warning working women against aspirations. It is a reminder of the close surveillance over women, especially when they ventured in public, and how their clothes and demeanour were scrutinised in order to get at who exactly this woman was—respectable, or sexually available, or perhaps a class and gender trespasser like 'Ria.

Further investigation, however, uncovers more complexity to *'Ria*, and more in line with Bailey's theory of conspiratorial knowingness. It is also possible to read this as a story of female assertiveness and vitality. Although 'Ria's actions are curtailed by her environment, she exudes independence, both financial and in terms of decision-making. After all, she works, which implies a freedom of movement and a power to purchase and consume autonomously. She exhibits the 'competitive individualism [... and] self-advertisement' characteristic of her trade.[61] She also seems to know what she wants and has aspirations that she is not afraid to try to realise without consultation with others. Also, when her elegant evening out doesn't turn out as expected, it does not seem (from the score at least) that she is heartbroken about it, but quite resilient. This story can then also be read as a triumph of competence and a confident opening of a dialogue about female ambition and independence. An audience could experience a more complex knowingness, acknowledging the hierarchy yet questioning why someone could not step down from the gallery into the stalls if they wished, as well as sympathy for someone attempting to push against convention. It is a triumph story also in the fact that actual, non-fictional women were there, on the stage and in the audience, singing, laughing and claiming their rights to work and leisure. Finally, 'Ria did try to find a place for herself in the stalls, but she doesn't seem to mind too much going back to the gallery, and in that sense this narrative is also about the celebration of working-class identity.

In 'Ria, music-hall experiments with self-reflexivity. Firstly, Bellwood, marketed as 'our Bessie' and one of the people, had in fact achieved her aspirations. She had forged a lucrative career despite her class and gender, working her way from rabbit skinning in Bermondsey to star status. Bellwood not only knew working-class struggles first-hand, she was also a woman who had frequent brushes with the law due to her temper. Second, 'Ria can be interpreted as a metaphor for the music hall itself, its struggle to rise out of controversy and gain respectability, and to match financial success with social recognition. Third, how *'Ria* appealed to its audiences was to switch the performance round on to them with Bellwood/'Ria standing on the stage looking at the audience, describing what they were experiencing on a regular basis. Four, the song was probably a veridical account of some of music hall's attractions and drawbacks, like the loud singing and boisterous behaviour of those in the gallery, or the difficulties facing unaccompanied women. During this period there was a link, actual or imagined, between an unaccompanied, well-dressed woman (like 'Ria) in the stalls of a music hall and prostitution.[62]

The song was also inward-looking in its intertextual connections with other music-hall texts.[63] 'Ria looks back to another popular song, Cockney swell Arthur Lloyd's 1873 hit 'Immenseikoff, or the Shoreditch toff'. Here we also find incongruity between one's station and aspirations, but less self-awareness than in 'Ria's account. 'Ria is echoed in 1891 song 'Wot cher' popularised by Albert Chevalier, not only in shared musical and linguistic elements, but also in the theme of the poor trying to rise above their station. Such porousness not only of texts but also of stage performances, termed 'intertheatricality' by Bratton (2003), depends on and nurtures mutual familiarity between performer, text and audience. It is a 'mesh of connections between all kinds of theatre texts, and between texts and their users'.[64] This concept highlights the fact that, in order to interpret new performances, audiences reused their popular culture and entire world knowledge and experience. In this light, 'knowingness' emerges as the shared (or not) experience and memory of what came before this specific performance.

The multiple layers of meaning but also the specificity of music-hall audience composition meant that Bellwood could have adapted the song's content by describing specific audience members or performing certain lines to one, thus heightening their involvement. Skilful performance could highlight mutually opposed readings, tweaking them to resonate with differently ideologically and geographically positioned audiences. As Kift notes, there were many different audiences present at any one time, depending on location, period and specific seating plan in each hall, and, while diverse, they remained segregated by class and purchasing power.[65] With a song like this, addressing class tensions inherent in the hall itself, singers may have addressed different portions of their performance to different portions of their audience,[66] 'setting them laughing at each other, calling on the powerful emotional force of their rivalries and antagonisms to reinforce a climactic endorsement of the song and the singer [her]self'.[67] The song's popularity with West and East End audiences alike suggests the text's openness to interpretations, as well as ambiguity or adaptability in its performance. In an 1893 interview with the *Era*, Jenny Hill explained that West End audiences preferred her comic personations of coster girls and East End life, whereas East End audiences enjoyed dramatic songs and were less impressed with coster renditions, particularly in venues where costermongers frequented the gallery.[68] This did not mean that she didn't perform coster renditions for East End audiences, but that, in order for the personation to be a success, it needed to be 'performed without exaggeration or satire'.[69] Hill explained that '[i]f your song strikes a coster as a natural, inoffensive ditty, he will tolerate it; but begin to stroke an imaginary curl on your cheek, to crane your neck, or thrust your lower jaw out, and he is annoyed in a minute'.[70] The level of detail in her description indicates that this was a practical aspect of performance and repertoire development discovered by Hill in praxis. As Bailey also notes, the same performance could afford quite different pleasures to different audiences. What was a caricature to the outsider could be a source of pride and identity for the insider—'the small man [or woman] writ large'. Indeed, 'parody might march hand in hand with validation, [...] exploiting sectional antipathies within the audience'.[71]

3   'Bother the Men!': Feminism and Purity

Although street humour and knowable characters were a staple of the serio-comedienne's repertoire, Hill in particular also used her stage time to perform more controversial and political personations such as a Bluestocking in *Bother the Men*, which offers a more nuanced view of the material of the serio-comedienne, her appeal to audiences and interaction with the rapidly shifting society around her. *Bother the Men* (1870–1877) appears right at the start of Hill's solo career. It was originally performed in 1869 by Mrs. Howard Paul (Isabella Hill), a well-known legitimate theatre and burlesque actress who headed her own company. Jenny Hill's decision to include this song in her turn at the Eastern music hall in Limehouse in 1870,[72] only a year after the original performance, may have been motivated by a desire to attract an audience with something familiar. However, if the audience favoured the original, Hill risked failure. The Eastern was located in a dockland area with 'dozens of cheap lodging houses and brothels, public-houses, beer-shops and dance halls',[73] making Hill's decision to perform a women's rights character as part of her turn curious. However, the fact that she later performed the song at both East- and West End venues suggests that her treatment of the women's rights activist was sufficiently ambiguous and adaptable to be popular with a diverse audience.

The song featured Jenny Hill as the 'quaintly dressed old maid who screams as well as sings',[74] although the comedienne was in her early twenties at the time. The sheet music for *Bother the Men* portrays a women's rights campaigner and platform woman as unfeminine, in opposition to marriage and overly vocal in her opinions. Regardless of an audience's potential familiarity with the song, the choice of such potentially controversial content during Hill's establishing career phase makes its repertoire inclusion, on the face of it, perplexing. Although the suffrage movement did not gain wider prominence and discussion until later in the nineteenth-century, the discussion of women's rights and their movement from the private to public sphere was already signalling instability in Britain's gender and social hierarchies. As music-hall relied on a reflection of life that joined an audience together rather than splintering them with differing opinions, the presence of such material on the repertoire presupposes a multi-layered performance style, reliant on the plurality of intentions and interpretations inherent in the text to appeal to many audience members.

Few accounts are available of Hill's performance of *Bother the Men*; however, those found indicate that her portrayal of Miss Grym caricatured women's rights activists and middle-class women in a similar way to the image depicted on the sheet music cover. Miss Grym, it is said, 'speaks her mind freely about the lords of creation'.[75] Later reviews added that 'her umbrella was a "caution", and as she upheld the rights of women, and advocated their claims to wear breeches, the chairman, at whom she levelled many of her remarks, had a rather bad time of it'.[76] These reviews, combined with mentions of her 'sneeringly' describing men as 'the lords of the creation'[77] and holding 'antiquated' views,[78] result in a reduction of Miss Grym to one of caricatured bitterness. Rather than offering a realistic reflection of contemporary women's rights campaigners, Hill's portrayal exaggerates the lack of femininity and belligerence with which these women were publicly regarded. The character's aggressive temperament and insulting of the chairman imply that Miss Grym's comic appeal was partly found in her anger, with the audience laughing at the character rather than laughing in agreement with her and her opinions. Hill's personation of such an exaggerated image of platform women, however, does not mean that *Bother the Men* lacks subtext. Instead, an understanding of both the complexity of the figure socially, and parallels between the reception of platform women/women's rights campaigners and serio-comediennes, is clearly evident in this song.

Contemporary caricatured portrayals of women's rights campaigners provide a reflection of social concerns about 'excess women' and the increasing anxiety regarding women's movement from the private to public sphere. By 1861, it was estimated that there were over a million unmarried women, half of whom were estimated to be 'excess women' as they were not engaged in what was considered to be worthwhile work. A considerable proportion of these women were well-educated and belonged to the middle and upper classes. It became apparent that 'excess women' needed to gain employment in order to support themselves in the absence of husbands, helping fuel the fight for the wider inclusion of women in the workforce. Working-class women already often continued working even after marriage in order to support their families, setting the precedent for the fight for women's rights to become more central to the lives of middle- and upper-class women. A stereotypical image presented female campaigners as out of touch with the lower classes. The result was that the humour in *Bother the Men* was as much about class as it was about gender, widening its appeal in the halls. It was frequently stressed that, 'exploited by their husbands, by their employers, by society at large, most working-class women were in no position to rebel against social injustice'[79] whereas those campaigning for equality did not understand the larger picture, which detracted from their message. Marital status was another point on which campaigners were mocked, leading to general questioning of their femininity and labelling them as men-hating. With the purpose of creating an instantly recognisable women's rights campaigner character, an exaggerated, unfeminine caricature was created. However, the lyrics and subtext of the song held a more complex interpretation.

It was not only excess women that fuelled fears of shifts in gender hierarchy. Platform women more generally were increasing the presence of women's political voices in the public sphere. Their public visibility and audience familiarity with them affected the ways in which songs such as *Bother the Men* were understood. They also shared similarities with serio-comediennes as women presenting themselves and their views to an audience. In 1870 school boards were set up to establish and administer elementary education, and, by 1879, seventy women had been elected to these boards. To be elected, women had to canvass and speak in public, 'performing "turns" for voters, sometimes as many as three per night, dashing around in carriages'.[80] As suggested by Walkowitz's use of 'turns' and 'performing', there were parallels between platform women and female performers. Though performing in different venues and for different reasons, both were gradually normalising the image of a woman, whatever her class, presenting herself and her opinions in public.

By performing speeches in music halls, a space separate from 'real life' and designated for entertainment, performers like Hill could speak their mind without breaking social conventions. Hill recalled anti-patter clauses in her contracts and censorship on direct address as prominent at this time, with managers striving for respectability trying to prevent performers from saying inappropriate things. However, patter was an important aspect of a serio-comedienne's appeal. It was a form of conspiratorial direct address that allowed an audience to feel connected to a performer and that could make a performance feel authentic and unscripted, making audiences think that they had a connection with the performer that other audiences hadn't had. Therefore, spoken word sections in songs were a compromise. The performer was able to engage the audience in direct address, talking to them conspiratorially or informally, but censors and managers were able to have their minds put at ease by viewing them in advance. As a result, the speeches were often quite ambiguous. For example, in *P's and Q's* (1888), Hill sings about female education, with her stance unequivocal in the chorus:

> I don't believe in teaching girls
> Such twaddle as the rules of three.
> If they only know their P's and Q's
> They can do without your ABCs.

However, one of three spoken words sections declares:

> Females ought not to be married with school figures – they've got their own to think about. Fancy worrying about Addition! When she gets married she soon learns what that is – and it ain't long before somebody, her husband – instructs her in Multiplication – that generally leads to a row – which causes division. If they don't soon make it up its Long Division

– if they do it's Short division – and then they begin with Bills of Parcels, which is arithmetic for babies. Then we come to the Rule of Three. Is it likely anyone can endure the rule of three? Why, she often goes stark staring mad with the rule of one – so don't let your daughters be taught such rubbish…

Though the speech appears to show a woman against female education, the underlying argument for its usefulness is more complex. The very fact that the jokes in the speech revolve around a knowledge of arithmetic shows Hill/her character to be intelligent and educated, and gives a knowing nod to the more complex social reasons pertaining to the debate on female education, implying that the song is a satiric caricature. On the other hand, to those opposed to female education, the speech appears to be in keeping with their opinions. Speeches therefore allowed serio-comediennes to connect to an audience in a potentially more conspiratorial and also more ambiguous way, leaving the text to be decoded as desired by audiences. Middle-class platform women, however, generally performed speeches in spaces not designated for performance, and so their deviation from convention was arguably more upsetting to the equilibrium. Also for the sake of respectability and propriety, they had to couch their arguments 'within culturally acceptable modes of address such as the "appeal"'.[81]

These scripted addresses further strengthen the link between platform women and performers. In the fight for female suffrage, the Actresses Franchise League actively trained women in public speaking in order to better spread their message and deal with hecklers and crowds.[82] Women were increasingly visible, expressing their opinions publicly rather than remaining in private roles, so techniques perfected by stage performers became important to platform women in order to be heard. This created an unlikely alliance between the 'disreputable' stage women and the middle and upper-classes. Fenwick Millar, standing for a school board election in the 1880s, was described as a 'master orator',[83] a phrase that was also regularly used by reviewers to describe Hill. Such parallels and their implications become clearer in Hill's performance of *Bother the Men*, as well as later political material such as the *Female Politician* (1880), where the image of a woman chastised for speaking publicly is superimposed onto a woman celebrated for speaking publicly. Here, Hill balanced the stereotypical campaigner image with an actual discussion of politics and women's rights:

Lords of creation they're pompously dubb'd;
We, so downtrodden, neglected, and snubb'd,
Must not complain, tho' an angel 'twould vex,
Being of course the inferior sex.

Chorus
Bother the men!
Bother the men!
Quite out of patience I get with them when,
Bother the men!
Bother the men!
I think of them; bother them!
Bother the men!

Full of conceit, women they treat
More like the ground that is under their feet;
Such their pretense,
'tis an offence
Merely to hint we have got common sense!
In our anatomy brain forms no part!
While as for poetry, Science, or Art,
Physic, Theology, Politics – what?
We comprehend them? Oh certainly not!

Chorus
Well we may dread,
Having to wed,
(Strange that so many are into it led)
Sad is their fate!
But to alter their state
We're out of the frying pan into the grate!
See what old maids are compelled to go thro'!
If clever they're either "strong minded," or "blue."
Should they start as M.D's, they're derided and mocked!
And the 'Lords of creation' are dreadfully shock'd!

Chorus
Ah, but I know what makes them so,
Jealousy, which they are too proud to show!
Give us a chance, they with a glance
See we'd ahead of them quickly advance!
Only let government

Bring in a bill
To give us the franchise, and have it we will!
Women we'll send into parliament! Then
O, you will see how they'll bother the men!

The lyrics are fascinating in the included details and reflections of the ongoing debates on women's suffrage, but the way they were probably presented allows for much ambiguity. Again, this had the potential to unite an audience of very differing opinions: to those against the song is mocking these unreasonable and undesirable women, whereas to a woman it could entertain based on its ability to level abuse at men as well as the middle-classes, but also based on its content. The polysemy of *Bother the Men* allowed audiences to, even unwittingly, engage in a live and current debate. The message of the song could be taken at face value or decoded as desired, keeping the atmosphere convivial. Whereas platform women could be dismissed when performing such speeches in public, politically minded performers like Hill could showcase debates to their audiences under the guise of entertainment, negotiating a continued popularity with people watching from varied viewpoints, in a space where it was already acceptable for a woman to sass back and be listened to.

NOTES

1. Jerome K. Jerome, 'Variety Patter,' *The Idler* 1, no. 2 (March 1892): 123–135.
2. Peter Bailey, 'Conspiracies of Meaning: Music-Hall and the Knowingness of Popular Culture,' *Past & Present* (1994): 138–170 (p. 144).
3. Bailey, 'Conspiracies of Meaning,' 168.
4. Michael J. Childs, *Labour's Apprentices: Working-Class Lads in Late Victorian and Edwardian England* (London: McGill-Queen's University Press, 1992), 123.
5. Barry J. Faulk, *Music Hall and Modernity: The Late-Victorian Discovery of Popular Culture* (Athens: Ohio University Press, 2004), 30.
6. Songwriter Richard Morton in *The Era*, 1 April 1914.
7. Richard Anthony Baker, *British Music Hall: And Illustrated History* (Barnsley: Pen and Sword History, 2014), 34.
8. Bailey, 'Conspiracies of Meaning,' 139.
9. Max Beerbohm, 'Demos' Mirror,' in *More Theatres 1898–1903* (New York: Taplinger Publishing Company, 1969), 276.
10. Gail Marshall, *Actresses on the Victorian Stage: Feminine Performance and the Galatea Myth* (Cambridge: Cambridge University Press, 1998).

11. Susan Glenn, *Female Spectacle: The Theatrical Roots of Modern Feminism* (Cambridge, MA and London: Harvard University Press, 2000), 6.

12. Lois Rutherford, '"Managers in a small way": The Professionalisation of Variety Artistes, 1860–1914,' in *Music Hall: The Business of Pleasure*, ed. Peter Bailey (Milton Keynes: Open University Press, 1986), 116.

13. Tracy Davis, *Actresses as Working Women—Their Social identity in Victorian Culture* (London: Routledge, 1991), 17.

14. Davis, *Actresses as Working Women*, 24–26.

15. Davis, *Actresses as Working Women*, 30.

16. Martha Vicinus, *The Industrial Muse: A Study of Nineteenth-Century British Working-Class Literature* (New York: Barnes and Noble, 1974), 240.

17. Glenn, *Female Spectacle*, 3.

18. Beerbohm, 'Demos' Mirror,' 274.

19. Max Beerbohm, 'In a Music Hall,' in *More Theatres 1898–1903* (New York: Taplinger Publishing Company, 1969), 397.

20. Gareth Stedman Jones, 'Working-Class Culture and Working-Class Politics in London, 1870–1900; Notes on the Remaking of a Working Class,' *Journal of Social History* 7, no. 4 (1974): 460–508. Peter Bailey, 'Conspiracies of Meaning: Music-Hall and the Knowingness of Popular Culture,' *Past & Present*, no. 144 (1994): 138–170.

21. Bailey, 'Conspiracies of Meaning,' 128, 148.

22. Peter Bailey, ed., *Music Hall: The Business of Pleasure* (Milton Keynes: Open University Press, 1986), xvii.

23. Bailey, *Conspiracies of Meaning*, 151.

24. Jacqueline S. Bratton, 'Jenny Hill: Sex and Sexism in the Victorian Music Hall,' in *Music Hall: Performance and Style*, ed. J. S. Bratton (Milton Keynes: Open University Press, 1986), 103–104.

25. *The Era*, 24 October 1885.

26. Faulk, *Music Hall and Modernity*, 23.

27. T. S. Eliot, 'London Letter,' *The Dial*, New York, LXXIII, no. 6 (December, 1922), 659–663.

28. *The North-Eastern Gazette*, 22 January 1984.

29. Bailey, 'Conspiracies of Meaning,' 146.

30. Bratton, 'Introduction,' in *Music Hall: Performance and Style*, xiv.

31. Bridget Elliott, 'Much Ado About Money—Reading British Music Hall in the Nineties,' in *Literature and Money*, ed. Anthony Purdy (Amsterdam: Rodopi, 1993): 45–77 (p. 65); cf. Bratton 1986, 94–95.

32. Elliott, 'Much Ado About Money,' 68–70.

33. *The Era*, 5 May 1894.

34. Judith Walkowitz, *City of Dreadful Delight* (Chicago: University of Chicago Press, 1992), 46.

35. Walkowitz, *City of Dreadful Delight*, 45.

36. Glenn, *Female Spectacle*, 14.
37. *The Era*, 10 May 1884.
38. *The Era*, 25 July 1885.
39. *The Era*, 10 January 1885.
40. *The Era*, 18 September 1886.
41. Judith Flanders, *The Victorian City* (London: Atlantic Books, 2012), 20.
42. Ibid., 422.
43. Faulk, *Music Hall and Modernity*, 13.
44. Peter Bailey, *Popular Culture and Performance in the Victorian City* (Cambridge: Cambridge University Press, 1998), 117.
45. *The Era*, 15 May 1886.
46. Ibid.
47. Flanders, *The Victorian City*, 293.
48. See interview with Jenny Hill in *Era*, 17 June 1893.
49. *Nottingham Guardian*, 4 July 1896.
50. *The Era*, 30 April 1887.
51. *The Era*, 31 October 1885.
52. *The Era*, 6 March 1886.
53. Henry Mayhew, *The Illustrated Mayhew's London*, ed. John Canning (London: Guild Publishing, 1986), 14.
54. John Canning in ibid., 7.
55. Ibid., 30.
56. Ibid., 26.
57. Ibid., 33.
58. Alisun Pawley and Daniel Müllensiefen, 'The Science of Singing Along: A Quantitative Field Study on Sing-Along Behavior in the North of England,' *Music Perception: An Interdisciplinary Journal* 30, no. 2 (2012): 129–146, https://doi.org/10.1525/mp.2012.30.2.129.
59. Noorden, 2010, 155, in Pawley and Müllensiefen, 'The Science of Singing Along,' 130.
60. Stedman Jones, 'Working-Class Culture.'
61. Bailey, *Popular Culture and Performance*, 123.
62. Penelope Summerfield, 'Patriotism and Empire: Music Hall, 1870–1914,' in *Imperialism and Popular Culture*, ed. John MacKenzie (Manchester: Manchester University Press, 1986), 23.
63. Derek B. Scott, *Sounds of the Metropolis: The 19th Century Popular Music Revolution in London, New York, Paris and Vienna* (Oxford: Oxford University Press, 2008), 184–185.
64. Jacky Bratton, *New Readings in Theatre History* (Cambridge: Cambridge University Press, 2003), 37–38.
65. Dagmar Höher, 'The Composition of Music Hall Audiences 1850–1900,' in Bailey, *Music Hall*, 72–92.

66. Elliott, 'Much Ado About Money,' 60–61.
67. Bratton, 'Introduction,' in *Music Hall: Performance and Style*, xii.
68. *The Era*, 17 June 1893.
69. Ibid.
70. Ibid.
71. Bailey, *Popular Culture and Performance*, 122–123.
72. *The Era*, 16 October 1870.
73. J. Seed, 'Limehouse Blues: Looking for "Chinatown" in the London Docks, 1900–40,' *History Workshop Journal* 62 (2006): 59.
74. *The Era*, 16 October 1870.
75. *The Era*, 28 January 1877.
76. *The Era*, 7 January 1872.
77. *The Era*, 17 April 1872.
78. Ibid.
79. Walkowitz, *City of Dreadful Delight*, 73.
80. Ibid., 66.
81. J. Schroeder, 'Speaking Volumes: Victorian Feminism and the Appeal of Public Discussion,' *Nineteenth-century Contexts* 25, no. 2 (2003): 100.
82. J. Holledge, *Innocent Flowers. Women in Edwardian Theatre* (London: Virago Press, 1981), 59.
83. Walkowitz, *City of Dreadful Delight*, 67.

WORKS CITED

Bailey, Peter. 'Conspiracies of Meaning: Music-Hall and the Knowingness of Popular Culture.' *Past and Present* 144 (1994): 138–170.

Bailey, Peter, ed. *Music Hall: The Business of Pleasure*. Milton Keynes: Open University Press, 1986.

Bailey, Peter. *Popular Culture and Performance in the Victorian City*. Cambridge: Cambridge University Press, 1998.

Baker, Richard Anthony. *British Music Hall: An Illustrated History*. Barnsley: Pen and Sword History, 2014.

Beerbohm, Max. *More Theatres 1898–1903*. New York: Taplinger Publishing Company, 1969.

Bratton, Jacky. *New Readings in Theatre History*. Cambridge: Cambridge University Press, 2003.

Bratton, Jacqueline S. *Music Hall: Performance and Style*. Milton Keynes: Open University Press, 1986.

Childs, Michael J. *Labour's Apprentices: Working-Class Lads in Late Victorian and Edwardian England*. London: McGill-Queen's University Press, 1992.

Davis, Tracy. *Actresses as Working Women—Their Social Identity in Victorian Culture*. London: Routledge, 1991.

Eliot, T. S. 'London Letter.' *The Dial* 73, no. 6 (December 1922): 659–663.

Elliott, Bridget. 'Much Ado About Money—Reading British Music Hall in the Nineties.' In *Literature and Money*, edited by Anthony Purdy. Amsterdam: Rodopi, 1993.

Era, 16 October 1870.

Era, 7 January 1872.

Era, 17 April 1872.

Era, 28 January 1877.

Era, 10 May 1884.

Era, 10 January 1885.

Era, 25 July 1885.

Era, 24 October 1885.

Era, 31 October 1885.

Era, 6 March 1886.

Era, 15 May 1886.

Era, 18 September 1886.

Era, 30 April 1887.

Era, 17 June 1893.

Era, 5 May 1894.

Era, 1 April 1914.

Faulk, Barry J. *Music Hall and Modernity: The Late-Victorian Discovery of Popular Culture*. Athens: Ohio University Press, 2004.

Flanders, Judith. *The Victorian City: Everyday Life in Dickens' London*. London: Atlantic Books, 2012.

Glenn, Susan. *Female Spectacle: The Theatrical Roots of Modern Feminism*. Cambridge, MA: Harvard University Press, 2000.

Höher, Dagmar. 'The Composition of Music Hall Audiences 1850–1900.' In *Music Hall: The Business of Pleasure*, edited by Peter Bailey. Milton Keynes: Open University Press, 1986.

Holledge, J. *Innocent Flowers: Women in Edwardian Theatre*. London: Virago Press, 1981.

Jerome, Jerome K. 'Variety Patter.' *The Idler* 1, no. 2 (March 1892): 123–135.

Jones, Gareth Stedman. 'Working-Class Culture and Working-Class Politics in London, 1870–1900: Notes on the Remaking of a Working Class.' *Journal of Social History* 7, no. 4 (1974): 460–508.

Marshall, Gail. *Actresses on the Victorian Stage: Feminine Performance and the Galatea Myth*. Cambridge: Cambridge University Press, 1998.

Mayhew, Henry. *The Illustrated Mayhew's London*. London: Guild Publishing, 1986.

North-Eastern Gazette, The, 22 January 1984.

Nottingham Guardian, 4 July 1896.

Pawley, Alisun, and Daniel Müllensiefen. 'The Science of Singing Along: A Quantitative Field Study on Sing-Along Behaviour in the North of England.' *Music Perception: An Interdisciplinary Journal* 30, no. 2 (2012): 129–146. https://doi.org/10.1525/mp.2012.30.2.129.

Rutherford, Lois. '"Managers in a Small Way": The Professionalisation of Variety Artistes, 1860–1914.' In *Music Hall: The Business of Pleasure*, edited by Peter Bailey. Milton Keynes: Open University Press, 1986.

Schroeder, J. 'Speaking Volumes: Victorian Feminism and the Appeal of Public Discussion.' *Nineteenth-Century Contexts* 25, no. 2 (2003): 97–117.

Scott, Derek B. *Sound of the Metropolis: The 19th Century Popular Music Revolution in London, New York, Paris and Vienna*. Oxford: Oxford University Press, 2003.

Seed, J. 'Limehouse Blues: Looking for "Chinatown" in the London Docks, 1900–40.' *History Workshop Journal* 62 (Autumn 2006): 58–85.

Summerfield, Penelope. 'Patriotism and Empire: Music Hall, 1870–1914.' In *Imperialism and Popular Culture*, edited by John MacKenzie. Manchester: Manchester University Press, 1986.

Vicinus, Martha. *The Industrial Muse: A Study of Nineteenth-Century British Working-Class Literature*. New York: Barnes & Noble, 1974.

Walkowitz, Judith. *City of Dreadful Delight*. Chicago: University of Chicago Press, 1992.

'Deliberately Shaped for Fun by the High Gods': Little Tich, Size and Respectability in the Music Hall

Oliver Double

Little Tich (1867–1928) was one of the most popular comedians of the music hall, inducing extraordinary enthusiasm in audiences, and earning higher rates of pay than many of his rivals. In 1898, he toured in a musical comedy entitled *Billy*, playing the title role in what was very much a star vehicle. Reviewing the show at the Prince's Theatre in June, the *Manchester Guardian* remarked that, 'The bulk of the work falls on Little Tich, and it is not stretching probability very far to suppose that the piece was written to exploit his peculiar talents...He is almost constantly on the stage'.[1] In November, the same newspaper reviewed the show again, this time at the Comedy Theatre, and identified the key element of its comedy:

> It is the size of the Hon. Billy that gives point to most of the fun, and he is made all the smaller by bringing him into contrast with such a giant as Mr

O. Double (✉)
School of Arts, University of Kent, Canterbury, UK

© The Author(s) 2020
L. Lee (ed.), *Victorian Comedy and Laughter*,
https://doi.org/10.1057/978-1-137-57882-2_9

Picton Roxborough. The line of humour is legitimate enough, if it is not overdone. In the present case Little Tich seems to enjoy the joke quite as much as the audience.[2]

It is a simple enough comment and, on the face of it, perfectly valid. Tich was only 4'6" tall, and undoubtedly played on his diminutive stature in his comedy throughout his career. *Billy* made a special feature of his size, casting him opposite Picton Roxborough, who was known as 'the tallest actor on the English stage'.[3] At 6'5", Roxborough would have towered over Tich, and if the difference in heights was not enough, there was even a scene in which the two men wrestled.[4] This comic contrast clearly had legs, because they had already been cast against each other in *Lord Tom Noddy*, a similar musical comedy star vehicle for Tich which toured in 1896–1897.

However, the idea that Little Tich *seemed* to enjoy the jokes about being small as much as the audience demands closer examination. Behind his onstage enjoyment of the gags, Tich's private attitudes towards his size were more complex. Offstage, he desired acceptance and craved the kind of middle-class respectability which was not easy to come by for a humble comic. In touring *Uncle Tom Noddy* and *Billy* to venues like the Comedy Theatre and Manchester's Prince's Theatre, Tich was a low culture music-hall interloper breaking into the high culture world of the legitimate theatre, and that might account for some of the more negative critical responses.

Moreover, gags about his smallness and the high-jinks with Picton Roxborough played to what Lillian Craton has called 'the Victorian fascination with physical difference'.[5] Craton argues that following the Industrial Revolution, 'Middle-class identity was not conferred at birth, but continually earned and always at risk, and so physical markers of economic or moral status took on new importance for defining the middle class'. This gave 'new significance to representations of abnormality' because of 'the importance of *image* – comportment, reputation, and physical appearance – as a sign of social status'.[6] For Tich, respectability was hard won, and the fact that he seemed to enjoy jokes about his physical difference is more a testament to the subtlety of his performance skills than an accurate reflection of how he felt as a small person within the world of popular entertainment.

1   'So Much Amusement That the Audience Refused to Listen to Anyone Else'[7]

Little Tich was born Harry Relph on 21 July 1867, the youngest of 16 children fathered by the 77-year-old landlord of the Blacksmith's Arms in Cudham, Kent. He started performing in local pubs while still a child, dancing, playing the tin whistle and developing a blackface act. By 1880 he was getting his first major public engagements at venues like the Rosherville Gardens in Gravesend, and he made his London Debut at the Foresters Music Hall in 1884. Around this time, he was billing himself as 'Young Tichborne', a reference to the infamous Tichborne Claimant case, and in November 1884 adapted this to Little Tich.

Between 1887 and 1889, Tich toured America with the company of the great vaudeville impresario Tony Pastor, dropping the use of blackface and developing what would become the most celebrated element of his act: the Big Boot Dance. His American experiences were the making of him, and after returning to the UK, he was engaged at the prestigious Empire Music Hall in Leicester Square for £12 a week. In the 1890s, he became one of the biggest stars in British music hall, playing the most important venues and being cast in the celebrated Drury Lane pantomime, as well as starring in musical comedies like *Lord Tom Noddy* and *Billy*. Throughout that decade he also became famous in Europe, appearing at theatres in Berlin, Geneva, Rotterdam, Brussels, Marseilles, Barcelona and Budapest, among others. He lived in Paris for several years, and made his debut in that city at the Folies Bergère in December 1896 to great acclaim. Continuing to enjoy great success at home and abroad, in June 1912 he was one of the acts honoured by being chosen to appear at the first Royal Variety Show at the London Palace.

By the 1920s, his career was suffering from a climate of change in popular entertainment, the music halls increasingly coming under threat from cinema and revue. His earnings in 1925–1926 had dropped by over 80% since the height of his fame. However, he was still making a good living and the following year his income doubled. In November 1927, he was performing a new routine as a charlady when he had an accident and was struck on the head by a mop. A few days later he had a stroke, which left him incapacitated, and he died on 10 February 1928.[8]

Little Tich's craving for recognition and respectability should be seen in the light of the sheer scale of his success. He had remarkable market value, securing frequent bookings at the very best halls. He appeared at the Tivoli for 17 years and at the Palladium for nine consecutive years. This meant his earning power was prodigious. In 1907, the *Daily Mail* published an article about the money made by music-hall artistes, claiming that the going rate for Tich was £150 per week, the equivalent of over £16,000 today. The only acts listed as making better money than this were Arthur Roberts (at £160 per week) and Joe Elvin and company (at £175 per week), although this last sum was for a whole cast rather than a solo act.[9] A 1914 article gave his earnings as £300 per week, suggesting that they had doubled.[10] Even during a career slum, he still earned as much as £2200 in 1925–1926,[11] which would now be worth over £121,000.

He also enjoyed both popularity and critical acclaim, not just in Britain but also in France. The effect he had on audiences was extraordinary. In 1906, a review claimed that, 'At the Manchester Hippodrome on Monday Little Tich caused so much amusement with his dancing and drollery that the audience refused to listen to anyone else, and the bioscope, with pictures of King Haakon's coronation, was brought to the rescue'.[12] It takes a very special kind of comedian to be unfollowable, pleasing the people in the auditorium so much that they will not accept that he has to leave the stage. Nor was this the only time Little Tich created such an effect. In 1922, an act called Charles Althoff had to follow Tich's 45-minute act at the Finsbury Park Empire and found himself facing such a tired audience that he eventually tore his wig off in despair at his inability to register with them.[13]

2   'A HOUSEHOLD WORD TO THOUSANDS WHO HAD NEVER SEEN HIM IN THE FLESH'[14]

Given Tich's success, it is perhaps unsurprising that he spawned many imitators, including Little Pich, Little Ditch and Little Ganty.[15] Indeed, Little Pich made a considerable career out of ripping off Tich's act. Oscar Dreyer, a German agent, suggested to a Hungarian performer named Carl that he should see Little Tich at the Berlin Wintergarten and then provided with the finance to develop his own copycat version of the act.[16] Pich worked internationally, appearing in London and Paris

Alhambra as well as touring the Orpheum vaudeville circuit across the USA. His career lasted at least five years, with references to him cropping up in the trade press between 1906 and 1911, albeit sometimes under the name 'Little Carl' which he was occasionally forced to adopt.[17]

Critics' attitude towards Pich tended to be scornful, a review of his appearance at the Empire, Leicester Square in September 1906, noting that although he 'models himself closely on Little Tich, even to the make-up and the long boot... his method is more extravagant, and his voice is both unmelodious and inaudible'.[18] Pich clearly knew the value of his stolen stage routines, and—with delicious irony—in 1911 refused to go on at the Paris Alhambra in protest at one of the other acts which he believed to be imitating him:

> There was an amusing incident at the Alhambra June 16, when the new program was presented by the summer tenants. Little Pich refused to go on, affirming that a couple of English comics were 'copying' a part of his act. This consisted of reaching over, stiff-backed, and picking up a hat direct by the head. Little Tich (I mean Little Pich) does this in his big boots; the English couple do it by slipping a foot into a loop on the table. It was certainly similar in effect, and hence the alleged 'copy.' The program continued that evening without the appearance of Pich, but there was no riot in the hall.[19]

Imitations of Tich did not just appear on the stage. Craftsmen depicted him in the form of tiny automata that were used in seaside slot machines or sold as music boxes to decorate private homes. When operated, they would come to life, performing his famous Big Boot Dance.[20] Little Tich starred in his own comic strip, in the children's comic *Merry and Bright*. The cover of the issue dated 15 January 1916, for example, features a strip in which he performs a fantastical version of his stage act, using his big boots to steal the cigar of an aristocratic heckler sitting in one of the boxes. He also licensed his likeness to be used in advertising, like the newspaper advert for Odol mouthwash which shows him wearing his big boots, inclining his body towards the product and saying, 'I felt a decided leaning towards that bottle'.[21]

Thus, Tich's act spilled off the stage into everyday life, leaving a lasting impact on popular culture. He was seen as a symbol of Britishness, representing his country and its capital city. Reporting Harry Relph's death in 1928, the *Daily Mirror* recalled that the French actor, Sacha

Guitry's first words on arriving at Victoria Station a few years earlier were, 'Where is Little Tich?'; and argued that the diminutive music-hall comic 'was, evidently, for M. Guitry, as for hundreds of other Frenchmen, a being typically *Londonian*. It was as though the question had been: "Why is there not a fog? Show me some *rosbif* and a police-man!"'[22] Indeed, Tich's impact in France was considerable, another journalist arguing that 'he was probably more esteemed [in Paris] than in [his] native haunts' and noting that the French Minister of Public Instruction had conferred the Ordre des Palmes Académiques on him in 1910.[23] Tich was remembered long after his death, with critics denigrating contemporary comedians in comparison with him right up to the mid-1960s.[24] More than four decades after his death, he was still famous enough to merit a blue plaque being erected on a house in Hendon where he had lived.[25]

Perhaps his most important legacy was the fact that he gave a word to the English language. The word 'titch', used to refer to any small person, derives from Harry Relph's stage name. Remarkably, this had come into common usage well within his own lifetime. On his death, the variety critic Archibald Haddon noted that, 'So famous was the name that innumerable under-sized boys and men throughout the country have been nicknamed Tich by their mates. It was, indeed, a household word to thousands who had never seen him in the flesh'.[26] The ventriloquist A. C. Astor expanded on the idea:

> There is for me something of magic in the name of Little Tich. It conjures up an astonishing little man whose name had trickled even so far as the remote North Country village where I spent my early years, for the son of a gardener in the village, being very diminutive, was, and probably still is, known as 'Tich.' And since Harry Relph first achieved fame with the then topical name of Little Tich, there have sprung into existence thousands of little Tiches. Every big workshop has one, in almost any walk of life the small man responds to the kindly nickname of Tich, and usually accepts it with such grace that he doubtless quite forgets his real cognomen.[27]

This suggests that the word 'Tich' was long-established when Relph died, and there is plenty of evidence that 'Tich' and 'Little Tich' were popular references even while he was still in his twenties. In 1892, a race-horse named Little Tich ran at Lincoln.[28] In 1897, the *Times* published a letter which includes 'Little Tich' as an example of well-known phrases charged as two words when sending a telegram.[29] In 1899, 'Little Tich' was being used as an alias by a 44-year-old criminal appearing at Bow Street.[30] In 1910, it was reported that Claude Hay, the Conservative MP for Hoxton and Shoreditch, had been nicknamed Little Tich 'because he was at once the smallest and the most irrepressible person at Westminster'.[31] In 1914, a polo pony named Little Tich was sold at Tattersall's for 110 guineas.[32] In 1915, a tiny schoolboy cricketer was nicknamed Little Tich by the soldiers watching him play in a match at Lords.[33]

'Tich' is still commonly used today, although it is more usually spelled 'titch', and—as the *OED* points out–has also spawned the adjective 'titchy'. 'Titch' was used as the name for the title character in a series of children's books by Pat Hutchins, the first of which was published in 1971, and these later became an animated series.

There is a certain irony about the fact that we refer to small people as 'titch', given the origins of the word. Arthur Orton, the Tichborne Claimant, had been conspicuously corpulent at the time of the legal case in which he falsely claimed to be Roger Tichborne, the heir to a wealthy family, who had been lost at sea in 1854. Thus 'Tichborne' was often used as a nickname for fat people, and in his childhood Harry Relph was overweight enough to be known as 'Young Tichborne'. He had lost the weight by the time he adopted the stage name Little Tich, so the word 'Tich' or 'Titch' became associated with shortness of stature rather than stoutness of girth. Thus, the name of a famously large man eventually mutated into a word that refers to smallness.

3   'FULLY-GROWN ADULTS WITH FULLY ADULT FEELINGS'[34]

Onstage, Little Tich was happy to make use of his size, deciding in his teens that 'a diminutive stature might be an aid to humour' and acknowledging that 'it has been an important part of my stock-in-trade ever since'.[35] It was a similar decision to that taken by the tiny Miss Mowcher in Charles Dickens's *David Copperfield* (1850) who declares: 'If there are people so unreflecting or so cruel, as to make a jest of me, what is left for me to do but to make a jest of myself, them, and everything?'[36]

Tich's act was littered with gags about his lack of height. In one routine, he refers to his wife as his better half, adding, 'Or to be more correct, my better two and three quarters'. In another, an old maid picks him up in the mad rush of a sale, mistaking him for a 'fourpenny gol-liwog'. A typical line uses his size as the basis of a self-deprecating gag about his intellect: 'I'm a bigger fool than I look. Er, or I should say to be more correct, I, I don't look as big a fool as I am. Er – and now I'm not right'. His tininess is often exaggerated to the point of absurdity, showing him getting lost down a rabbit hole, or sitting in the whip-hole of a horse-drawn cab.[37] In one song, he points out a distinct advantage to being so surreally small:

> The Don of the Don Juans,
> The ladies around me throng,
> They can hide me under their Dorothy bags
> If their husbands come along.[38]

Beyond specific gags, his size seems to have fuelled his comedy in a more general sense, playing an intrinsic part in his characterisations. J. B. Priestley, a big fan of Tich, recalled that all of his parodies of social types 'were seen as if through a diminishing glass, or as visitors from some society of gnomes, and you began laughing at the first sight of them, all the more because they looked intensely serious, often arriving in a furi-ous state of indignation'.[39] This echoed the critics of Tich's time. One, for example, wrote that, 'Little Tich, being short of inches, makes us laugh by mocking dignity'.[40] The idea here seems to be that seriousness, indignation or dignity become inherently ridiculous when they are pre-sented by a conspicuously short man.

However, offstage Tich was himself a serious man, often indignant about his struggle for dignity as a small person. Like Miss Mowcher, he was well aware of the ignorance and cruelty that lay behind the laugh-ter at his size. The social model of disability, developed from the ideas of the Union of Physically Impaired Against Segregation in the 1970s, separates a person's impairments from their disability, instead suggesting that 'Disability is something imposed on top of our impairments by the way we are unnecessarily isolated and excluded from full participation in society'.[41] To be disabled, then, a person must have both physical impair-ments and social factors which mean that these impairments restrict the possibilities available to them. Tich had physical differences from those about him which made him conspicuous, but there is little evidence that he had any significant functional impairment. The abnormalities in his hands created slight restrictions in his use of them, but he had enough manual dexterity to paint and play the piano and cello well. A boyhood accident left him with a right foot that turned slightly inwards, but his dancing and acrobatics show that this must have created no real physical restrictions. Indeed, the eloquence of his legs was remarked on in reviews, one of which praised the 'little waggles of the leg [which] one would lose a few years of life to describe'.[42]

In terms of sheer physical ability, the feats he accomplished in his act suggest that far from being disabled, he was, if anything, supremely able. However, the disabling social factor of Victorian attitudes to physical difference, and the barrier they posed to middle-class respectability, meant that he often felt isolated and excluded. He was regarded as deformed, not just for his unusual shortness but because he also had an extra finger on each hand—something which made him extremely self-conscious. Sometimes critics were cruel about his size, a review of his performance in *Lord Tom Noddy* describing him as a 'debauched homunculus'.[43] Others were more patronising, as in the review of the same show which suggested that 'his performance has doubtless its attractions', but only 'for those who can get over the painfulness of seeing capital made of physical defects'.[44] Writing in the *World*, William Archer even suggested that there was something uncivilised about allowing somebody who looked like Harry Relph to appear on the stage for the entertainment of audiences:

> I have seen 'Little Tich' before, in the distance, so to speak, at Drury Lane. The grotesque surroundings of pantomime seemed his natural habitat; he appeared to enjoy his antics, and one accepted him as a gnome in the fairy world. But to see him in close quarters in a small theatre, figuring as a real human being, and the hero, forsooth, of what purports to be a love story! I can only say that I would rather be 'Little Tich' himself than the man or woman who can find pleasure in such a spectacle. He, poor fellow, cannot help his diminutiveness, his crookedness, his superfluity of fingers, and if he can make money by exhibiting these things, who shall blame him for doing so? The true hideousness is that of a society which pays to see him and laugh at such spectacles, instead of paying liberally to have them kept out of sight.[45]

A review of *Billy* in 1898 praised Tich's performance and had no problem with his penchant for 'eccentric humour', but shared Archer's distaste at the suggestion that the comedian should be capable of romance:

'[I]t is a mistake to represent him as the hero of what is meant to be a serious love interest, ending with marriage bells'.[46]

Such comments highlight the attitudes Tich faced as both a little person and a music-hall performer. It is fine for him to appear in his 'natural habitat' of low culture music hall or pantomime, but not in a musical comedy at a legitimate theatre like the Garrick. Similarly, it is fine for him to appear as a comic grotesque, but not as 'a real human being', still less one who marries and thus acquires a physical marker of moral status that affords middle-class respectability. Archer's solution of barring people like Tich from appearing in public seems to be driven by what Craton calls 'a fear that middle-class normalcy...faced contamination from freaks'.[47] Tich not only faced this kind of prejudice in his stage work, but also in his everyday life. It was impossible to shed the comic novelty of his stature when he left the stage, as Benny Green pointed out in 1986: 'Unlike most of his fellow-artists, he could not take off his make-up once the act was finished. His whole comic persona was built on his tiny body. When he left the stage door, his freakishness went with him'.[48] He hated being pointed at, and preferred Paris to London because fewer people stared at him there.

He was not just indignant on his own behalf, though, and was angered by prejudice on the basis of physical smallness, no matter who was on the receiving end of the sniggering. Seeing a Toy Town scene at a circus, featuring a cast of 'midgets' who were personally known to him, he carefully explained to his young daughter, 'Although they may look like children, they are fully grown adults with fully adult feelings'. Similarly, on a ship bound for Australia he came across a group of passengers laughing at some performers from the Lester's Midgets troupe in the swimming pool, and furiously chided them: 'You seem to forget that these are men and women just the same as you. But a good deal more intelligent than *you* are'.[49]

4   'Not a Midget, Nor Was He a Dwarf'[50]

However, although Tich felt kinship with other little people, his daughter was insistent that he 'was certainly not a midget, nor was he a dwarf, although he has often been inaccurately described as one'.[51] This seems to be a simple enough statement, pointing out that her father did not have either of the medical conditions associated with those two terms (which are now seen as rather archaic or insulting). However, there is more to it than that, because 'midget' and 'dwarf' are also part of the lexicon of the freak show, and Relph must have been keen to dissociate himself from that world. Early in his career, he accepted being marketed as a freak, using publicity materials which included the sentence: 'The Wonder of the Age, having Six Fingers and one Thumb on each Hand. A Decided Novelty'. He even sang a song called 'Six Fingers and a Thumb',[52] which similarly played up the freakishness of his extra digits, if exaggerating their number.

As Robert Bodgan has eloquently argued, '"Freak" is not a quality that belongs to the person on display. It is something that we created: a perspective, a set of practices—a social construction'.[53] As with the social model of disability, in the freak show physical difference is less important than the social frame that gives it meaning. The condition of being a freak is not inherent, but is constructed in order to frame disability or deformity to suggest that it is something marvellous, grotesque or intriguing, purely for the purposes of commercial entertainment. Freak show impresarios would take people—sometimes even people without any abnormality whatsoever—and turn them into freaks by providing them with a new name, image and even a fake biography. As one sideshow manager put it, '[F]reaks are what you make them. Take any peculiar looking person, whose familiarity to those around him makes for acceptance, play up that peculiarity and add a good spiel and you have a great attraction'.[54]

Bogdan points out that, within the conventions of the freak show, the terms 'midget' and 'dwarf' had particular meanings, relating to the way that different types of freak were created by being framed in different ways:

> Small people who were well proportioned – 'perfect humans in miniature' – in particular coveted the term *midget* for themselves as a way of disaffiliating from the more physically deformed 'dwarf' exhibits. For midgets, who were typically cast in the high aggrandized mode, to be called a 'dwarf' was like being called a 'child': it was an insult. 'Dwarfs' were associated with exotic freak or circus clown roles, and these roles 'midgets' shunned.[55]

Thus, 'midget' and 'dwarf' were terms used to denote position within the hierarchy of the freak show, and Tich would have not want to be described with either word as he did not want to be seen as part of that

world. As somebody who craved middle-class respectability, he would
have been keenly aware that within the hierarchy of live performance,
a star of the music-hall occupied a far more respectable position than a
mere sideshow freak.

That he saw the difference as important is suggested by an anecdote he shared more than once, about something that happened to
him while touring America in the late 1880s. During an engagement at
the Chicago Opera House, he decided to pay a visit to a dime museum—a typical venue for the exhibition of freaks—which he describes in
his memoir as 'a sort of chamber of horrors and lunatic asylum combined!' As the museum fills up, he finds the curious customers who
have paid a dime to see such wonders as a bearded lady and a 'live mer-
maid' instead start paying attention to him: 'I found…that the people
were crowding round and staring at *me!* …Everybody was staring at me
and whispering. I was feeling most embarrassed and annoyed. So out
I went'. On leaving, he discovers the proprietor of the museum shouting, 'Step this way, ladies and gentlemen! The opportunity of a lifetime!
Little Tich, the famous comedian from the Opera House, *now on view!*'
While being struck by the proprietor's impudence, he also feels 'a certain
pride' because 'I could see that I was getting on! Already I had become a
"draw"!'[56]

The humour in the story relies on the audience in the dime museum
mistaking Relph for an exhibit, and although it is never explicitly stated,
the clear suggestion is that he initially thinks they are staring at him
because of his size. For this moment, he thinks he is being viewed as
a midget or a dwarf and is suitably annoyed by the audience's mistake.
The conclusion—in which it is revealed that they simply want to stare at
a star of the stage—is a happy ending, because it shows him that he has
acquired precisely the kind of star status that would allow him to avoid
being exhibited in a dime museum. This is the basic incongruity which
gives the anecdote its comic quality.

5   'He Surprises and Amuses His Audience a Hundred Times in as Many Seconds'[57]

However, it was more than status that separated Little Tich from the
freaks of the dime museum and the side show. There was also the crucial
matter of his talent. According to Bogdan, many freaks 'were presented
as "human wonder", but they did not sing opera or claim heroic feats;

rather, they merely performed pedestrian tasks which the marks assumed were too difficult for them given their physical disabilities'.[58] Similarly, Julie Anderson argues that when freaks 'demonstrated how they managed their daily chores', this 'appeared wondrous and amazing' because of 'the public's perception of the limitation of their bodies'.[59]

By contrast, Tich's act was wondrous and amazing not merely because of the audience's limited expectations of him. There was nothing *pedestrian* about him, and many of his routines could accurately be described as *heroic feats*. The Big Boot Dance is a case in point. There are two films of this routine in existence, the better known of which was made by Alice Guy and shown at the 1900 Paris Universal Exposition, as a very early attempt to use synchronised sound, which was played on a cylinder.[60] Here, Little Tich is shown performing in front of a painted backdrop depicting a street scene, and this short version of the routine contains many of its trademark stunts.

Tich wrings a good deal of comic business out of the process of putting on his boots, which are long, thin and flattish, extending forwards to make each foot almost as long as his legs. Having put them on, and let them flap about for a second or two, he moves from sitting to standing. This is achieved in one blink-and-you-miss-it move, splaying his legs outwards, then sliding them back together so that the soles end up on the floor as his torso rises up. He follows this with a couple of moves which involve swinging the boots around in mad circles, knocking his battered top hat off his head. This takes him into a series of stunts in which he leans forward—keeping his legs and body in a rigid straight line—at a crazy angle which appears to be only about 45 degrees from the stage. The first lean allows him to retrieve his hat, which he places on his head before doing a series of similar leans to left and right.

After a couple of bits of business, including balancing his hat on his nose by the brim, he sits back down on the floor, and does a gag in which he traps his hand between the boots. Then he flips over onto his front and walks on his hands back up to standing, pivoting over the toes of the big boots in the process. This allows him to walk towards his hat—which is now upside down on the floor in front of him—and lean down in such a way as to scoop it up onto his head. It is time for the climax. He goes up onto tiptoes, his absurd footwear becoming a ridiculously rickety-looking pair of stilts, and takes a couple of precarious steps. His final move is to walk off stage right, giving his farewell bow by leaning back into the frame with one last crazy-angled lean.

Although it is played for laughs, it is an unmistakable display of physical skill, and this version does not even include all the stunts in the routine. A later film shows him doing the tiptoe stilt stunt in the middle of some furious tap dancing[61]—no mean feat in such improbably big boots. Nor was the Big Boot Dance the sum total of Tich's achievements. Indeed, J. B. Priestley recalled being 'glad' when he made less use of the boots, because 'after all they were just a gimmick and he remained a great comedian without any help from them'.[62] Tich had a large repertoire, and also performed numerous comic songs in character, not to mention other dance routines like his celebrated Loie Fuller parody.[63]

Contemporary commentators suggest that his real strength lay not in his material but in the way he performed it. A review from March 1901 suggests that 'songs are the mere incidentals of Little Tich's entertainment', and another from September that same year makes a similar point: 'It is not his songs that make Little Tich the great man of the music-hall stage, nor yet his singing, but the innumerable asides and tricks and mannerisms with which he surprises and amuses his audience a hundred times in as many seconds'.[64]

The recollections of those who actually saw Tich's act suggest that there were a number of key elements to his performance style. Firstly, whether doing a dance routine or delivering comic patter, he was an intensely physical performer. J. B. Priestley's account gives an idea of the extraordinary energy of his act:

> The tale of his grievances was illustrated by nothing less than a fury of movement and gestures...He only had to say 'I went in', and his tiny legs went hurtling across the stage and we saw him bursting through an invisible door. If he said he would show us what he thought about some obstreperous fellow, his dumbshow would almost explode into wild careering round the stage, punching and kicking away, defying men of any weight to come near him.[65]

Secondly, in spite of the manic energy his physicality was also capable of fine detail, like the 'little waggles of the leg' which led a critic to claim that 'one would lose a few years of life to describe'.[66] There is a lovely gag in the Big Boot Dance in which he takes one of his crazy straight-bodied leans a degree or two too far. He only takes an instant to communicate the idea that he has overshot, pulling a face and flapping his hands in alarm. Having pulled himself back to perpendicular, he takes his hat off, ruefully looks off to his left as if catching the eyes of some-body in the wings, and wipes imaginary fear-sweat off his forehead. The fake mistake gag could have ended there, but he takes it a step further, shaking the sweat from his hand into his hat, swirling it around in the bottom for a moment, then emptying it onto the stage.

All of this is mimed with utter precision and economy, the whole sequence lasting no more than five seconds. Developing bits of business like this allowed him to spin out the sequence of putting his boots on at the beginning of the dance longer and longer, until it became the main body of the routine. As he put it, 'I am able to make so much play of putting them on now that I hardly need to dance in them'.[67]

The third key element of his performance was his ability to connect with the audience. As with many of his contemporaries, the songs he sang were not what we would recognise as conventional songs. They would start with a couple of verses and choruses, then go into a long patter routine before going into a final chorus. This was the direct pre-cursor to stand-up comedy, and just like today's comedians, Tich had the invisible skill—sometimes called 'charisma' or 'presence'—of forging an immediate, powerful rapport with the people watching him. According to Mary Tich's biography, 'As soon as he came on the stage he con-nected with the emotional voltage in the auditorium, concentrated it and somehow intensified it, by the power that great performers often apply'.[68]

Of course, this phenomenon is extremely difficult to pin down, and in his memoir Tich himself makes a gag out of floundering around in the attempt to define it: 'That how-shall-we-term-it whereby one man can as-it-were a song in such a way as to you-grasp-the-idea, when another man, with the same song, would draw tears of anguish from a laughing hyena, is something very slippery'.[69]

Fourthly, there was a knowing sophistication to his comedy. He would draw attention to his own technique, laying bare his processes in order to focus on the here and now and eliminate any barriers of artifice between performer and audience. J. B. Priestley was not the only person to allude to this, but his account is the most precise:

> His act, for all its mad energy, kept moving into another and cool dimen-sion, where we observed and estimated it with him. The clever eyes would give us a wink or at least a twinkle, asking us to join him as a sophisticated performer, pretending for our amusement to be an indignant jockey or

outraged lady in court dress. He would suddenly take us behind the scenes with him, doing it with a single remark. He would offer us a joke and then confide that it went better the night before. He would drop a hat and be unable to pick it up, because he kicked it out of reach every time, and then mutter, half in despair, 'Comic business with *chapeau*'.[70]

This kind of sophisticated frame-breaking brings to mind the work of present-day comedians like Stewart Lee, and the use of the French word for hat highlights a link with another of Tich's comic descendents: Eddie Izzard. Like Izzard, Tich performed in France to French audiences, using his own unique version of their language, supplemented by the odd English phrase. C. B. Cochrane's account gives an idea of the overall effect: "*Je m'appelle Clarice*", said Tich, with that chuckle...Continuing, in French – more or less: "I am an admiral's daughter – I've just come from the Court ball – oh, my success! – what a *succès fou!* – *beaucoup de success* – very nice!" – the "very nice" always in English'.[71] According to one source, he could also perform his act in German.[72]

6   'I SPEND MONTHS IN PERFECTING MYSELF IN A SONG'[73]

In 1900, an interviewer asked Tich if he worked the act out beforehand, to which he replied, 'Oh, no. That wouldn't work. Of course, we must have some idea of what we are going to do. But I always find it best to depend upon the jeu d'esprit of the moment. See how I get on with the audience and so forth'.[74] By suggesting that his act was simply fuelled by 'jeu d'esprit', he was denying the toil and danger that he put himself through to attain the level of skill seen in his act, and playing along with the idea that what the audience saw onstage was a simply outpouring of natural talent. Indeed, it was fancifully suggested that there was some special scientific link between his talent as a comedian and his stature:

> One laughs at him wonderingly; indulging in such speculations as whether his smallness of stature may not have contributed by some physiological process to his success as a comedian. So great and expansive a spirit of fun is compressed within so diminutive a body that in its efforts to find expression it uses every avenue of escape.[75]

Another commentator alluded to the metaphysical to explain his funniness, suggesting that he was 'deliberately shaped for fun by the high gods'.[76] Many agreed that there was something other-worldly about Tich, comparing him with a range of mythical creatures. He was 'a being sprung out of one of Grimm's Fairy Tales', a 'rum elfin creature', a 'droll dwarf comedian', an 'incomparable gnome of fantasy', an 'entertaining Lilliputian', and was 'like a Norwegian troll in his minute, terrific sprightliness'.[77] This kind of language echoes Dickens' descriptions of small characters like Miss Mowcher—referred to as an 'imp of supernatural intelligence'—and the 'perfectly goblin-like' Quilp in *The Old Curiosity Shop*.[78]

If all this magical imagery suggested that Tich was somehow inhuman, in some cases this idea was explicitly stated. A review of an appearance at the Manchester Hippodrome in 1928 argues that:

> He does not imitate human beings, and when he is on the stage he hardly seems to be a human being. Not an action is normal; not a word is other than impish; there is not a twist of the features that might not appropriately belong to an incarnation of mockery and mischief which would cause but little surprise if it were suddenly to fly up the ray of the limelight on a broomstick.[79]

Such whimsy denied the fact that Tich was an extremely talented and hardworking professional, but he occasionally opened up to interviewers about the toil that lay behind his act: 'It may seem very easy for me to come on to the stage and deliver my patter, but I may tell you that I spend months in perfecting myself in a song with its accompanying make-up and actions before I think of submitting it to my audiences'.[80] He never shied away from putting in these months of graft, introducing new songs into his repertoire throughout his career.

The act involved not just skill and hard work, but also risk. There are many accounts of how difficult and painful it was for him to perform the Big Boot Dance. In 1909, he was doing the routine on a raked stage in Belfast and fell during the tiptoe stunt where the boots became stilts, dislocating his knee in the process. Subsequently, he dropped this bit from the dance, and later omitted the whole routine from his act. Cutting his signature bit from his repertoire was a brave choice, and could lead to trouble. Earlier, in 1905, when he missed the boot routine at the Tivoli in Sydney, the audience got so annoyed at the lack of big boots that they 'guyed' him, leading to an altercation in which he suggested that they were not 'decent and respectable' and they 'howled at the comedian'.[81]

The dislocated knee was by no means the most serious injury to befall him in the course of making people laugh—it is thought that his accident with the mop while performing 'The Charlady' at the Alhambra in 1927 brought on the stroke which led to his death a few months later.

Given the toil and risk, it might seem odd that Tich would tell a reporter that the whole act was just a bit of spontaneous *jeu d'esprit*, but in fact it is not surprising that Tich would promote the idea that his act was essentially improvised. Like stand-up comedy, music-hall performance was firmly rooted in the present tense, and the powerful connection between performer and audience relied on creating the illusion of spontaneity even when presenting frequently repeated material. One critic was perceptive enough to realise this, writing that Tich displayed 'a spontaneity – or a splendid imitation of it – that is irresistible'.[82]

7   'TICH HE WAS IN PUBLIC AND RELPH IN PRIVATE'[83]

The subtle performance skills of comics like Little Tich meant that music hall was shot through with this kind of ambiguity, and this made it hard to draw a clear line between the world of the stage and everyday life. Not only was it hard to tell the prepared from the spontaneous, there was also an essential ambiguity about just how the comedian seen onstage related to the performer in private life. In legitimate theatre there was no such confusion. Henry Irving may have been extremely engaging as Mathias in *The Bells*, but it is unlikely that audiences would have had problems distinguishing between the actor and the character he played.

In music hall it was not so simple. The onstage role was much more closely associated with the offstage performer, and there was a notion that the comedy performed onstage was an expression of self. Indeed, special efforts were made by some in the business to maintain the image created onstage in everyday life. For example, in the 1860s, George Leybourne was contracted to appear in public every day and buy drinks for members of the public to maintain his 'Champagne Charlie' persona.[84] Having said this, it was not uncommon for comedians to stress the difference between their onstage and offstage identities, portraying themselves as much more respectable and middle-class in their private lives than the personas they adopted in the music halls. This was particularly true of Little Tich, whose daughter recalled that his private life was 'kept rigidly separate from his professional career'.[85]

Offstage, Harry Relph was very different from the grotesques he played onstage. Photographs show him as a serious, smartly dressed man, striking rather formal poses. He was well-read and cultured, painting watercolours, playing the piano and the cello, and learning to speak French, German, Spanish and Italian. He tended to stay outside of the music-hall social scene, but counted among his friends artists like Paul Nash and Toulouse-Lautrec, who was supposedly exactly the same height as him. Nash wrote that Tich's public personality was 'a very different personality from his private character which was rather grave and inclined to studiousness',[86] and many more made the same observation. For Archibald Haddon, the use of different names to indicate onstage and offstage identities was crucial:

> The famous stage name of this wonderful little artist – the greatest music-hall grotesque of his time – is here placed in inverted commas because that is how he signed his letters to me. In his dressing room, where I chatted with him many times of late, the basket containing his costumes bore the letters 'H.R.' for he was born and christened Harry Relph; so Tich he was in public and Relph in private.[87]

In his ghost-written memoir, Tich used his keen awareness of the difference between stage persona and private self as the basis of an amusing anecdote. In 1898, the Belgian painter Jan van Beers saw Tich perform at the Olympia in Paris, and after the show approached him to ask him to pose for a painting. Van Beers said Tich's smile reminded him of Mr. Punch, and in the memoir this becomes a comic moment in which Tich 'weighed [the comment] up awhile before I thanked him!'—clearly not sure quite what to make of an apparently unflattering comparison. To clarify the situation, he asks, 'You refer to my *stage* smile?' The implication is that it is fine for the stage persona to be compared to a grotesque puppet, but not the private man. Subsequently, Tich 'paid a visit to [van Beers'] house...taking the smile with me'—humorously referring to his own facial expression as if it were as artificial and separable from himself as a prop or item of costume.[88]

However, it must have been difficult for the comedian to maintain a clear separation between Relph and Tich given the extent to which his act spilled off the stage into everyday life, what with multiple imitators, appearances in adverts and comic strips, his likeness being used in music boxes and automata, and his stage name becoming a common phrase. He would often be reminded of his stage identity when going about his business. To give one example, his daughter recalled that the tune that accompanied his Big Boot Dance—especially written for him by the composer Auguste Bosc—was often played by restaurant and theatre orchestras if he was known to be present.[89]

8   'A PERFORMER ENTITLED TO BE CALLED AN ARTIST'[90]

It might have seemed to the reviewer of *Billy* that Tich enjoyed the jokes about his size 'quite as much as the audience', but offstage he did not care for such humour. As one of his obituaries noted:

> Although Little Tich made full artistic use of his littleness he was not at all disposed to allow any humorous references to the stature of Mr. Harry Relph. He was, indeed, very sensitive about it, and was mortally offended at being regarded as a freak, as facetious colleagues would discover.[91]

Such sensitivity is understandable given that he was framed as a freak at the beginning of his career. His daughter argued that 'he could not only acquiesce but actively co-operate in marketing this exaggeration of his own disability—about which he felt such self-humiliation in private' because of 'desperate economic pressures'.[92] It was only his talent and the hard work he put into the act that allowed him to move up from being a humble freak to a more respectable music-hall comic, and one who appeared in musical comedies in legitimate theatres to boot. Given this experience, it is easy to understand his keen awareness of the precariousness of his position within the hierarchies of show business and society at large.

In joking at the expense of his height Harry Relph was taking a pragmatic decision, which he probably could not have avoided. Even today, it is a standard ploy for comedians to joke about their inherent physical properties, no matter what shape or size they are—but given the Victorian fascination with physical difference, he had little choice but to frame his size as something comical for audiences to laugh freely at. The fact that he seemed to enjoy the size jokes as much as the audience was probably, in fact, a manifestation of his comic skill. When comedians corpse at their own gags, this is often part of the 'splendid imitation' of spontaneity, which allows them to forge such a strong relationship with the audience. As Priestley pointed out, Tich's clever eyes would give a wink or a twinkle to communicate to the people watching him that he was in on the joke, thus 'asking us to join him as a sophisticated performer'. It seems likely that it was just this kind of technique which led critics to suggest he enjoyed joking about how small he was.

What this reveals is the sophistication of music-hall technique, which involved a far more complex and ambiguous relationship between onstage and off, between fiction and reality, than in legitimate theatre. Much of what appears to be natural and spontaneous is actually carefully planned and repeated night after night, and the completeness of this illusion can lead to confusion between onstage persona and the private person of the offstage world. Harry Relph was keen to separate himself from his Little Tich persona, not least because he wanted to avoid the indignity of being pointed at and patronised in his everyday existence.

Privately—as well as craving middle-class respectability for himself—he had a strong sense of justice and fairness, and his dislike of being treated differently was not just a matter of personal pride. Seeing other little people being ridiculed or mistreated angered him just as it would if that disdain were directed against him. He also felt strongly about the way his own profession was seen. Relph stood up for other music-hall performers, and was a leading player in the Music Hall War of 1907, an industrial dispute against the managements of the syndicates which were becoming increasingly dominant.

The artistes felt that pay and conditions were worsening, particularly for the lowest-paid acts, and went on strike in support of their demands. Relph eagerly participated, failing to turn up for an engagement at the Tivoli and sending the humorous message: 'I am learning a new cornet solo, cannot tear myself away'.[93] He allowed a strike meeting to be held at his flat, at which he donated £20 towards the 'emergency fund for poor artists',[94] this being the equivalent of over £2100 today. Given the skill, dedication and risks involved in his act, it is perhaps not surprising that he was also infuriated by the comparatively humble position which music-hall occupied in the hierarchy of theatre. During Tich's career music hall was shifting its identity, with the syndicates that ran it actively seeking to shed its raucous, working-class image and gain respectability among the middle classes.[95] The Royal Variety Performance of 1912 was a very tangible sign of success in this respect. However, although more dignified than the freak show, music-hall continued to be seen as culturally lower than legitimate theatre, entertainment rather than art.

This rankled with Relph, as Archibald Haddon recalled shortly after his death, talking of a 'personal grievance which he aired to me repeatedly. He loved to think of himself, before all, as a performer entitled to be called an artist, and he imagined that newspaper critics begrudged him the distinction'.[96] When his friend George Robey was knighted, Relph was indignant that this was to recognise his war work and not his achievements as a music-hall comedian:

> Why is it that a variety artiste is never singled out for distinction of this kind on his professional merits, while actors in the so-called legitimate and even managers in variety are considered eligible to have handles to their names? ...This country...is supposed to be more democratic than ever it was. Yet the line of demarcation between variety artistes and 'actors' is, in this respect, drawn as rigidly as ever. No such division is made in France or in America. There an actor is an actor, whether he plays Hamlet or wears the red nose and sloppy trousers of a vaudeville comedian...I maintain that on the score of individual ability the variety star is usually the better actor of the two. He has to do everything off his own bat, as it were, whereas the actor gets the support of his company. This makes a vast difference in the demand on the individual. Moreover, a variety star contributes individually much more to the general scheme of entertainment and the gaiety of nations. And I think it will be admitted that he enjoys, at least, an equal amount of popularity among his fellow-countrymen.[97]

This last point hits home particularly hard, coming from a man so popular with his fellow-countrymen that he added a new word to their language within his own lifetime.

NOTES

1. 'Prince's Theatre, Billy,' *Manchester Guardian*, 7 June 1898, 8.
2. 'Comedy Theatre, Billy,' *Manchester Guardian*, 8 November 1898, 9.
3. 'Prince's Theatre, Lord Tom Noddy,' *Manchester Guardian*, 26 May 1896, 5.
4. 'Alexandra Theatre,' *Morning Post*, 24 August 1898, 2.
5. Lillian Craton, *The Victorian Freak Show* (Amherst, NY: Cambria Press, 2009), 2.
6. Craton, 30.
7. 'Variety Theatres,' *Manchester Guardian*, 4 July 1906, 12.
8. Much of this information is taken from Mary Tich and Richard Findlater, *Little Tich: Giant of the Music Hall* (London: Elm Tree Books, 1979).

9. 'What Artistes Earn,' *Daily Mail*, 24 January 1907, 8.
10. 'King's Bench Division. The Action by Miss Vesta Victoria. Terry v Moss' Empires (Limited), *The Times*, 12 December 1914, 3.
11. Tich and Findlater, 140.
12. 'Variety Theatres,' *Manchester Guardian*, 4 July 1906, 12.
13. 'Althoff's Comeback,' *Variety*, 6 October 1922, 2.
14. Archibald Haddon, '"Little Tich." Memories and Anecdotes. The Evolution of the Boots,' *The Observer*, 12 February 1928, 23.
15. See 'London Notes,' *Variety*, 14 September 1907, 8; Edward G. Kendrew, 'Paris Notes,' *Variety*, 2 January 1909, 9.
16. C. C. Bartram, 'London Notes,' *Variety*, 6 October 1906, 8.
17. 'London Notes,' 14 September 1907.
18. 'His Child,' *Manchester Guardian*, 16 September 1906, 8.
19. Edward G. Kendrew, 'Paris Notes,' *Variety*, 8 July 1911, 16.
20. See Tich and Findlater, 88, https://www.youtube.com/watch?NR=1&feature=endscreen&v=wunRAOn7nQs, accessed 21 August 2014, which features charming footage of a Little Tich music box.
21. 'Little Tich on the "Odol Smile",' *The Stage*, 6 February 1908, 5.
22. 'Little Tich,' *Daily Mirror*, 11 February 1928, 7.
23. 'Our London Correspondence,' *Manchester Guardian*, 11 February 1928, 12.
24. 'Notes on Broadcasting. Making Comic Talent Go a Long Way,' *The Times*, 2 January 1965, 12.
25. 'Little Tich,' *The Guardian*, 19 May 1969, 18.
26. Archibald Haddon, '"Little Tich ." Memories and Anecdotes. The Evolution of the Boots,' *The Observer*, 12 February 1928, 23.
27. A. C. Astor, "Just Jottings", *The Stage*, 14 July 1927, 18.
28. 'Lincoln Spring Meeting, Tuesday,' *Manchester Guardian*, 23 March 1892, 3.
29. 'Word-Counting in Telegrams,' *The Times*, 27 August 1897, 4.
30. 'Police,' *The Times*, 27 January 1899, 12.
31. Miscellany, *Manchester Guardian*, 24 January 1910, 5.
32. 'Tattersall's Sale. Good Prices for Polo Ponies,' *The Times*, 21 July 1914, 16.
33. 'County Cricket in Miniature. A Small Boy's Match at Lord's,' *The Times*, 28 August 1915, 9.
34. Tich and Findlater, 95.
35. Ibid., 31.
36. Quoted in Craton, 70.
37. These examples can all be found on Little Tich, *In Other People's Shoes*, Windyridge, 2002, WINDY CDR9. See 'The Toreador,' 'The Sale,' 'The Gas Inspector' and 'The Gamekeeper'.

38. 'The Don of the Don Juans,' *In Other People's Shoes.*
39. J. B. Priestley, *Particular Pleasures* (London: Heinemann, 1975), 189.
40. 'Variety Theatres,' *Manchester Guardian*, 8 February 1911, 3.
41. Quoted in Michael Oliver and Bob Sapey, *Social Work with Disabled People* (2nd Edition) (Houndmills and London: Macmillan, 1999), 22.
42. 'The Hippodrome. "Little Tich",' *Manchester Guardian*, 2 February 1926, 12.
43. Quoted in Tich and Findlater, 53.
44. 'Musical Farce' at the Garrick Theatre, *Manchester Guardian*, 16 September 1896, 5.
45. This quote is reconstructed from two sources: Tich and Findlater, 53; 'Theatrical Notes,' *Pall Mall Gazette*, 23 September 1896, n.p.
46. 'Prince's Theatre, Billy'.
47. Craton, 2.
48. Benny Green, *The Last Empires: A Music Hall Companion* (London: Pavilion/Michael Joseph, 1986), 134.
49. Tich and Findlater, 95.
50. Ibid., 30.
51. Ibid.
52. Ibid.
53. Robert Bogdan, *Freak Show: Presenting Human Oddities for Amusement and Profit* (Chicago and London: University of Chicago Press, 1988), xi.
54. Quoted in Bogdan, 95.
55. Bogdan, 175.
56. Little Tich, *Little Tich: A Book of Travels (and Wanderings)* (Baileyton, Alabama: A&B Treebooks, 2007), 52–54. Also see 'How I Sang for a Shilling A Week,' *Red Letter*, 13 January 1912, 42, 45.
57. 'The Palace Theatre,' *Manchester Guardian*, 19 March 1901, 8; 'The Palace of Varieties,' *Manchester Guardian*, 17 September 1901, 6.
58. Bogdan, 200.
59. In Bridget Telfer, Emma Shepley, and Carole Reeves eds., *Re-framing Disability: Portraits from the Royal College of Physicians* (London: Royal College of Physicians, 2011), 26.
60. Alice Guy, *Little Tich et ses 'Big Boots'*, USA & France: Gaumont, 3 mins.
61. This footage can be found in compilation of clips here: http://www.britishpathe.com/video/flashbacks-extracts/query/little+tich, accessed 27 August 2014.
62. Priestley, 189.
63. Very grainy footage of this can be found at https://www.youtube.com/watch?v=RfZ9dQ9Umqs, accessed 26 August 2014.
64. 'The Palace Theatre,' *Manchester Guardian*, 19 March 1901, 8; 'The Palace of Varieties,' *Manchester Guardian*, 17 September 1901, 6.
65. Priestley, 189.

66. 'The Hippodrome. "Little Tich",' *Manchester Guardian*, 2 February 1926, 12.
67. Tich and Findlater, 39.
68. Ibid., 4.
69. Little Tich, 2007, 26.
70. Priestley, 190.
71. Quoted in Green, 133.
72. James M. Glover, 'The Music Box,' *The Stage*, 15 February 1928, 17.
73. 'In the Green Room,' *Penny Illustrated Paper*, 24 August 1912, 247.
74. '"Little Tich" at Cardiff,' *Western Mail*, 11 April 1900, n.p.
75. 'The Hippodrome,' *Manchester Guardian*, 14 July 1914, 10.
76. 'Variety Theatres,' *Manchester Guardian*, 27 August 1918, 6.
77. See, respectively, 'Prince of Wales Theatre,' *Birmingham Daily Post*, 26 May 1891, n.p.; 'The Hippodrome,' *Manchester Guardian*, 21 September 1926, 11; 'Music Hall Gossip,' *Era*, 4 April 1891, n.p.; Green, 133; 'Prince's Theatre, Lord Tom Noddy'; 'Royalty in the Music Hall, The "Command" Performance at the Palace,' *Manchester Guardian*, 2 July 1912, 9.
78. Quoted in Craton, 54, 73.
79. 'Variety Theatres,' *Manchester Guardian*, 11 May 1920, 11.
80. 'In the Green Room,' *Penny Illustrated Paper*, 24 August 1912, 247.
81. 'Little Tich's Retort,' *Daily Mail*, 4 May 1905, 5.
82. 'Variety Theatres,' *Manchester Guardian*, 16 December 1908, 14.
83. Haddon, op. cit.
84. For more on this, see 'Chapter 10: Onstage, Offstage,' in Oliver Double, *Getting the Joke: The Inner Workings of Stand-Up Comedy* (London: Bloomsbury, 2014), 141–158.
85. Tich and Findlater, 6.
86. Paul Nash, *Outline: An Autobiography* (London: Columbus Books, 1988), 170.
87. Haddon, op. cit.
88. See Little Tich, 2007, 82–84.
89. Tich and Findlater, 88.
90. Haddon, op. cit.
91. 'Our London Correspondence,' 11 February 1928.
92. Tich and Findlater, 28.
93. 'Music Hall Strike Amusing Incidents,' *Manchester Guardian*, 23 January 1907, 12.
94. 'Eager for the Fray,' *Daily Mirror*, 23 January 1907, 3.
95. See Oliver Double, *Britain Had Talent: A History of Variety Theatre* (Basingstoke and New York: Palgrave, 2012), 37–50.
96. Haddon, op. cit.
97. Tich and Findlater, 68–69.

Works Cited

Astor, A. C. 'Just Jottings.' *The Stage*. July 14, 1927.

Bartram, C. C. 'London Notes.' *Variety*. October 6, 1906.

Birmingham Daily Post. 'Prince of Wales Theatre.' 26 May 1891.

Bogdan, Robert. *Freak Show: Presenting Human Oddities for Amusement and Profit*. Chicago and London: University of Chicago Press, 1988.

British Pathé. 'Flashback Extracts: 1910–1919.' Accessed August 27, 2014. http://www.britishpathe.com/video/flashbacks-extracts/query/little+tich.

Craton, Lillian. *The Victorian Freak Show*. Amherst, NY: Cambria Press, 2009.

Daily Mail. 'Little Tich's Retort.' 4 May 1905.

Daily Mail. 'What Artistes Earn.' 24 January 1907.

Daily Mirror. 'Eager for the Fray.' 23 January 1907.

Daily Mirror. 'Little Tich.' 11 February 1928.

Double, Oliver. *Britain Had Talent: A History of Variety Theatre*. Basingstoke: Palgrave Macmillan, 2012.

Double, Oliver. *Getting the Joke: The Inner Workings of Stand-Up Comedy*. London: Bloomsbury, 2014.

Era. 'Music Hall Gossip.' 4 April 1891.

Glover, James M. 'The Music Box.' *The Stage*. February 15, 1928.

Green, Benny. *The Last Empires: A Music Hall Companion*. London: Pavilion, Michael Joseph, 1986.

Guy, Alice. *Little Tich et ses 'Big Boots'*. USA and France: Gaumont.

Haddon, Archibald. '"Little Tich" Memories and Anecdotes. The Evolution of the Boots.' *The Observer*. February 12, 1928.

Kendrew, Edward G. 'Paris Notes.' *Variety*. January 2, 1909.

Kendrew, Edward G. 'Paris Notes.' *Variety*. July 8, 1911.

Manchester Guardian. 'Comedy Theatre, Billy.' 8 November 1898.

Manchester Guardian. 'His Child.' 16 September 1906.

Manchester Guardian. 'Lincoln Spring Meeting, Tuesday.' 23 March 1892.

Manchester Guardian. 'Miscellany.' 24 January 1910.

Manchester Guardian. 'Music Hall Strike Amusing Incidents.' 23 January 1907.

Manchester Guardian. 'Musical Farce at the Garrick Theatre.' 16 September 1896.

Manchester Guardian. 'Our London Correspondence.' 11 February 1928.

Manchester Guardian. 'Prince's Theatre, Billy.' 7 June 1898.

Manchester Guardian. 'Prince's Theatre, Lord Tom Noddy.' 26 May 1896.

Manchester Guardian. 'Royalty in the Music Hall, The "Command" Performance at the Palace.' 2 July 1912.

Manchester Guardian. 'The Hippodrome.' 14 July 1914.

Manchester Guardian. 'The Hippodrome.' 21 September 1926.

Manchester Guardian. 'The Hippodrome. "Little Tich".' 2 February 1926.

Manchester Guardian. 'The Palace Theatre.' 19 March 1901.

Manchester Guardian. 'The Palace of Varieties.' 17 September 1901.
Manchester Guardian. 'Variety Theatres.' 4 July 1906.
Manchester Guardian. 'Variety Theatres.' 16 December 1908.
Manchester Guardian. 'Variety Theatres.' 8 February 1911.
Manchester Guardian. 'Variety Theatres.' 27 August 1918.
Manchester Guardian. 'Variety Theatres.' 11 May 1920.
Morning Post. 'Alexandra Theatre.' 24 August 1898.
Nash, Paul. *Outline: An Autobiography.* London: Columbus Books, 1988.
Oliver, Michael, and Bob Sapey. *Social Work with Disabled People.* 2nd ed. London: Macmillan, 1999.
Pall Mall Gazette. 'Theatrical Notes.' 23 September 1896.
Penny Illustrated Paper. 'In the Green Room.' 24 August 1912.
Priestley, J. B. *o.* London: Heinemann, 1975.
Red Letter. 'How I Sang For A Shilling A Week.' 13 January 1912.
Telfer, Bridget, Emma Shepley, and Carole Reeves, eds. *Re-framing Disability: Portraits from the Royal College of Physicians.* London: Royal College of Physicians, 2011.
The Guardian. 'Little Tich.' 19 May 1969.
The Stage. 'Little Tich on the "Odol Smile".' 6 February 1908.
The Times. 'County Cricket in Miniature. A Small Boy's Match at Lord's.' 28 August 1915.
The Times. 'King's Bench Division. The Action by Miss Vesta Victoria. Terry v Moss' Empires (Limited).' 12 December 1914.
The Times. 'Notes on Broadcasting. Making Comic Talent Go a Long Way.' 2 January 1965.
The Times. 'Police.' 27 January 1899.
The Times. 'Tattersall's Sale. Good Prices for Polo Ponies.' 21 July 1914.
The Times. 'Word-Counting in Telegrams.' 27 August 1897.
Tich, Little. *In Other People's Shoes.* Windyridge, 2002. CDR9.
Tich, Little. *Little Tich: A Book of Travels (and Wanderings).* Baileyton, AL: A&B Treebooks, 2007.
Tich, Mary, and Richard Findlater. *Little Tich: Giant of the Music Hall.* London: Elm Tree Books, 1979.
Variety. 'Althoff's Comeback.' 6 October 1922.
Variety. 'London Notes.' 14 September 1907.
Western Mail. '"Little Tich" at Cardiff.' 11 April 1900.
YouTube. 'Little Tich: Loie Fuller.' Accessed August 26, 2014. https://www.youtube.com/watch?v=RfZ9dQ9Umqs.
YouTube. 'Rare English comedian—Little Tich Automaton.' CollectorsChannel, 19 December 2007. https://www.youtube.com/watch?NR=1&feature=endscreen&v=wunRAOn7nQs

Dissent

Laughing Out of Turn: *Fin de Siècle* Literary Realism and the Vernacular Humours of the Music Hall

Peter T. A. Jones

> It is the laughter of the music halls which is all wrong. [...] Hookey, I think, discerned unwonted gravity in my expression. At any rate she bade me cheer up... (Albert Neil Lyons, *Hookey*, 1902)[1]

> Why not woo the muse of the suburban drawing-room, nay, even the muse of the halls? (George Gissing, 'The Muse of the Halls,' 1893)[2]

In assessing the place of humour within literary realism during the *fin de siècle*, we can begin by making an axiomatic claim. As the geniality and '*charmisma*' associated with the Dickensian or Thackerean corpus faded away, the disenchanted stance of naturalism became entrenched.[3] Laughter gained little purchase with the socially conscious narratives of George Gissing, Emile Zola, Arthur Morrison or Thomas Hardy, which sought to illuminate the enervating effects of modern conditions on the individual and the masses. Even as late as 1903 Jack London held fast

---

P. T. A. Jones (✉)
Queen Mary, University of London and the New College
of the Humanities at Northeastern, London, UK

© The Author(s) 2020
L. Lee (ed.), *Victorian Comedy and Laughter*,
https://doi.org/10.1057/978-1-137-57882-2_10

to a pessimistic vision, when he framed the London slum or 'Ghetto' as a place that 'like an infuriated tigress turning on its young [...] blots out the light and laughter'.[4] According to Aaron Matz, a 'non- or even anti-comic' form of satire was integral to the diagnostic pathologies of a 'bleaker' school of realism which was sceptical about the possibility of social regeneration or renewal. Within these works of 'satirical realism', laughing in the face of social ills effectively meant laughing out of turn: 'After Thackeray, after Dickens, once the gap between satiric and realist treatment had narrowed, comedy was displaced by a far bleaker and more heartrending form of representation'.[5] I want to extend Matz's claim by proposing that despite being displaced into the domain of the trivial and the popular, that untimely laughter continued to act as a destabilising force within works which appeared steadfastly committed to extreme forms of mordant solemnity. How is it possible, given the influence of this pessimistic creed, that nineteenth-century realism was profoundly shaped by the flexible morphology of comic speech?

By exploring the ways that the gestures and routines of the music hall stage feed into literary discourse, I will make the case that vernacular humour had a determinative role in shattering the tonal decorum and compositional codes of realism. J. L. Austin's and Michel De Certeau's theories of performative utterance and the 'speech act' are central to this enquiry's efforts to chart the disruptive powers of music hall speech and song. The 'present', 'discrete' and 'phatic' components embedded within 'turns (*tours*) and detours' of the music hall act, interfere with seemingly stable procedures of speech presentation, narration and character formation.[6] Gestures and styles that provoked amusement in music hall theatres helped to fuel fitful but significant experiments in genre formation that obtruded upon, or directly took issue with, the gloomy temper of realism. These were manifested in the 1890s and into the Edwardian era through the raucous emergence of upstart forms such as the 'New Humour' spearheaded by Barry Pain and Jerome K. Jerome, and the closely intersecting group of 'cockney school' writers such as William Pett Ridge, Rudyard Kipling, Henry Nevinson, Israel Zangwill and Albert Neil Lyons.[7] Rather than understanding these deviations from type as symptomatic of a terminal state of affairs in socially conscious fiction, a more acute conception of the genealogy of realism can be attained by considering the process through which a firm disjunction between earnest literary diction and popular comic laughter was abraded during the *fin de siècle*. At the close of the nineteenth century, literary realism was vitiated by an essential paradox. In one sense, its purposes were aligned towards a defensive position of beleaguered authorship, which watched vigilantly 'over the "propriety" of terms' and became increasingly withdrawn in its efforts to ward off the humours of mass culture.[8] A second movement sought deliverance from this cloistered and dejected condition by looking outwards towards the sphere of popular expression. As the tension between embattled intellectualism and sensitivity to public sentiment began to build, it became ever more imperative to find an aesthetic solution to manage the consequences of this split motive.

1   WOUNDED DISPOSITIONS: SPLITTING
THE SIDES OF PESSIMISM

George Gissing's 'The Muse of the Halls' appeared in the Christmas edition of *English Illustrated Magazine* in 1893. This short story follows the career of a struggling musician who fears his artistic and personal integrity will be compromised by being sucked into the popular marketplace. Denis's fiancé, Hilda Paget, announces her intention to perform on the music hall stage in pursuit of 'filthy lucre'. This disharmonious interposition of the materials of mass leisure into the wrong domain—specifically a 'faded little parlour' in suburban Brixton—leads to a break in decorum and a displacement of genre towards the comic, which is likened to 'a crisis in domestic drama'. Denis is appalled by Hilda's decision, despite her protestations that 'I shall come forward just as I do in concert-rooms–just!'[9] The crisis is aggravated by Hilda's willingness to import catchphrases, raillery and slang, which she has picked up from her acquaintances at the music hall.

> The corruption of the music-hall, already! I can't help it. If I degrade myself, I am only following the general example of our time. Everybody, in every kind of art, is beginning to play to the gallery. We have to be democratic, or starve. And we don't like starving. We've got to *climb down*–there's a phrase for you, Denis! We have to *get a show*–there's another! We must find tunes that'll *knock 'em*—
>
> The musician seized his hat and strode from the room; a moment, and the front door sounded behind him.[10]

Hilda is possessed by the eccentric tongues of the music hall and made to bare her ill-humours even despite professed best intentions. She reassures her mother that this 'isn't my natural way of talking'.[11] Fragments of speech are italicised in a way that graphically distinguishes them as discrepant false notes or rogue elements in proper patterns of verbal composition. Despite its involuntary foreignness, this act of glossolalia is a potent means for deflating Denis's idealised version of 'Art'.

> I don't want to call names, Denis, but when you first knew me you talked about a comic opera–indeed you did. And you whistled several bars to me one day–very jolly music. But since our engagement you've grown so awfully solemn. I suppose you meant to correct my frivolity.
> When I first met you, I was busy with my Concerto in A flat—
> And very flat it was—
> "Hilda!" protested Mrs. Paget.[12]

Modes of cross-talk that are characteristic of the staged knockabout humour of the music hall, provide a means for sending up a code of composition that must eschew 'frivolity' at all costs. Denis links the stability of his attachment to Hilda with the success of the work that will 'correct' his fiancé's predilection to trade in forms of demotic and comical expression. Denis insists that Hilda abandon her career on the stage as 'Miss Lilian Dove' as a condition of their marriage. Ironically, he gives up on his 'Cantata' and begins a successful career writing music hall songs for another star named Bella Lancey. Denis reaches a compromise solution which allows him to preserve a fragile veneer as a 'serious composer', while disguising baser popular allegiances under the pseudonymous persona of 'Thomson of the halls, the organs, the popular echoes'. There is an added layer of equivocation here, because this stability comes at the cost of an admission that 'Denis Bryant of the serious public' is only a convenient fiction.[13]

In 'My Great and Only' (1890), Rudyard Kipling dramatised the permeation of his own work with the patter of Gatti's music hall. In this short story, an unnamed author responds positively to the monetary enticements of the popular marketplace by writing a song for the halls. '*That's what the girl told the soldier*' gains a rapturous response from the 'sea of tossing billycocks and rocking bonnets'. The author bathes in 'Perfect Felicity' but the cost of success is to remain anonymous, while the reputation of the comic singer 'the Great and Only' begins to swell.[14]

They do not call for authors on these occasions, but I desired no need of public recognition. I was placidly happy. The chorus bubbled up again and again throughout the evening, and a redcoat in the gallery insisted on singing solos about "a swine in the poultry line," whereas I had written "man," and the pewters began to fly, and afterwards the long streets were vocal with various versions of what the girl had really told the soldier, and I went to bed murmuring: "I have found my destiny."[15]

The author's advancement is rooted in his ability to recognise and then to accommodate the punning logic of the music hall. An authoritative account of 'what the girl had really told the soldier' is not discovered in the original lyric but becomes transposed into it, through the verbal substitutions and multiplications of the chorus. This process is analogous to the challenges faced by the embattled intellectual, who risks being subsumed by the antiphonal and polysemic structure of his own work. Only by renouncing the bonds of authorship entirely, can the artist discover a cultural product whose broad appeal lies in its ability to blend together the seemingly irreconcilable moods of seriousness and frivolity.

Some day a man will rise up from Bermondsey, Battersea or Bow, and he will be coarse, but clear-sighted, hard but infinitely and tenderly humorous, speaking in the people's tongue, steeped in their lives and telling them in swinging, urging, clinging verse.[...] And all the little poets who pretend to sing to the people will scuttle away like rabbits, for the girl (which, as you have seen, of course, is wisdom) will tell that soldier (which is Hercules bowed under his labours) all that she knows of Life and Death and Love.[16]

In Gissing's and Kipling's tales, struggling and ambitious young artists arrive at different solutions to the same aesthetic conundrum. Denis Bryant goes to any length (including ruining his wife's career) to preserve his artistic ideals, whereas for Kipling's narrator, literary prestige has utterly lost its currency. Both examples are united in their seeming inability to square an intention to hold onto cultural authority with a compulsion to channel popular echoes that appeal to the tastes of the masses. The music hall's value lies in its ability to act as a space of abstraction, degeneration or fantasy, where a marriage of opposing dispositions—'aureate and ordinary language, the serious and the grotesque'—seemed possible.[17]

Importantly, it is not exclusively in shorter, ephemeral or ostensibly lighter works that we find popular humour leaving its mark. Even in gloomier novels of social realism laughter could erupt in all the wrong places. Preserving some degree of mimetic fidelity meant confronting forms of merriment in pubs, streets or dwellings, which seemed glaringly dissonant within these works. In his first published novel *Workers in the Dawn* (1880), George Gissing's narrator makes the following avowal regarding the shoppers in a working-class street market: 'It must be confessed that the majority do not seem unhappy; they jest with each other amid their squalor; they have an evident pleasure in buying and selling; they would be surprised if they knew you pitied them'.[18] Laughter is diagnosed as a symptom of unconscious disengagement on the part of the crowd, from the immiserating effects of the slum environment. This state of blindness and moral laxity can only exist because the 'majority' do not have access to an aesthetic framework which would enable them to measure their conduct against a criterion of good taste.

Gissing's early works rejected positivism and instead embraced Arthur Schopenhauer's pessimism, 'detached asceticism' and commitment to the 'sublime force' of artistic experience.[19] The German philosopher—best known for his gloomy views regarding the futility of biological life— also wrote about the causes of laughter in the first book of *The World as Will and Representation* (1818/1819) and then expanded these terse remarks in a later edition.[20] George Gissing had read this study in German before an English translation appeared between 1883 and 1886.[21] Schopenhauer suggested that laughter is activated by a perceived incongruity between the 'concept' and the 'real objects which have been thought through it in some relation'.[22] The free display of merriment is deemed to be particularly problematic, especially when this act departs from the ameliorating influence of 'seriousness' [*ernst*].[23] 'The opposite of laughing and joking is seriousness. Accordingly, it [seriousness] consists in the consciousness of the perfect agreement and congruity of the conception, or thought, with what is perceived, or the reality'.[24]

For Schopenhauer, unless popular laughter was leavened by cultivated discernment and an earnest disposition, it could not properly be designated as humour at all. He castigated writers who allowed facile 'jokes and buffoonery' to be erroneously framed as humour within their works. Uncouth jests purportedly generated 'flat and vulgar' prose and literary culture ought to avoid incorporating comic diction characterised by 'high words and a low meaning' that indulged the uncultivated tastes of the public. Accommodating this species of unrefined comedy led to cultural miscategorisation that was equivalent to calling 'every concert a music academy'.[25] Schopenhauer intended this rather myopic critique to act as an antidote to the infectious ubiquity of popular mirth. This account testifies to the intractable difficulties faced by aesthetic arbiters who sought to defend the purity of literary culture by distinguishing it from the conduits, domains and personae that abetted the issuance of popular laughter. Schopenhauer's express desire was for a disposition to emerge within European literary culture, which had the power to neutralise the disruptive powers of vernacular humour. Forms of expression that Bakhtinian scholars designate as a *'grammatica jocosa'* (laughing grammar) would not find a place within this programme for canonicity and grammaticality.[26] Even in Gissing's imagined slum, the objective validity of this programme of reactionary pessimism—of wounded melancholy, of irony and of moral failure—is compromised by the 'evident' merriment of the market crowd which acts as a gelastic irritant disrupting tonal consistency. The intermixing of serious and comic dispositions, produces a volatile compound which has the effect of decomposing the orchestration of realist presentation.

2   A Comic *Volte-Face* and the 'Novel of Misery'

The music hall 'grew rapidly to dominate the commercialized popular culture of the late nineteenth century'.[27] This increasing primacy had a major role in galvanising debates about the problematic status of vernacular (especially cockney) humour within literary culture. In *Confessions of a Young Man* (1888) the Irish novelist George Moore advocated for the reinvigorating influence that the music hall might have on the 'worn-out rhetoric' of dramatic and literary culture. 'The music-hall is a protest against the villa, the circulating library, the club, and for this the "'all" is inexpressibly dear to me'.[28] For dissenting critics such as Robert Buchanan, a perceived coarsening of cultivated thought by music-hall vulgarity, should properly have been confined to the 'Arry and 'Arriet sketches by E. J. Milliken, which appeared in *Punch* magazine between 1877 and 1897. In *The Coming Terror* (1891) Buchanan maintains that Moore was culpable for tarring literature with the dialectical heterodoxy of the music hall:

> *He* utters his detestation, and boldly pictures to us the literary future:
> 'Arry triumphant, the tongue loosened, the morals and manners free and
> easy, the old gods of letters set up for cockshies, the music-hall turned into
> a Temple of all the arts, and 'Arriet, *alma Venus* of Seven Dials, *hominum*
> *divumque voluptas*, at her apotheosis.[29]

By the 1890s, these debates had entered a phase of marked intensity,
spurred by the rise of 'Kiplingism' which followed the publication of
Barrack-Room Ballads and Other Verses in 1892. By 1900 Buchanan was
convinced that the ascendency of 'Cockneydom' or 'Hooliganism' had
irrevocably tarnished high literary culture with the coarse and Jingoistic
sentiments of the crowd.

> Hooliganism, not satisfied with invading our newspapers, should already
> threaten to corrupt the pure springs of our literature. These noisy strains
> and coarse importations from the music-hall should not be heard where
> the fountains of intellectual light and beauty once played, where Chaucer
> and Shakespeare once drank inspiration, and where Wordsworth, Hood,
> and Shelley found messages for the yearning hearts of men.[30]

Despite his railing at the deep infelicity of disquieting trends, Buchanan
clearly recognised that his worst fears for the 'literary future' had been
realised, at least in part. The tongue was loosened and 'importations'
from the music hall were shaping the evolution of literary realism.

The story of a comic *volte-face* within literary realism is intimately
connected with the evolution of the 'novel of misery'. Employed in an
unsigned article that was published in the *Quarterly Review* in October
1902, this term was used to distinguish pessimistic literature influenced
by the philosophy of Schopenhauer, biological determinism and the
'latest scientific and pathological hypotheses' espoused by Hippolyte
Adolphe Taine. Works by Gissing and Emile Zola constituted an aesthetic rejoinder to the humane Idealism of writers like Victor Hugo and
Charles Dickens who 'lacked the central conviction that the life of man
was a nightmare of sensuality, crime, drunkenness and nervous disorders'.[31] Even though it contained 'as much reality as any of the realists',
one 'cockney school' novel is presented as a glaring exception that stood
apart from a descending curve of narratives that 'formed a code of composition in which charm was interdicted'. It is the willingness of William
Pett Ridge's *Mord Em'ly* (1898) to pay tribute to the 'rough humour of

the London crowd' that marks this tale as an outlier within the canon.[32] An earlier 1898 review from the *Academy* contends that the distinctiveness of Ridge's approach stems from his incorporation of a peculiar dialogic mode:

> For just as mediæval scholars passed from city to city to hold disputations, so do Mr Ridge's characters pass from street corner to street corner to exchange personalities. This is a novel of repartee. Gathered in its pages are retorts enough to furnish forth a wilderness of bus drivers. Mr. Ridge knows the cockney resources of invective to their ultimate depths; he can supply you in a moment with the appropriate answer, in any given case, of a policeman, a cabman, a pot-boy, a barmaid, a drunkard, an organ-grinder, and Mord-Em'ly, who stands for young Walworth-road womanhood generally, which is simply to say that Mr. Ridge knows his subject.[33]

The mention of the philosopher-cum-bus driver highlights a connection with Barry Pain's *De Omnibus: By the Conductor* sketches which in 1898 had appeared adjacent to the serialised instalments of *Mord Em'ly* in *To-Day*, the weekly journal edited by Jerome K. Jerome. Pain's sketches sought to capture the sharp-witted diction of a bus conductor in creatively enumerated cockney dialect: 'little perrygrawfts in the pipers on the subjic of smokin' on the tops o' 'buses'.[34] Adrian Poole argues that a 'mania for phonetic accuracy' has the effect of obstructing 'the expression of anything at all' in the cockney sketches of Pain, Edwin Pugh, Ridge and Clarence Rook.[35] The quality of these sketches is doubtless very patchy and their slangy commentary on topical issues can be difficult to decipher. Nevertheless, within these stories, a fascination with vernacular speech is not generally reducible to the phoneticist's pedantic concern with idiomatic classification. The attempt to decode the contents and commitments of the cockney 'novel of repartee' must remain cognizant of the ways that 'resources of invective' constitute rhetorical forms that give impetus to a 'dialogic interchange' between page and stage; 'between the humorous text and its culture'.[36]

The clear-cut definition of the novel of misery in the *Quarterly Review* article, might lead us to assume that George Gissing expurgated the rambunctious humour of the music hall from his novels, to preserve the acuity of his disenchanted vision. Yet, works that seem only to dramatise 'the difficult life and sad death of realism', can also gesture towards the parturition of new modes of enlivened humourous presentation.[37] Particularly in the latter stages of his career, Gissing's pessimistic sensibility is periodically superseded by a mood characterised by playful experimentation with the resources of vernacular comedy. In 1898, the same year as *Mord Em'ly* appeared, Methuen published Gissing's *The Town Traveller*. This was an 'uncharacteristically comic novel' which was intended as a knowing parody of the Dickensian comic method. *The Town Traveller* bore a much closer resemblance to the cockney school sketch, than to any determinist study of social and moral dysfunction. Perhaps problematically for Gissing, this work elicited a 'widespread and favourable critical response' and proved his ability to successfully 'compromise with the market'.[38] Gissing scholars have tended to find this novel 'remarkable for its comic vein' and to write it off as a 'minor' work which was the result of 'mere hack work'.[39] Like *Mord Em'ly*, this work occupies an anomalous place within the canon. Where we might expect caustic refutation of a Dickensian comic mode, *The Town Traveller* in fact offers something closer to a sensitive homage that is inflected with a relatively light-touch dramatic irony. The plot is orientated around the flirtatious friendship between Mr. Gammon—typified by his 'unfailing humour'—and a younger cockney woman named Polly Sparkes, who openly seeks a degree of self-determination and pleasure.

Polly engages in the 'agreeable business of selling programmes at a fashionable theatre' and in the evening, unashamedly accepts an invitation to join a party of her fellow lodgers, when she hears them singing a 'popular refrain'. Vernacular speech is incorporated into typography without any discernible effort to mitigate its perceived infirmities. Characters are given room to laugh without facing immediate reprisal.

> Polly Sparkes throughout her leisurely toilet was moved to irritation and curiosity by the sound of frequent laughter on the other side of the party wall — uproarious peals, long chucklings in a falsetto key, staccato bursts of mirth.

> "That is the comic stuff in *Clippings*," she said to herself with an involuntary grin. "What a fool he is! And why's he staying in bed this morning? Got his holiday, I suppose. I'd make better use of it than that."[40]

Gammon's leisured consumption of 'comic stuff' signals Gissing's willingness to allow popular laughter to reverberate through and shape the dynamics of his plot. The fictional title of *Clippings* refers to weekly publications such as *Tit-Bits*, *Pick-Me-Up* or Jerome's *To-Day* that contained 'short vignettes and tales about ordinary British subjects in everyday situations' and were pitched to an expanding mass market for comic literature.[41] In one respect, publications like *Clippings* are understood to spread a type of pseudo-literacy. Nevertheless, Polly's 'involuntary grin' dramatises the infectious appeal of these idioms and their capacity to foster communities of shared sentiment and meaning.

Recent scholarship is principally committed to the conception that a lapse into the crudities of comic and ephemeral subject matter, was a function of the unswerving descent of realism. Regenia Gagnier argues that the aesthetic veracity of the cockney school is compromised by the use of humour that is tantamount to a form of political bad faith, because it transcends the insurmountable conditions of 'scarcity and violence' experienced by the working classes.[42] Roger Henkle concedes that jocular portraits of urban life provide insights into the 'vital popular culture' which subsisted in working-class communities but supports the key premise of Gagnier's argument: 'The writers of the "cockney school",[...] created an individual subject that could be brought within the hegemonising of middle class English culture'. Images of mass culture are co-opted with a view to throwing a comfort blanket over the 'alienated domain' which is evoked in the works of Gissing, Zola or Morrison. This explanation risks introducing a heavy-handed distinction between the ideological commitments of the cockney school and pessimistic fictions that ostensibly sought to identify the corrupted foundations of demotic expression from a neutral standpoint. Both literary lineages were prone to their own forms of partisanship and bigotry. To complicate matters further, the forces of respectabilisation and conservatism that created 'individualistic, spirited, jingoistic, hard-playing, blunt, beef-eating, beer-drinking, and for all that, ultimately law-abiding' individuals were also pre-eminent on the popular stage.[43] Historians such as Peter Bailey, Dagmar Kift and Andy Medhurst have sought to elaborate upon a critical assessment of the music hall's 'sensibility of consoling resignation', by drawing attention to the significance of a culturally charged, collectively encountered space where 'small joys' and 'alternative values' were articulated amid 'the material realities of hardship'.[44] The cockney school was not exempted from tutelary value systems, which sought to neutralise the disruptive capacity of popular sentiment stirred up by the 'expressive range' of music-hall performance.[45]

Nevertheless, if this corpus was prone to rely upon inert and consoling types, then it could also harness the verbal dexterity by which music hall acts 'broke through the fictions of their impersonations'.[46]

3   'ENTANGLE HIM': LASHED BY THE TONGUE OF THE COCKNEY *SOUBRETTE*

At a surface level, the vocalisations of comic speech can be considered apart from their setting as what Austin calls 'locutionary' acts. To be fully realised, though, speech acts must also be '"explained" by the "context" in which they are designed to be or have actually been spoken in linguistic interchange'.[47] As Bailey points out, the 'complexity of popular cultural forms' which were occasioned by the music hall can only be fully conceived 'in terms of the specific determinants of situation and experience which typify this particular milieu'.[48] Literary accounts that seek to defuse the resistant capacity of the 'cross-talk, puns, malapropisms and catchphrases' of the music hall, by deflecting their situationally specific meanings, must also struggle to paper over the consequential effects of comic utterance.[49] Barry Faulk argues that the 'literature of the hall in the 1890s' inclines towards a culturally conservative 'reactive formation' against the comic and sentimental excesses of popular entertainment. These texts are united by their complicity in the work that recuperates mass culture 'to healthy, manly, and middle-class norms'. The possibility of a restrained, even and uniform grammaticality is set up as an alternative to the feminising effects of the music hall act, which provoke a 'sentimental, hysterical, irrational' audience response.[50] Despite its unquestionable centrality, it is also essential to explore the vulnerabilities of a 'rhetoric of cultural expertise' which endeavours to render the music hall into something amenable to middle-class desires.[51] This regulating framework is placed under strain by the recalcitrant voices of young female personae in the examples that follow. Rather than preserving decorum, wilful characters laugh out of turn, answer back or (like Hilda Paget) allow the refrains of the music hall to resound in spite of mechanisms of recuperation.

> It is not the mere lewdness that matters–though that has served an ill-purpose in obscuring the true evil.[...] This does not lie in the plump calf or exaggerated leer of a vain soubrette. It is the laughter of the music halls which is all wrong. For it concerns gin and glorious beer; the

'bashing' of mothers-in-law; the 'pinching of watches'; the humours of bilking; the vanity of thrift.[...] You invent systems by which the infant soul receives a daily scouring.[...] Here it gazes upon jesters, clothed in dirty rags; and upon whose faces warts and pimples are painted.[...]

Hookey, I think, discerned unwonted gravity in my expression. At any rate she bade me cheer up.[52]

In this excerpt from *Hookey* (1902), by the cockney school novelist and playwright Albert Neil Lyons, the music hall routine can be understood as operating at different dialogic levels across which meaning is generated. In one sense, the performance can be construed as a locutionary act considered apart from local conditions of reference and filtered through partisan diegetic presentation. Laughter is deemed to be corrupting vulnerable youngsters and is a symptom of a retrogressive failure of the public education system. Behind this superficial formulation, lies a recognition that this utterance has a complex set of context-dependent meanings. The 'unwonted' implications of errant laughter are embedded within what Austin designates as the 'perlocutionary act', that relates only 'obliquely' or 'not at all' to the act of locution.[53] In this case, friction is generated when the delight of a young working-class woman called Hookey, rubs up against the pertinacious 'gravity' of the narrator. The power of the narrator's sober and didactic broadside collapses in the face of perlocutionary meanings generated by comradely intimacy, resulting from a preoccupation with Hookey's carefree disposition. The peculiar humours of the music hall leave the diegetic voice verbally incapacitated and lacking composure. Moralistic homily is rendered inoperative because it is uncoupled from the embedded dialogic interchange between the narrator and Hookey, that acts as the cynosure driving forward Lyons's plot: 'Because I am afflicted with a club foot and some grosser infirmities, peculiar to middle age, I think she suspected me of evangelistic tendencies. At any rate, her indifference to my patronage was marked'.[54] The laughing grammar of the music hall had the power to generate resistant structures within literary discourse and narration. Importantly, these interferences create a shifting nomenclature which has the potential to upset stable ontologies and procedures of character formation.

Jerome K. Jerome became a key exponent of the New Humour at 'a time when *The Idler* (set up by Robert Barr in 1892 but edited by Jerome alone from 1895) and *To-day* (launched by Jerome at the end of 1892) were drawing a number of talented writers into their orbit'. Carolyn Oulton contends that Jerome was acutely aware that the amusing stories which he published lacked cultural authority and that he struggled to reconcile the 'idea of humour with literary work'. In many respects, the content of *Idler* and *To-day* accorded with the consoling vision outlined by Gagnier and Henkle, by fostering a parochial 'clubbishness' and a 'conservative critique of psychological and New Woman fiction'.[55] This comforting veneer is readily discernible in a short story which Jerome published in the 1893 edition of *The Idler*, entitled 'Variety Patter'. Jerome begins his semi-autobiographical tale by recounting his 'temptation' and 'first appearance' at a music hall at the age of fourteen, presumably in 1873.[56] This departure from decorum leaves the youthful narrator feeling beset with guilt and penitential fantasies. During a later visit to the 'Pav' (the Pavillion in Piccadilly Circus), a sense of self-reproach is dispelled by the reassuring prospect of an affable, gentlemanly and beer-swilling fraternity. Finally, the narrator relates his impressions of a 'disturbance' witnessed during a third outing to a less prestigious London hall 'in a southeast district'.[57]

The restive audience led by a coal-heaver vehemently agitate for the appearance of a well-known performer 'Joss Jessop, the Monarch of Mirth'. These wishes are rebuffed by the chairman who introduces 'Signorina Ballatino', a novelty performer who struggles to play the 'zither' successfully.[58] The impotence and failure of the chairman to silence the audience means that the Signorina is forced to take matters into her own hands.

> She did not waste time on the rest of the audience. She went straight for that coal-heaver, and thereupon ensued a slanging match the memory of which sends a thrill of admiration through me even to this day. [...] She announced her intention of 'wiping down the bloomin' 'all' with him, and making it respectable; and, metaphorically speaking, that is what she did. Her tongue hit him between the eyes, and knocked him down and trampled on him. It curled round and round him like a whip, and then it uncurled and wound the other way.[...] It played around him like forked lightening, and blinded him.[...] The people sitting near him drew away, not feeling it safe to be near, and left him alone, surrounded by space, and language.
>
> It was the most artistic work of its kind I have ever heard. Every phrase she flung at him seemed to have been woven on purpose to entangle him and to embrace in its choking folds his people and his gods, to strangle

with its threads his every hope, ambition and belief. Each term she put
upon him clung to him like a garment, and fitted him without a crease.
The last name that she called him one felt to be, until one heard the next,
the one name that he ought to have been christened by.[59]

The coal-heaver enjoins the audience to certify a set of commitments
according to which habituated and reassuring laughter is directed at the
familiar persona of 'Joss'. At first, the zither playing actress is subjected
to jeers and compelled to adopt a 'fixed smile of ineffable sweetness',
while she inhabits the role of a voiceless manikin.[60] In De Certeau's
terms, the coal-heaver and his adherents seek to 'postulate the constitution of a space of their own [...] in which they can construct a system
based on rules ensuring the system's production, repetition, and verifica-
tion'.[61] The intervention of the Signorina causes this system (the comforting homosocial circuitry of audience expectation) to be shattered and
turned towards new ends. By breaking character, the actress restyles and
reconceives the grammatical rules of the game that govern the 'dynamics
of engagement in the stage form'.[62] Her voice is operational and transformative rather than simply being locutionary, iterative and perfunctory.
The outsized, figurative dimensions of these 'popular tactics' take on a
kinesic power that grasps hold of the discourse that regulates bodies,
gestures and actions. The 'choking folds' of her visceral speech stifle the
breath that gives volition to a set of prescribed routines. Her 'styles of
action intervene in a field which regulates them at the first level [...] but
they introduce into it a way of turning it to their advantage that obeys
other rules and constitutes something like a second level interwoven into
the first'.[63]

A contest, which resembles the *agon* (a dialogue or debate) at
the heart of Aristophanic comedy, is only resolved when the stricken
coal-heaver is finally overcome by what De Certeau frames as an 'open
sea of common experience that surrounds, penetrates, and finally carries
away every discourse'.[64] Informed by something akin to folk wisdom,
the speaker's idiom is vested with the power to counteract the resources
of invective that her opponent has picked up 'in the course of his many
wanderings from Billingsgate to Limehouse Hole'.[65] Her knowledge of
the idiosyncratic involutions of common experience provides a means
for anticipating the elliptical wishes and desires of audience members.
An aperture of 'space and language' opens and engulfs her victim who
can no longer summon the fidelity of a constituency ('his people and

his gods') who have abandoned him for a more appealing prospect. This chorus presides over a form of ritual immolation which frees the Signorina from obsolescence and causes a new persona to be brought forth, who can now command the breath of popularity: 'But she does not call herself Signora Ballatino'.[66] The '"Turns" (or "tropes")' of the music hall 'constitute "proper" meanings' and perpetuate fixed types, such as the doll-like Signorina. But the 'practice of these ruses'—the disruptive tactics of popular performance—leaves a trace which is discernible in the same '"literary zones" into which they have been repressed'.[67] The enunciative practices of vernacular comedy generate antiphonal or discordant patterns of meaning as they pass across and are interpolated into literary discourse.

4   GETTING CARRIED AWAY: THE 'HUNGRY EARS' OF THE MUSIC HALL

The 'auditory appeal' of the music hall had the capacity to 'forge and sustain communal life' in a way that circumvented regimes of standardisation, elocution or control.[68] Popular tactics intervened in the domains which were designed to regulate them, whether this was in the theatre, the suburban parlour or reformatory. Modes of retort challenged the perspectives of social purity campaigners who claimed that the music-hall audience was uniquely 'disposed to see in indecency a comic as well as an enticing effect'.[69] They also set up an unsettling alternative to the 'seductive discourse' of music-hall cultists like Arthur Symons and Theodore Wratislaw, whose critical authority rested upon the 'ability to evaluate, and "rescue," formerly illegitimate cultural expression' in a way that 'occluded the complexities of music-hall audiences'.[70] The performed speech of the incorrigible, malapert young woman acts as a vehicle for exploring how dialectical fluidity can expose infirmities in the rhetorical stance of the discerning amateur or expert. This intervention subsequently blurs firm distinctions between serious artistic presentation and culturally displaced frivolity. Mord Em'ly, for example, is sent to a reformatory called 'Faith Cottage' after being wrongly accused of stealing cream meringues from a shop in the Walworth Road. Having offered an irreverent but perfectly accurate response to an arithmetical problem posed by her tutor, Mord recognises an opportunity to performatively disrupt the solemnity, composure and reserve of Faith Cottage with a 'comic song'.

It was this attitude of independence, following the period of sullenness, that demanded all the efforts of the mistresses. They conspired to make a special effort; one or two of them were maladroit enough to let this be seen, with the result that Mord Em'ly, fearing that she had encouraged them by a too complaisant manner, broke out one summer afternoon, sang a comic song, and on the floor of the schoolroom, with the sun blazing though the window upon her queer figure, danced a frenzied, excited solo.[71]

Following this exuberant outburst, Mord is put into solitary confinement for two weeks under the superintendence of Mrs. Batson (who 'had been a prison wardress') at 'Pleasant Cottage'.[72] This act separates Mord from her would-be audience and 'the congratulations that she would receive that night in the bedroom at Faith Cottage'.[73] Efforts to curtail the deleterious effects of popular leisure, rest upon separating the infected party from the roots of collective expression. The intention is that those who have become prey to the morally discomposing effects of music hall, can be restored to themselves through measures of correction and reform.

In Gissing's *Thyrza* (1887) a process of attempted recuperation and control transpires between the correspondingly titled Chapter 4 'Thyrza Sings' and Chapter 13 'Thyrza Sing Again'. Thyrza lives with her sister Lydia in a house characterised by its fading working-class gentility and situated in Lambeth. On a summer night, the windows of their top floor room are thrown open and Thyrza finds herself drawn to sounds that are evidence of an 'abundance of coarse humour' in the street market.[74] She departs and meets her boisterous friend Totty Nancarrow, 'who relished life with so much determination, yet to all appearance so harmlessly'.[75] Thyrza is persuaded to enter a 'friendly lead' (a small music hall), where a concert is taking place. During the performance, the laughter of her friend 'sounded above the hubbub of voices' but Thyrza shrinks self-reproachfully into 'as little space as possible'.[76] In time, however, Thyrza is convinced by the chairman to sing a 'half-mirthful, half-pathetic' refrain. The audience are beguiled by her 'pure, sweet tones', and will not 'be left with hungry ears after a song like that'. A potential disjunction only arises when the 'hungry ears' of the audience begin to corrupt the stable locutionary sense of Thyrza's song through the voracious and excessive gaiety of their response. The personality that instinctively wanted to 'shrink' from those who 'knew her by sight', is now magnified and 'borne upwards' into celebrity by the 'clamour' of the audience. There are also hints that members of the crowd read coarser implications into this ostensibly unblemished performance: 'There were remarks aside between men with regard to Thyrza's personal appearance'.[77]

Thyzra sings again while visiting the building where the Oxford-educated Walter Egremont is endeavouring (ultimately unsuccessfully) to set up a working men's college. The 'sense of being quite alone, together with the sudden radiance, affected her with a desire to utter her happiness'.[78] Thyzra is not aware of Walter's presence and is unwittingly overheard by him singing 'in the undertone of one who sings but half consciously'.[79] A sense of moral stability can only be restored once her song has been wrenched away from the hungry ears of the crowd and rehearsed in a new context. Egremont seeks to detain her voice and to cut it away from the cultural conditions where it is vocalised in dialogic interchange. Thyrza's reputation is guaranteed by entering a state of seclusion where she modestly performs for no one. She falls under the tutelage (and ultimately in love with) the qualified intellectual who must be the sole witness to her popular allure. Thyrza's song is sheltered from the unrestrained gaiety of the crowd who (unlike Egremont) cannot properly control their sentiments and get carried away. The impossibility of producing an ideally sanitised space that can accommodate Thyrza's buoyant personality is anticipated in the strange unfurnished emptiness of Egremont's 'cheerless chambers'.[80] In both Chapters 4 and 13, Thyrza's performance is overheard by male admirers except in the former episode she faints into the arms of a working-class radical with a 'strain of sensuality' whose subsequent declarations of affection leave her unmoved.[81] The uncanny symmetry of Thyrza's two recitals indicates that Egremont's elocutionary regime of silence is intercut by the same modes of audition which it was designed to extinguish.

The transmutative influence of the hungry ears and the loosened tongue of the public who are carried away by comic turns, was difficult to contain because it travelled well beyond the walls of the theatre. Jacqueline Bratton highlights that music hall refrains 'would be carried away from the hall and used, perhaps with quite different meanings, by members of the audience singing it at home, in the street or at other gatherings'.[82] In 1900 G. F. Scotson-Clark averred that the 'melodies' and 'catch-words' which 'fill the public mouth' were being spoken by an increasingly broad public, who hailed from across the class spectrum:

> But for the fecundity of the music-hall, how barren would be the land, how void the chit-chat of the drawing-rooms, the parlours, the sculleries!

In what way, rather than by apeing the latest contortion, could 'Arry make 'Arriet guffaw? In what way, other than by parodying the latest witticism, could Edwin make Angelina giggle? And in what way, other than by ambling through the latest skirt dance, could Gwendolen captivate the soul of Algernon?[83]

In this instance, shared merriment provides a means of establishing romantic bonds and functions as a type of social binding agent. The catchy routines of the music hall constitute popular tactics which De Certeau distinguishes for their capacity to act as 'phatic topoi', which like snatches of song hailed across the street, function to 'initiate, maintain or interrupt contact'. Part of the efficacy of these idioms, stems from their applicability to different fields of usage. Phatic utterances remain 'anterior or parallel to informative speech' and can be spoken across and through different registers.[84]

A narrow-sighted critique of the recuperative endeavours of literary culture can tend to miss the punchline.[85] Despite being subject to correction, the punning logic of popular culture (like the 'frenzied, excited' soloist Mord Em'ly) repeatedly performs in a way that departs from the script. The 'wisdom' unheard in 'what the girl had really told the soldier' and the rhetorical alterations of the music hall, turn realism towards brighter ends. Long after the popularity of music hall had begun to fade, its aesthetically transformative powers continued to occupy literary professionals. This concern is reflected in the sentiments of T. S. Eliot, who, in works such as the unfinished *Sweeney Agonistes* (1932), laboured to escape 'modernist alienation' and recover a sense of cultural belonging. Eliot modelled himself after the music-hall star Marie Lloyd who, 'could be both an artist *and* popular'. According to David Chinitz, the music hall 'for Eliot, represents a vanishing possibility of reconciliation between diverging levels of culture that ought to have been simultaneously available to him'.[86] Eliot's desire was that a lost alliance between demotic expression and ideals of high culture, could be restored through his act of aesthetic recovery. In *Sweeney Agonistes*, the attempt to marry Aristophanic comedy and music-hall song was ultimately an abortive one. Eliot inclined towards the utopian *volkgeist* or 'elegiac narrative' fashioned by the likes of Max Beerbohm and Arthur Symons to capture the mystique of 'the halls'.[87] Eliot spoke of being 'haunted' by *fin de siècle* poets such as John Davidson who used colloquial idioms to lend 'dignity' to the presentation of humble characters.[88] An example of such characterisation emerges in Davidson's 'In a Music Hall' (1891) through the 'limber' performance of Julian Aragon 'the famous Californian Comique':

> Cheeks nothing; no, by Jingo! I'm obscene!
> My gestures, not my words, say what I mean
> And the simple and the good,
> They would hiss me if they could,
> But I conquer all volition where I'm seen.[89]

Aragon's performance captures the peculiar acrobatic tenor of music-hall speech, gesture and song. The speaker quietens the hisses of morally scrupulous critics and deflects the resolution of those (including the poet himself) who strain to convert antic routines into conventional diction.

NOTES

1. Albert Neil Lyons, *Hookey: Being a Relation of Some Circumstances Surrounding the Early Life of Miss Josephine Walker* (London: T. Fisher Unwin, 1902), 16–17.
2. George Gissing, 'The Muse of the Halls,' *The Gissing Journal* 42, no. 3 (2006), 8.
3. William Oddie, 'Mr. Micawber and the Redefinition of Experience,' in *Charles Dickens*, ed. Harold Bloom, rev. edn (New York: Infobase Publishing, 2006), 98.
4. Jack London, *The People of the Abyss*, Centenary edn (London: Pluto, 2001), 147.
5. Aaron Matz, *Satire in an Age of Realism* (Cambridge: Cambridge University Press, 2010), 34–35; Revealingly, Matz emphasises that in the case of Thomas Hardy's *Jude the Obscure* (1895), an apparently uncompromising commitment to a 'tragic' or 'sad' outlook, 'yields to a much more bizarre, carnivalesque wretchedness' that 'disrupts that late sequences of *Jude*'. Jude is haunted by the 'inescapable sound of discordant laughter' and when 'realistic manifestations of tragedy have been exhausted, there remains nothing else for us to do but laugh'. See Matz, 60–61.
6. Michel De Certeau, *The Practice of Everyday Life* (Berkeley: University of California Press, 1984), 98.
7. Peter Keating usefully differentiates between two definitions of the 'cockney school', the first of which takes in 'all of those novelists in

the nineties who wrote about East End working class life.' The second is adopted in this investigation because of its aptness and frequency of usage. This delimits a strand of literature that is characterised by offering an unusually 'optimistic, happy and culturally inclusive portrait' of everyday, humdrum existence. Buoyant cockney stories are juxtaposed with a group of writers including Arthur Morrison who follow the 'spiritually cramped, narrow and one-sided picture of working-class life.' See P. J. Keating, *The Working Classes in Victorian Fiction* (London: Routledge and Kegan Paul, 1979), 199.

8. De Certeau, 39.
9. Gissing, 'The Muse of the Halls,' 2.
10. Ibid., 4 (emphasis in original).
11. Ibid., 4.
12. Ibid., 3.
13. Ibid., 10–11.
14. Rudyard Kipling, 'My Great and Only,' in *Abaft the Funnel* (New York: Doubleday, Page and Co., 1909), 272 (emphasis in original).
15. Ibid., 272–273.
16. Ibid., 273.
17. John Sloan, *John Davidson, First of the Moderns: A Literary Biography* (Oxford: Clarendon Press, 1995), 223.
18. George Gissing, *Workers in the Dawn*, ed. Debbie Harrison (Brighton: Victorian Secrets, 2010), 8.
19. Debbie Harrison, 'The Triumph of Schopenhauer's Pessimism Over Comte's Positivism in George Gissing's Early Writing,' *Literature Compass* 9, no. 11 (2012), 831, 883.
20. See Arthur Schopenhauer, *The World as Will and Idea*, trans. R. B. Haldane and John Kemp, 1st edn, 3 vols. (London: Trübner & Co., 1883–1886).
21. See Gissing, *Workers*, 'Explanatory Notes,' 609.
22. Schopenhauer, I, 67.
23. See Magda Romanska and Alan Ackerman, 'The Industrial Age: Introduction,' in *Reader in Comedy: An Anthology of Theory and Criticism*, ed. Magda Romanska and Alan Ackerman (London: Bloomsbury, 2016), 179–181.
24. Schopenhauer, II, 280.
25. Ibid., 283–284.
26. See Peter Stallybrass and Allon White, *The Politics and Poetics of Transgression* (London: Methuen, 1986), 10.
27. Peter Bailey, 'Conspiracies of Meaning: Music-hall and the Knowingness of Popular Culture,' *Past and Present* 144 (1994), 138.
28. George Moore, *Confessions of a Young Man* (London: Swan Sonnenschein, Lowry & Co., 1888), 242, 245.

29. Robert Buchanan, *The Coming Terror and Other Essays and Letters* (London: William Heinemann, 1891), 180.
30. Robert Buchanan and Sir Walter Besant, *The Voice of 'The Hooligan':* A *Discussion of Kiplingism* (New York: Tucker, 1900), 24.
31. Anonymous, 'The Novel of Misery,' *Quarterly Review* (October 1902): 391, 393, 401.
32. *Quarterly Review*, 394, 412, 413.
33. Anonymous, '*Mord-Em'ly* by W. Pett Ridge,' *The Academy*, 5 November 1898, 199.
34. Barry Pain, 'De Omnibus: By the Conductor,' *To-Day*, 16 April 1898, 328.
35. Adrian Poole, *Gissing in Context* (London: Macmillan, 1975), 51.
36. Jennifer A. Wagner-Lawlor, 'Introduction' in *The Victorian Comic Spirit: New Perspectives*, ed. Jennifer A. Wagner-Lawlor (Aldershot: Ashgate, 2000), xvi.
37. Matz, 101.
38. Simon J. James, *Unsettled Accounts: Money and Narrative in the Novels of George Gissing* (London: Anthem Press, 2003), 52, 98.
39. John Spiers, *Gissing and the City: Cultural Crisis and the Making of Books in Late Victorian England* (Basingstoke: Palgrave Macmillan, 2006), 72; Jacob Korg, 'Review of *The Town Traveller*,' *The Gissing Newsletter* 20, no. 4 (April 1984), 31.
40. George Gissing, *The Town Traveller* (London: Methuen & Co., 1898), 5, 6, 36, 37.
41. John D. Cloy, *Muscular Mirth: Barry Pain and the New Humor* (Victoria, BC: University of Victoria Press, 2003), 7.
42. Regenia Gagnier, *Subjectivities: A History of Self-Representation in Britain, 1832–1920* (Oxford: Oxford University Press, 1991), 127.
43. Roger Henkle, 'Morrison, Gissing, and the Stark Reality,' *NOVEL: A Forum on Fiction* 25, no. 3 (1992): 302–320, 312.
44. Andy Medhurst, *A National Joke: Popular Comedy and English Cultural Identities* (Abingdon: Routledge, 2007), 65–66.
45. Barry J. Faulk, *Music Hall and Modernity: The Late-Victorian Discovery of Popular Culture* (Athens: Ohio University Press, 2004), 139.
46. Bailey, 144.
47. John Langshaw Austin, *How to Do Things with Words* (Cambridge, MA: Harvard University Press, 1975), 94, 100.
48. Bailey, 141–142.
49. David Russell, 'Varieties of Life: The Making of the Edwardian Music Hall,' in *The Edwardian Theatre: Essays on Performance and the Stage*, ed. Michael R. Booth and Joel H. Kaplan (Cambridge: Cambridge University Press, 1996), 70.
50. Faulk, 122.
51. Ibid., 25.
52. Lyons, *Hookey*, 16–17.

53. Austin, 101.
54. Lyons, *Hookey*, 2.
55. Carolyn Oulton, '"Making Literature Ridiculous": Jerome K. Jerome and the New Humour,' *Dickens Studies Annual: Essays on Victorian Fiction* 48 (2017): 279, 280, 282, https://www.jstor.org/stable/10.5325/dickstudannu.48.2017.0273.
56. Jerome K. Jerome, 'Variety Patter,' in *The Other Jerome K. Jerome*, selected and intro. by Martin Green (Stroud: The History Press, 2009), 43.
57. Ibid., 46–47.
58. Ibid., 47; Bratton notes that this performance has variously been attributed to Jenny Hill and Bessie Bellwood, serio-comediennes who were both capable of demonstrating 'an awesome power over strong men'. See Bratton, 95.
59. Jerome, 49.
60. Ibid., 48.
61. De Certeau, 24.
62. Bailey, 142.
63. De Certeau, 26, 30.
64. Douglas Kerr offers an illuminating reading of ways that 'the staged cross-talk of misunderstanding or contestation or complicity,' associated with the music hall double act, forms a 'template' for dialogue in Joseph Conrad's fictions. See 'Conrad and the Comic Turn,' *Victorian Literature and Culture* 43, no. 1 (2015), 158; De Certeau, 15.
65. Jerome, 49.
66. Ibid., 50.
67. De Certeau, 24.
68. Faulk, 140.
69. Anonymous, 'Music Hall Morality,' *The Spectator* (12 October 1889), 462.
70. Faulk, 27.
71. William Pett Ridge, *Mord Em'ly* (London C. Arthur Pearson Ltd., 1898), 84.
72. Ibid., 80.
73. Ibid., 81.
74. George Gissing, *Thyrza*, 3 vols. (London: Smith, Elder & Co., 1887), I, 63.
75. Ibid., 66.
76. Ibid., 70.
77. Ibid., 74–75.
78. Ibid., 265–266.
79. Ibid., 266.
80. Ibid., 265.
81. Ibid., 41.

82. Jacqueline S. Bratton, *Music Hall: Performance and Style* (Milton Keynes: Open University Press, 1986), xii.
83. G. F. Scotson-Clark, *The 'Halls'* (London: T. Fisher Unwin, 1900), 21.
84. De Certeau, 99.
85. Ibid., 3.
86. David Chinitz, *T. S. Eliot and the Cultural Divide* (Chicago: University of Chicago Press, 2003), 103 (emphasis in original).
87. Faulk, 3.
88. T. S. Eliot, 'Preface' to *John Davidson: A Selection of his Poems*, ed. Maurice Lindsay (London: Hutchinson & Co., 1961), xii.
89. John Davidson, *In a Music Hall, and Other Poems* (London: Ward & Downey, 1891), 12.

WORKS CITED

Anonymous. '*Mord-Em'ly* by W. Pett Ridge.' *The Academy.* November 5, 1898.

Anonymous. 'Music Hall Morality.' *The Spectator* (12 October 1889): 461–462.

Anonymous. 'The Novel of Misery.' *Quarterly Review* (October 1902): 391–414.

Austin, John Langshaw. *How to Do Things with Words.* Cambridge, MA: Harvard University Press, 1975.

Bailey, Peter. 'Conspiracies of Meaning: Music-Hall and the Knowingness of Popular Culture.' *Past and Present* 144 (1994): 138–170.

Bratton, Jacqueline S. *Music Hall: Performance and Style.* Milton Keynes: Open University Press, 1986.

Buchanan, Robert, and Sir Walter Besant. *The Voice of 'The Hooligan': A Discussion of Kiplingism.* New York: Tucker, 1900.

Chinitz, David. *T.S. Eliot and the Cultural Divide.* Chicago: The University of Chicago Press, 2003.

Cloy, John D. *Muscular Mirth: Barry Pain and the New Humor.* Victoria: University of Victoria Press, 2003.

de Certeau, Michel. *The Practice of Everyday Life.* Berkeley: University of California Press, 1984.

Davidson, John. *In a Music Hall, and Other Poems.* London: Ward & Downey, 1891.

Eliot, T. S. 'Preface.' In *John Davidson: A Selection of His Poems*, edited by Maurice Lindsay. London: Hutchinson & Co., 1961.

Faulk, Barry J. *Music Hall and Modernity: The Late-Victorian Discovery of Popular Culture.* Athens: Ohio University Press, 2004.

Gagnier, Regenia. *Subjectivities: A History of Self-Representation in Britain, 1832–1920.* Oxford: Oxford University Press, 1991.

Gissing, George. 'The Muse of the Halls.' *The Gissing Journal* 42, no. 3 (2006): 1–14.

Gissing, George. *The Town Traveller*. London: Methuen & Co., 1898.

Gissing, George. *Thyrza in Three Volumes*. Vol 1. London: Smith, Elder & Co., 1887.

Gissing, George. *Workers in the Dawn*. Brighton: Victorian Secrets, 2010.

Harrison, Debbie. 'The Triumph of Schopenhauer's Pessimism over Comte's Positivism in George Gissing's Early Writing.' *Literature Compass* 9, no. 11 (2012): 826–836.

Henkle, Roger. 'Morrison, Gissing, and the Stark Reality.' *NOVEL: A Forum on Fiction* 25, no. 3 (1992): 302–320.

James, Simon J. *Unsettled Accounts: Money and Narrative in the Novels of George Gissing*. London: Anthem Press, 2003.

Jerome, Jerome K. 'Variety Patter.' In *The Other Jerome K. Jerome*, selected and introduced by Martin Green. Stroud: The History Press, 2009.

Keating, P. J. *The Working Classes in Victorian Fiction*. London: Routledge and Kegan Paul, 1979.

Kerr, Douglas. 'Conrad and the Comic Turn.' *Victorian Literature and Culture* 43, no. 1 (2015): 149–168.

Kipling, Rudyard. 'My Great and Only.' In Kipling. *Abaft the Funnel*. New York: Doubleday, Page & Co., 1909.

Korg, Jacob. 'Review of The Town Traveller.' *The Gissing Newsletter* 20, no. 4 (April, 1984): 29–32.

London, Jack. *The People of the Abyss*. London: Pluto, 2001.

Lyons, Albert Neil. *Hookey: Being a Relation of Some Circumstances Surrounding the Early Life of Miss Josephine Walker*. London: T. Fisher Unwin, 1902.

Matz, Aaron. *Satire in the Age of Realism*. Cambridge: Cambridge University Press, 2010.

Medhurst, Andy. *A National Joke: Popular Comedy and English Cultural Identities*. Abingdon: Routledge, 2007.

Moore, George. *Confessions of a Young Man*. London: Swan Sonnenschein, Lowry & Co., 1888.

Oddie, William. 'Mr. Micawber and the Redefinition of Experience.' In *Charles Dickens*, edited by Harold Bloom, rev. edn, 91–104. New York: Infobase Publishing, 2006.

Oulton, Carolyn. '"Making Literature Ridiculous": Jerome K. Jerome and the New Humour.' *Dickens Studies Annual: Essays on Victorian Fiction* 48 (2017): 273–284, https://www.jstor.org/stable/10.5325/dickstudannu.48.2017.0273.

Pain, Barry. 'De Omnibus: By the Conductor.' *To-Day*. April 16, 1898.

Poole, Adrian. *Gissing in Context*. London: Macmillan, 1975.

Romanska, Magda, and Alan Ackerman. 'The Industrial Age: Introduction.' In *Reader in Comedy: An Anthology of Theory and Criticism*, edited by Magda Romanska and Alan Ackerman, 179–181. London: Bloomsbury, 2016.

Russell, David. 'Varieties of Life: The Making of the Edwardian Music Hall.' In *The Edwardian Theatre: Essays on Performance and the Stage*, edited by Michael R. Booth and Joel H. Kaplan, 61–85. Cambridge: Cambridge University Press, 1996.

Schopenhauer, Arthur. *The World as Will and Idea*. Translated by R. B. Haldane and John Kemp. 1st edn, 3 vols. London: Trübner & Co., 1883–1886.

Scotson-Clark, G. F. *The 'Halls'*. London: T. Fisher Unwin, 1900.

Sloan, John. *John Davidson, First of the Moderns: A Literary Biography*. Oxford: Clarendon Press, 1995.

Spiers, John. *Gissing and the City: Cultural Crisis and the Making of Books in Late Victorian England*. Basingstoke: Palgrave Macmillan, 2006.

Stallybrass, Peter, and Allon White. *The Politics and Poetics of Transgression*. London: Methuen, 1986.

Wagner-Lawlor, Jennifer A. 'Introduction.' In *The Victorian Comic Spirit: New Perspectives*, edited by Jennifer A. Wagner-Lawlor, xiii–xx. Aldershot: Ashgate, 2000.

What Was *New* About the 'New Humour'?: Barry Pain's 'Divine Carelessness'

Jonathan Wild

The emergence of what came to be known as the 'new humour' stimulated considerable debate among critics of comic writing during the final decade of the nineteenth century. This term emerged alongside other cultural and social forms which were designated by critical commentators as 'new': these included the 'new drama', a term associated with the emergence of an Ibsen-influenced theatre in Britain in the 1890s; the 'new woman', who typically populated the 'new drama' and was marked out by her independence of mind and action; and the 'new journalism', a category of writing identified with the growth of the popular press in the late-Victorian period. As with other categories labelled 'new' in the period, the application of this prefix to 'humour' was rhetorical rather than methodical. Those writers who were associated with 'new humour', including in particular Jerome K. Jerome, W. L. Aldin, Robert Barr, G. B. Burgin, W. W. Jacobs, W. Pett Ridge and Israel Zangwill, shared only broad similarities as writers in this field. This is equally the case for Barry Pain, a writer whose work was the first to be identified under the 'new humour' designation. The aim

J. Wild (✉)
University of Edinburgh, Edinburgh, Scotland, UK

of this chapter is to identify the emergence of 'new humour' by tracing the early pejorative application of what became a remarkably enduring label. By examining the controversy surrounding the reception of Pain's first book, *In a Canadian Canoe* (1891), we are better able to understand why and how a schism developed in the last years of the Victorian period between what were perceived as old and new forms of humour. Moreover, this chapter offers the chance to reassess the work of Pain, a once highly regarded but now largely overlooked author. My aim in offering this reassessment is to unshackle Pain from the monolithic 'new humour' label and to situate his writing instead within a revealing continuum of British comic literature.

* * *

Barry Pain is a name little recognised today. While a variety of the sixty volumes published in his lifetime are now available via online book sites, few of these books have been republished since the 1930s. This neglect mirrors the fate of other writers once labelled as 'new humourists'; the exception to this rule is Jerome K. Jerome, the enduring popularity of whose *Three Men in a Boat* (1889) has ensured his longevity as a comic writer. In Pain's case, there was never a single representative volume of his work which, in standing for the rest of his output, was likely to keep his name in the consciousness of the reading public. Aside from the neglect of Pain's writing by general readers since at least the Second World War, critics have also been slow to reassess his work. To date only one study of his literary career has emerged, John D. Cloy's *Muscular Mirth: Barry Pain and the New Humor* (2003), and this critique, though useful, provides more of an overview of his career than a detailed investigation into his oeuvre. More recently, where internet interest in his writing has emerged, these sources have tended to focus on Pain's weird and supernatural fiction rather than his prolific output as a writer of comedy: Pain's work in the former genre was collected together in volumes with evocative titles such as *Stories in the Dark* (1901), *The Shadow of the Unseen* (co-authored by James Blyth) (1907) and *Here and Hereafter* (1911). But it was comic writing that provided Pain with his start in publishing in the late 1880s and early 1890s. Pain, unlike his fellow 'new humourists', was university educated, having gained a scholarship to study at Cambridge in 1884. During and immediately after his time at university Pain wrote for student publications, in particular *Granta*, which published the original versions of stories that would subsequently appear in the wider periodical press. Key among this early material was his story 'The Hundred Gates', which after its initial publication in *Granta* was reissued in 1889 in the *Cornhill Magazine*. The essence of Pain's style as a writer of comedy in this period is already in place in this fledgling work. In particular, we can recognise the employment of an arresting conceit (here, the narrator's dream of a field with one hundred gates, each topped by a stock character from light literature); his engagement with contemporary intellectual concepts (the narrator recalls his dream to a member of the 'Psychical Society'); and a final plot twist which adds a degree of edge to the foregoing humour. The latter of these conceptual features emerges when the narrator, having encountered various stock characters from 'bad books', on recognising that one of the gates is vacant, is informed by an 'uncommon curate' atop the adjacent gate that 'we've been waiting for you'; the curate adds that 'the man who tries to get a cheap reputation for wit by sneering at things not worth the sneer is the most commonplace character of all'.[1] This story also heralds Pain's characteristic fondness for puns; here the stock characters sit on gates because, as one of them confirms, 'those who use us have no style; so we're compelled to sit on gates'.[2] While the unsigned nature of Pain's *Cornhill* story meant that the reading public were largely unaware of his name at this time, the favourable impression made by 'The Hundred Gates' on influential editors such as James Payn (*Cornhill*'s editor at this time) and F. C. Burnand of *Punch*, proved invaluable in helping him secure commissions elsewhere; the remarkable volume of Pain's contributions to periodicals (such as *Punch, To-Day*, the *Idler, Black and White*, and the *Windsor Magazine*) in the 1890s testifies to the opportunities then available to an energetic and talented young writer with powerful connections.

These influential contacts certainly expedited the next stage of Pain's development as an author: the publication of his first book. The appearance of *In a Canadian Canoe* in 'The Whitefriars Library of Wit and Humour', a series of monthly volumes that had already included work by established writers such as G. Manville Fenn, G. A. Henty, and Percy Fitzgerald, meant that Pain's debut was widely circulated and reviewed. By including Pain, then a relatively unknown twenty-seven-year-old, in this 'Library', his publisher Henry & Co, and series editor W. H. Davenport Adams, were evidently looking to contemporise their list. In this regard they were following the lead of the Bristol publisher J. W. Arrowsmith, whose highly successful 'Three-and-Sixpenny Series' had already featured Jerome's *Three Men in a Boat* (a book that would come to epitomise 'new humour'), alongside work by established names such as Grant Allen and Max O'Rell. It was this blending of old and new writers in the 'Whitefriars Library' that would lead directly to the coining of the term 'new humour'. This occurred after the distinguished literary figure Andrew Lang (whose *Essays in Little* [1891] had formed the series' first volume) read a rave review of Pain's book in *Punch*. The review, published in *Punch*'s regular column 'Our Booking-Office', twice implored the public to 'buy and read' the book, which was described as 'not only witty and humorous but fresh and original in style'.[3] Lang's own volume in the series had been respectably reviewed in the press, but as the *Academy* noted, it was somewhat out-of-step with contemporary taste: 'the wide public, though they may just tolerate the scholarly refinement of Mr. Lang's less serious style, will demand in future issues [of the Whitefriars Library] a coarser stimulus and a more direct appeal to the wit and humour of their own daily life'.[4] While Pain's book could hardly be described as offering a coarse stimulus, it certainly provided the sort of fresh and innovative material that was well-judged to appeal to modern readers. Instead of welcoming this innovation, however, Lang, in a *Longman's Magazine* article entitled 'The New Humour', professed himself to be comprehensively baffled by Pain's work. After quoting several laudatory comments from the *Punch* review, Lang countered this evidently misguided praise by reprinting short extracts from *In a Canadian Canoe*. He then followed these quotations by asking 'now, is all this quaint, witty, humorous, refined, original' (terms which offered the gist of the *Punch* reviewer's praise), 'or is it mere gabble?'[5] Later in this article, and turning up the heat of his criticism, Lang argued that 'these new jokes vanquish me; they make me feel more than commonly suicidal. Anyone can put together incongruous bosh'.[6] Then, while acknowledging the likely clash of generations between himself (born in 1844) and Pain (born in 1864), he concluded his attack by stating that 'it seems pretty certain that the same mind cannot appreciate both the New Humour and the old'.[7] Lang's response to *In a Canadian Canoe* now appears a curious mixture of exasperated ill temper and a more clear-sighted recognition of the sort of shift in focus common to most cultural forms over time. While the latter of these qualities is intriguingly evident in Lang's acknowledgement that 'a new kind of humour may have arisen, and may demand in its consumers a new kind of intellectual palate',[8] he makes abundantly clear elsewhere that the impoverished nature of this 'New Humour' could only appeal to a deeply corrupted sensibility.[9]

Lang's article was widely commented upon in the periodical press during the ensuing month. Rather than uniting with Lang against the upstart 'new humour', critics tended to side with youth against age. The *Speaker*, for example, remarked that Pain had 'weathered so gallantly' the 'tea-cup storm' caused by Lang's *Longman's* article, and added that although the term 'New Humour' had been used 'slightingly to begin with, [it] is now being applied not by any means as a term of reproach'.[10] Taking a similar line, *Tinsley's Magazine* called this matter 'the sensation of the month, in the English world of letters', before remarking that Pain's 'brilliant little book' had been subjected to an 'injudicious and unfair attack' by Lang.[11] And even the conservative *Bookman* censured Lang for the vehemence of his criticism: under a heading entitled 'To an Old Humorist', their correspondent argued that 'there is a good deal of the colt in Mr. Barry Pain's work; but as promising colts have to be broken, it was surely worth Mr. Lang's while to employ the friendly discipline of a trainer who has kept some astonishing animals in his stable, and not to decide all at once that the newcomer deserved nothing but a contemptuous whip'.[12] For Pain, the fallout from Lang's critique of his book clearly helped to raise his profile and increase sales of his work; the *Bookman*'s October 1891 issue records a 'leading West End [of London] bookseller' placing *In a Canadian Canoe* as his fourth 'best selling' book, after work by established writers Lucas Malet, Rudyard Kipling and Mary E. Wilkins.[13] Sales of the book received a further stimulus when *Punch*'s reviewer, 'The Baron De Book-Worms' Assistant Reader', returned fire on Lang, calling his review an 'ugly piece of bludgeon work', before facetiously asking how his 'admirers would have protested had any sacrilegious critic ventured to treat one of your own immortal works in this manner'.[14] This drew a testy defence of his original critique from Lang in his subsequent *Longman's* column. But Lang's justification was tempered by an acknowledgement that he now realised that he had earlier read some 'really humorous pieces' by Pain. These, he reflected, he had failed to connect with the book he reviewed because they had appeared anonymously. Lang then offered the curious remark that, had he earlier linked this admirable humour with Pain, 'I would not have spoken my mind about his *Canadian Canoe* at all'.[15] Armed with this foreknowledge, one assumes, Lang would have treated

Pain's book as a local aberration rather than something symptomatic of a new and malign current in modern literature.

Taking Lang's original article as a guide, it is difficult to understand what particular features of *In a Canadian Canoe* mark out this book as a representative example of 'new humour'. No list of writers is offered by Lang to indicate whose work might also be associated with this school, indeed the only other contemporary 'humourists' mentioned—F. Anstey, James Payn, F. C. Burnand and Walter Besant—are all cited approvingly; even Jerome, whose name would come to exemplify 'new humour', is described by Lang as a writer 'I can even laugh with', although, as he further avers, only 'rarely'.[16] Without a wider context of work in which to situate the 'new humour', we are left to identify Lang's understanding of this type from the comments he makes on Pain's work alone. But as Lang's critique is typically composed of dismissive phrases such as 'mere gabble', 'irrelevant rubbish' and 'incongruous bosh', it makes any attempt to identify the salient features of the 'new humour' difficult to establish. Clues in Lang's article, however, do allow us some understanding of his conception of the 'new' aspects represented by Pain's writing. He identifies, for example, a sketch entitled 'On Art and Sardines', as representing 'Cambridge fun'.[17] This sketch, which is first among nine short pieces (voiced by a narrator musing from his Canadian canoe on the Cambridge Backs) that make up the book's opening section, includes a 'doe' sardine who after reading a novel by the popular Victorian novelist Ouida, thrown overboard in disgust by a young man from a P.N.O. steamer, 'was haunted by an awful vision of a man soldering up tins of fish':

> The doctors prescribed narcotics. When she had taken the morphia of the doctors she had no more fear of the dream. But she took too much of it. She took all there was of it. Then the doctors prescribed coral, and she took any amount of the coral. She would have taken in a reef; but the auctioneer was away for his Easter holidays, and consequently there were no sales. So she took in washing instead.[18]

After describing this sketch as 'mere gabble', Lang continues 'I vow that I fail to see this fun merely because it is Cambridge fun'.[19] He concludes this withering assessment of Pain's surreal apologue, or moral fable, by pronouncing it indicative of "an author trying his hardest to be funny",[20] while making clear that Pain fails to rise much above mere undergraduate foolery. In a further donnish put-down, Lang reasons that 'it is not original to utter propositions never advanced before, if these propositions are merely meaningless'.[21] So it appears that, for Lang, the modish surrealism of Pain's humour is what comprises its newness, and it is especially the wilful unfathomableness of this 'nonsense' (as Lang describes it) that marks out its novelty. While one might reasonably remark that nonsense in its various manifestations is the enemy of reasonable interpretation, Lang is quick to distinguish earlier healthy nonsense—in this case that of Edward Lear—from the decadent variety found in Pain's work: Lear's 'Yongi Bongi Bo *(sic)* and Mrs. Jingley Jones' provide 'witty and diverting nonsense' that is 'really amusing', while Pain's efforts offer 'mere gabble'.[22] This judgement is presented by Lang as self-evident, with no supporting rationale other than the quotations from and paraphrase of Pain's work.

The vehemence of Lang's reaction to *In a Canadian Canoe* becomes more explicable when reading two of the stories identified by contemporary reviewers as representing its best and most innovative work: 'The Girl and the Beetle' and 'The Celestial Grocery'. Like 'The Hundred Gates', these stories offer perspectives on modern life that are designed to distort and reimagine the familiar. The humour in both stories is, because of this process of radical distortion, unsettling and thought-provoking. In this respect, if we follow Lang in considering Pain as an inheritor of earlier British nonsense writers, his work is much closer to the disorienting angularity of Lewis Carroll than to the warmth and reassurance of Lear. The first of these stories, 'The Girl and the Beetle', is a simultaneously playful and serious apologue, which begins with the imminent death of a beetle named Thomas. Pain uses this arresting opening to develop a social comedy in which Thomas, whose life had been one of immorality, is encouraged to address his end by Mary, his simpering 'wife', and the 'Dear Friend', a pious beetle who had 'lived a very good life, and...wanted other beetles to be good'.[23] During the Dear Friend's attempt to make Thomas confront the 'disgusting, and loathsome, and abominable' nature of his life, he is 'interrupted by a curious stridulating noise which Thomas made'.[24] This noise distracts the 'Dear Friend' from his earlier spiritual 'enthusiasm' and encourages him to approach the dying beetle's need for repentance from a different angle. Being unable to stridulate himself (and having 'sometimes felt the want of it') the 'Dear Friend' decides to show some interest in the process, before gradually returning to more serious subjects:

He waited till the last whir had died away, and then he said:
'May I inquire how you make that noise? It is most interesting.'
Thomas knew all about it.
'It is caused,' he answered dryly, 'by the friction of a transversely striated
elevation on the posterior border of the hinder coxa against the hinder
margin of the acctabulum, into which it fits.'
'Ah!' gasped the Dear Friend; but he speedily recovered himself. 'That is
indeed interesting – really, extremely interesting.' He was trying to think
in what way it would be possible to connect this with more important matters. 'Talking about fits,' he said, 'I have just come away from such a sad
case, quite a young-'
'I was not talking about fits, sir,' interrupted Thomas, a little irritably.[25]

This early set-piece in the story, satirising Victorian piety and death,
then spools out into broader philosophical humour questioning the rel-
ative positions of man and beetle in the cosmic order. Drawing upon
and subverting the comedy of Aristophanes' *Peace*, Pain reimagines the
scene from that play in which the Athenian Trygaeus is carried heaven-
wards on the back of a giant dung beetle so that he can hold a private
audience with the Gods. In Thomas's interpretation, Aristophanes has
invented this scenario 'to account for a prevalent belief that man could
rise to higher things'.[26] For Thomas, the beetle is a higher organism than
man, a species that he categorises as 'the very lowest of all creatures'. But
Thomas concedes that even man is on his 'way to a hereafter', because in
a well-ordered universe 'nothing's wasted: the very strictest economy is
practised'.[27] The patronising attitude of Thomas the beetle to 'inferior'
creatures deftly plays with man's hubristic sense of his own place in the
order of things.
Pain develops this idea further following Thomas's death, at which
point the story becomes centred on the human world. Here in a modern suburban setting, people are gathered together for a tennis party
in the grounds of a detached villa. One member of this party, Maurice
Grey, picks up and pockets Thomas's now dead body before later hand-
ing it over to Marjorie, the 'Girl' of the story. This pair, understanda-
bly ignorant of Thomas's perorations on the spiritual hierarchy of the
animate world, are set up by Pain to reflect humourously the self-en-
closed world of man. A form of enlightenment for both takes place when
Thomas appears to them in separate dreams. Now swelled to human
size, the beetle carries Marjorie Trygaeus-like into the firmament, where

he corrects her misapprehensions about the ordering of the universe ('Poor little Marjorie! They've taught you all wrong'), before seeming to reveal a key moment from her future.[28] Later, Maurice reveals his own beetle-dream, in which Thomas tells him 'everything [he] wanted to know' about the psychological studies he had 'been working at for the last two years'. Like Marjorie's dream, Maurice's moment of enlightenment is 'all gone' when he wakes, but both sense that they will gain access 'one day' to the truths revealed in the dream.[29] The story's final twist, foreshadowed in both of these dreams, sees Maurice, now Marjorie's fiancé, killed after a fall into a quarry, with the beetle's revelations implicitly clear to him at the moment of his death. Likewise, Marjorie, on hearing of Maurice's death, is now able to understand the consoling vision Thomas had revealed to her of a 'soul going home' to the 'River of Light'.[30] This outline indicates the formally ambitious nature of Pain's story, while also offering a sense of the variety of modes and moods that it incorporates. Although these sometimes abrupt tonal shifts—from sophisticated social comedy, through philosophical wit, and finally to a melodramatically pathetic ending (with Maurice's body brought back from the quarry 'broken and ghastly')—suggest a youthful writer still getting to grips with the medium, they also reveal a freedom from constraint.[31] Writing for the commercial marketplace during his ensuing years of professional authorship, Pain would be hidebound by strict formal conventions governing word length and content, but here over the story's forty-five pages he was able to offer free rein to his imagination. While the resulting freedom led Pain towards some degree of stylistic discordance (the pathetic and rather leaden conclusion, although a key aspect of Pain's apologue, jars with the liveliness of the writing elsewhere), it also yielded notable dividends. In particular, it allowed the philosophical elements embedded within the humour to percolate and develop across the story's interlocking sections. What emerges here is a confidently uninhibited piece of writing, one perhaps calculated to inspire admiration and irritation from separate cohorts of its Victorian readers.[32]

These qualities are equally evident in 'The Celestial Grocery', a story which Pain, in an interview conducted early in his career, considered 'the best thing I have ever done'. In the same interview Pain described it as 'a fairy [story] for grown-up people', adding that this form of writing allowed him to 'to treat a purely fanciful and impossible subject as real'.[33] The story begins with the narrator, a pompous boarding-house-dwelling schoolmaster, remembering a night at the theatre, after which he had decided to splash out on a cab to take him home: the unaccustomed luxury of a seat in the stalls (his ticket given to him by a more affluent friend) had inspired this further extravagance. Having fallen into a doze in the cab, he wakes up in an empty street opposite a brightly lit grocery shop. Walking into this shop across paving stones of crystal and with the 'wildest music' in the air[34] (and after an elliptical exchange with the sharp-witted cab-horse), the narrator encounters Mr. Joseph, the shop's proprietor. In conversation with Joseph, who is invisible having absent-mindedly left his body in the cellar, the narrator discovers that the shop deals in abstract concepts rather than material goods. As Joseph confirms, 'we supply, or, to speak more accurately, we groce, all Emotions to the Solar System, and trade's very slack just now in that branch', but he continues: 'we are doing rather better in States of Being, and we've just got a new assortment of Deaths'.[35] While these 'Deaths' do not appeal to the narrator, he decides instead to sample some of the shop's supply of 'Pure white, Crystallised, Disinterested Love'. When asked by Joseph, 'Do you like it?' he replies:

> 'Yes...it is grand, it is sublime. But I don't think I could stand very much of it. How much is it a pound?'
> 'We don't sell it by the pound; we sell it by the spasm.'
> 'Then,' I said, 'I'll take six spasms.'
> 'James [the grocer then instructs his assistant], six of the pure white.'[36]

Also on offer in this grocery is 'real happiness' (a compound for which 'you buy the ingredients and you blend them yourself'), and 'Requited love', which, as the grocer remarks, is 'not expensive', but had resulted in 'complaints that it doesn't wear well'.[37] The narrator then samples 'Political Success', which offers him 'a delightful sense of exhilaration, triumph, and power', even though he is unable to understand from this brief taster 'what [his] politics were': this commodity is, the grocer declares, 'very expensive' and can only be sold in 'bursts'.[38] Excited by the seemingly limitless possibilities on offer, the narrator places a large order for commodities such as 'Literary Fame, Musical Ability, Personal Charm, Popularity, and Contentment', and offers to 'pay two pounds on account'.[39] But in common with the ending of 'The Girl and the Beetle', Pain then tempers this exuberance before moving towards a pathetically sombre conclusion. This occurs when the spectral grocer and his assistant, Joseph and James, disappear downstairs to 'feed Joseph's body', and are replaced by a female figure, 'full of the most spiritual beauty'.[40] This angelic character informs the narrator that 'he had not bought the best things' at the shop, and encourages him instead to make a more selfless purchase on behalf of his insane asylum-dwelling father.[41] By making this purchase, for which he pays with his flower buttonhole rather than with tainted cash, the narrator seemingly gains liberation from his self-centred existence, along with the freedom to experience the 'new love' inspired by his interlocutor. But the conclusion of Pain's story thwarts this optimism, revealing instead the mental breakdown of the narrator whose destiny seems set to follow that of his father: the narrator's closing lines, 'I have resigned my post, and to-night I leave my lodging. I am very lonely', provide a grim (if formally appropriate when considered in its apologue context) finale to the lively and original humour of the tale's earlier sections.[42]

Writing at the end of 1891, a year that had marked his remarkable arrival on the literary scene, Pain reflected on the new humour controversy that he had unconsciously spearheaded. In an article in the *Speaker* entitled 'The Old Humour and the New', he self-deprecatingly referred to *In a Canadian Canoe* as 'a little book of unimportant experiments which I brought out this year'. These experiments, he suggested, were conducted in the spirit of what he called 'divine carelessness', a concept he elucidated in the following terms:

> If there is one gift more than another which opens to a man the world of the imagination, that gift is humour. Here that divine carelessness which is essential to true humour can move unimpeded: there are no stupid limitations; one needs no paltry research to acquire the local colour; one need not consult the lawyer, the doctor, nor the antiquarian, in order to gain a mean and stupid accuracy. The world of the imagination has no laws and no limitations but those which the instinct of the artist imposes upon him. It is not easy, as it may seem to some, to acquit one's self well in that world; it is not true that anyone can write a story of the imaginary world. There is a distinction between carelessness, the habit of merely making mistakes, and that divine carelessness which belongs to true humour.[43]

For Pain, the apologue offered the perfect vehicle for achieving this 'divine carelessness'. But, as he noted in his *Speaker* article, this form of writing was not currently considered a commercial proposition: 'As a rule, the editors will not look at it, and the critics hate it'. For Pain, however, the apologue offered a format capable of providing fresh impetus for literature, being 'much less exhausted than the lump of stirring incidents which is welcomed as a novel of adventure', and furthermore, 'in its delicate fantasy and suggestiveness' it was designed to appeal to the 'qualities of the humourist'.[44] All humour written today, Pain declared, should be 'new humour,' but to truly embrace this form of literary modernity writers needed to free themselves from modes that had become 'exhausted', pursuing instead those 'measureless tracts still unexplored'. As Pain went on, 'any quite ordinary person, with only a small experience of life, may have noticed in the merciless tricks of destiny, in the unthinking doggedness of natural law, in the ghastly incongruities with which Nature spoils her most beautiful scenes and stories, room for humour of a more grim and, possibly, less pleasing kind. Laughter is better than impotent anger'.[45] In this way, Pain argued, the sort of new humour that he advocated might provide an effective weapon in addressing the challenges of the modern world.

Among the areas of humour that Pain in his *Speaker* article considered relatively exhausted by 1891 were those that focused exclusively on 'the characters and incidents of real life'.[46] The lobbying carried out by Pain in this article was clearly directed to magazine editors who he felt commissioned only material that they perceived to be popular while remaining suspicious of innovation. In choosing more overtly imaginative settings and incidents for his own work, Pain looked to expand the field of humourous writing in Britain, offering in the process a radically different form of comic writing from that currently proliferating. But it is difficult to find much evidence that Pain's contemporaries shared his faith in imaginative writing, the work of those writers who were closely associated with the 'new humour' label (including Jerome K. Jerome, Robert Barr, G. B. Burgin, W. W. Jacobs, W. Pett Ridge and Israel Zangwill) being consistently rooted in 'real life' over the ensuing decade. Jerome, described later by his contemporary Coulson Kernahan as 'the chieftain of the clan of The New Humour', led the way in this respect by constructing his material from recognisably contemporary people and scenes.[47] In *Three Men in a Boat*, for example, the narrator reports laconically on his own experience (and that of his clerkly companions) of 'the cussedness of things' that they encounter on their journey down the Thames. Jerome's extensive use of contemporary clerks' slang helps to embed his lower-middle class characters in a present immediately evident to his readers.[48]

It would be wrong, however, to suggest that Pain and Jerome led differing and antagonistic factions of humour writers during the 1890s. Indeed, both of them were heavily involved with publications that became closely associated with the 'new humour' phenomenon: the *Idler*, a sixpenny monthly magazine that first appeared in February 1892, and *To-Day*, a two-penny weekly appearing from November 1893. The *Idler*'s first edition included contributions by Jerome, who acted as co-editor, and Pain who contributed to a feature entitled 'The Idlers' Club'. This 'Club' feature took the form of a roundtable discussion by the magazine's regular contributors, and its first appearance provides evidence of the intended readership for this new humourous publication. Robert Barr (the *Idler*'s co-editor), in opening the Club's discussions, addressed the paucity of material available for a readership who had grown up in 'our present system of education'. This readership, the inheritors of the 1870 Education Act and subsequent legislation were, Barr further averred, 'a great reading population crying out for printed matter, and yet nobody seems to pay any attention to the appeal'.[49] The unspoken implication here is that this readership had evolved beyond the more modest penny papers previously available to them, and now had the desire and the disposable income to purchase better quality publications. The relatively high production values of the *Idler* were indicated by its sixpenny price, a feature that marked it out from many of the comic papers then available: typical among these was *Pick-Me-Up*, a weekly comic penny paper which first appeared in October 1888. The *arrival* of this readership is inextricably linked with the class-bound application by critics of the 'new humour' label, and the poems, sketches and stories that appeared in the *Idler* tend to reflect the social status of this assumed audience. Pain's own contribution to the 'Idlers' Club' suggests that he felt that the magazine would, in addition to publishing much Jerome-inspired comedy of real life, also provide a potential platform for his own humour of 'divine carelessness'. The imaginative flight of fancy represented by his suggestion, for example, of a club for millionaires, in which they might 'find the absence of luxury which they must miss so much', or alternately of the wisdom of a 'red and white bullock' that he saw 'soliloquise the other day' (*Idler*, June 1892, 604), appears in direct dialogue with the topsy-turveydom of his *Canadian Canoe* writings.[50] Pain's presence in the *Idler* (and *To-day* which Pain edited between 1897 and 1905) suggests the happy coexistence of his favoured brand of surreal humour alongside the humour of everyday life favoured by Jerome and others.

* * *

Writing an anonymously published review in 1908 of Jerome's new story collection, *The Angel and the Author—And Others*, E. V. Lucas offered what amounted to an obituary for the term 'new humour'. After confidently noting that it was Jerome who had founded this 'school', Lucas went on to suggest that the 'new humour' (which he also argued was 'one of the silliest catch phrases ever invented') had become both 'a cult and a target'. Of those writers who were once associated by critics with the 'new humour', Lucas felt that there were 'but few survivors'. These 'survivors', now 'chastened', he went on, had left behind their new humourous past and embarked on more serious literary pursuits:

> Mr. Zangwill would lead his brethren back to Zion and give women a vote. Mr. Robert Barr is a sensational novelist. Mr. Burgin is a domestic novelist. Mr Pett Ridge is a London novelist with leanings towards the Y.M.C.A. Mr. Alden is dead. Mr. Jerome is resolutely funny still, but even he is oftener in the pulpit than not.[51]

Although Lucas offers a tongue-in-cheek account of these writers forswearing their membership of the 'school' of 'new humour', what is implicitly clear here is that this movement never actually existed other than in the minds of indolent critics. The 'new humourists' were only ever a collection of contemporary authors whose comic work had shared places of publication and often a focus on the lives of those 'ordinary' people who also constituted their assumed readership. Lucas' failure to include in this list the name of the writer who had originally inspired the 'new humour' label further confirms the imprecision of this catch-all phrase. The qualities that Lucas considered typical of what had come to be known as the 'new humour' were emphatically those that characterised Jerome's own work. These features of Jerome's style, in particular 'his exaggerations, his facetiousness', were declared now comprehensively 'out of date'. Lucas, however, saw in one section of the book under review a way forward for Jerome in his career as a writer of humour. It was in his use of the apologue, Lucas declared, a form Jerome had employed in his title story, 'that he is now at his best'. Some sixteen years after Pain's initial challenge to editors to broaden the field of humourous writing in the periodical press he found his views belatedly echoed in a review that also belatedly removed him from the pantheon of 'new humourists'.

While there is little evidence to suggest that the apologue grew in popularity as a genre of humourous publication after 1908, the later twentieth century certainly saw the emergence of comic writing and performance that was significantly in tune with the wider currents of Pain's early work. This is evident, for example, in the surreal humour that Spike Milligan and others created for the *Goon Show*, a BBC radio programme that ran from 1951 to 1960. A direct line from Pain's comedy can also be traced in the later 'Cambridge fun' devised by the team behind *Monty Python's Flying Circus*. Their imaginative and irreverent sketch comedy (which appeared on BBC television between 1969 and 1974, and subsequently in several films), typically relied on unexpected reversals of expectation which often incorporated academic points of reference. The reception of *Monty Python* indeed brought with it a fresh sense of a 'new humour' made provocatively incomprehensible to an older generation of consumers. Writing in *The Times*, following the broadcasting of an episode of the first *Monty Python* television series, Henry Raynor outlined his own experience of watching the show:

> There was a point last week at which John Cleese interviewed the only descendent of a German baroque composer whose surname included every commonly-known German word, including greetings and an order for sausages, an incredible rigmarole repeated with the utmost seriousness in every question and answer. Many of our activities and convictions need only a slight nudge to the left to become patently lunatic, and *Monty Python* nudges vigorously and unobtrusively.[52]

While Raynor's review was much more accepting of this brand of 'new humour' than Lang's had been in 1891, both critics united in their sense of the shock brought about by this radical and disorienting newness. This sense of disorientation was clearly what Pain set out to achieve when he published *In a Canadian Canoe*. In providing his Victorian readers with work that emerged from the imaginative freedom of what he called 'divine carelessness', Pain intended to write humour that was avowedly *new*. While Lang was therefore correct in labelling it as such, as this chapter has demonstrated, the utility of his enduring classification began and ended at this point.

NOTES

1. Barry Pain (originally published anonymously), 'The Hundred Gates,' *Cornhill Magazine*. New Series XIII, 76 (1889), 415, 416.
2. Ibid., 409.
3. Baron de Book-Worms, 'Our Booking Office,' *Punch*, 101 (29 August 1891), 99.
4. Unsigned review, *The Academy*, 989 (18 April 1891), 368. The work collected in *Essays in Little* consisted of literary essays that Lang had originally published in a variety of newspapers and magazines. Any wit or humour they offered readers was therefore only a by-product of their function as critical essays.
5. Andrew Lang, 'At the Sign of the Ship,' 'The New Humour,' *Longman's Magazine*, 18.108 (October 1891), 660–662.
6. Ibid., 662.
7. Ibid.
8. Ibid., 661.
9. It is clear from the context of the review that Lang does not draw directly here upon George Meredith's influential 'An Essay on Comedy' (1877) in making this distinction. Meredith's essay had contrasted 'comedy' with its ability to manifest what he defined 'the Comic Spirit', and 'humour' which could only provide earthly forms of laughter. The 'comic', he argued, 'is the governing spirit, awaking and giving aim to these powers of laughter, but it is not to be confounded with them; it enfolds a thinner form of them, differing from satire in not sharply driving into the quivering sensibilities, and from humour in not comforting them and tucking them up, or indicating a broader than the range of this bustling world to them'. Lang's distinction by contrast implicitly opposes the healthy 'humour' of the past with its modern upstart counterpart. Wylie Sypher, ed., *Comedy* (Baltimore and London: The Johns Hopkins University Press, 1983), 43.
10. Unsigned review, 'The Week,' *The Speaker*, 4 (17 October 1891), 468.
11. Unsigned, 'Current Literature,' *Tinsleys' Magazine*, 30 (November 1891), 559.
12. Unsigned, 'To an Old Humorist,' *The Bookman*, 1.2 (November 1891), 62.
13. Unsigned, 'Sales of Books During the Month,' *The Bookman*, 1.1 (October 1891), 31.
14. An A. R. in the B. de B.-W.'s Office, *Punch*, 101 (10 October 1891), 179.

15. Andrew Lang, 'At the Sign of the Ship,' *Longman's Magazine*, 19.109 (November 1891), 112.

16. Andrew Lang, 'The New Humour,' 662.

17. Ibid., 661.

18. Barry Pain, *In a Canadian Canoe* (London: Henry, 1891), 5–6.

19. Lang, 'The New Humour,' 661.

20. Ibid., 661.

21. Ibid., 662.

22. Ibid., 661.

23. Barry Pain, *In a Canadian Canoe*, 166.

24. Ibid., 168.

25. Ibid., 168–169.

26. Ibid., 175.

27. Ibid., 178.

28. Ibid., 194.

29. Ibid., 205.

30. Ibid., 196.

31. Ibid., 210.

32. A review of *In a Canadian Canoe* in the periodical *Hearth and Home* recognised that the collection was likely to polarise opinion among readers: 'Mr. Pain is over the heads of the million, but those who can discover his charm will find it irresistible'. *Hearth and Home*, 19 (24 September 1891), 609.

33. Raymond Blathwayt, 'A Chat with Barry Pain,' *The Novel Review*, 1.7 (October 1892), 571.

34. Barry Pain, *In a Canadian Canoe*, 132.

35. Ibid., 134, 135.

36. Ibid., 137.

37. Ibid., 138.

38. Ibid., 139.

39. Ibid., 140.

40. Ibid., 141.

41. Ibid., 143.

42. Ibid., 149.

43. Barry Pain, 'The Old Humour and the New,' *The Speaker*, 4 (19 December 1891), 741.

44. Ibid.

45. Ibid.

46. Ibid. Pain himself would later specialise in character comedy that was centred on the daily life of ordinary people; examples include his 'Eliza' tales (1900–1913), focused on the life of an office clerk and his wife, and *De Omnibus* (1901), featuring the musings of a London 'bus conductor'.

47. Coulson Kernahan, *Celebrities: Little Stories About Famous Folk* (London: Hutchinson, 1923), 243.

48. In an intriguing foreshadowing of Lang's 'new humour' critique, *Punch*'s 1890 review of *Three Men in a Boat* had dismissed Jerome's wearisome modishness: as the 'Baron de Book-Worms' (whose Assistant Reader's high praise for Pain's book had inspired Lang's ire) proclaimed, 'I'm hanged if I see where the fun of this is'. The Baron went on to declare that Jerome's slang-ridden book was merely a 'weak imitation of American fun', implying that this new and up-to-date humour was merely a passing fad: Dickens' *Pickwick Papers* is employed by the 'Baron' to cleanse his palate, and this venerable text works within minutes to shake him with laughter. It is, perhaps, appropriate then to date the actual birth of the critical concept of 'new humour' to this review, although the label only emerged the following year in Lang's *Longman's* column.

49. Robert Barr, The Idler's Club, *The Idler* (February 1892), 106.

50. Barry Pain, ibid., 109.

51. E. V. Lucas (originally unsigned), *Times Literary Supplement*, 335 (11 June 1908), 187.

52. Henry Raynor, 'Television,' *The Times Saturday Review*, 57730 (29 November 1969), III.

Works Cited

Cloy, John D. *Muscular Mirth: Barry Pain and the New Humor*. Victoria, BC, Canada: English Literary Studies Monograph Series, 2003.

Jerome, Jerome K. *The Angel and the Author—And Others*. London: Hurst and Blackett, 1908.

Jerome, Jerome K. *Three Men in a Boat*. Bristol: J. W. Arrowsmith, 1889.

Kernahan, Coulson. *Celebrities: Little Stories About Famous Folk*. London: Hutchinson, 1923.

Lang, Andrew. *Essays in Little*. London: Henry, 1891.

Pain, Barry. *De Omnibus*. London: T. Fisher Unwin, 1901.

Pain, Barry. *Here and Hereafter*. London: Methuen, 1911.

Pain, Barry. *In a Canadian Canoe*. London: Henry, 1891.

Pain, Barry. *Stories in the Dark*. London: Grant Richards, 1901.

Pain, Barry. 'The Hundred Gates.' *The Cornhill Magazine*. New Series XIII, 76 (1889), 405–416.

Pain, Barry and James Blyth. *The Shadow of the Unseen*. London: Chapman & Hall, 1907.

Sypher, Wylie, ed., *Comedy*. Baltimore and London: The Johns Hopkins University Press, 1983.

Just Laughter: Neurodiversity in Oscar Wilde's 'Pen, Pencil and Poison'

Matthew Kaiser

I am now a *neurasthenic*. My doctor says I have all the symptoms. It is comforting to have them *all*, it makes one a perfect type.

—Oscar Wilde[1]

1   POISONING OUR MINDS

'Pen, Pencil and Poison' recounts the life and career of the 'extremely artistic' Thomas Griffiths Wainewright, who murdered two women and two men, and attempted to kill two Australians.[2] Critics generally agree that Wilde's admiring sketch of the Regency dandy is a clever but minor work, more notable for its devil's advocacy than for its philosophical profundity. Wainewright, Wilde explains, was 'not merely a poet and painter, an art-critic, an antiquarian, and a writer of prose, an amateur of beautiful things, and a dilettante of things delightful, but also a forger of no mean or ordinary capabilities, and a subtle and secret poisoner almost

M. Kaiser (✉)
Department of Literatures and Languages, University of California,
Merced, CA, USA

© The Author(s) 2020   309
L. Lee (ed.), *Victorian Comedy and Laughter*,
https://doi.org/10.1057/978-1-137-57882-2_12

without rival in this or any age'. As Lawrence Danson notes, Wilde's deadpan equation of art with murder, and his alliterative insertion of strychnine into Wainewright's art box, differs from satirical classics such as Jonathan Swift's *A Modest Proposal* (1729) or Thomas De Quincey's *On Murder Considered as One of the Fine Arts* (1827), in that readers are not asked to 'invert the initial shocking assumption'.[3] Wilde wallows in the unhealthiness of his enterprise: 'The fact of a man being a poisoner', he professes, 'is nothing against his prose'.[4] The essay is meant to act on its readers as a discursive poison, muddling their aesthetic and ethical priorities, destabilising the logical oppositions that structure their moral equilibrium. Wilde presents Wainewright's 'lemon-coloured kid gloves', his 'aesthetic eclecticism', 'his citron morocco letter-case', and his 'archaeological accuracy in costume' as more biographically relevant than his lack of 'moral instinct': 'To those who are pre-occupied with the beauty of form nothing else seems of much importance'.[5] The pillbox ring into which Wainewright stuffs his lethal powder is 'beautiful', Wilde assures us, and 'served to show off … his delicate ivory hands'.[6] At those terrible rumours that Wainewright's wife was 'privy' to his crimes, Wilde recoils, but *amorally*: 'Let us hope that she was not. Sin should be solitary, and have no accomplices'.[7]

Joseph Bristow and Rebecca Mitchell declare 'Pen, Pencil and Poison' 'daring' and 'ingenious': a 'rollicking endorsement of unabashed deviance'.[8] To others, however, the essay suffers in comparison to Wilde's more nuanced and less cold-blooded efforts in 'The Portrait of Mr. W.H', 'The Critic as Artist' and 'The Decay of Lying' to free art from the normative demand that it be morally uplifting. Wilde's claim that Wainewright's crimes 'gave a strong personality to his style', improving his art, and his breezy dismissal of the dandy's victims, can sound at times like cynical echoes of his more genial, albeit autotelic, aestheticism, for 'it is through joy', Wilde insists in 'The Soul of Man Under Socialism', 'that the Individualism of the future will develop itself'.[9] One reviewer wondered whether 'the joke has gone far enough', whether Wilde's laughter seemed a bit strained.[10] Wilde himself viewed 'Pen, Pencil and Poison' as an amusing but lesser experiment. His favourite child was 'The Decay of Lying', a dialogue spoken in the voices of his sons Cyril and Vyvyan. He wrote both works in late 1888, as London reeled from the Ripper murders, as the winter fogs encroached. They appeared in print in January 1889: 'Pen, Pencil and Poison' in Frank Harris's *Fortnightly Review*, 'The Decay of Lying' in *Nineteenth Century*. Two years later, Wilde revised both essays for *Intentions*, 'the book', Danson reminds us, 'on which his claims as a theorist and critic chiefly rest'.[11] It was obvious from the start, however, which of the two essays Wilde preferred. In a January 1889 letter to Henry Lucy, he brushes aside his friend's praise of 'Pen, Pencil and Poison', redirecting him to 'my *Nineteenth Century* article', which 'is so much the better of the two[,] that I should like to know your views on my new theory of art contained in it'.[12]

In the pages that follow, I make the case for reading 'Pen, Pencil and Poison'—if not as a major work—as a theoretically innovative text nonetheless. The essay's profundity, I argue, has never been fully appreciated, perhaps not even by its author, in part because Wilde anticipates a theory of mind for which we only now are developing a vocabulary. 'Pen, Pencil and Poison' is important not so much as a statement of Wilde's views on art (I defer to him on that matter), but as an incisive critique of nineteenth-century ideologies of health and mental fitness, of the normative fantasy that a 'good' or mentally fit reader exists. This normative fantasy has deep roots in Victorian eugenics, in political, cultural and governmental efforts to improve the nation's 'stock', 'the inborn qualities of a race', as Francis Galton, the father of modern eugenics, succinctly put it, and to purge British culture of its diseased, degenerate and defective elements.[13] The implicitly eugenic fantasy of a healthy reader—of an optimal mind, of a 'good' reader *improved* or refined by literature—is the structuring logic of modern literary studies and is inextricably linked to the rise of English as an academic discipline in the late nineteenth century. The Victorian architects of English literary studies justified their enterprise ideologically on therapeutic grounds, presenting the idea of literature, Terry Eagleton explains in his now canonical account, as a moral and cultural corrective to the incipient anarchism and epistemological relativism that Matthew Arnold and his followers feared had loosened the bonds of society.[14]

With 'Pen, Pencil and Poison' Wilde poisons the late-Victorian body politic, frees his readers from the strictures of health. Rather than advocating pathology, however, as a new, better, or alternative readerly norm, for that would be equally prescriptive and onerous, Wilde embraces an anti-therapeutic politics of neurodiversity, or neurological pluralism, wherein differences in our capacity as complex organisms for sociability, rationality, concentration and productivity, among other culturally privileged traits, are viewed nonhierarchically and nonpathologically, as differences in cognitive style, rather than as defects or deficits. Implicit, then, in

Wilde's epistemological relativism, in his radical subjectivism, is a neurological relativism, a political and ethical commitment to cultivating critical distance from our own healthy or conventional thoughts. We must be prepared as readers to poison our minds, to read against the grain of our cognitive health. Forget, for a moment, the 'remarkable' Wainewright, or the witty Wilde: the *reader* is the true hero, or anti-hero, in 'Pen, Pencil and Poison'.[15] The subject of Wilde's essay is our laughter: our susceptibility or resistance to his cruel jokes. Wilde prods us into questioning our ideological—our neuronormative—investment in being perceived by our peers as intellectually 'healthy' readers.

My reading of 'Pen, Pencil and Poison' is informed by recent scholarship—in particular the work of Elisha Cohn—on Wilde's long-standing interest in brain science.[16] It is also informed by the political concerns of the nascent neurodiversity movement, a global movement for social justice, which seeks an end to the marginalisation of neurological 'Others'. How does the concept of neurodiversity challenge the tenets of reader-response criticism, and of literary studies more generally? How might the academy's embrace of neurodiversity as an intellectual and political value compel us to rethink the practice of reading? Despite the progress made by literary studies in the areas of gender and cultural diversity, despite our efforts as a discipline to grapple with our imperial origins, the fact remains: the implied reader who makes literature cohere, the phantasmatic beneficiary of literary studies itself, is a neuronormative fiction, a cognitive ideal, to whom, a century and a half after the rise of English studies, we still stubbornly or unwittingly cling.

2   Those Ankles

The comedic weight of 'Pen, Pencil and Poison', and its ethical complexity, rests upon two thick ankles. They are the most famous ankles in Victorian literature, ankles that launched a thousand quips. For decades, critics have circled them warily, snickered at them, or winced, but have seldom failed to mention them. Wainewright, Wilde informs us, murdered his uncle in 1829 'to gain possession' of his estate, 'Linden House, a place to which he had always been very much attached'.[17] Next he killed his wife's mother. '[T]he following December he poisoned the lovely Helen Abercrombie, his sister-in-law', whose life he had insured for 18,000*l*.[18] 'When a friend', Wilde writes, 'reproached him with the murder of Helen Abercrombie he shrugged his shoulders and said,

"Yes; it was a dreadful thing to do, but she had very thick ankles"'.[19] The quotation and the accompanying shrug are likely apocryphal, but Wilde, shameless borrower that he was, did not invent the story out of whole cloth. A version of this 'unforgettable phrase', as Bristow and Mitchell describe it, is 'commonly repeated in biographical sketches of Wainewright'.[20] In his 1880 'Introduction' to Wainewright's *Essays and Criticisms*, W. Carew Hazlitt, upon whom Wilde relied for most of his facts, quotes the dandy as saying that his sister-in-law's fatal flaw was her 'thick legs'.[21]

'Thick ankles' is funnier than 'thick legs'. It is also crueler, for it renders Wainewright's crime more absurd and petty. With his more 'heartless' formulation of the joke, presented without judgment or commentary, Wilde puts his readers in a cognitive and ethical bind.[22] Whereas 'thick legs' suggests that Wainewright's aversion to Helen Abercrombie is global, inspired by a general air of plumpness or stockiness, 'thick ankles' is a more fussy complaint, suggesting that, to a fastidious aesthete like Wainewright, who collects gems, miniatures, antique bronzes, and teapots, any stray or anomalous detail has the power to undermine the pleasing effect of the whole. Wainewright's sensitivity to detail is the source of his insensitivity to women. 'Ankles' also underscores the sexually violent nature of Helen Abercrombie's death. More than an aesthetic object, she is an inventory of female parts, a collection of weights and measurements. Wilde recasts violence against women as aesthetic critique. But even as Wilde exposes Wainewright's self-justifying misogyny, highlighting with his ankle joke the absurdly trivial criterion used to determine whether women live or die, he trivialises the victim's death by rendering it so absurd, by casting her killer in a comic light, as an overly zealous aesthete. Meanwhile, behind a door never mentioned, in a room only ever implied, Helen Abercrombie dies in agony, for strychnine poisoning leads to violent muscle spasms and eventually to respiratory and brain failure.

Here is where Wilde's reader—a complicated creature, more a gaggle of contending perspectives than a personage—comes into play. Wilde understands that it is cognitively impossible to experience horror and hilarity simultaneously. By heightening the horror and hilarity of Helen Abercrombie's murder, linking it causally to her ankles, Wilde triggers cognitive dissonance in his readers: oscillation between incommensurable states of amusement and disgust. This cognitive dissonance manifests itself as guilty laughter. Wilde actively encourages his readers to be of two minds, indeed, to be of four minds, or more, cognitively diversified. Wilde turns the mind of the reader into his paradox. Walker Gibson's classic distinction between the 'real' reader, on the one hand, the flesh-and-blood individual 'upon whose crossed knee rests the volume', and the 'mock' or implied reader, on the other, 'whose mask and costume the individual takes on in order to experience the language', does not come close to explaining Wilde's trick.[23] 'Pen, Pencil and Poison' addresses itself simultaneously to at least four implied or mock readers: a socially conscious reader fascinated but troubled by the idea of Wainewright; a dispassionate and clinically detached reader who views Wainewright as a metaphor or conceptual abstraction rather than as an actual person; a sociopathic reader who smiles indulgently at Wainewright's unconventional and unsentimental attitude; and an aesthetically sensitive reader engrossed in the play of Wilde's language, in the illusion produced. All four of these implied readers think the joke is on the other three readers. All four are correct. In 'Pen, Pencil and Poison', Wilde encourages us to laugh behind our own multiple backs. In contrast to Swiftian satire, Wildean humour emerges from its author's pluralistic and anti-therapeutic refusal to privilege one implied reader over another, to hierarchise, let alone reconcile or integrate, the dissonant cognitive states that he induces in us. Wilde refuses to provide us with an ideal mind, a standard of mental and hermeneutic health, towards which to strive, or with which we might synthesise and make sense of our contradictory and multiplicitous interpretive and emotional impulses. As a result, those troublesome ankles linger, casting a pall over his essay.

Naturally, some flesh-and-blood readers, those in the public eye, will have an allergic reaction to cognitive dissonance, to Wilde's rhetorical assumption that a small part of them *smiles* at the murder of a young woman. These readers typically react in one of three ways. Some turn indignantly from his essay, as did the anonymous reviewer cited above. Others, if they admire Wilde, avert their eyes, ignoring or downplaying the essay's distressing notes. Still others, if they identify strongly with Wilde, engage in heroic acts of interpretive contortion in order to explain the problem away, in the process redeeming Wilde, wiping the smile off our faces. Rare is the critic who shamelessly *enjoys* Wilde's ankle joke, who, like Julia Prewitt Brown, cites it approvingly as evidence for why 'Pen, Pencil and Poison' is a 'highly amusing essay'.[24] Philip Smith and Michael Helfand win the award for best contortionists.

After mistakenly claiming that Wainewright 'kills his wives', they argue that Wilde's equation of art with murder is meant to raise awareness of the financial difficulties faced by 'the middle-class artist', for if Wainewright had 'inherited wealth', they maintain, he would not have had to resort to murder.[25] Other critics find solace in diagnosing 'Pen, Pencil and Poison' as satire. They put all their eggs into the basket of one implied reader, reassuring us that naughty Wilde means well. Josephine M. Guy, for instance, reads Wilde's essay as a 'witty attack' on Paterian aestheticism, and painstakingly lists every ironic echo of Pater—his love of cats, his attraction to the colour green—that reverberates in Wilde's portrait of Wainewright.[26] Regenia Gagnier, too, urges calm, encourages us to view 'Pen, Pencil and Poison' as parody, to treat Wilde's narrative voice as a rhetorical pose, with which he distinguishes his own aestheticism from his narrator's 'limited conception of social life and ... dangerously isolated egotism'.[27] Others implore us to look past the whole murder thing, to focus instead on the less vexing trope of forgery. Bristow and Mitchell acknowledge that Wainewright's crimes were 'heinous', and they take pains not to downplay them, and then proceed to downplay them, claiming that Wainewright the bank-forger held greater intellectual attractions for Wilde than Wainewright the killer, for 'the primary connection that drove Wilde's writing on ... Wainewright' was 'how the deft criminality of forgery spurs the brilliant creativity of art'.[28] Reader-response critic Michael Patrick Gillespie, too, works diligently to keep our focus on forgery, which he reads as a therapeutic metaphor for the 'amalgamative creativity' of reader and writer, encouraging us to view 'Pen, Pencil and Poison' as an 'invitation' to readers 'to become forgers in the most complex sense of the word: to shape order from chaos'.[29] Thus, like Gagnier, Gillespie discovers medicinal and redemptive properties in the essay's 'dialogism' and 'polyvocality'.[30]

The problem with these readings—for all their flashes of brilliance—is that they let readers off the hook. They go to extraordinary lengths to protect us from the consequences of our laughter, to rescue us from our own cruelty. They are constrained by ideologies of mental health. They drain the poison from 'Pen, Pencil and Poison'. They present themselves as epistemological antidotes to cognitive dissonance. They offer safety, ethical and hermeneutic coherence, respectability, fitness. Wilde does the opposite. He sickens us. Keep in mind that Wilde wrote his ankle joke in the late autumn of 1888, at the height of the media storm over the Ripper murders, and mere weeks, perhaps days, after Mary Jane

Kelly, the sixth victim, was discovered anatomically dismantled on a bed in her Whitechapel room, her internal organs, breasts and thighs distributed ritualistically around her corpse, her liver between her ankles. Wainewright's aesthetic dissection of Helen Abercrombie should be read in this context. So should Wilde's decision to make light of her murder. Historian Judith Walkowitz provides a grim account of the misogynous humour inspired that autumn by media coverage of Jack the Ripper, of the popular sport among London men of terrorising prostitutes by impersonating the Ripper, or of newspaper reports of abusive husbands taunting their wives with 'I'll Whitechapel You' or 'Look out for Leather Apron'.[31] In the end, it's the same joke: the working-class bloke, his mates in tow, sneaking up on the neighbourhood whore; the gentleman with his glass of port and *Fortnightly Review*, smiling at those ankles.

3   FROM PATHOLOGY TO NEURODIVERSITY

Of Wilde's many nineteenth-century detractors, whose ranks swelled in the wake of his 1895 conviction for gross indecency, few expressed greater disgust at his writings than physician and eugenist Max Nordau. Today, Nordau 'is typically treated', Steven Aschheim notes, 'as little more than a "symptom," a textbook example of hopelessly outmoded and misguided cultural and intellectual postures built upon thoroughly discredited psycho-physiological premises'.[32] In Nordau's *Degeneration* (1892), however, it is Wilde who is the symptom. Nordau describes the 'deranged' and 'hysterical' Wilde as symptomatic of the 'pathological aberration of a racial instinct', indeed, of the 'ego-maniacal recklessness' and 'perversion' of fin-de-siècle culture itself, the primary aim of which, he claims, is to 'irritate' one's 'moral and sane' 'fellow-creatures'.[33] 'Pen, Pencil and Poison' sends the verbose clinician into a wordless rage, which manifests itself as furious quotation: a dumb-show rehearsal of Wilde's most self-evidently revolting statements, including the line about Helen Abercrombie's ankles. Nordau stops himself, presumably to spare the reader further pain, only to condemn Wilde's essay as 'tortuously disdainful prattling' and 'heckling'.[34]

Nordau grounds his critique of Wildean aestheticism in nineteenth-century brain science. As George Mosse explains, Nordau's sweeping indictment of modern culture—of Ibsen, Nietzsche, Zola, Whitman and Wilde, among others—is motivated by his eugenic fear that 'industrial society' has caused 'the human organism' to 'become fatigued with nervous excitement', to 'suffer from decayed brain centers'.[35] Nordau diagnoses Wilde's art, then, as literally *sick*, as emanating from the 'degenerate' 'nervous system' and weakened cellular 'protoplasm' of an 'ego-maniac': an individual with '[b]adly-conducting sensory nerves', whose 'organic ego-sensibility' had 'advance[d] irrepressibly into the foreground', 'fill[ing]' his defective brain 'with obsessions which are not inspired by the events of the external world, and by impulsions which are not the reaction against external stimulation'.[36] Worse than sick, however, worse than being trapped in the narcissistic echo chamber of his antisocial mind, Wilde is *sickening*. His unsanitary ideas threaten to infect border-line healthy nervous systems. Because the population's neurophysiological fragility has reached pandemic proportions, and because so many suscep-tible brains teeter on the brink of egomania, Wilde's ideas constitute a biohazard.

Wildeans seldom pass up an opportunity to poke fun at Nordau. Who doesn't love a good melodramatic villain? The problem, however, is that Wilde's aestheticism is inspired by the same neurological theo-ries of mind with which Nordau attacks him. Elisha Cohn traces Wilde's career-long interest in brain science, and his flirtation with scientific materialism, to his Oxford days, to the remarkable notebooks that he kept as an undergraduate. These notebooks 'track[] ... his burgeoning interest in Greek philosophy and his dedication to Pater's art history, but also his fascination with debates in the sciences', in particular his attraction to theories of the 'physical basis of mind'.[37] Wilde's fragmen-tary scientific musings range widely and contain some comical flashes of earnestness, as when he contemplates the 'unconscious' 'movement of algae', or expresses concern that '[t]he navicula of the oyster ... causes ... extraordinary mortality among young oysters'.[38] Taking a break from his blue-and-white china, Wilde ponders the consequences of removing 'the hemispherical ganglia from a pigeon'.[39] He marvels at how 'the elabo-rate cerebral cells of the human brain' can be traced to the 'structureless albumenoid matter (Bathybius Haeckelii) which the depths of the north Ocean hide'.[40] A common theme in the notebooks is the intrinsic flesh-iness of thought, the physiological underpinnings of all 'psychical activ-ity': 'Is thought', Wilde wonders, 'a property of the cerebral protoplasm in the same sense as irritability is?'[41] At the end of his career, from his cell in Reading Gaol, Wilde continues to turn his thoughts brainward: 'We know now that we do not see with the eye or hear with the ear', he muses in *De Profundis* (1897), for '[i]t is in the brain that the poppy

is red, that the apple is odorous, that the skylark sings'.[42] Turning to
The Picture of Dorian Gray (1890), Cohn heroically corrals every stray
reference to 'pearly' 'brain' cells and 'white nerve[s]' into a compelling
account of Wilde's 'neurological aestheticism': the myriad ways in which
neurological discourses structure and legitimise his aestheticism, but also
enable him to synthesise the various intellectual traditions that inform his
understanding of subjectivity.[43]

Given the extent to which Wilde's aestheticism leans on brain science, Nordau's medical denunciation of 'Pen, Pencil and Poison' is more
savvy and apt than one might think. Uncanny similarities exist between
Wilde and Nordau, especially on the subject of neural plasticity in readers. Both envision the reader as physically susceptible to literary texts,
which, like opium, can 'make[ ] one think in a circle', as Dorian discovers, 'one thought' creeping '[f]rom cell to cell of his brain', modifying
his cellular structure, until it is too late: 'Dorian Gray had been poisoned
by a book'.[44] Wilde openly admits that his authorial aim is to weaken
his readers' grips on their minds, shake loose their healthy thoughts.
Towards the end of 'Pen, Pencil and Poison', he expresses his misgivings
about having subjected them to his poisonous essay. With a note of mock
concern, he warns readers that their minds might be too premature, too
impressionable, to contemplate the deleterious and epistemologically
uncontainable dandy: '[H]e is far too close to our own time', 'a little too
modern', 'for us to be able to form any purely artistic judgment about
him'.[45] Without the palliative and protective benefits of critical distance
or historical perspective, the unprepared mind of the reader succumbs to
disorienting emotion: 'It is impossible', Wilde adds, 'not to feel a strong
prejudice against a man who might have poisoned Lord Tennyson, or
Mr. Gladstone, or the Master of Balliol'. Wilde, too, is a 'subtle and
secret poisoner', agitating the nervous systems of his unwitting guests,
asking them to cultivate a stance of Arnoldian disinterestedness vis-à-vis
their own mental health.

Nordau's considerable limitations as a thinker should not be attributed to his biological determinism per se. The problem with Nordau is
the neuronormative model of mind at the heart of his book: his therapeutic fantasy of a healthy or 'neurotypical' reader assailed by Wilde
and his ilk.[46] Nordau defines 'sanity' primarily in terms of sociability, as
one's capacity for empathy: the 'organic' ability 'to know [oneself] in
emotional communion with the species'.[47] Without empathy, 'the social
edifice' collapses. While Nordau concedes that criticising 'the vulgar

herd' sometimes proves necessary, the 'sane man' experiences 'combat
... in the cause of truth and knowledge' as a 'painful' 'duty', whereas
Wilde, who has a 'mania for contradiction', experiences it as a sadistic
pleasure.[48] Wilde emerges from the pages of *Degeneration* a molester of
brains. Gallant Nordau offers himself as their therapeutic saviour.

Wilde famously deflected eugenic and neuronormative attacks on his
art by making a virtue of pathology. It was one of his favourite rhetorical
tactics, though not his most effective or groundbreaking. Art and madness, Wilde declared, spring from the same sacred corner of the human
mind. 'There is nothing sane about the worship of beauty', he asserts
in 'The Critic as Artist': 'It is too splendid to be sane'.[49] Wilde cloaked
himself in genius, as well as in cloaks that only a genius would wear,
turning the eugenic argument against him on its head, for eugenists like
Galton, Cesare Lombroso, John Ferguson Nisbet and Nordau 'associated genius', Anne Stiles notes, 'with evolutionary regression, asym-
metrical brain development, and medical conditions such as hysteria and
epilepsy'.[50] Wilde sought political agency and artistic legitimacy in the
very disease paradigms with which others sought to contain him. 'I quite
agree with Dr. Nordau's assertion that all men of genius are insane', he
informed journalist Chris Healy, 'but Dr. Nordau forgets that all sane
people are idiots'.[51] As far as political agency goes, pathology only gets
us so far. A declaration of insanity or perversion that sounds charming
on Wilde's lips falls flat when entrusted to a less skillful, charismatic or
ironic speaker. In a 1911 speech before the Eugenics Education Society,
Edith Ellis, a lesbian proponent of eugenics, and the wife of Havelock
Ellis, attempts with a palpable air of desperation to reconcile her eugenic
commitment to race improvement with her 'abnormal' and biologically
inconvenient sexual identity, offering her sceptical audience the example
of Oscar Wilde, 'one of Nature's satires', a 'perplexing mixture' of 'man'
and 'woman', as proof that homosexuality might function as a genetic
mutation with 'possibly a sacred function in the human scheme'.[52] Cue
the polite applause, shuffle of middle-class feet.

Wilde's most anti-authoritarian and epistemologically sophisticated
refutation of eugenic neuronormativity takes the form, then, not of his
defensive efforts to romanticise or to reappropriate pathology, but rather
his untimely commitment to the principle of neurodiversity, his pluralistic resistance to the idea of a healthy reader, to the idea, that is, that
the contradictory responses inspired in us by a literary text refine us,
sharpen our minds, or make us better people. Wilde is not interested in

improving our health. Wilde's praise of the pathological Wainewright is less groundbreaking, in the end, than his cultivation of a neurodiverse practice of reading, his refusal to privilege one implied reader over another, or even to see this refusal as symptomatic of cognitive limberness. Celebrating pathology and promoting neurodiversity are only superficially related activities; they can often be antithetical. To promote neurodiversity means to reimagine mental health, mental illness and cognitive disabilities as ideological constructs; it means to deny the existence of a standard or neurotypical nervous system; and most crucial of all, as I mentioned earlier, it means to view neurophysiological differences nonhierarchically and nonpathologically as differences in cognitive style, rather than as defects or anomalies to be managed therapeutically. Promoting neurodiversity is not the same thing, then, as inverting the classical sanity–insanity hierarchy, crowning madness king, making a virtue of abnormality, deviance, and disease. Any celebration of pathology, however well-meaning or refreshing it may be, risks reproducing the very neuronormativity that it critiques, only counterculturally, with insanity or criminality presented as new cognitive ideals, the world's 'sane' population dismissed as idiots or as cognitively deficient. As we've seen, when backed into a corner, Wilde will deploy pro-pathology rhetoric, at times flippantly. When he is at his best, however, his deployment is more tactical. He invokes insanity not as a political end in itself but as a necessary step on the path to neurodiversity. Hence, Wainewright's pathology triggers the essay's neurodiversity.

With his radically anti-utilitarian and pluralistic ethic of reading, Wilde exposes the eugenic underbelly of modern literary criticism, the ideologies of cognitive health that structure Western bourgeois understandings of what it means to be a 'good' reader. His own anti-utilitarian '[c]riticism', he hopes, 'will annihilate race-prejudices, by insisting upon the unity of the human mind in the variety of its forms'.[53] In its purest form, Wildean individualism defines itself against competition, against judgment, against the hierarchical impulse to measure one thing against another, against the 'conformity to rule', whether that rule is health or madness, law or crime.[54] 'A red rose is not selfish because it wants to be a red rose', Wilde writes in 'The Soul of Man Under Socialism', but '[i]t would be horribly selfish if it wanted all the other flowers in the garden to be both red and roses'.[55] It is Oscar Wilde's most beautiful and revolutionary idea: his rose-coloured answer to the Golden Rule. Around Helen Abercrombie's ankles Wilde plants implied readers of many shapes and hues: autists and artists, sadists and mums. It is a garden around which no selfish giant builds a wall. Readers proliferate, tangling their heads. No gardener dares untangle them.

4   AGAINST HEALTH

Victorian eugenics haunts twenty-first-century literary studies. It is time to acknowledge the ghost at our banquet. When Merton Professor of English George Stuart Gordon declared that 'England is sick', in his 1922 inaugural lecture at Oxford, and that 'English literature must save it', he was invoking Galton as much as Arnold, couching his call for a new culture in the rhetoric of eugenics: an enfeebled nation in need of iatric intervention, undergraduate minds in need of literary medicine.[56] Eugenics might conjure images of forced sterilisation and ethnic cleansing, but from the late 1880s to the Second World War, at least in Great Britain, 'Galton's eugenics made for a church as broad', Donald Childs reminds us, 'as that of his opponents'.[57] Proponents of eugenics included the Fabian socialist George Bernard Shaw, as well as Virginia Woolf, W. B. Yeats, Olive Schreiner, H. G. Wells and D. H. Lawrence. Angelique Richardson exposes the eugenic foundations of New Woman feminism, with its call for the 'rational reproduction of a new healthy race', and of Sarah Grand's vision of literature as 'a medicinal drug' taken 'to effect health'.[58] With her utilitarian motto 'art for man's sake', Grand 'set[] herself in opposition to Oscar Wilde's camp'.[59] More than a pseudoscience or a hereditary explanation for social problems, eugenics is a 'technology of life', a therapeutic rhetoric of normalization, regulation and correction: the body as an expression of national and racial health.[60] In Britain, eugenic proposals to incentivise sexual reproduction by the strong and to discourage it by criminals, the feeble-minded, and the degenerate 'never left the realm of theory', Nicholas Wade observes.[61] The *rhetoric* of eugenics, however, was ubiquitous, Marouf Hasian explains, and remains so to this day, shaping late-nineteenth- and twentieth-century representations of the poor, the mentally ill, and women, legitimising hygienic campaigns to eliminate 'race poisons', such as smoking and alcohol, and bolstering political movements for 'birth control, prohibition, scouting, intelligence testing, conservation, immigration restriction', and community childcare.[62]

The rise of English studies in the late nineteenth century is inseparable from the rise of eugenics, its mushroom growth occurring, Eagleton notes, 'in the Mechanics' Institutes, working men's colleges and extension lecturing circuits', where the study of literature, it was hoped, would exert a pacifying influence on working-class minds, as religion once did, would instil in young men a sense of national and racial pride, teach them to transcend their self-interested thoughts, 'curb in them any disruptive tendency'.[63] Literature served not merely as a vehicle for ideological control: it was a therapeutic technology for the maintenance of cognitive health, refining, managing, cultivating the reader's unruly brain, which was bombarded by toxiferous influences from popular and consumer culture. Literature became 'a holy sacrament of the mind', in the words of nineteenth-century lecturer Henry Hudson.[64] A moral tonic, yes, but in an age of scientific materialism, literature also functioned as a salutary tool, Nordau reminds us, for developing psycho-physiological 'sympathy' with one's 'own species', strengthening the 'organic base of the social edifice'.[65]

Literary studies has long since abandoned its social-engineering pretensions, but the therapeutic benefit of literature remains, for many humanists today, an indispensable arrow in the quiver of disciplinary self-justification. Martha Nussbaum's 1997 defence of humanities education contains uncanny echoes of Gordon's demand that England take its medicine. The scholarly contemplation of art and literature, Nussbaum insists, is 'vital' to 'cultivating powers of imagination that are essential to citizenship', for 'narrative imagination is an essential preparation for moral interaction'.[66] Suzanne Keen deftly dismantles Nussbaum's argument, questioning her assumption that 'reading certain novels is good for people', or that the empathy inspired by literary texts 'necessarily translates into what Steven Pinker calls "nicer" human behavior'.[67] And yet neuronormativity haunts even Keen's scepticism, so unyielding is our ideal of the healthy reader. Even if novel-reading does not inspire altruism, 'empathy', she argues, remains 'a core component' of literary studies, 'the loss of which ... is indeed to be regretted'.[68] The 'atrophy' of 'empathy', she adds, would 'impoverish humans', for '[d]eficiencies in empathy impair human relationships and contribute to psychopathology'.[69] Aware perhaps of her neurologically elitist definition of good reading, Keen gestures weakly towards neurodiversity: 'Having no empathy does not necessarily indicate low intelligence, however: Asperger's sufferers can be exceptionally bright'.[70] Send them to the Science Building! Thus does Victorian neuronormativity rear its head, the ghost at our banquet. Set Keen's Asperger's 'sufferer' alongside Wilde's ankle joke for a moment. What are these discordant notes of unsociability, but the cognitive remainder, the pesky residuum, the whiff of disease, that literary studies cannot reconcile with its ideal of reading?

Here we are—at the end of a chapter on laughter, at the end of a book on Victorian comedy—contemplating ethnic cleansing, forced sterilization and the eugenic foundations of literary studies. I'm afraid that I've spoiled the fun. Let's give Oscar Wilde the last laugh, shall we? Wilde teaches us the unhealthy art of laughter. Laugh, he urges us, in the face of modern medicine. Laugh at the eugenic pronouncements of the Max Nordaus and Francis Galtons of the world. Laugh at the idea of good health. Laugh until your brain hurts and your sides ache. Wilde's jokes may be cruel, his humour, poisonous. But it is just laughter.

NOTES

1. Oscar Wilde, 'Letter from Oscar Wilde to Robert Ross,' in *The Complete Letters of Oscar Wilde*, eds. Merlin Holland and Rupert Hart-Davis (New York: Henry Holt, 2000), 1174.
2. Oscar Wilde, *Intentions*, in *The Artist as Critic: Critical Writings of Oscar Wilde*, ed. Richard Ellmann (Chicago: University of Chicago Press, 1969), 321.
3. Lawrence Danson, *Wilde's Intentions: The Artist in His Criticism* (Oxford: Oxford University Press, 1997), 88.
4. Wilde, *Intentions*, 339.
5. Ibid., 321, 322, 323, 325, 330.
6. Ibid., 333.
7. Ibid., 334.
8. Joseph Bristow and Rebecca N. Mitchell, *Oscar Wilde's Chatterton: Literary History, Romanticism, and the Art of Forgery* (New Haven: Yale University Press, 2015), 215, 227, 230.
9. Wilde, *Intentions*, 338; Oscar Wilde, 'The Soul of Man Under Socialism,' in *The Artist as Critic: Critical Writings of Oscar Wilde*, ed. Richard Ellmann (Chicago: University of Chicago Press, 1969), 286.
10. Anonymous, Review of *Intentions*, in *Literary Opinion* (July 1891), 10.
11. Danson, *Wilde's Intentions*, 1.
12. Oscar Wilde, 'Letter from Oscar Wilde to Henry Lucy,' in *The Complete Letters of Oscar Wilde*, eds. Merlin Holland and Rupert Hart-Davis (New York: Henry Holt, 2000), 384.
13. Francis Galton, *Essays in Eugenics* (Honolulu: University Press of the Pacific, 2004), 35.

14. See Terry Eagleton, *Literary Theory: An Introduction*, 2nd ed. (Minneapolis: University of Minnesota Press, 1996), 15–46.

15. Wilde, *Intentions*, 321.

16. See Elisha Cohn, '"One Single Ivory Cell": Oscar Wilde and the Brain,' *Journal of Victorian Culture* 17, no. 2 (2012): 183–205.

17. Wilde, *Intentions*, 333.

18. Ibid., 333–334.

19. Ibid., 337.

20. Bristow and Mitchell, *Oscar Wilde's Chatterton*, 230.

21. W. Carew Hazlitt, 'Introduction,' in *Essays and Criticisms* by Thomas Griffiths Wainewright, ed. W. Carew Hazlitt (London: Reeves and Turner, 1880), lxix.

22. Bristow and Mitchell, *Oscar Wilde's Chatterton*, 230.

23. Walker Gibson, 'Authors, Speakers, Readers, and Mock Readers,' in *Reader-Response Criticism: From Formalism to Post-structuralism*, ed. Jane P. Tompkins (Baltimore: The Johns Hopkins University Press, 1980), 2.

24. Julia Prewitt Brown, *Cosmopolitan Criticism: Oscar Wilde's Philosophy of Art* (Charlottesville and London: University of Virginia Press, 1997), 44.

25. Philip E. Smith II and Michael S. Helfand, *Oscar Wilde's Oxford Notebooks: A Portrait of Mind in the Making* (New York: Oxford University Press, 1989), 65.

26. Josephine M. Guy, 'Introduction,' in *Criticism: Historical Criticism, Intentions, The Soul of Man, The Complete Works of Oscar Wilde*, vol. 4 (Oxford: Oxford University Press, 2007), xxxii.

27. Regenia Gagnier, *Idylls of the Marketplace: Oscar Wilde and the Victorian Public* (Stanford: Stanford University Press, 1986), 39.

28. Bristow and Mitchell, *Oscar Wilde's Chatterton*, 222.

29. Michael Patrick Gillespie, *Oscar Wilde and the Poetics of Ambiguity* (Gainesville: University Press of Florida, 1996), 37.

30. Gillespie, *Oscar Wilde and the Poetics of Ambiguity*, 40.

31. Judith R. Walkowitz, *City of Dreadful Delight: Narratives of Sexual Danger in Late-Victorian London* (Chicago: University of Chicago Press, 1992), 219.

32. Steven E. Aschheim, 'Max Nordau, Friedrich Nietzsche and Degeneration,' *Journal of Contemporary History* 28, no. 4 (1993): 643.

33. Max Nordau, *Degeneration*, ed. George L. Mosse (Lincoln: University of Nebraska Press, 1968), 318–319.

34. Nordau, *Degeneration*, 320.

35. George L. Mosse, 'Introduction,' in *Degeneration* (Lincoln: University of Nebraska Press, 1968), xxi.

36. Nordau, *Degeneration*, 253–254, 256–257.

37. Elisha Cohn, 'Oscar Wilde and the Brain Cell,' in *Progress in Brain Research* 205 (2013): 23; Oscar Wilde, 'Commonplace Book,' in *Oscar Wilde's Oxford Notebooks: A Portrait of Mind in the Making*, eds. Philip E. Smith II and Michael S. Helfand (New York: Oxford University Press, 1989), 121.

38. Wilde, 'Commonplace Book,' 112, 126.

39. Ibid., 136.

40. Ibid., 112.

41. Ibid., 111.

42. Oscar Wilde, *De Profundis* (New York: The Modern Library, 1992), 80.

43. Oscar Wilde, *The Picture of Dorian Gray*, ed. Norman Page (Peterborough, ON: Broadview Press, 1998), 166; Cohn, 'One Single Ivory Cell,' 185.

44. Wilde, *The Picture of Dorian Gray*, 178, 215.

45. Wilde, *Intentions*, 339–340.

46. See Thomas Armstrong, *The Power of Neurodiversity: Unleashing the Advantages of Your Differently Wired Brain* (Cambridge, MA: Da Capo Press, 2010), viii.

47. Nordau, *Degeneration*, 325.

48. Ibid., 318–319.

49. Wilde, *Intentions*, 393.

50. Anne Stiles, *Popular Fiction and Brain Science in the Late Nineteenth Century* (Cambridge: Cambridge University Press, 2012), 128.

51. Quoted in Richard Ellmann, *Oscar Wilde* (New York: Vintage, 1987), 550.

52. Mrs. Havelock Ellis, 'Eugenics and the Mystical Outlook,' in *Nineteenth-Century Writings on Homosexuality: A Sourcebook*, ed. Chris White (London: Routledge, 1999), 113–114.

53. Wilde, *Intentions*, 405.

54. Wilde, 'The Soul of Man,' 286.

55. Ibid., 285.

56. Quoted in Eagleton, *Literary Theory*, 20.

57. Donald J. Childs, *Modernism and Eugenics: Woolf, Eliot, and the Culture of Degeneration* (Cambridge: Cambridge University Press, 2001), 7.

58. Angelique Richardson, *Love and Eugenics in the Late Nineteenth Century: Rational Reproduction and the New Woman* (Oxford: Oxford University Press, 2003), 26, 119.

59. Richardson, *Love and Eugenics*, 120.

60. Michel Foucault, *The History of Sexuality: An Introduction*, vol. 1, trans. Robert Hurley (New York: Vintage Books, 1978), 145.

61. Nicholas Wade, *A Troublesome Inheritance: Genes, Race and Human History* (New York: Penguin, 2014), 33.

62. Marouf A. Hasian, Jr., *The Rhetoric of Eugenics in Anglo-American Thought* (Athens: The University of Georgia Press, 1996), 5, 28.
63. Eagleton, *Literary Theory*, 22–23.
64. Quoted in Lionel Gossman, 'Literature and Education,' *New Literary History* 13, no. 2 (1982): 355.
65. Nordau, *Degeneration*, 327.
66. Martha C. Nussbaum, *Cultivating Humanity: A Classical Defense of Reform in Liberal Education* (Cambridge: Harvard University Press, 1997), 85, 90.
67. Suzanne Keen, *Empathy and the Novel* (Oxford: Oxford University Press, 2007), ix, xxv.
68. Keen, *Empathy and the Novel*, ix.
69. Ibid., 9, 167.
70. Ibid., 10.

WORKS CITED

Anonymous. Review of *Intentions*, by Oscar Wilde. *Literary Opinion* (July 1891), 10.

Armstrong, Thomas. *The Power of Neurodiversity: Unleashing the Advantages of Your Differently Wired Brain*. Cambridge, MA: Da Capo Press, 2010.

Aschheim, Steven E. 'Max Nordau, Friedrich Nietzsche and *Degeneration*.' *Journal of Contemporary History* 28, no. 4 (1993): 643–657.

Bristow, Joseph and Rebecca N. Mitchell. *Oscar Wilde's Chatterton: Literary History, Romanticism, and the Art of Forgery*. New Haven and London: Yale University Press, 2015.

Brown, Julia Prewitt. *Cosmopolitan Criticism: Oscar Wilde's Philosophy of Art*. Charlottesville and London: University of Virginia Press, 1997.

Childs, Donald J. *Modernism and Eugenics: Woolf, Eliot, and the Culture of Degeneration*. Cambridge: Cambridge University Press, 2001.

Cohn, Elisha. '"One Single Ivory Cell": Oscar Wilde and the Brain.' *Journal of Victorian Culture* 17, no. 2 (2012): 183–205.

Cohn, Elisha. 'Oscar Wilde and the Brain Cell.' *Progress in Brain Research* 205 (2013): 19–39.

Danson, Lawrence. *Wilde's Intentions: The Artist in His Criticism*. Oxford: Oxford University Press, 1997.

Eagleton, Terry. *Literary Theory: An Introduction*. 2nd ed. Minneapolis: University of Minnesota Press, 1996.

Ellis, Mrs. Havelock. 'Eugenics and the Mystical Outlook.' In *Nineteenth-Century Writings on Homosexuality: A Sourcebook*, edited by Chris White, 113–114. London: Routledge, 1999.

Ellmann, Richard. *Oscar Wilde*. New York: Vintage, 1987.

Foucault, Michel. *The History of Sexuality: An Introduction.* 1st Vol. Translated by Robert Hurley. New York: Vintage Books, 1978.

Gagnier, Regenia. *Idylls of the Marketplace: Oscar Wilde and the Victorian Public.* Stanford: Stanford University Press, 1986.

Galton, Francis. *Essays in Eugenics.* Honolulu: University Press of the Pacific, 2004.

Gibson, Walker. 'Authors, Speakers, Readers, and Mock Readers.' In *Reader-Response Criticism: From Formalism to Post-Structuralism,* edited by Jane P. Tompkins, 1–6. Baltimore: The Johns Hopkins University Press, 1980.

Gillespie, Michael Patrick. *Oscar Wilde and the Poetics of Ambiguity.* Gainesville: University Press of Florida, 1996.

Gossman, Lionel. 'Literature and Education.' *New Literary History* 13, no. 2 (1982): 341–371.

Guy, Josephine M. 'Introduction.' In *Criticism: Historical Criticism, Intentions, The Soul of Man. The Complete Works of Oscar Wilde.* Vol. 4, edited by Josephine M. Guy, xix–lxxxvi. Oxford: Oxford University Press, 2007.

Hasian, Jr., Marouf A. *The Rhetoric of Eugenics in Anglo-American Thought.* Athens: The University of Georgia Press, 1996.

Hazlitt, W. Carew. 'Introduction.' In *Essays and Criticisms* by Thomas Griffiths Wainewright. Edited by W. Carew Hazlitt, ix–lxxxi. London: Reeves and Turner, 1880.

Keen, Suzanne. *Empathy and the Novel.* Oxford: Oxford University Press, 2007.

Mosse, George L. 'Introduction.' In *Degeneration* by Max Nordau. Edited by George L. Mosse, xiii– xxxvi. Lincoln: University of Nebraska Press, 1968.

Nordau, Max. *Degeneration.* Edited by George L. Mosse. Lincoln: University of Nebraska Press, 1968.

Nussbaum, Martha C. *Cultivating Humanity: A Classical Defense of Reform in Liberal Education.* Cambridge: Harvard University Press, 1997.

Richardson, Angelique. *Love and Eugenics in the Late Nineteenth Century: Rational Reproduction and the New Woman.* Oxford: Oxford University Press, 2003.

Smith II, Philip E. and Michael S. Helfand. *Oscar Wilde's Oxford Notebooks: A Portrait of Mind in the Making.* New York and Oxford: Oxford University Press, 1989.

Stiles, Anne. *Popular Fiction and Brain Science in the Late Nineteenth Century.* Cambridge: Cambridge University Press, 2012.

Wade, Nicholas. *A Troublesome Inheritance: Genes, Race and Human History.* New York: Penguin, 2014.

Walkowitz, Judith R. *City of Dreadful Delight: Narratives of Sexual Danger in Late-Victorian London.* Chicago: University of Chicago Press, 1992.

Wilde, Oscar. 'Commonplace Book.' In *Oscar Wilde's Oxford Notebooks: A Portrait of Mind in the Making*. Edited by Philip E. Smith II and Michael S. Helfand, 107–152. New York: Oxford University Press, 1989.

Wilde, Oscar. *De Profundis*. New York: The Modern Library, 1992.

Wilde, Oscar. *Intentions*. In *The Artist as Critic: Critical Writings of Oscar Wilde*. Edited by Richard Ellmann, 290–432. Chicago: University of Chicago Press, 1969.

Wilde, Oscar. *The Complete Letters of Oscar Wilde*. Edited by Merlin Holland and Rupert Hart-Davis. New York: Henry Holt, 2000.

Wilde, Oscar. *The Picture of Dorian Gray*. Edited by Norman Page. Peterborough, ON: Broadview Press, 1998.

Wilde, Oscar. 'The Soul of Man Under Socialism.' In *The Artist as Critic: Critical Writings of Oscar Wilde*. Edited by Richard Ellmann, 255–289. Chicago: University of Chicago Press, 1969.

BIBLIOGRAPHY

Ablow, Rachel. 'Introduction: The Feeling of Reading.' In *The Feeling of Reading: Affective Experience & Victorian Literature*, edited by Rachel Ablow, 1–10. Ann Arbor, MI: The University of Michigan Press, 2010.

Alberini, Cristina, ed. *Memory Reconsolidation*. London: Academic Press, 2013.

Altick, Richard D. *Punch: The Lively Youth of a British Institution, 1841–1851*. Athens: Ohio State University Press, 1997.

Anderson, Amanda, and Harry E. Shaw, eds. *A Companion to George Eliot*. Hoboken, NJ: Wiley, 2016.

Anderson, Benedict. *Imagined Communities: Reflections on the Origin and Spread of Nationalism*. London: Verso, 1991.

Andrews, Malcolm. *Charles Dickens and His Performing Selves*. Oxford: Oxford University Press, 2007.

Andrews, Malcolm. *Dickensian Laughter*. Oxford: Oxford University Press, 2013.

Anonymous. 'A Chat with Jenny Hill.' *The Era*. June 17, 1893.

Anonymous. 'Advertisement.' *The Athenaeum*. January 21, 1888.

Anonymous. 'Advertisements and Notices.' *The Era*. October 24, 1885.

Anonymous. 'Alexandra Theatre.' *Morning Post*. August 24, 1898.

Anonymous. 'Althoff's Comeback.' *Variety*. October 6, 1922.

Anonymous. 'Astley's Amphitheatre.' *Morning Post*. May 29, 1862.

Anonymous. 'Chips.' *The North-Eastern Daily Gazette*. January 22, 1894.

Anonymous. 'Chips.' *The North-Eastern Gazette*. January 22, 1894.

Anonymous. 'Comedy Theatre Billy.' *Manchester Guardian*. November 8, 1898.

Anonymous. 'County Cricket in Miniature. A Small Boy's Match at Lord's.' *The Times*. August 28, 1915.

Anonymous. 'Du Maurier's "Joke Pots."' *London Journal*. October 15, 1904.

© The Editor(s) (if applicable) and The Author(s) 2020
L. Lee (ed.), *Victorian Comedy and Laughter*,
https://doi.org/10.1057/978-1-137-57882-2

Anonymous. 'Eager for the Fray.' *Daily Mirror*. January 23, 1907.

Anonymous. 'Gossip of the Week.' *Nottinghamshire Guardian*. July 4, 1896.

Anonymous. 'Grains of Gall.' *Hampshire Telegraph*. July 21, 1888.

Anonymous. 'Half-a-Crown Every Week for a Joke.' *Belfast Telegraph*. November 24, 1887.

Anonymous. 'Half-a-Crown Every Week for a Joke.' *Dundee Weekly News*. February 19, 1887.

Anonymous. 'His Child.' *Manchester Guardian*. September 16, 1906.

Anonymous. 'Hoods Whims. Second Series.' *London Magazine*. December 1827.

Anonymous. 'Imitation The Sincerest Flattery.' *Dundee Courier*. November 19, 1887.

Anonymous. 'Imported Humour.' *Leeds Mercury*. April 29, 1882.

Anonymous. 'In a Joke Factory.' *Hampshire Telegraph*. April 22, 1899.

Anonymous. 'In the Green Room.' *Penny Illustrated Paper*. August 24, 1912.

Anonymous. 'Jenny Hill in South Africa.' *The Era*. May 5, 1894.

Anonymous. 'Jokes by Our Readers.' *Illustrated Chips*. March 23, 1895.

Anonymous. 'King's Bench Division. The Action by Miss Vesta Victoria. Terry v Moss.' *The Times*. December 12, 1914.

Anonymous. 'Life in Cardiff.' *Western Mail*. January 26, 1880.

Anonymous. 'Lincoln Spring Meeting, Tuesday.' *Manchester Guardian*. March 23, 1892.

Anonymous. 'Little Tich on the "Odol Smile."' *The Stage*. February 6, 1908.

Anonymous. 'Little Tich.' *Daily Mirror*. February 11, 1928.

Anonymous. 'Little Tich.' *The Guardian*. May 19, 1969.

Anonymous. '"Little Tich" at Cardiff.' *Western Mail*. April 11, 1900.

Anonymous. 'Little Tich's Retort.' *Daily Mail*. May 4, 1905.

Anonymous. 'London Notes.' *Variety*. September 14, 1907.

Anonymous. 'Men Who Write Jokes.' *Newcastle Weekly Courant*. June 16, 1894.

Anonymous. 'Miscellany.' *Manchester Guardian*. January 24, 1910.

Anonymous. '*Mord-Em'ly* by W. Pett Ridge.' *The Academy*. November 5, 1898.

Anonymous. 'Motley.' *Bristol Mercury*. November 28, 1896.

Anonymous. 'Mr Gladstone and the Jokes.' *Dundee Weekly News*. September 21, 1889.

Anonymous. 'Music Hall Gossip.' *The Era*. April 4, 1891.

Anonymous. 'Music Hall Morality.' *The Spectator*. October 12, 1889.

Anonymous. 'Music Hall Strike Amusing Incidents.' *Manchester Guardian*. January 23, 1907.

Anonymous. '"Musical Farce" at the Garrick Theatre.' *Manchester Guardian*. September 16, 1896.

Anonymous. 'New Publications.' *Hampshire Advertiser*. May 8, 1858.

Anonymous. 'Notes—Mainly Personal.' *Dundee Evening Telegraph*. January 14, 1898.

Anonymous. 'Notes on Broadcasting, Making Comic Talent Go a Long Way.' *The Times*. January 2, 1965.

Anonymous. 'Original Correspondence.' *The Era*. February 11, 1866.

Anonymous. 'Our Captious Critic.' *Illustrated Sporting and Dramatic News*. January 6, 1877.

Anonymous. 'Our Joke Competition.' *Dundee Weekly News*. October 5, 1899.

Anonymous. 'Our London Correspondence.' *Manchester Guardian*. February 11, 1928.

Anonymous. 'Police.' *The Times*. January 27, 1899.

Anonymous. 'Prince of Wales Theatre.' *Birmingham Daily Post*. May 26, 1891.

Anonymous. 'Prince's Theatre Billy.' *Manchester Guardian*. June 7, 1898.

Anonymous. 'Prince's Theatre, Lord Tom Noddy.' *Manchester Guardian*. May 26, 1896.

Anonymous. 'Provincial Theatricals.' *The Era*. October 31, 1885.

Anonymous. 'Provincial Theatricals.' *The Era*. September 18, 1886.

Anonymous. 'Review of *Intentions*, by Oscar Wilde.' *Literary Opinion* (July 1891): 10.

Anonymous. 'Royalty in the Music Hall, The "Command" Performance at the Palace.' *Manchester Guardian*. July 2, 1912.

Anonymous. 'Satires and Caricatures of the Eighteenth Century.' *Blackwood's Edinburgh Magazine*. November 1848.

Anonymous. 'Selected Anecdotes, &c.' *Lancaster Gazette*. January 25, 1845.

Anonymous. 'Sinclair and Croueste's Circus.' *The Era*. October 16, 1870.

Anonymous. 'Stories of the Sanctum.' *Hartlepool Northern Daily Mail*. June 23, 1894.

Anonymous. 'Tattersall's Sale. Good Prices for Polo Ponies.' *The Times*. July 21, 1914.

Anonymous. 'The Autobiography of a Good Joke.' *Bentley's Miscellany*. July 1837.

Anonymous. 'The Business of Joke-Making.' *Derry Journal*. March 6, 1895.

Anonymous. 'The Hippodrome. "Little Tich."' *Manchester Guardian*. February 2, 1926.

Anonymous. 'The Hippodrome.' *Manchester Guardian*. July 14, 1914.

Anonymous. 'The Hippodrome.' *Manchester Guardian*. September 21, 1926.

Anonymous. 'The Joke Copyright Protective Company.' *Lancaster Gazette*. January 25, 1845.

Anonymous. 'The London Music Halls.' *The Era*. January 7, 1872.

Anonymous. 'The London Music Halls.' *The Era*. January 10, 1885.

Anonymous. 'The London Music Halls.' *The Era*. January 28, 1877.

Anonymous. 'The London Music Halls.' *The Era*. March 6, 1886.

Anonymous. 'The London Music Halls.' *The Era*. April 30, 1887.

Anonymous. 'The London Music Halls.' *The Era*. May 10, 1884.

Anonymous. 'The London Music Halls.' *The Era*. May 15, 1886.

Anonymous. 'The London Music Halls.' *The Era*. July 25, 1885.

Anonymous. 'The Modern Circus.' *The Era*. August 4, 1883.

Anonymous. 'The Novel of Misery.' *Quarterly Review* 196, no. 392 (October 1902): 391–414.

Anonymous. 'The Palace of Varieties.' *Manchester Guardian*. September 17, 1901.

Anonymous. 'The Palace Theatre.' *Manchester Guardian*. March 19, 1901.

Anonymous. 'The Wit and Wisdom of George Eliot.' *The Spectator*. January 13, 1872.

Anonymous. 'Theatrical Notes.' *Pall Mall Gazette*. September 23, 1896.

Anonymous. 'Unassorted Fun.' *Hampshire Telegraph*. April 22, 1899.

Anonymous. 'Unsigned Letter.' *The Era*. August 4, 1883.

Anonymous. 'Unsigned Review.' *Saturday Review*. February 26, 1859.

Anonymous. 'Variety Theatres.' *Manchester Guardian*. February 8, 1911.

Anonymous. 'Variety Theatres.' *Manchester Guardian*. May 11, 1920.

Anonymous. 'Variety Theatres.' *Manchester Guardian*. July 4, 1906.

Anonymous. 'Variety Theatres.' *Manchester Guardian*. August 27, 1918.

Anonymous. 'Variety Theatres.' *Manchester Guardian*. December 16, 1908.

Anonymous. 'What Artistes Earn.' *Daily Mail*. January 24, 1907.

Anonymous. 'Wit and Humour.' *British Quarterly Review*. July, 1872.

Anonymous. 'Wit and Humour.' *Cardiff Times*. January 23, 1897.

Anonymous. 'Word-Counting in Telegrams.' *The Times*. August 27, 1897.

Anonymous. 'Worthy of Attention.' *Punch Almanac*. 1845.

Anonymous. *The Book of Humour, Wit, and Wisdom: A Manual of Table-Talk*. London: Routledge, 1867.

Armstrong, Thomas. *The Power of Neurodiversity: Unleashing the Advantages of Your Differently Wired Brain*. Cambridge, MA: Da Capo Press, 2010.

Aschheim, Steven E. 'Max Nordau, Friedrich Nietzsche and *Degeneration*.' *Journal of Contemporary History* 28, no. 4 (1993): 643–657.

Astor, A. C. 'Just Jottings.' *The Stage*. July 14, 1927.

Atkinson, Juliette. 'Critical Responses: to 1900.' In *George Eliot in Context*, edited by Margaret Harris, 65–73. Cambridge: Cambridge University Press, 2013.

Auden, W. H. *The English Auden: Poems, Essays, and Dramatic Writings 1927–1939*. Edited by Edward Mendelson. London: Faber and Faber, 1977.

Austin, John Langshaw. *How to Do Things with Words*. Cambridge, MA: Harvard University Press, 1975.

Bailey, Peter. 'Conspiracies of Meaning: Music-Hall and the Knowingness of Popular Culture.' *Past and Present* 144 (1994): 138–170.

Bailey, Peter, ed. *Music Hall: The Business of Pleasure*. Milton Keynes: Open University Press, 1986.

Bailey, Peter. *Popular Culture and Performance in the Victorian City*. Cambridge: Cambridge University Press, 1998.

Bain, Alexander. *The Emotions and the Will*. London: John W. Parker and Son, 1859.

Baker, Richard Anthony. *British Music Hall: An Illustrated History*. Barnsley: Pen and Sword History, 2014.

Bakhtin, Mikhail. 'From Notes Made in 1970–71.' In *Speech Genres and Other Late Essays*. Translated by Vern W. McGee, edited by Caryl Emerson and Michael Holquist, 132–158. Austin, TX: University of Texas Press, 1986.

Bakhtin, Mikhail. *Problems of Dostoevsky's Poetics*. Translated by Caryl Emerson. Minneapolis, MN: University of Minnesota Press, 1984.

Bakhtin, Mikhail. *Rabelais and His World*. Translated by Helene Iswolsky. Cambridge, MA: MIT Press, 1968.

Barber, C. L. *Shakespeare's Festive Comedy: A Study of Dramatic form and Its Relation to Social Custom*. Princeton, NJ: Princeton University Press, 1959.

Barthes, Roland. *Barthes: Selected Writings*. Edited by Susan Sontag. Glasgow: Fontana Press, 1983.

Barthes, Roland. *The Pleasure of the Text*. Translated by Richard Miller. New York: Hill and Wang, 1975.

Barthes, Roland. 'The Reality Effect.' In *The Rustle of Language*, translated by Richard Howard and edited by François Wahl, 141–148. Berkeley: University of California Press, 1989.

Barton, Anna. 'Delirious Bulldogs and Nasty Crockery: Tennyson as Nonsense Poet.' *Victorian Poetry* 41, no. 1 (2009): 313–330.

Bartram, C. C. 'London Notes.' *Variety*. October 6, 1906.

Baudelaire, Charles. 'Of the Essence of Laughter, and Generally of the Comic in the Plastic Arts.' In *Selected Writings on Art and Literature*. Translated by P. E. Charvet. London: Penguin, 2006.

Baudelaire, Charles. *Oeuvres Complètes*. Paris: Gallimard, 1975.

Beals, M. H. 'Musings on a Multimodal Analysis of Scissors-and-Paste Journalism (Parts 1–4).' https://www.mhbeals.com (accessed May 14, 2018).

Beer, Gillian. *Darwin's Plots: Evolutionary Narrative in Darwin, George Eliot and Nineteenth-Century Fiction*. Cambridge: Cambridge University Press, 1983.

Beer, Gillian. 'The Reader as Author.' *Authorship* 3, no. 1 (April 2014): 1–9.

Beerbohm, Max. *More Theatres 1898–1903*. New York: Taplinger Publishing Company, 1969.

Benjamin, Walter. *Selected Writings. Vol. 4, 1938–1940*, edited by Howard Eiland and Michael W. Jennings. Cambridge, MA: Belknap Press of Harvard University Press, 2003.

Bergson, Henri. 'Laughter.' In *Comedy*, edited by Wylie Sypher. Baltimore: Johns Hopkins University Press, 1956.

Bergson, Henri. *Laughter: An Essay on the Meaning of the Comic*. Translated by C. Brereton and F. Rothwell. Rockville Maryland: Arc Manor, 2008.

Berlant, Lauren. 'Humorlessness (Three Monologues and a Hairpiece).' *Critical Inquiry* 43 (Winter 2017): 305–340.

Bevis, Matthew. 'Edward Lear's Lines of Flight.' *Journal of the British Academy* 1 (2013): 31–69.

Bevis, Matthew, and James Williams, eds. *Edward Lear and the Play of Poetry*. Oxford: Oxford University Press, 2016.

Billig, Michael. *Laughter and Ridicule: Towards a Social Critique of Humour*. New York: Sage, 2005.

Bogdan, Robert. *Freak Show: Presenting Human Oddities for Amusement and Profit*. Chicago and London: University of Chicago Press, 1988.

Booth, Michael R. *English Plays of the Nineteenth Century. V. Pantomimes, Extravaganzas and Burlesques*. Oxford: Oxford University Press, 1976.

Bowen, John. *Other Dickens: Pickwick to Chuzzlewit*. Oxford: Oxford University Press, 1999.

Bown, Alfie. 'Eventual Laughter: Dickens and Comedy.' PhD thesis, University of Manchester, 2014.

Bown, Alfie. *In the Event of Laughter: Psychoanalysis, Literature and Comedy*. New York: Bloomsbury, 2018.

Bratton, Jacky. 'Pantomime and the Experienced Young Fellow.' In *Victorian Pantomime: A Collection of Critical Essays*, edited by Jim Davis. London: Palgrave Macmillan, 2010.

Bratton, Jacky. *New Readings in Theatre History*. Cambridge: Cambridge University Press, 2003.

Bratton, Jacky, and Ann Featherstone. *The Victorian Clown*. Cambridge: Cambridge University Press, 2006.

Bratton, Jacqueline S. 'Jenny Hill: Sex and Sexism in the Victorian Music Hall.' In *Music Hall: Performance and Style*, edited by J. S. Bratton. Milton Keynes: Open University Press, 1986.

Bratton, Jacqueline S. *Music Hall: Performance and Style*. Milton Keynes: Open University Press, 1986.

Bristow, Joseph, and Rebecca N. Mitchell. *Oscar Wilde's Chatterton: Literary History, Romanticism, and the Art of Forgery*. New Haven and London: Yale University Press, 2015.

British Pathé. 'Flashback Extracts: 1910–1919.' http://www.britishpathe.com/video/flashbacks-extracts/query/little+tich (accessed August 27, 2014).

Brough, Lawrence, and John R. Kemble, eds. *Jokelets, Being the Merry Book of the Moore & Burgess Minstrels*. London: Saxon & Co., 1901.

Brown, Julia Prewitt. *Cosmopolitan Criticism: Oscar Wilde's Philosophy of Art*. Charlottesville and London: University of Virginia Press, 1997.

Bruns, John. *Loopholes: Reading Comically*. New Brunswick and London: Transaction Publishers, 2009.

Buchanan, Robert. *The Coming Terror and Other Essays and Letters*. London: William Heinemann, 1891.

Buchanan, Robert, and Walter Besant. *The Voice of 'The Hooligan': A Discussion of Kiplingism*. New York: Tucker, 1900.

Buckmaster, Jonathan. 'Ten Thousand Million Delights.' In *Dickens and the Imagined Child*, edited by Peter Merchant and Catherine Waters. Farnham: Ashgate, 2015.

Burnand, F. C. 'Punch Notes—II.' *The Pall Mall Magazine*. July 1899.

Burton, Alan, and Laraine Porter. *Crossing the Pond: Anglo-American Film Relations Before 1930*. Towbridge: Flicks Books, 2002.

Cammaerts, Émile. *The Poetry of Nonsense*. London: Routledge, 1925.

Carey, John. *Here Comes Dickens: The Imagination of a Novelist*. Ann Arbor, MI: University of Michigan Press, 1974.

Carey, John. *The Intellectuals and the Masses: Pride and Prejudice Among the Literary Intelligentsia*. London: Faber and Faber, 1992.

Carey, John. *The Violent Effigy—A Study of Dickens' Imagination*. London: Faber and Faber, 1973.

Carlyle, Thomas. 'Jean Paul Friedrich Richter.' In Carlyle. *Critical and Miscellaneous Essays*. Boston: James Munroe and Co., 1838.

Carlyle, Thomas. 'John Paul Friedrich Richter.' In *Critical and Miscellaneous Essays Collected and Republished*, 5–27. New York: Alden, 1885.

Carroll, David. *George Eliot: The Critical Heritage*. London: Routledge, 2000.

Carroll, Lewis. *Through The Looking-Glass*. London: Macmillan & Company, 1872.

Carroll, Nöel. *Comedy/Cinema/Theory*. California: University of California Press, 1991.

Chesterton, G. K. 'A Defence of Nonsense.' In *The Defendant*, 42–50. London: R. Brimley Johnson, 1901.

Chesterton, G. K. *Orthodoxy*. New York: Lane, 1909.

Childs, Donald J. *Modernism and Eugenics: Woolf, Eliot, and the Culture of Degeneration*. Cambridge: Cambridge University Press, 2001.

Childs, Michael J. *Labour's Apprentices: Working-Class Lads in Late Victorian and Edwardian England*. London: McGill-Queen's University Press, 1992.

Chinitz, David. *T.S. Eliot and the Cultural Divide*. Chicago: University of Chicago Press, 2003.

Chorley, H. F. 'Review of *National Tales*.' *London and Westminster Review*. April 1838.

Cloy, John D. *Muscular Mirth: Barry Pain and the New Humor*. Victoria: University of Victoria Press, 2003.

Cohn, Elisha. '"One Single Ivory Cell": Oscar Wilde and the Brain.' *Journal of Victorian Culture* 17, no. 2 (2012): 183–205.

Cohn, Elisha. 'Oscar Wilde and the Brain Cell.' *Progress in Brain Research* 205 (2013): 19–39.

Collins, Charles Allston. 'To Be Taken at the Dinner Table.' *Doctor Marigold's Prescriptions; Being the Christmas Number of All the Year Round*. December 1865.

Crangle, Sara. *Prosaic Desires: Modernist Knowledge, Boredom, Laughter, and Anticipation*. Edinburgh: Edinburgh University Press, 2010.

Craton, Lillian. *The Victorian Freak Show: The Significance of Disability and Physical Differences in 19th-Century Fiction*. Amherst, NY: Cambria Press, 2009.

Cronin, Richard. 'Edward Lear and Tennyson's Nonsense.' In *Tennyson Among the Poets: Bicentenary Essays*, edited by Robert Douglas-Fairhurst and Seamus Perry. Oxford: Oxford University Press, 2009.

Dallas, E. S. 'Adam Bede.' *The Times*, April 12, 1859.

Dames, Nicholas. 'On Not Close Reading: The Prolonged Excerpt as Victorian Critical Protocol.' In *The Feeling of Reading: Affective Experience & Victorian Literature*, edited by Rachel Ablow, 11–26. Ann Arbor, MI: University of Michigan Press, 2010.

Dames, Nicholas. *The Physiology of the Novel: Reading, Neural Science, and the Form of Victorian Fiction*. Oxford: Oxford University Press, 2007.

Danson, Lawrence. *Wilde's Intentions: The Artist in His Criticism*. Oxford: Oxford University Press, 1997.

Darwin, Charles, and Paul H. Barrett. *Charles Darwin's Notebooks 1836–1844*. Cambridge: Cambridge University Press, 1987.

Davidson, John. *In a Music Hall, and Other Poems*. London: Ward & Downey, 1891.

Davis, Jim. *Victorian Pantomime: A Collection of Critical Essays*. London: Palgrave Macmillan, 2010.

Davies, Luke. 'The Way of the World: Franco Moretti, The Bourgeois: Between History and Literature.' *Review 31*. http://review31.co.uk/article/view/158/the-way-of-the-world (accessed January 20, 2020).

Davis, Tracy. *Actresses as Working Women: Their Social Identity in Victorian Culture*. London: Routledge, 1991.

de Certeau, Michel. *The Practice of Everyday Life*. Berkeley: University of California Press, 1984.

'delight, n.' OED Online. June 2019. Oxford University Press. https://www.oed.com/view/Entry/49382rskey=20qfXM&result= (accessed July 16, 2019).

Dibdin, Thomas. *Harlequin and Mother Goose, or, The Golden Egg!* Reprinted in Andrew McConnell Stott. *The Pantomime Life of Joseph Grimaldi*. Edinburgh: Canongate, 2009.

Dickens, Charles. *Barnaby Rudge*. Edited by Kathleen Tillotson. Oxford: Oxford University Press, 1982.

Dickens, Charles. *Dombey and Son.* Edited by Alan Horsman. Oxford: Clarendon Press, 1974.

Dickens, Charles. 'Dullborough Town.' In *The Uncommercial Traveller,* edited by Daniel Tyler. Oxford: Oxford University Press, 2015.

Dickens, Charles. 'Full Report of the First Meeting of the Mudfog Association for the Advancement of Everything.' In *Dickens' Journalism: 'Sketches by Boz' and Other Early Papers 1833–1839,* edited by Michael Slater. London: Dent, 1994.

Dickens, Charles. *Hard Times.* London and New York: Norton, 2001.

Dickens, Charles. 'Letter to Mary Tayler.' November 6, 1849. In *The Letters of Charles Dickens: 1847–1849,* edited by Graham Storey and K. J. Fielding. Oxford: Clarendon Press, 1980.

Dickens, Charles. *Martin Chuzzlewit.* Edited by Margaret Cardwell. Oxford: Clarendon Press, 1982.

Dickens, Charles. *Nicholas Nickleby.* Edited by Arthur Waugh, Hugh Walpole, Walter Dexter, and Thomas Hatton. Bloomsbury: Nonesuch Press, 1938.

Dickens, Charles. *Oliver Twist.* Edited by Fred Kaplan. London and New York: Norton, 1993.

Dickens, Charles. *Oliver Twist.* Edited by Philip Horne. London: Penguin Books, 2003.

Dickens, Charles. *Our Mutual Friend.* Edited by E. Salter Davies. Oxford: Oxford University Press, 1981.

Dickens, Charles, ed. *The Memoirs of Joseph Grimaldi.* 2 volumes. London: Richard Bentley, 1838.

Dickens, Charles. *The Old Curiosity Shop.* Edited by Elizabeth M. Brannan. Oxford: Clarendon Press, 1997.

Dickens, Charles. *The Pickwick Papers.* Edited by James Kinsley. Oxford: Clarendon Press, 1986.

Dickens, Charles. *The Pickwick Papers.* Hertfordshire: Wordsworth Editions, 1993.

Dickens, Charles, and George Augustus Sala. 'First Fruits.' *Household Words.* May 15, 1854.

Dickens, Charles, and William Henry Wills. 'A Curious Dance Round A Curious Tree.' *Household Words.* January 17, 1852.

Dickens, Mamie. *My Father as I Recall Him.* Westminster: Roxburghe Press, 1897.

Dickie, Simon. *Cruelty and Laughter: Forgotten Comic Literature and the Unsentimental Eighteenth Century.* Chicago: University of Chicago Press, 2011.

Double, Oliver. *Britain Had Talent: A History of Variety Theatre.* Basingstoke: Palgrave Macmillan, 2012.

Double, Oliver. *Getting the Joke: The Inner Workings of Stand-Up Comedy.* London: Bloomsbury, 2014.

Eagleton, Terry. *Literary Theory: An Introduction*. 2nd ed. Minneapolis: University of Minnesota Press, 1996.

Eliot, George. *Adam Bede*. 1859. Hertfordshire: Wordsworth Editions, 1997.

Eliot, George. *Daniel Deronda*. 1876. Hertfordshire: Wordsworth Editions, 1996.

Eliot, George. 'German Wit: Heinrich Heine.' *Westminster Review* 65 (January 1856): 1–33.

Eliot, George. *Middlemarch*. 1871–2. Hertfordshire: Wordsworth Editions, 1994.

Eliot, George. 'Notes on Form in Art.' In *George Eliot: Selected Essays, Poems and Other Writings*, edited by A. S. Byatt, 231–239. London: Penguin, 2005.

Eliot, George. 'Rachel Gray.' *Leader* 7. January 5, 1856, 19.

Eliot, George. *Scenes of Clerical Life*. 1857. Hertfordshire: Wordsworth Editions, 2007.

Eliot, George. *The George Eliot Letters*. 9 vols. Edited by Gordon S. Haight. New Haven and London: Yale University Press, 1954–1978.

Eliot, George. *The Mill on the Floss*. 1860. Hertfordshire: Wordsworth Editions, 1995.

Eliot, George. 'The Natural History of German Life.' *Westminster Review* 66 (July 1856): 51–79.

Eliot, T. S. 'From Poe to Valéry.' In *To Criticize the Critic and Other Essays*, 27–42. London: Faber and Faber, 1965.

Eliot, T. S. 'London Letter.' *The Dial* 73, no. 6 (December 1922): 659–663.

Eliot, T. S. 'Preface.' In *John Davidson: A Selection of His Poems*, edited by Maurice Lindsay. London: Hutchinson & Co., 1961.

Eliot, T. S. 'The Music of Poetry.' In *One Poetry and Poets*. London: Faber and Faber, 1957.

Eliot, T. S. *The Poems of T.S. Eliot: Volume I, Collected and Uncollected Poems*. Edited by Christopher Ricks and Jim McCue. London: Faber and Faber, 2015.

Elliott, Bridget. 'Much Ado About Money—Reading British Music Hall in the Nineties.' In *Literature and Money*, edited by Anthony Purdy. Amsterdam: Rodopi, 1993.

Ellis, Havelock. 'Eugenics and the Mystical Outlook.' In *Nineteenth-Century Writings on Homosexuality: A Sourcebook*, edited by Chris White, 113–114. London: Routledge, 1999.

Ellmann, Richard. *Oscar Wilde*. New York: Vintage, 1987.

Emanuel, Walter. 'A Note on British Wit and Humour.' *Pall Mall Magazine*. July 1901.

Emerson, Ralph Waldo. *English Traits*. Boston: Houghton, Mifflin, and Co., 1886.

Empson, William. 'Alice in Wonderland: The Child as Swain.' In *Some Versions of Pastoral*, 253–298. London: Chatto and Windus, 1935.

Ermarth, Elizabeth Deeds. 'Negotiating Middlemarch.' In *Middlemarch in the 21st Century*, edited by Karen Chase, 107–131. Oxford: Oxford University Press, 2006.

Ernest, Clown. 'Circus Clowning.' *Edinburgh Evening News*. January 2, 1882.

Faulk, Barry J. *Music Hall and Modernity: The Late-Victorian Discovery of Popular Culture*. Athens: Ohio University Press, 2004.

Feely, Catherine. '"What Say You To Free Trade in Literature?" The Thief and the Politics of Piracy in the 1830s.' *Journal of Victorian Culture* 19, no. 4 (2014): 497–506.

Flanders, Judith. *The Victorian City: Everyday Life in Dickens' London*. London: Atlantic Books, 2012.

Flint, Kate. 'The Materiality of Middlemarch.' In *Middlemarch in the Twenty-First Century*, edited by Karen Chase, 65–86. Oxford: Oxford University Press, 2006.

Forster, John. *The Life of Charles Dickens*. London: Cecil Palmer, 1928.

Foster, Stephen. 'Old Dog Tray.' http://www.love-poems.me.uk/foster_old_dog_tray.htm (accessed April 29, 2016).

Foucault, Michel. *The History of Sexuality: An Introduction*. 1st vol. Translated by Robert Hurley. New York: Vintage Books, 1978.

Foucault, Michel. *The History of Sexuality: An Introduction*. 1st vol. Translated by Robert Hurley. New York: Vintage Books, 1990.

Fowler, Rowena, ed. *Edward Lear: The Cretan Journal*. Euboea: Denise Harvey, 1984.

Freud, Sigmund. *The Joke and Its Relation to the Unconscious*. Translated by Joyce Crick. London: Penguin, 2003.

Freud, Sigmund. *The Standard Edition of the Complete Psychological Works of Sigmund Freud, Volume V: The Interpretation of Dreams (Second Part) and On Dreams*. Edited and translated by James Strachey. London: Vintage, 2001.

Gagnier, Regenia. *Idylls of the Marketplace: Oscar Wilde and the Victorian Public*. Stanford: Stanford University Press, 1986.

Gagnier, Regenia. *Subjectivities: A History of Self-Representation in Britain, 1832–1920*. Oxford: Oxford University Press, 1991.

Galton, Francis. *Essays in Eugenics*. Honolulu: University Press of the Pacific, 2004.

Gibson, Walker. 'Authors, Speakers, Readers, and Mock Readers.' In *Reader-Response Criticism: From Formalism to Post-Structuralism*, edited by Jane P. Tompkins, 1–6. Baltimore: Johns Hopkins University Press, 1980.

Gillespie, Michael Patrick. *Oscar Wilde and the Poetics of Ambiguity*. Gainesville: University Press of Florida, 1996.

Gillooly, Eileen. *Smile of Discontent: Humor, Gender, and Nineteenth-Century British Fiction*. Chicago: University of Chicago Press, 1999.

Gissing, George. 'The Muse of the Halls.' *The Gissing Journal* 42, no. 3 (2006): 1–14.

Gissing, George. *The Town Traveller*. London: Methuen & Co., 1898.

Gissing, George. *Thyrza in Three Volumes*. London: Smith, Elder & Co., 1887.

Gissing, George. *Workers in the Dawn*. Brighton: Victorian Secrets, 2010.

Glenn, Susan. *Female Spectacle: The Theatrical Roots of Modern Feminism*. Cambridge, MA: Harvard University Press, 1998.

Glover, James M. 'The Music Box.' *The Stage*. February 15, 1928.

Gold, Tanya. 'Have You Heard the One About Rape? It's Funny Now.' *Guardian*. August 17, 2012.

Gossman, Lionel. 'Literature and Education.' *New Literary History* 13, no. 2 (1982): 341–371.

Gray, Donald J. 'A List of Comic Periodicals Published in Great Britain, 1800–1900.' *Victorian Periodicals Newsletter*, no. 15 (1972): 2–39.

Green, Benny. *The Last Empires: A Music Hall Companion*. London: Pavilion, Michael Joseph, 1986.

Greiner, Rae. *Sympathetic Realism in Nineteenth-Century British Fiction*. Baltimore: Johns Hopkins University Press, 2012.

Griffiths, Devin. *The Age of Analogy*. Baltimore: Johns Hopkins University Press, 2016.

Guy, Josephine M. 'Introduction.' In *Criticism: Historical Criticism, Intentions, The Soul of Man. The Complete Works of Oscar Wilde*. Vol. 4, edited by Josephine M. Guy, xix–lxxxvi. Oxford: Oxford University Press, 2007.

Haddon, Archibald. '"Little Tich." Memories and Anecdotes. The Evolution of the Boots.' *The Observer*. February 12, 1928.

Halliday, Andrew. *Comical Fellows*. London: J. H. Thomson, 1863.

Harrison, Debbie. 'The Triumph of Schopenhauer's Pessimism Over Comte's Positivism in George Gissing's Early Writing.' *Literature Compass* 9, no. 11 (2012): 826–836.

Hasian, Jr., Marouf A. *The Rhetoric of Eugenics in Anglo-American Thought*. Athens: The University of Georgia Press, 1996.

Haughton, Hugh, ed. *The Chatto Book of Nonsense Poetry*. London: Chatto and Windus, 1988.

Hazlitt, William. 'Introduction.' In *Essays and Criticisms* by Thomas Griffiths Wainewright, edited by W. Carew Hazlitt, ix–lxxxi. London: Reeves and Turner, 1880.

Hazlitt, William. 'On Wit and Humour.' In *Lectures on the English Comic Writers*, 1–31. New York: Russell & Russell, 1969.

Henkle, Roger. 'Morrison, Gissing, and the Stark Reality.' *NOVEL: A Forum on Fiction* 25, no. 3 (1992): 302–320.

Hennefeld, Maggie. *Specters of Slapstick and Silent Film Comediennes*. New York: Columbia University Press, 2018.

Hillis-Miller, J. 'Optic and Semiotic in *Middlemarch.*' In *The Worlds of Victorian Fiction*, edited by Jerome Hamilton Buckley, 125–148. Cambridge, MA: Harvard University Press, 1975.

Hobbes, Thomas. *Leviathan.* 1651. Peterborough, Canada: Broadview Press, 2002.

Holledge, J. *Innocent Flowers: Women in Edwardian Theatre.* London: Virago Press, 1981.

Hollington, Michael. *Dickens and the Grotesque.* London: Croon Helm, 1984.

Hood, Tom, ed. *The Book of Modern English Anecdotes, Humour, Wit and Wisdom.* London: Routledge, 1872.

House, M., G. Storey, et al., eds. *The Letters of Charles Dickens.* Oxford: Oxford University Press, 2015.

Hughes, Kathryn. *George Eliot: The Last Victorian.* Lanham, MD: Rowman and Littlefield, 2001.

Hutton, R. H. 'The Humour of Middlemarch.' *The Spectator.* December 14, 1872.

Huxley, Aldous. 'Edward Lear.' In *On the Margin*, 167–172. London: Chatto and Windus, 1923.

Hyman, Susan, ed. *Edward Lear in the Levant: Travels in Albania, Greece and Turkey in Europe, 1848–1849.* London: John Murray, 1988.

Irvine, Mark. 'Mrs (Polly) Lewes's Comic *Middlemarch.*' *George Eliot–George Henry Lewes Studies*, no. 34/35 (September 1998): 28–47.

James, Henry. Unsigned Review. *Galaxy* 15 (March 1873): 424–428.

James, Henry. *The Tragic Muse.* London: Macmillan and Co., 1921.

James, Simon J. *Unsettled Accounts: Money and Narrative in the Novels of George Gissing.* London: Anthem Press, 2003.

Jerome, Jerome K. 'Variety Patter.' *The Idler* 1, no. 2 (March 1892): 123–135.

Jerome, Jerome K. 'Variety Patter.' In *The Other Jerome K. Jerome*, edited by Martin Green. Stroud: The History Press, 2009.

Jerome, Jerome K. *The Angel and the Author—And Others.* London: Hurst and Blackett, 1908.

Jerome, Jerome K. *Three Men in a Boat.* Bristol: J. W. Arrowsmith, 1889.

John, Juliet. *Dickens's Villains: Melodrama, Character, Popular Culture.* Oxford: Oxford University Press, 2003.

Jones, Emrys. 'Pop and Dulness.' *Proceedings of the British Academy* 52 (1970): 240–241.

Jones, Gareth Stedman. 'Working-Class Culture and Working-Class Politics in London, 1870–1900: Notes on the Remaking of a Working-Class.' *Journal of Social History* 7, no. 4 (1974): 460–508.

Kaminsky, Alice. 'George Eliot, George Henry Lewes, and the Novel.' *PMLA* 70, no. 5 (December 1955): 997–1013.

Kant, Immanuel. *Critique of Judgement*. Translated by J. H. Bernard. London: Macmillan, 1914.

Keating, P. J. *The Working Classes in Victorian Fiction*. London: Routledge and Kegan Paul, 1979.

Keen, Suzanne. *Empathy and the Novel*. Oxford: Oxford University Press, 2007.

Keene, Charles. 'Thrift.' *Punch*. December 5, 1868.

Kendrew, Edward G. 'Paris Notes.' *Variety*. January 2, 1909.

Kendrew, Edward G. 'Paris Notes.' *Variety*. July 8, 1911.

Kernahan, Coulson. *Celebrities: Little Stories About Famous Folk*. London: Hutchinson, 1923.

Kerr, Douglas. 'Conrad and the Comic Turn.' *Victorian Literature and Culture* 43, no. 1 (2015): 149–168.

Kierkegaard, Søren. *Concluding Unscientific Postscript to the Philosophical Crumbs*, edited and translated by Alastair Hannay. Cambridge: Cambridge University Press, 2009.

Kincaid, James. *Dickens and the Rhetoric of Laughter*. Oxford: Oxford University Press, 1971.

Kincaid, James. 'Laughter and "Oliver Twist."' *PMLA* 83, no. 1 (March 1968): 63–70.

Kipling, Rudyard. 'My Great and Only.' In Kipling, *Abaft the Funnel*. New York: Doubleday, Page & Co., 1909.

Koestler, Arthur. 'Joking Apart.' In *Bricks to Babel: Selected Writings with Comments by the Author*, 321–343. London: Hutchinson, 1982.

Koestler, Arthur. *The Act of Creation*. London: Hutchinson and Company, 1964.

Kuipers, Giselinde. *Good Humor, Bad Taste: A Sociology of the Joke*. New York: Mouton de Gruyter, 2006.

Lane, Christopher. *Hatred & Civility: The Antisocial Life in Victorian England*. New York: Columbia University Press, 2004.

Lang, Andrew. 'At the Sign of the Ship: The New Humour.' *Longman's Magazine* 18, no. 108 (October 1891): 660–666.

Lang, Andrew. *Essays in Little*. London: Henry, 1891.

Lear, Edward. *A Book of Nonsense*. London: Frederick Warne and Co., 1846.

Lear, Edward. *More Nonsense, Pictures, Rhymes, Botany, Etc*. London: Robert John Bush, 1872.

Lear, Edward. *Nonsense Songs, Stories, Botany, and Alphabets*. London: Robert John Bush, 1871.

Leary, Patrick. *The Punch Brotherhood: Table Talk and Print Culture in Mid-Victorian London*. London: British Library, 2010.

Lecercle, Jean-Jacques. *Philosophy of Nonsense: The Intuitions of Victorian Nonsense Literature*. London: Routledge, 1994.

Levine, Caroline. 'Victorian Realism.' In *The Cambridge Companion to the Victorian Novel*, edited by Deirdre David, 84–106. Cambridge: Cambridge University Press, 2012.

Levine, George. 'Introduction: George Eliot and the Art of Realism.' In *The Cambridge Companion to George Eliot*, edited by George Levine, 1–19. Cambridge: Cambridge University Press, 2001.

Lewes, G. H. 'Dickens in Relation to Criticism.' *Fortnightly Review* 11, no. 62 (February 1872): 141–158.

Lippitt, John. 'Humor and Irony in the *Postscript.*' In *Kierkegaard's 'Concluding Unscientific Postscript': A Critical Guide*, edited by Rick Anthony Furtak, 149–169. Cambridge: Cambridge University Press, 2010.

Lodge, Sara. *Thomas Hood and Nineteenth-Century Poetry: Work, Play, and Politics.* Manchester: Manchester University Press, 2007.

London, Jack. *The People of the Abyss.* London: Pluto, 2001.

Lyons, Albert Neil. *Hookey: Being a Relation of Some Circumstances Surrounding the Early Life of Miss Josephine Walker.* London: T. Fisher Unwin, 1902.

Mars-Jones, Adam. 'Queerer and Queerer: "Edward Lear: The Complete Verse and Other Nonsense."' *The Guardian.* November 11, 2001. https://www.theguardian.com/books/2001/nov/11/classics.highereducation.

Marshall, Gail. *Actresses on the Victorian Stage: Feminine Performance and the Galatea Myth.* Cambridge: Cambridge University Press, 1998.

Martin, Robert Bernard. *The Triumph of Wit: A Study of Victorian Comic Theory.* Oxford: Clarendon Press, 1974.

Marx, Karl. *The Communist Manifesto.* New York: Simon & Schuster, 2013.

Massey, Gerald. 'American Humour.' *North British Review.* November 1860.

Masson, Thomas L. 'How I Wrote 50,000 Jokes.' In Masson. *Our American Humorists*, 432–448. New York: Moffat, Yard & Company, 1922.

Matthews, Brander. 'On the Antiquity of Jests.' *Longman's Magazine.* February 1885.

Matz, Aaron. *Satire in an Age of Realism.* Cambridge: Cambridge University Press, 2010.

Mayer, David. *Harlequin in His Element: The English Pantomime, 1806–1836.* Cambridge, MA: Harvard University Press, 1969.

Mayhew, Henry. *The Illustrated Mayhew's London.* London: Guild Publishing, 1986.

McGill, Meredith L. *American Literature and the Culture of Reprinting, 1834–1853.* Philadelphia: University of Pennsylvania Press, 2003.

Medhurst, Andy. *A National Joke: Popular Comedy and English Cultural Identities.* Abingdon: Routledge, 2007.

Meredith, George. 'On the Idea of Comedy, and of the Uses of the Comic Spirit.' *New Quarterly Magazine* 8 (January–July 1877): 1–40.

Miles, Henry Downes. *The Life of Joseph Grimaldi: With Anecdotes of His Contemporaries*. London: Charles Harris, 1838.

Moore, George. *Confessions of a Young Man*. London: Swan Sonnenschein, Lowry & Co., 1888.

Moretti, Franco. 'Serious Century.' In *The Novel: History, Geography, and Culture*, vol. 1, edited by Franco Moretti, 365–400. Princeton, NJ: Princeton University Press, 2006.

Moretti, Franco. *The Bourgeois: Between History and Literature*. London: Verso Books, 2013.

Morton, Richard. 'London Pavilion Memories.' *The Era*. April 1, 1914.

Mosse, George L. 'Introduction.' In *Degeneration* by Max Nordau, edited by George L. Mosse, xiii–xxxvi. Lincoln: University of Nebraska Press, 1968.

Motley, John, ed. *Joe Miller's Jests or, the Wits Vade-Mecum*. London: T. Read, 1739.

Mulholland, Clara. 'Molly's Fortunes.' *Hampshire Telegraph*. April 22, 1899.

Murphy, Ray, ed. *Edward Lear's Indian Journal*. Peterborough: Jarrolds, 1953.

Nash, Paul. *Outline: An Autobiography*. London: Columbus Books, 1988.

Ngai, Sianne. *Ugly Feelings*. Cambridge, MA: Harvard University Press, 2005.

Nicholson, Bob. 'You Kick the Bucket; We Do The Rest!: Jokes at the Culture of Reprinting in the Transatlantic Press.' *Journal of Victorian Culture* 17, no. 3 (2012): 273–286.

Nietzsche, Friedrich. *Ecce Homo: How to Become What You Are*. Translated and edited by Duncan Large. Oxford: Oxford University Press, 2009.

Nietzsche, Friedrich. *The Gay Science: With a Prelude in German Rhymes and an Appendix of Songs*. Translated by Josefine Nauckhoff and Adrian Del Caro. Cambridge: Cambridge University Press, 2001.

Nietzsche, Friedrich. *Twilight of the Idols*. Translated and edited by Duncan Large. Oxford: Oxford University Press, 2008.

Noakes, Vivien. *Edward Lear: The Life of a Wanderer*. Stroud: Alan Sutton, 2004.

Nordau, Max. *Degeneration*. Edited by George L. Mosse. Lincoln: University of Nebraska Press, 1968.

Nussbaum, Martha C. *Cultivating Humanity: A Classical Defense of Reform in Liberal Education*. Cambridge: Harvard University Press, 1997.

Oddie, William. 'Mr. Micawber and the Redefinition of Experience.' In *Charles Dickens*, edited by Harold Bloom. New York: Infobase Publishing, 2006.

Oliver, Double. *Britain Had Talent: A History of Variety Theatre*. Basingstoke: Palgrave, 2012.

Oliver, Michael, and Bob Sapey. *Social Work with Disabled People*. London: Macmillan, 1999.

Orwell, George. 'Nonsense Poetry.' In *The Collected Essays, Journalism and Letters of George Orwell*, Volume 4, 64–68. Harmondsworth: Penguin, 1970.

Oulton, Carolyn. '"Making Literature Ridiculous": Jerome K. Jerome and the New Humour.' *Dickens Studies Annual: Essays on Victorian Fiction* 48 (2016): 1–16.

P., F. 'Circus Procedure.' *Edinburgh Evening News.* December 21, 1881.

Pain, Barry. 'De Omnibus: By the Conductor.' *To-Day.* April 16, 1898.

Pain, Barry. *De Omnibus.* London: T. Fisher Unwin, 1901.

Pain, Barry. *Here and Hereafter.* London: Methuen, 1911.

Pain, Barry. *In a Canadian Canoe.* London: Henry & Co., 1891.

Pain, Barry. *Stories in the Dark.* London: Grant Richards, 1901.

Pain, Barry. 'The Hundred Gates.' *The Cornhill Magazine* 76 (1889): 405–416.

Pain, Barry. 'The Old Humour and the New.' *The Speaker* 4 (19 December 1891): 740–742.

Pain, Barry, and James Blyth. *The Shadow of the Unseen.* London: Chapman and Hall, 1907.

Partington, Alan. *The Linguistics of Laughter: A Corpus-Assisted Study of Laughter-Talk.* New York: Routledge, 2006.

Parvulescu, Anca. *Laughter: Notes on a Passion.* Cambridge, MA: MIT Press, 2010.

Pater, Walter. 'Charles Lamb.' In *Appreciations: With an Essay on Style,* 107–127. London: Macmillan and Co., 1889.

Paterson, Peter. *Glimpses of Real Life as Seen in the Theatrical World and in Bohemia: Being the Confessions of Peter Paterson, a Strolling Comedian.* Edinburgh: William P. Nimmo, 1864.

Paulus, Tom, and Rob King. 'Introduction.' In *Slapstick Comedy,* edited by Tom Paulus and Rob King, 1–18. Abingdon-on-Thames: Routledge, 2010.

Pawley, Alisun, and Daniel Müllensiefen. 'The Science of Singing Along: A Quantitative Field Study on Sing-along Behaviour in the North of England.' *Music Perception: An Interdisciplinary Journal* 30, no. 2 (2012): 129–146. https://doi.org/10.1525/mp.2012.30.2.129.

Peck, Robert McCracken. 'The Natural History of Edward Lear: Exhibition Catalog.' *Harvard Library Bulletin* 22, nos. 2–3 (Summer–Fall 2011): 125–159.

Peck, Robert McCracken. *The Natural History of Edward Lear.* Boston: David R. Godine, 2016.

Pfaller, Robert, ed. *Stop That Comedy! On the Subtle Hegemony of the Tragic in Our Culture.* Wien: Sonderzahl, 2005.

Pigeon, Stephen. 'Steal It, Change It, Print It: Transatlantic Scissors-and-Paste Journalism in the Ladies Treasury, 1857–1895.' *Journal of Victorian Culture* 22, no. 1 (2017): 24–39.

Pitman, Ruth. *Edward Lear's Tennyson.* Manchester: Carcanet Press, 1988.

Plotz, John. *Portable Property: Victorian Culture on the Move.* Princeton, NJ: Princeton University Press, 2008.

Plotz, John. 'Review of *The Bourgeois: Between History and Literature* by Franco Moretti.' *Victorian Studies* 56, no. 4 (Summer 2014): 734–736.

Poole, Adrian. *Gissing in Context*. London: Macmillan, 1975.

Priestley, J. B. *Particular Pleasures*. London: Heinemann, 1975.

Ray, Gordon N., ed. *Thackeray's Contributions to the Morning Chronicle*. Urbana: University of Illinois Press, 1955.

Ray, Martin. *Thomas Hardy Remembered*. London: Routledge, 2017.

Richards, Jeffrey. *The Golden Age of Pantomime: Slapstick, Spectacle and Subversion in Victorian England*. London: I.B. Tauris, 2014.

Richardson, Angelique. *Love and Eugenics in the Late Nineteenth Century: Rational Reproduction and the New Woman*. Oxford: Oxford University Press, 2003.

Ridge, William Pett. *Mord Em'ly*. London: C. Arthur Pearson Ltd., 1898.

Romanska, Magda, and Alan Ackerman, eds. *Reader in Comedy: An Anthology of Theory and Criticism*. London: Bloomsbury, 2016.

Russell, David. 'Varieties of Life: The Making of the Edwardian Music Hall.' In *The Edwardian Theatre: Essays on Performance and the Stage*, edited by Michael R. Booth and Joel H. Kaplan. Cambridge: Cambridge University Press, 1996.

Rutherford, Lois. '"Managers in a Small Way": The Professionalisation of Variety Artistes, 1860–1914.' In *Music Hall: The Business of Pleasure*, edited by Peter Bailey. Milton Keynes: Open University Press, 1986.

Sammons, Jeffrey L. *Heinrich Heine: A Modern Biography*. Princeton NJ: Princeton University Press, 1979.

Schopenhauer, Arthur. *The World as Will and Idea, in Three Volumes*. Translated by R. B. Haldane and John Kemp. London: Trübner & Co., 1883–1886.

Schopenhauer, Arthur. *The World as Will and Presentation, Vol. I*. Translated by Richard E. Aquila. New York: Pearson Longman, 2008.

Schopenhauer, Arthur. *The World as Will and Idea: Vol. II*. Translated by R. B. Haldane and J. Kemp. Boston: Ticknor and Company, 1887.

Schroeder, J. 'Speaking Volumes: Victorian Feminism and the Appeal of Public Discussion.' *Nineteenth-Century Contexts* 25, no. 2 (2003): 97–119.

Scotson-Clark, G. F. *The 'Halls.'* London: T. Fisher Unwin, 1900.

Scott, Derek B. *Sound of the Metropolis: The 19th Century Popular Music Revolution in London, New York, Paris and Vienna*. Oxford: Oxford University Press, 2003.

Seed, J. 'Limehouse Blues: Looking for "Chinatown" in the London Docks, 1900–40.' *History Workshop Journal* 62 (Autumn 2006): 58–85.

Seville, Catherine. *Literary Copyright Reform in Early Victorian England: The Framing of the 1842 Copyright Act*. Cambridge: Cambridge University Press, 1999.

Sewell, Elizabeth. *The Field of Nonsense.* London: Chatto and Windus, 1952.

Shaw, Harry E. *Narrating Reality: Austen, Scott, Eliot.* Ithaca, NY: Cornell University Press, 1999.

Simpson, Richard. 'Richard Simpson on George Eliot.' In *George Eliot: The Critical Heritage*, edited by David Carroll, 221–250. Abingdon-on-Thames: Routledge, 2013.

Sloan, John. *John Davidson, First of the Moderns: A Literary Biography.* Oxford: Clarendon Press, 1995.

Smith, David A., Ryan Cordell, and Abby Mullen. 'Computational Methods for Uncovering Reprinted Texts in Antebellum Newspapers.' *American Literary History* 27, no. 3 (2015): 1–15.

Smith, Sydney. *Elementary Sketches of Moral Philosophy.* London: Spottiswoodes & Shaw, 1849.

Smith II, Philip E., and Michael S. Helfand. *Oscar Wilde's Oxford Notebooks: A Portrait of Mind in the Making.* Oxford: Oxford University Press, 1989.

Spencer, Herbert. 'The Physiology of Laughter.' *Macmillan's Magazine* 1 (March 1860): 395–402.

Spielmann, M. H. *The History of Punch.* London: Cassell & Company, 1895.

Spielmann, M. H. 'The Rivals of Punch.' *The National Review.* July 1895.

Spiers, John. *Gissing and the City: Cultural Crisis and the Making of Books in Late Victorian England.* Basingstoke: Palgrave Macmillan, 2006.

Spiers, John. 'Review of *The Town Traveller.*' *The Gissing Newsletter* 20, no. 4 (April 1984): 29–32.

Stallybrass, Peter, and Allon White. *The Politics and Poetics of Transgression.* London: Methuen, 1986.

Stephen, Leslie. 'Humour.' *Cornhill Magazine* 33 (March 1876): 318–326.

Stewart, Susan. *Nonsense: Aspects of Intertextuality in Folklore and Literature.* Baltimore: Johns Hopkins University Press, 1979.

Stiles, Anne. *Popular Fiction and Brain Science in the Late Nineteenth Century.* Cambridge: Cambridge University Press, 2012.

Stoker, Bram. *Dracula.* London: Penguin Books, 2009.

Strachey, Lady, ed. *Later Letters of Edward Lear.* London: T. Fisher Unwin, 1911.

Strachey, Lady, ed. *Letters of Edward Lear.* London: T. Fisher Unwin, 1907.

Strachey, Lytton. *Cornerstones: Portraits of Four Eminent Victorians.* Tucson, AZ: Fireship Press, 2009.

Summerfield, Penelope. 'Patriotism and Empire: Music Hall, 1870–1914.' In *Imperialism and Popular Culture*, edited by John MacKenzie. Manchester: Manchester University Press, 1986.

Surridge, Lisa. *Bleak Houses—Marital Violence in Victorian Fiction.* Athens: Ohio University Press, 2005.

Swaab, Peter, ed. '*Over the Land and Over the Sea': Selected Nonsense and Travel Writings of Edward Lear.* Manchester: Carcanet Press, 2005.

Swaab, Peter. "'Some Think Him … Queer": Loners and Love in Edward Lear.' In *Edward Lear and the Play of Poetry*, edited by James Williams and Matthew Bevis, 89–114. Oxford: Oxford University Press, 2016.

Sypher, Wylie, ed. *Comedy.* Baltimore and London: Johns Hopkins University Press, 1983.

Telfer, Bridget, Emma Shepley, and Carole Reeves, eds. *Re-framing Disability: Portraits from the Royal College of Physicians.* London: Royal College of Physicians, 2011.

Thompson, E. P. *The Making of the English Working Class.* London: Pelican Books, 1963.

Thwaite, Ann. *Glimpses of the Wonderful: The Life of Philip Henry Gosse.* London: Faber, 2002.

Tich, Little. 'How I Sang for a Shilling a Week.' *Red Letter.* January 13, 1912.

Tich, Little. *In Other People's Shoes.* Windyridge, 2002. CDR9.

Tich, Little. *Little Tich: A Book of Travels (and Wanderings).* Baileyton, AL: A&B Treebooks, 2007.

Tich, Mary, and Richard Findlater. *Little Tich: Giant of the Music Hall.* London: Elm Tree Books, 1979.

Tromp, Marlene. *The Private Rod: Marital Violence, Sensation, and the Law in Victorian Britain.* Charlottesville: University Press of Virginia, 2000.

Verene, Donald Phillip. *The Philosophy of Literature: Four Studies.* Eugene, OR: Cascade Books, 2018.

Vicinus, Martha. *The Industrial Muse: A Study of Nineteenth-Century British Working-Class Literature.* New York: Barnes & Noble, 1974.

Wade, Nicholas. *A Troublesome Inheritance: Genes, Race and Human History.* New York: Penguin, 2014.

Wagner-Lawlor, Jennifer A. 'Introduction.' In *The Victorian Comic Spirit: New Perspectives*, edited by Jennifer A. Wagner-Lawlor. Aldershot: Ashgate, 2000.

Walkowitz, Judith R. *City of Dreadful Delight: Narratives of Sexual Danger in Late-Victorian London.* Chicago: University of Chicago Press, 1992.

Wallet, W. F. *The Public Life of W. F. Wallett, the Queen's Jester: An Autobiography of Forty Years' Professional Experience & Travels in the United Kingdom, the United States of America (inc. California), Canada, South America, Mexico, the West Indies, etc.*, edited by John Luntley. London and Derby: Bemrose & Sons, 1884.

Wells, Carolyn. 'The Senses of Nonsense.' *Scribner's Magazine* 29. 1901.

Welsh, Alexander. *The City of Dickens.* Cambridge, MA: Harvard University Press, 1986.

West, Anna. *Thomas Hardy and Animals.* Cambridge: Cambridge University Press, 2017.

Wickberg, Daniel. *The Senses of Humor: Self and Laughter in Modern America.* Ithaca, NY: Cornell University Press, 1998.

Wilde, Oscar. 'Commonplace Book.' In *Oscar Wilde's Oxford Notebooks: A Portrait of Mind in the Making*, edited by Philip E. Smith II and Michael S. Helfand, 107–152. New York: Oxford University Press, 1889.

Wilde, Oscar. *De Profundis.* New York: The Modern Library, 1992.

Wilde, Oscar. *Intentions.* In *The Artist as Critic: Critical Writings of Oscar Wilde*, edited by Richard Ellmann, 290–432. Chicago: University of Chicago Press, 1969.

Wilde, Oscar. *The Complete Letters of Oscar Wilde.* Edited by Merlin Holland and Rupert Hart-Davis. New York: Henry Holt, 2000.

Wilde, Oscar. *The Picture of Dorian Gray.* Edited by Norman Page. Peterborough, ON: Broadview Press, 1998.

Wilde, Oscar. 'The Soul of Man Under Socialism.' In *The Artist as Critic: Critical Writings of Oscar Wilde*, edited by Richard Ellmann, 255–289. Chicago: University of Chicago Press, 1969.

Williams, James. 'Nineteenth-Century Nonsense Writing and the Later Work of James Joyce.' PhD thesis, University of Cambridge, 2008.

Wisse, Ruth. *No Joke: Making Jewish Humor.* Princeton, NJ: Princeton University Press, 2015.

Wister, Sarah Butler. 'A Plea For Seriousness.' *Atlantic Monthly.* May 1892.

YouTube. 'Little Tich: Loie Fuller.' https://www.youtube.com/watch?v= RfZ9dQ9Umqs (accessed August 26, 2014).

INDEX

© The Editor(s) (if applicable) and The Author(s) 2020
L. Lee (ed.), *Victorian Comedy and Laughter*,
https://doi.org/10.1057/978-1-137-57882-2